CHUTES AND LADDERS

CHUTES

AND

LADDERS

*Navigating the Low-Wage
Labor Market*

Katherine S. Newman

RUSSELL SAGE FOUNDATION
New York

HARVARD UNIVERSITY PRESS
*Cambridge, Massachusetts
London, England*
2006

Copyright © 2006 by the Russell Sage Foundation
All rights reserved
Printed in the United States of America

Library of Congress Cataloging-in-Publication Data

Newman, Katherine S., 1953–
  Chutes and ladders : navigating the low-wage labor market / Katherine S. Newman.
    p. cm.
  Includes bibliographical references and index.
  ISBN-13: 978-0-674-02336-9 (alk. paper)
  ISBN-10: 0-674-02336-6 (alk. paper)
    1. Minorities—Employment—New York (State)—New York.   2. Career development—
United States.   3. Social mobility—United States.   4. Working poor—United States.
5. United States—Economic conditions—1981–2001.   6. United States—Economic
policy—1993–2001.   I. Title.

HD8081.A5N49 2006
305.5′690973—dc22   2006044340

To my colleagues in Cambridge:

Mary Brinton, Prudence Carter, Mariko Chang, Lizbeth Cohen,
Diane Davis, Frank Dobbin, Susan Eckstein, David Ellwood, Drew Faust,
Jennifer Hochschild, Sandy Jencks, Michele Lamont, Frank Levy,
Jenny Mansbridge, Dick Murnane, Paul Osterman, Bob Putnam, Bob Reich,
Rob Sampson, Bish Sanyal, Theda Skocpol, Mary Waters, Bill Wilson,
and Chris Winship.

And to the Harvard students I was privileged to teach:

Victor Tan Chen, Cybelle Fox, David Harding, Tomás Jiménez,
Shelley McDonough, Jal Mehta, Gesemia Nelson, Wendy Roth,
Mario Small, Ruth Turley, Celeste Watkins, and Dan Zuberi.

Contents

✿

Acknowledgments

The debts I accumulated in the course of this project are many, since it unfolded over a nine-year period. The graduate students who started it with me have completed their studies and launched careers of their own. I was especially gratified that a number of them stuck with me in this endeavor, returning to connect with our informants, joining me for reunion dinners with the main characters and their families. Those occasions made it possible to thank the men and women who opened their lives to us over these many years; without them there would be no story to tell. I hope that this book contributes to an understanding of their struggles, their triumphs, and the aspirations they share with millions of other, more fortunate Americans. Having promised to keep their identities to myself, I cannot thank them by name, but they know who they are, and I trust they will see in this volume a faithful reflection of their lives.

Among those who contributed to this research effort, I want to acknowledge first and foremost the labor of Dr. Chauncy Lennon, who worked with me as a postdoctoral scholar, lent me a helping hand even as he worked full-time for the Ford Foundation, and met with me weekly even after he became senior program manager for SeedCo, a nonprofit organization that provides workforce training. Jennifer Lee, associate professor of sociology at the University of California, Irvine, managed the first wave of follow-up interviews in 1997–98 and was both a creative partner and an incredibly disciplined manager. Many of those interviews were conducted by Prudence Carter, associate professor of sociology at Harvard University, who also took the first wave of quantitative data in hand to give us a picture of the mobility patterns in the first follow-up.

Cathryn Ellis started working on this project when she was in graduate school and came back to it many years later, despite her busy schedule as a producer for National Public Radio. Travis Jackson, now an associate professor of music at the University of Chicago, committed precious time to tracking down one of the key figures in this story who had long since moved out of New York. Magdelena Rodriguez, who came to the project in 2001, is one of the most gifted fieldworkers I have ever encountered. Ana Ramos-Zayas, now in the Department of Anthropology and the Department of Puerto Rican/Caribbean Studies at Rutgers University, conducted many of the original interviews with our Puerto Rican and Dominican workers and helped Magdelena reconnect with them for follow-up interviews in 2001.

During the years I taught at Harvard University, several students in the Sociology and Social Policy Program contributed to this project, mainly by helping to analyze the data that poured in from several waves of follow-up surveys and interviews. Wendy Roth and Joel Horwich were instrumental in that phase of the research, not to mention Victor Tan Chen, who not only helped to mine some of the materials in Chapters 6 and 7 but also coauthored Chapter 6. Victor came to Harvard an accomplished journalist-turned-sociologist, and I am indebted to him for working with me and for lending his talent as a writer to this endeavor.

One of the benefits of working at Harvard was the access it provided to the dense network of academics that inhabit the greater Boston area. It was my good fortune to get to know labor economists Peter Gottschalk and Helen Connolly, who have spent many years mastering the Survey of Income and Program Participation (SIPP), a mammoth and complicated federal data resource. When I wanted to know whether the findings that came from my fieldwork made any sense in a national context, Peter and Helen willingly joined me in an exploration of the question using the SIPP data (presented in Chapter 5). Collaborations across disciplines are all too rare; this one was especially fruitful. My Princeton colleague Marty Gilens was equally generous with his time when I needed to understand better the patterns of stability and fluctuation in political opinions and policy preferences, particularly with respect to welfare and social spending. I thank him for his input to this volume.

Projects as long and elaborate as *Chutes and Ladders* require considerable resources to sustain. I am pleased to express my abiding gratitude to a number of foundations that supported this work and remain committed to the community of scholars who care about poverty, whether or not it is politically popular. First among them is the Russell Sage Foundation, which supported the original research for my previous book, *No Shame in My Game*, and then stepped forward once again to underwrite *Chutes and Ladders*. Many scholars have thanked Eric Wanner, the foundation's imaginative president, but I owe him more than most. Eric has stuck with me through two books and waited patiently while I completed several others (which delayed this one). Without him, I doubt any of them would have seen the light of day.

The collaboration of Russell Sage with the Rockefeller Foundation to create their joint research program, the Future of Work, reflects the leadership of Katherine McFate and Julia Lopez, whose support has been crucial for many researchers, myself included. The Ford Foundation, which also supported *No Shame*, provided the funds I needed to finish the data analysis and write this book. I am particularly grateful to Mel Oliver, now dean of social science at the University of California, Santa Barbara; as a vice president at the Ford Foundation, he helped to sustain the foundation's interest in asset building among the poor. Helen Neuborne, the senior program manager of Ford's Community Development Division, and Nancy Sconyers, who served as my program officer, were instrumental in persuading the foundation that this project was a worthy cause.

The National Science Foundation is the nation's most valued peer-reviewed source of support for research. I would like to thank Stuart Plattner, who recently announced his retirement as director of the Cultural Anthropology Program at NSF, which contributed precious funds (Award No. 9802726) to the support of this effort. No less important have been the enthusiasm of Michael Aronson at Harvard University Press and the intellectual engagement of Andrew Cherlin and one anonymous reviewer, whose comments helped to shape the final form of this book. My copyeditor, Julie Ericksen Hagen, worked wonders on the original manuscript.

I began writing *Chutes and Ladders* during my years at Harvard University, and the insights contained here reflect the input of dozens of colleagues and students who participated in Harvard's Multidisciplinary Program on Inequality and Social Policy, also supported by NSF. It was a privilege to work with them and to see the fruits of our collective labor blossom. The book was finally completed not long after I took a new job in the Department of Sociology and the Woodrow Wilson School at Princeton University. Princeton's generosity made it possible for me to concentrate on getting the work done, and I am grateful to my new colleagues for the warm welcome I have received. Special thanks go to Noel Hunt, who put a great deal of time into the preparation of this manuscript, just one of the many ways she has helped me since we began working together.

My family, as always, deserves my thanks for putting up with the many hours I had to leave them on their own while I worked on *Chutes and Ladders*. My husband, Paul Attewell, sociologist extraordinaire, and my sons Steven (now twenty-three) and David (seventeen) have appeared in the acknowledgments of all of my books because they make everything I do worthwhile.

CHUTES AND LADDERS

Prologue

The prosperity of the late 1990s—sustained by low interest rates and low levels of unemployment—shifted the economic landscape nationwide. Roaring growth lasted for an unprecedented length of time; miraculously, inflation remained under control. Those glory years led to an expansion in home ownership, the mass movement of ordinary Americans into the stock market, and the growth of the minority middle class. True, the benefits of this expansion accrued disproportionately to those at the top of the income distribution, who pulled away from the rest in a dizzying accumulation of wealth, but the poorest among us caught the rising tide as well: "The wages of America's worst-paid workers rose faster than prices for the first time in a generation. Real hourly wage rates among the bottom 20 percent of workers rose about 11 percent between 1995 and 2000. Mean family income among single mothers in the bottom half of the earnings distribution for all single mothers grew 16 percent during this period."[1]

What did these historic trends mean for the nation's working poor? Did new occupational avenues open for them, and who among them was able to seize these opportunities? These are the central questions of this book. To answer them, we must examine the pathways through the low-wage labor market that blossomed into opportunity for some, while leaving others mired in poverty. This is not a story of averages but rather a tale of divergent trajectories that derived from differences in human capital, the bur-

dens of children, the willingness of kin to lend a hand, the vagaries of social networks, and the ins and outs of social policies that either made it
possible for workers to gain more education or slammed that door tight.
Most of all, the pathways that led to upward mobility depended on access
to jobs that paid a living wage, that offered much-needed benefits, and that
opened up opportunities for advancement in firms that were growing.
Chutes and Ladders takes a close look at a group of poor workers who had
none of these advantages in the early 1990s and then asks which of them
moved up and out of the low-wage world and which remained mired in the
nether regions of entry-level employment, episodic welfare, and a low
standard of living, even as the economy around them changed for the
better.

The people whose experiences are recounted here lived in segregated
black neighborhoods in Harlem and in equally impoverished Puerto Rican
and Dominican enclaves of Washington Heights, on the far Upper West
Side of Manhattan. I came to know them in the early 1990s when I first
began focusing my attention on low-wage workers. The ethnography that
emerged from my first encounter with their world, *No Shame in My Game:
The Working Poor in the Inner City*, described how poor job seekers in the
city landed work, battled the stigma that came with a low station in life,
learned new skills, and made ends meet with the help of parents, siblings,
lovers, spouses, and friends. These workers came from the ranks of the
fast-food labor force. Second only to the armed forces, businesses like
McDonald's, Burger King, White Castle, Kentucky Fried Chicken, Arby's,
and Taco Bell are the proving ground of the nation's low-skilled workforce.[2]

As it happened, the Harlem residents who landed those jobs flipping
burgers were the lucky ones. When my research commenced in 1993–94,
the labor market in central Harlem was in terrible shape. More than 18
percent of the workforce was unemployed; more than 40 percent of the
households fell below the official poverty line, and 30 percent relied on
welfare. The fieldwork for *No Shame in My Game* lasted for about eighteen
months, long enough to chart the efforts that many of my informants
made to find better jobs. The fortunate few, who had relatives to shelter
them while they used their earnings to go to school, left Burger Barn behind for good. Most got nowhere. They were still working and hence had
not been reduced to the unemployment line, but by 1995, when I set my
fieldwork aside to write up the results in *No Shame in My Game*, their future looked like the monotonous past: poor.

The drumbeat of good news—high growth, low unemployment, negligible inflation—began sounding in the late 1990s, much to the surprise of most observers. The long-sustained boom that began during President Clinton's first term continued well into the early years of the new millennium. Though I began my research on the working poor with no intention of following my sample over a long period of time, it became clear to me that their lives represented an acid test for the theories of labor market progression at the heart of the debate over welfare reform, and, more generally, that they offered a way of learning about the new dynamics of poverty in a postwelfare world. Growing inequality was pushing millions of poorly educated Americans—native born and new immigrants alike—into low-wage work. With welfare a thing of the past, the dynamics of poverty had become most centrally a function of movement through this end of the labor market. Who got stuck in poverty and who graduated out of it would now be a matter of how they fared in the world of work.

One wouldn't want to pin all hope on extraordinarily favorable labor markets, for they come along rarely. If it turned out that only under these conditions could we hope for progress for the nation's poor workers, the policy remedies would be much harder to identify. As it turned out, moving up did get easier during the boom years of the late 1990s and early years of the new century, but it also happens even in slack labor markets, and the difference between the two contexts is not as large as I first expected. This means that there is good reason to focus on the factors that make it possible for some poor workers to grab the brass rings, as well as on the barriers that interfere with upward mobility for others.

Chutes and Ladders charts the movement of the workers and unsuccessful job seekers I first met in 1993, whom I have now followed through two waves of follow-up studies, in 1997 and 2001–2002. Rather than dwelling on averages, I ask how these people—who all began as fast-food workers or rejected applicants for those minimum-wage jobs—fanned out into "high flyers" and "low riders," how some managed to get more education, good jobs, or both, while others struggled and floundered, weighed down by family obligations, poor training, and racial discrimination. I consider how these pathways through the labor market affected their family lives, especially the formation of the households they lived in and the movements their children made through the education system.

But as a sociological project, this book is more than an attempt to examine the labor market behavior of the inner-city working poor. It is also a study of how the paths they took shaped their understanding of how the economy works, their sense of purpose, their beliefs about good fortune and bad luck, their attitudes toward others who succeeded more than they did or fell by the wayside. That is, it is a study of the cultural orientation of the fortunate workers who emerged from working poverty into the working or middle class and of their counterparts, who remained locked in hardship.

1

Lives, in the Long Run

❦

Highway 101 winds its way through the redwood country of northern California. Dappled sunlight peeks through the fog that shrouds the majestic sequoias lining the road. Deep greens alternate with brilliant yellows as the leaves of oak trees move in the breeze that whips off the Pacific Ocean. When the sun sets, even the highway patrol's cars slow to a crawl, for visibility is limited here and the small country towns that beckon in the distance provide little light to guide a newcomer. We are a long, long way from Harlem, which is precisely what Jamal was after when he first ventured to his rural outpost near Hamilton, California.[1]

Jamal's Journey

When I first met Jamal, he was twenty-two years old, stood six feet tall, and packed 250 pounds underneath his hooded gray sweatshirt. Round faced, with huge brown eyes and dark brown skin, he seemed a gentle giant most of the time, but he was known to erupt with rage without much warning. The object of his affection at the time, his common-law wife, Kathy, was a slender seventeen-year-old white girl who had long, shiny red fingernails, short brown hair, rings on every finger, and bangles on her wrists that rang against the table when we would sit down to talk.

In 1993, the year I began to study low-wage workers in the inner city,

Jamal was working the early morning shift in a Burger Barn restaurant in central Harlem, scrambling to get as many hours as the manager would give him.[2] Kathy worked the grill there for a time as well, but quit when their little girl, Tammy, was born. Jamal struggled to support the family on his own but was having a hard time making ends meet. Managers didn't really like Jamal and the feeling was often mutual, so they tended to squeeze him out by cutting his hours back until his daily take-home pay dwindled to twenty-five dollars (minus the two-dollar subway fare). Jamal would quit in disgust and move on to the next minimum-wage job; he worked for a time in a C'est Bon café and at several other Burger Barns. With only a GED to his name and sweatshirts in his wardrobe, Jamal could not find a job that paid any better. As a teenager, Jamal had made good money in the auto factories near his grandmother's house in Delaware. By the mid-1990s, though, those kinds of jobs were much harder to find, so Jamal cycled from one minimum-wage stint to another. But he was never out in the cold. Jamal always worked, never asked anyone for a handout, and took some pride in his self-reliance.

Jamal's "associates"—friends, acquaintances, and antagonists—could not figure out why he bothered. They laughed in Jamal's face when he shook himself out of bed at 5:00 AM every morning to board a cross-town bus for work, all for a meager paycheck that they swore he could double in half an hour's work as a runner for a drug dealer. His Burger Barn uniform sparked a round of smirks, eyes rolled back and heads shaking back and forth. "Trust us," they told him, "you could do better." From the stoop of Jamal's building, it was easy to spot the characters that had gone down that path. They were the ones hanging on the corner all day, smoking weed, leaning into cars to make a deal, scowling at competitors.

Jamal was having none of this. He was not above a joint or two for himself, but he steadfastly refused entreaties to jump into the trade. Too many years in close company with a drug-addicted mother had taught Jamal all he needed to know about the dangers of getting in too deep. When he was a young boy, Jacqueline, Jamal's mother, had had a good job in the post office on a military base in Florida. She was rolling in money, so much so that it almost didn't matter when Jamal's father disappeared soon after the boy was born. Jacqueline could manage on her own, thank you very much. By the time Jamal was eleven, though, Jacqueline had a serious drug habit. Snorting heroin gave way to mainlining, her concentration at work faltered, and she was fired from the post office. The more erratic Jacqueline's behavior became, the more Jamal sought refuge with his solid, stable grandmother. He hopped busses and hitchhiked to Delaware, where he stayed as long as Grandma would have him. Eventually, though, she would tire of having a teenage boy in the house, even if he was working, and she'd ship him back down to Tallahassee.

Jamal's home life was becoming increasingly impossible. By the time he was eighteen, Jacqueline was broke, with an expensive habit to maintain. She wasn't making much of a living. Jamal himself had started working at thirteen, bagging groceries for tips, doing odd jobs, and finally landing a position on the clean-up crew at a local Burger Barn. During one particularly long stint in Delaware, he managed to find a job in an auto plant that gave him by far his best paycheck. Most of his jobs hovered around the minimum wage, which might have been enough for a teenager, but by his eighteenth birthday he was facing some serious demands for money: Jacqueline wanted a cut. What cash she couldn't score off of her son, she took in through prostitution. In a few short years, she had descended into an inescapable morass of dope, Johns, and petty crime. Along the way, she had hooked up with the man who fathered her second son, a boy who doted on Jamal—the big brother. Jamal was very fond of his brother, but he could not stick around to protect him from an increasingly desperate home life.

It was during one of his runaway stints that Jamal met Kathy, who was looking for an escape of her own. Kathy's father had died when she was ten, and her relationship with her mother had deteriorated steadily throughout her adolescence. Kathy's Supplemental Security Income (SSI) survivor benefits helped to sustain the household, although Kathy's mother also did jobs here and there. Kathy saw that government check as her property; her mother claimed it for the family. It was just one of the many sore points between them. Kathy stormed out of the house after one of their worst fights and vowed to run away from home. Not long thereafter, she met Jamal and discovered a kindred spirit in him. They hit the road together, making their way to New York City without telling anyone in their families where they were headed. Once in a while Kathy would disappear into a phone booth and call her younger brother, for whom she had a real soft spot, emerging with tears streaming down her face. She swore him to secrecy and promised to keep calling. Kathy knew her mother was looking for her, but finding a runaway girl in New York City is rarely easy.

Jamal and Kathy had a lot in common: they did not know their fathers;

both had cut their ties to their mothers; and they were hungry for affection. They also had problems managing anger. By 1994, two years after they had run away from Florida, some of the heady romance between them was starting to wear a little thin. Money was a constant headache. Between them, Jamal and Kathy pulled in about nine dollars an hour. On such a meager income, they could afford only a single room in an old building that had been subdivided into a low-rent tenement. Their rapacious landlord was bent on extracting the maximum rent for minimum service. Rats scurried across the floors at night and nibbled at their shoes. Heat was sporadic, and when the icy winter winds whipped across the Harlem River, a steady draft seeped through the broken seals around their windows. The streets surrounding the rooming house were no treat either. Jamal worried about Kathy's safety when he was away from home.

Into this unsavory situation came little Tammy, a low-birth-weight daughter who got off to a colicky start in life. Kathy quit work because they had no one to look after Tammy and applied for food stamps. Alone with a temperamental baby, staring at the four walls and cursing their loud neighbors, Kathy was not enjoying a glowing motherhood. And at seventeen, she was hardly prepared for the 24/7 obligation of caring for a newborn. Neither, it must be said, was Jamal. Cooped up in a single room, with no way to get away from his howling daughter, one day Jamal reached his limit and did something he regretted the instant it happened. The episode was so shameful to him that he would not talk about it. Social services had intervened, though, so it undoubtedly involved a serious injury. They took Tammy into foster care six months before we began our fieldwork.

Jamal and Kathy were remorseful, anxious to get their daughter back, and willing to do whatever the supervising judge in family court asked of them. They enrolled in parenting classes. The judge had insisted they find an apartment that would provide a separate bedroom for the baby. She had told Kathy that she had to stay home rather than work, so as not to be neglectful. Dutifully they visited their daughter under the strict supervision of her foster-care mother, seeing her once a week in a playroom in a city social worker's office.

As Tammy's first birthday drew close, Jamal and Kathy were increasingly desperate to satisfy the family court judge so that they could have her back. But meeting the court's conditions for reinstituting their parental rights was proving to be a challenge. How were they to find a one-bedroom apartment when Jamal earned barely enough to pay for a single room in a slumlord's broken-down house? When we left Jamal and Kathy in the spring of 1994, they had finally made it to the top of the public-housing wait list and had located a modest apartment in the South Bronx. At $600 a month it was a steal by local standards, but the rent swallowed all of Jamal's take-home pay. They really did not know how they were going to manage, but the apartment was the key to getting Tammy back, so they took it. The wheels of bureaucracy turn slowly, and a month later they still did not have their daughter at home, but they were hopeful she would be returned by Christmas. Four months later, when we looked them up again just to see how they were doing, the apartment was empty. Neither Jamal nor Kathy could be found. Even Jacqueline, who had also moved up to New York, had disappeared—without a trace.

In 1997 I began a formal follow-up study to find out how the workers I had originally interviewed for my research on low-wage employment in 1993 were doing in the labor market. Of all the people I had come to know in the beginning, Jamal was the one I most wanted to find. I hadn't seen or heard from him since the middle of 1994, and I was worried that his frustrations might have gotten the better of him. Kathy had blamed him for the loss of the baby. Jobs that paid a decent wage had eluded him. A chip had been building on his shoulder about the unforgiving attitudes of employers, their unwillingness to give him a chance. His grandmother was no longer interested in sheltering him; his own mother was more of a drain than a resource. It occurred to me that he might have done something foolish just to get more money into the house. None of these unpleasant fantasies could be checked against reality though, because Jamal was nowhere to be found. We used every legal database and search firm. We checked with neighbors in his last apartment house and did the same around his mother's building. Nothing. Was he in jail? Was he alive? If we could not find him, perhaps it was because he had literally disappeared. It seemed quite plausible to me in 1997.

The third and final follow-up study for this book was conducted in 2001–2002, and it turned up a man who fit Jamal's description in a tiny town in the far northern reaches of California. I very nearly failed to track down this lead—even though the person's Social Security number matched my records—since it seemed so unlikely that Jamal could have migrated to a small town way out west. But there he was. Jamal's path represents one of the least likely exit routes from working poverty. He got out of the inner city and found his way to a part of the nation where decent blue-collar jobs that pay a living wage still exist: logging country. There are few such niches left in the American economy, for these days even factory owners demand more educational credentials than the GED Jamal had to offer.[3] But in the rural reaches of California, nearly 300 miles from the nearest big city, employers cannot be quite that picky. Besides, even though Jamal does not have a diploma, he is literate and can do the kinds of arithmetic calculations that his job requires. Indeed, Jamal has proven himself to be a good worker, as his several promotions suggest.

Wood Works, the firm that has employed Jamal on and off for nearly eight years now, is a subsidiary of a larger lumber company, responsible for the lamination process that glues handsome veneers to plain wood planks for use in manufacturing furniture.[4] The factory floor is covered with piles of thick sheets of wood. Workers cart the piles around on tow motors to different stations, where huge machines glue, press, heat, sand, and cut the lumber into plywood panels of different thicknesses and sizes.

Lumber plants make use of a wide range of skill profiles, from unskilled haulers who bend their backs moving planks from one station to another, to skilled workers who operate complicated laminating equipment, to first-line foremen who oversee a variety of operations in the production process. Jamal has held positions all along this continuum.

He began his career at Wood Works in April 1996, about eighteen months after I lost contact with him in New York. Starting out in the labor pool, Jamal's first job was as an "off-bearer," pulling wood that had just been steamed and dried off of a conveyer belt and examining it for the number of knots in each piece. This inspection determines the "grade" or quality of the wood, the basis of its subsequent sorting. Jamal remained in the labor pool for about six months, at which point he became a heister driver—loading wood into the dryers from which the off-bearers take it—on the graveyard shift, working from 11:00 PM to 7:00 AM. (The factory operates around the clock and has three shifts; workers with the least seniority are stuck with night work.) The new position was a promotion, moving Jamal up in skill, pay, and responsibility.

However, his good fortune did not last long. After two months Jamal was demoted back into the labor pool, the victim (as he saw it) of a personality conflict with the supervisor. "That's pretty much the way the company was run at the time," he recalled. "If you had a problem and they didn't like you . . . they'd just replace you." Undaunted, he worked another two months as an off-bearer and then applied for a job as a press operator on the swing shift (from 3:00 to 11:00 PM). In luck once again, Jamal got the new position, which required him to learn more skills than either of the previous jobs. Press operators take over at the end of the manufacturing process that produces laminated wood. They make plywood panels of particular dimensions and thicknesses out of veneer. Sheets of veneer are glued together and heated at high temperatures, then sent elsewhere in the mill to be packaged.

Jamal proved to be a quick study, as he has in virtually all the jobs he has held. Though he has little education, he is both intelligent and intuitive, able to figure out what needs to be mastered. Moreover, he is wise in the ways of bureaucracy. Without being told this by anyone at Wood Works, Jamal figured out that if he were willing to bide his time on a bad shift, he could prove himself adept enough to merit a lateral move to the same job on a better shift. That is precisely what happened this time around: after two or three months as a press operator on the swing shift, his counterpart on the day shift quit and Jamal made his move, winning the more coveted spot. Not long thereafter, he was promoted into quality control. From there, it was one short leap to the best job he has ever had: weekend foreman.

Cockneys have a slang phrase that describes the process of deciphering hidden codes and tricks of survival: "sussing out" a situation. Someone who knows how to suss it out figures out the underlying rules of the game without being told. This is what Jamal is good at. What he seems to have trouble with is staying the course. Usually the honeymoon lasts for a few months and then something falls apart, he makes a serious mistake, and he finds himself cast back down into the depths. His positive qualities seem to ensure that those depths do not include unemployment, at least not for long. Jamal always lands a job. But he cannot seem to keep a hold on the positions that he has worked to secure. He lasted three or four months as a press operator and was then removed after a few "incidents." He did well as foreman for about four months, but was then demoted when his supervisors lost confidence in his leadership skills.

Jamal's mistakes ran the gamut from tardiness to failure to follow technical procedures. "I'm not much of a morning person," he noted sheepishly. This surprised me, since back in New York he got up before the sun rose to make his way across town for a lousy minimum-wage job that took almost an hour to get to. In Hamilton, he lives no more than an eight-minute drive from Wood Works. Nonetheless, Jamal was frequently late for the morning shift, which did not sit well with the powers that be. Some of his mistakes were more consequential and perhaps reflected a skill deficit. Press operators have to calculate time and temperature during the gluing process. At least once, Jamal blew it by using the wrong settings for a load of wood. The problem was compounded down the line when the operator on the next shift failed to notice that Jamal had used the wrong settings and ruined yet another batch. Both pressmen were reported for the errors because they had cost the firm money, albeit a minor amount. Jamal's last mistake, the third incident noted in his "disciplinary record," was dropping a load of wood from a hoist. The load splintered into pieces and was ruined.

Jamal bridles at these "write-ups." The system feels like it's a calculated effort to keep him on notice, to ride his back and refuse to let mistakes drop. Couldn't people just give him a break? That's what he wanted to know. Since he was willing to admit his mistakes, he reasoned, other people should let him off the hook rather than dwell on them. But no. "If you did one bad thing, and did it again," he complained, "you were considered bad. When you repeat a mistake, you can't really recover." The old Jamal, the one who burns inside when reminded of his failings, is still there.

Jamal's move to Hamilton, California, was not accidental. Not long after he landed in the West, he met Selina, a Mexican American girl who had her own family problems. Only fourteen at the time, Selina had dropped out of school after finishing seventh grade. Her father was a heavy drug user, which put a lot of strain on the family, especially on Selina's mother, who had some serious health problems to contend with. Selina was constantly in trouble at home and in school; she needed to get out of the house. Jamal was her savior. Late into the night he listened to her, without judgment. In offering Selina advice, Jamal drew on his own experience growing up with a heroin-addicted mother. As a newcomer to California, Jamal needed some comfort himself. One thing led to another, and they became romantically involved. Selina's parents, immigrants from Mexico and fairly traditional in their expectations (drug use notwithstanding), were not happy about this at all. They found out about Kathy and Tammy, and were not impressed that Jamal had abandoned them. The age gap between Jamal and Selina troubled them. The fact that Selina got pregnant a few months after she met Jamal sharpened their disapproval. As they saw it, there was only one solution: this young man was going to marry their daughter immediately. Jamal and Selina complied, but this won them no more than tolerance from her family.

The atmosphere in the family deteriorated as Jamal found he was unable to find a job that paid enough to cover the bills. Jamal and Selina decided to try their luck elsewhere and packed their bags for the East Coast. Jamal figured his grandmother would take him in again. By this time Jacqueline, Jamal's mother, was back at Grandma's place as well. Everyone converged on Delaware, where Jamal thought the jobs might be better and the family surroundings more congenial.

Always resourceful, Jamal set himself to find a job, and in short order he was hired into a nationally known moving and storage company. He drove a small truck, delivered goods, and did a lot of packing. Jamal stuck with the job until the union called a strike and a lockout forced him onto the unemployment lines. But he wasn't there for long. Jamal is not one to take a setback lying down. He put his mind to finding another position right away. This time the pickings were slim.

"I swore I'd never take another fast-food job," he recalled, "but there was nothin' else on tap." With money running low and his grandmother tapping her feet, waiting for him to produce some income, he donned a uniform not unlike the one he was wearing when I first met him in Harlem. Mopping the floors, tending the french fry vats, running around the freezer in search of meat patties—it was all very familiar to Jamal. Indeed that's why, despite his disdain for these jobs, he knows that he can land one in a pinch: he has the skills and experience and requires almost no training. It's comforting, on one level, to have such a fallback, but fast-food jobs were hardly the job of choice when Jamal was twenty. At twenty-six, it was an insult to need one. So when he heard about a position at an auto repair shop, he dropped the burger job in a nanosecond and jumped at the chance to work in the customer service department. Now this was more like it! Jamal was responsible for writing up orders for servicing vehicles. It didn't pay particularly well, but it was definitely a move up from flipping burgers.

Jamal's pattern of job-hopping is not unfamiliar to scholars of the youth labor market.[5] Of course, he was not exactly a youth by the time we caught up with him in Hamilton. He was in his late twenties and still moving from job to job. Yet, with the exception of the three-week interlude in the fast-food restaurant, most of his jobs required more skills and paid better than the positions in which I first found him in his early twenties. From Wood Works to the automotive job, Jamal found work that required writing skills, simple math, judgment, timing, and coordination with workmates. None of his jobs have been the sort that middle-class Americans

covet, and some have been stigmatized, but they have kept him off the unemployment lines.

Managing to stay "in work" without any gaps to speak of is an achievement in Jamal's circles. Most of his teenage associates from the old neighborhood lack this kind of work biography: they have experienced longer
gaps between jobs and have found fewer semiskilled opportunities. How
does Jamal manage to stay on the job, jumping tracks as often as he does?
Intelligent observation—not to mention trial and error—has led him to a
practical strategy for job hunting that he puts into play whenever he has to
find a new position. "Your best route," he explains, "is to find the source of
employment, find the source that will actually hire you." Jamal knows that
he could ask employees about openings, but he doesn't think they are always reliable or knowledgeable. A manager, in contrast, knows for sure
whether a firm is hiring and knows precisely what the company is looking
for. "I ask to speak to the 'hiring manager' and make my case. I want to
talk to the person who has the application on his desk." The secretaries
that might be in between are not the ones who can make decisions.

Once he has the right audience, Jamal sets about selling himself, or
rather putting his experience on display. "I go in with a positive mind,"
he says with conviction. "I try to find qualities in the job that I can actually
do. I basically go in and sell what I have knowledge of. I've done delivery,
I have some management experience, I've done sales. People I talk to
generally take those things and say, 'How's about a job doing this, this,
and this?'"

His strategy works, he notes, because he hasn't really tried to move very
far up the occupational ladder. "My jobs are labor-oriented, not technically oriented," he explains. Success has convinced Jamal that just about
anyone can get a job, for work is all about adaptation: jiggering what you
already know into a shape that makes sense for a new set of responsibilities. The capacity to adapt is one of his strengths, as he sees it. In any case,
he plans to depend on this quality until he can get his dream job as a motorcycle tester or a fighter pilot. Neither appears to be on the horizon, and
he is not exactly taking steps to bring that future about.

The dicey job situation in Delaware was not made easier by the fact that
Jamal's family did not approve of Selina any more than her family approved of Jamal. Jacqueline and her mother did not appreciate Selina's
pregnancy, did not want her to exercise a claim on Jamal's income, and
generally made life miserable for the couple. Selina, only fifteen by this

time, was thousands of miles from her own family, in a place that was entirely unfamiliar, and surrounded by hostile women. When Jamal came home from work, he would find his wife in tears, begging to go back home. He resisted for a time but finally gave in when Selina's own mother got sick and made it clear that she needed her daughter close by.

Once again they packed up, and Jamal made up his mind to give Wood Works another try. Despite the spotty nature of his prior experience with the firm, Jamal knew how to do a fair number of jobs on that shop floor. So long as he was willing to stoop to the "relief labor pool," the crew that works weekends on the swing shift, daytime on Monday, and graveyard shifts on Wednesdays and Thursdays, Wood Works was happy enough to have him back on the line. There weren't too many others willing to live with such an irregular schedule anyway. In 1998 Wood Works made Jamal a driver for the sander, which means he was labeling and sending finished materials to the next place they needed to go for processing (packaging, wrapping). He was working almost sixty hours a week, on shifts that sometimes lasted as long as twelve hours.

Sanders are the "last line of defense" in the mill, Jamal notes, and the final opportunity to make a piece of wood look high-quality. As such, sanders can be held over for many hours when a shift gets backed up on the work load. If the day crew slacks off, which they often do, the swing shift has to make up for it. If the sander goes down for half an hour, Jamal might find himself starting a shift with a huge backlog. One way or the other, Jamal makes sure the job gets done. If he could convince Wood Works that he would always take care of business, Jamal would probably be able to recapture the foreman's spot.

But his dedication is somewhat variable, and his lack of education undoubtedly affects his capacity to troubleshoot or improvise in situations where technical knowledge is required. For example, when he was responsible for quality control on the Wood Works shop floor, he managed to get the job done most of the time, but occasionally he made some spectacularly bad decisions, especially in anomalous situations. He misjudged timing or temperature, failed to ask advice when he was unsure of the right move, and left when his shift was over rather than waiting to see whether all was well. His supervisor reprimanded him for not sticking around an extra fifteen minutes to determine whether the wood was dry or bad, outcomes he should have been on the lookout for. Jamal was not sure how he was supposed to know that this was his responsibility. "They expect more from me than they do from other people," he asserted. Management thought he should be able to figure out the right course of action.

When it comes to absorbing the lessons that are put before him in a didactic and straightforward fashion, Jamal does well. When he has to figure out a new situation that he has not encountered before, his street smarts fail him and he feels too awkward about his lack of knowledge to ask someone else. Being the only black man on the shop floor does not make such a delicate situation any easier. Indeed, it inclines him to hope for the best rather than nail down the details, because he doesn't like asking questions that might single him out as a know-nothing.

These limitations have put the brakes on Jamal's occupational mobility. As a consequence, his growing family may feel the bite of hardship some day. Yet to conclude that Jamal's story is a tragedy in the making would be wrong. In 1994, he was earning the minimum wage and living in a rooming house in a slum, surrounded by crime and drugs. His child—born out of wedlock—had been placed in foster care, and he had no assurance he could get her back. No one in his family was willing to help him. By 2002, the year Jamal turned thirty, he was earning $32,500 a year, living in a two-bedroom trailer in a pleasant community, and was a married man with three children and a fourth on the way. In the course of his career in the laminating factory, he has been promoted twice. While his bosses sometimes lose patience with him, they also continue to employ him and have never fired him (though they have demoted him). Jamal has medical insurance for his family, although the policy is not exactly comprehensive and he currently faces nearly $5,000 in outstanding bills for health care. Jamal works long hours, but because his rent is only $400 a month and the cost of living is generally low in his rural community, he has the money to buy the kinds of creature comforts that would have been unthinkable in 1994. Measured by the distance he has traveled, Jamal has a lot to be proud of.

Still, it's never really enough. Long years of deprivation have left the man with a taste for extras that he cannot really afford. "Where did you get those new shoes?" Selina asks, clearly suspicious that he has been spending money without telling her. "Aw, these?" he answers. "I've had them for months!" New shoes, Yamaha motorcycles—these are the kinds of expenditures that a man with high medical debts might think twice about. Jamal is not a careful money manager, and Selina (who does not earn any income at all) is clearly worried about how they will survive with his tastes. Jamal is not unusual in this regard. Many working-poor parents

I have come to know in New York want to replace the old couch or take their children to visit family in the Dominican Republic once they are earning real money. Yet the wages they garner, while vastly better than the minimum wage they earned where I first met them, are rarely high enough to permit a lot of luxury spending. They end up in debt, at usurious interest rates on credit cards that are practically thrown at them by banks anxious for the business. Jamal and Selina are hardly alone in this pattern: American consumers are plunging into debt by the millions to satisfy their consumer desires.[6]

Jamal has come a long way in his work and family life, but he has also left some serious casualties along this road. Kathy is no longer part of his life. He has no idea what has become of Tammy, and he shows no curiosity about their welfare. On the contrary, he fears that some day the authorities will come knocking, looking to garnish his paycheck for their support. Conservatives and liberals alike would agree that he defaulted on this fundamental obligation. Selina is not eager to see any of their income disappear, but she is not happy that Jamal abandoned his first family. As they moved from place to place, she would carefully pack Tammy's baby pictures and other mementos to remind Jamal of the people he used to care about. Nevertheless, he has resisted Selina's efforts to connect her children with their stepsister, and one year Jamal took it upon himself to burn every last photo of Tammy.

Jamal is conscious of the mistakes he has made in the past and wants to do better this time around. Jamal and Kathy often came to blows during their arguments. Neither one of them would back down from a confrontation. Jamal works hard at controlling his temper with Selina, and she does the same. Though they do get angry with each other, they keep their hands to themselves.[7]

Jamal has trouble talking to people who are close to him, but he can jaw on for hours with those who are more distant. He spends many hours on his cell phone, discussing with his friends the pros and cons of various models of motorcycles. If Selina tries to interrupt or to engage him in conversation when he gets home from work, he shushes her. This drives her crazy because, by the end of a long day cooped up with three kids, she is desperate for some adult company. Jamal knows that he is not the easiest person to live with and wonders out loud whether he is too mean to his son or insufficiently sensitive as a husband. Jamal realizes that Selina feels cooped up during the day, and he tries to see to it that they go out to eat on the weekend. For her part, Selina recognizes that he puts in ten-hour days and needs to relax when the workday is done, so she doesn't make a fuss every time he heads for the motorcycle, even though she is really dying for some attention. Yet there are times when they get into screaming battles in front of their children.

Jamal is convinced he has changed a lot since we first met in 1994, and Selina attests to this. He is more responsible; he does try to please his family (planning a nice dinner out, taking the kids to play video games that, admittedly, he enjoys as much as they do). Most of all, he has worked at controlling his temper, or at least at getting angry without getting violent. Jamal never got into dealing drugs back in New York, but he was a devotee of marijuana and occasionally indulged in a hit of cocaine. No more. To-day he will have a cigarette or two in the bathroom, where there is a fan that blows the smoke away. He does not keep alcohol in the trailer at all. Selina has her own history with drugs, though nothing as serious as co-caine, and she too has left them behind. The change has done both of them some good, as they readily acknowledge.

Still, Jamal has trouble figuring out how to be a father, which is perhaps unsurprising since he never had a father himself. He fawns over his daughter but ignores his sons, who stand there hoping for some of their father's attention. When Jamal ignores them, they act up, which leads Jamal to bark at them or swat them. Standing six feet tall with an imposing girth, Jamal can be a scary sight, and Kyle (age six) and Jamal Junior (age three) sometimes cower in his presence. Jamal recognizes that he frightens his children at times, but he thinks that this reinforces his authority in the household. Only occasionally does he temper his angry outbursts with signs of affection. Jamal finds it hard to put his family's desires ahead of his own, and the time he spends with them is often dedicated to something that he cares about rather than the kinds of activities children look forward to.

Selina upbraids Jamal for these slights, insisting that he owes her and the kids an apology for promising them a nice family day, when instead he put them through a long drive in search of a new motorcycle. She berates Jamal for making them sit in a hot car for hours while he inspects new bikes in the shop, for the risks he takes on the road and the confusion he causes when he takes off on a motorcycle at ninety miles per hour, leaving her to try to find him in an unfamiliar area far from home. "If you would pay more attention to your kids, we wouldn't have this bed wetting problem with Jamal Jr.," she complains. The old Jamal would have stormed back at Selina with a litany of complaints. The new Jamal admits that he could do better and tries to hug Selina's anger away. She is not mollified and instead pushes him away. Jamal is stumped, so he retreats to an online chat room to post information about his new motorcycle.

Selina gave birth to Kyle only a few months after she and Jamal arrived in Hamilton. At fifteen, she was one of those rare first-time teen mothers who had a husband to rely on. Jamal quickly found a job, his first stint at the wood laminating factory, and began to bring home a decent paycheck for the first time in his life. Good thing, too, because within a few years they had a full house. Jamal Junior and Maria (now two), took their places in the tiny but tidy trailer, and by 2002, when we caught up with them, Selina was five months pregnant with their fourth child. She is a loving mother and has worked hard to make a nice home for all of them, which is not easy in the small trailer.

A narrow driveway strewn with toys announces the presence of Jamal's growing family. The front door of his trailer is fronted by a deck festooned with balls, water pistols, and action figures. Pictures of the whole family, each child, the grandparents, and various cousins cover the walls. Selina has taken great care—within a limited budget—in decorating her home with floral print curtains and scented candles. Cartoons are a fixture on the large television that sits in the middle of the living room, and a computer rests on a desk in the same room. Jamal likes to play video games on it, and Kyle tends to hang at his elbow. Selina uses the computer to access online chat rooms, her lifeline to the grown-up world during the many hours Jamal is gone. That depresses her at times, but she is also happy that she has a husband, they have a home, they can provide for their kids in most respects, and her family—just across the street—can help out if she needs them.

Jamal is living the kind of life that he would not have dreamed possible in 1994. That is not to say that he is perfectly content. On his bad days, when he can't get along with the boss or Selina is angry because he has indulged himself in a joyride instead of attending to his family, he can become sullen and withdrawn. But this is nothing compared with the outbursts of despair he was given to when I knew him in New York. He has managed to move beyond the troubles of his early twenties, out of the ghetto, up to a decent job that is basically his to keep so long as he doesn't blow it. Jamal can think of a lot of people who have not shared in his good fortune.

Kyesha's Miracle

The tall brick buildings of the Malcolm X Housing Project in Harlem tower over the clusters of mothers and children who spill out into its massive courtyard, on the lookout for the ice cream trucks that will be gathering on the street. Sunset brings relief from the heat of the summer's day, and children whiz around on the sidewalks, anxious to let off steam. Young men with gleaming, sweaty torsos lock shoulders and wave their arms skyward, blocking the basketballs in mid arc as they sail toward the hoops. Two thousand families dwell in this project, and though many of them don't know it, they all depend on one woman to make sure that their doors lock, the plumbing doesn't leak, and their heat comes on in the winter: Kyesha Smith.

A slender black woman of twenty-eight, Kyesha has green eyes and long, braided hair dyed maroon. She wears her New York City Housing Authority janitor's uniform—navy blue pants and a matching shirt—with a certain kind of pride, born less of the status it confers on her than the certain knowledge that without her, the Malcolm X Project would fall apart, literally. A ring of fifty keys is attached, permanently it seems, to her hip, and it jingles as she strides out of her office at the end of the day. Everyone in the yard greets Kyesha, and she, in turn, gives a high five. She knows "all their dramas," from the squalling newborns to the sob stories of the evicted to the pleas for new locks to keep unwanted boyfriends at bay.

Kyesha's official job title is "caretaker/janitor," but that hardly does justice to her responsibilities. She is in charge of a large warehouse of keys, tools, hardware, and plumbing supplies that are "mission critical" to the operation of this enormous public housing complex. Every piece of inventory required to keep the complex in order—from doorknobs to lug nuts, drills to space heaters—is under her watchful eye. From her gun-metal desk, she manages a command center covered in paperwork and pink message pads as residents call in with their complaints, work orders, and assorted mechanical failures. A steady parade of workmen, from janitors to plumbers, housing supervisors to construction guys, drop by to pick up instructions, leave supplies or just shoot the breeze. Kyesha greets everyone by name, invites a select few to join her in a dominoes game at lunch, and cracks blue jokes with the rest.

Everyone likes to goof off with Kyesha, and her sociability enhances her job performance. Ear to the ground, she keeps tabs on all of the gossip in this vertical neighborhood. Though she professes to prefer jobs that pay well and demand little, in fact Kyesha works hard, with admirable efficiency. What's more, she actually enjoys the job because it keeps her on her toes, with plenty of opportunities to socialize on the side. The money doesn't hurt either. With a base pay of $28,000 a year and ample opportunities for overtime (amounting to an additional $14,000 in 2002), Kyesha is earning a very good wage for someone who struggled through high school.

Her prospects can only improve in the long run. Advancement within the civil service depends on test performance, and it is only a matter of time before Kyesha will be able to move up. In 2002 she attended a dozen class sessions given by the union to prepare her for an exam that would qualify her for a supervisory job. Had she passed, she would have been promoted into management, to oversee a team of janitors like herself for the princely salary of $48,000 plus overtime. Three points shy of passing, Kyesha lost out on that opportunity. Days later she heard from a white co-worker, who has consistently urged her to seek promotions, that she needed to study the book rather than attend the classes. The test asked questions about how much gas you burn when you drive a car, something Kyesha has never done, and how to choose the right sealant for a new floor. All the answers were in the manual, but she didn't realize that, and now she has to wait another five years until there are enough openings for a new test to be offered.

Undaunted, she has set her sights on qualifying for a job as a heat and plant technician, which requires a certificate that is granted after completion of a training course. She has also considered applying for a spot in the Sanitation Department. It doesn't matter to her how smelly those trucks get on a hot summer day. That job pays a fortune, has full benefits, and is secure in an era when nothing else seems to be. For that matter, so is the janitor job she has now. Kyesha has finally landed in civil service paradise, which is exactly what she hoped for back in the years when she worked for minimum wage at Burger Barn. Her grandmother had paved the way, with a post office job that had enabled her to buy a house in a segregated suburb on Long Island. She was the first member of Kyesha's family to make it to the landed class, and her granddaughter absorbed that lesson in a hurry: city jobs make the good life possible.[8]

In the meantime, Kyesha is racking up a good record as a janitor in the housing project of her youth. Her success in running this blue-collar empire comes as little surprise to someone who studied her closely back in 1994, when she worked the drive-through window at one of Harlem's Burger Barn restaurants. Although she earned a paltry $4.75 an hour—after four years on the job—she held the most demanding position in the restaurant, one that fairly defeated my graduate student researchers, who were doing fieldwork on the shop floor. They valiantly tried to keep up with Kyesha as the orders poured in over the speaker, while she simultaneously picked up and bagged the food, took in money, and made change for the drivers at the window. No one else was able to handle the job as smoothly as Kyesha did. Her memory was excellent, her capacity to work under stress notable. Management certainly did see potential in her. She was promoted to crew chief in 1996 and then to swing manager not long thereafter. The trajectory was positive; the money was another story. "Six seventy-five an hour, [after] twelve freaking years," she remembered, shaking her braids. "[The owner] was definitely robbing us, for sure."

Making ends meet on an annual wage well below the poverty line was, to put it mildly, a challenge. When Kyesha first started working at the Barn, she was only fourteen (having lied about her age), so the paltry sum had to stretch only as far as the clothes and baubles that her mother, Dana, couldn't provide on her welfare stipend. At nineteen, though, Kyesha herself was a single mom and was expected to contribute more substantially to Dana's household coffer. Dana was looking after her grandson, Anthony, so that Kyesha could stay on the job, Kyesha was expected to turn over more of her income to the common good. Juan, Anthony's father, did what he could to help, buying Pampers and baby food when he had the money. But Juan faced demands on his earnings from his own mother, and since she controlled the roof over his head, Juan was not in a position to argue.

To be fair, Juan's mother did her share of caring for Anthony, especially on the weekends, even after Juan and Kyesha were no longer an item. That was something Juan could offer, even when his own earnings were too low for him to provide much financial support for his son. Until the welfare officials came looking for his mother and insisted that she get a real job, she was an important source of child care that freed Kyesha to work on weekends.

With money in short supply, Kyesha began looking around for second jobs, especially during the summer. Dana kept her ears open for opportunities she could pass on to her daughter. When she heard that the Malcolm X Housing Project was looking for cleaning staff, Dana nudged Kyesha to look into it. From that summer forward, Kyesha would come home from her Burger Barn job, rest for an hour or so, and then start her second shift, cleaning urine off of the elevator walls and picking up trash in the project courtyard. It was a nasty assignment but it paid well, and between the two jobs Kyesha was pocketing something close to a living wage. Of course, Dana waited for her share, foot tapping on the kitchen floor on payday. Kyesha dutifully complied, seeing as Dana gave her a roof over her head and free babysitting. She tried to hide the "windfall" tax rebate that arrived in her mailbox every year in March, but Dana was wise to that too.

Dana and Kyesha get along with each other, but there were tensions under the surface that started to bubble up with increasing frequency in the mid-1990s. During the daytime, when Anthony was in Dana's care, she was the boss. Shifting gears when his mother got home proved hard for the little boy. "Gram says . . ." came to be a constant refrain, and it got on Kyesha's nerves. It didn't feel right, seeing her authority displaced. "I don't care what Gram says," she would retort. Tension over money was relentless, as it is in most poor households. The uncomplicated relations between parents and children in most middle-class families are predicated on the relative abundance of resources. When money intrudes into family life, all kinds of confusions and moral ambiguities muddy the waters. Kyesha thought she should have a major voice in how household funds got spent, since a fair amount of it was hers. Dana saw herself as the woman in charge, providing services that made it possible for Kyesha to stay on the job, not to mention connections that gave her daughter a leg up on employment prospects that she could not have found on her own.

Instrumental reasoning was getting in the way of a family bond. Dana wanted to be paid fifty dollars a week to take Anthony to school and pick him up. "What a rip off," Kyesha muttered under her breath. Casting around for a less costly alternative, she approached her own grandmother, who was willing to accompany Anthony to and from school gratis. In short order, Dana was cut out of that deal. Evidently no offense was taken—at least not publicly—as Dana continued in her role as chief child care provider, with a heavy subsidy from the state welfare authorities, who continued to provide Dana with a stipend since she also had a child of her own under the age of two.

Kyesha was disturbed by her own dependence on Dana's goodwill and frustrated by the way she was tied down to the house and family. Although Dana's apartment was large, the walls seemed to be shrinking, or at least Kyesha's sense of privacy was diminishing. "Everybody's into my business," she complained, as she stuffed boxes full of supplies that would come in handy when the day came that she could move out on her own. She applied for a spot in public housing, and she sat for endless rounds of civil service exams in the vain hope of landing a job like her grandmother's, in the post office. Nothing came up on either front.

In the meantime, Kyesha's personal financial situation wasn't getting much better. Working two jobs—at Burger Barn and the summer job with the New York City Housing Authority—she earned too much to qualify for Medicaid. As a diabetic, Kyesha often found herself in the emergency room with a high sugar count, in need of an insulin shot. Anthony had some serious health problems as well; his teeth were decayed from sucking sweet juice from a baby bottle, and he had developed asthma, which sent him to the ER as well. Without insurance, Kyesha had nearly $8,000 in medical debts that were simply beyond her means to pay. Demands poured into her mailbox stamped with big red letters, "FINAL NOTICE," followed in short order by warnings that she would be hearing from collection agencies. Kyesha just tossed them out, since there wasn't much she could do about the bills and she had few assets for anyone to go after.

A fortuitous solution presented itself in the wake of the World Trade Center attack in 2001. Most of New York City's banking system was protected from catastrophe, but the small credit union where Kyesha banked had serious problems with its automatic teller machines in the aftermath of the terrorist attack. All of a sudden the ATMs were permitting customers to withdraw thousands of dollars that did not belong to them. In Kyesha's neighborhood word traveled fast that the floodgates had opened, and she rushed to the credit union and withdrew $6,000—enough, in conjunction with her savings, to pay off the hospital.[9] In due course, however, the bank caught up with Kyesha. "They sent me a letter saying if I don't pay them back, they're going to put that six grand on my credit report," she noted sheepishly. Her co-workers who had withdrawn excess funds had to pay the bank back to the tune of four or five hundred dollars a month.

Kyesha decided to take a different path, turning to her older half-brother, Reggie, who owns a restaurant down South, through which he launders drug money. In the past Kyesha had shunned Reggie's offers of financial assistance. This time, she was panicked enough about the bank's threats to accept his offer. And Reggie was only too happy to help. During his occasional bouts of prison time, Kyesha had been a loyal and support-ive sister, sending him cigarettes, underwear, magazines, and other good-ies to help pass the time. Reggie was glad to return the favor and offered up the entire $6,000 for her to return to the bank. He would not hear of her paying him back more than $250 a month because, as he put it, "You got to shop, you got to eat, whatever." One can criticize Kyesha for the fraud she committed, but it bears remembering that she got into this fix because she refused to go on welfare, which would have entitled her to Medicaid and protected her from sky-high hospital bills. Having chosen to work, she cut herself off from that benefit and exposed her family to ex-traordinary debt. That was the problem she was trying to cure on Septem-ber 12, 2001.

Kyesha's family is expert at maneuvering around public bureaucracies, bill collectors, and the patchwork quilt of their own private safety net composed of kin and friends. Without these skills, and the resources that flow in and out of various linked households, no one would be able to make ends meet.[10] Dana is practiced in the art of minor fraud. When Kyesha was born, Dana put her own maiden name on the baby's birth certificate. When her husband died, Dana then began to collect his Social Security as a widow and to receive SSI payments on behalf of her children. Meanwhile Aunt Beth, Dana's sister, who works out on Long Island, has been claiming Kyesha and her sister as dependents under their "real" last name—that is, their father's name—to get the tax deduction. Neither Kyesha nor her sister has ever lived with Aunt Beth.

Fortunately for all parties, Kyesha has never wanted to get a driver's li-cense. Living in New York City, where parking is a nightmare and public transportation is reliable, she has never needed a car. Lacking any money for travel, Kyesha had also never tried to get a passport. These days, however, she's thinking she might like to visit Aruba or Jamaica, and for that she would need a legal passport. Having lost her birth certificate, Kyesha hopped the subway to the registry to get a new copy, but there she discovered that there was no person on record with her name. After twenty-eight years as Kyesha Smith, it seemed that she was a nonentity.

Suddenly it dawned on Kyesha that if she tried to straighten out these legal records, she would run the risk of exposing Beth and Dana's fraudulent claims. Yet the longer she exists in officialdom under a fraudulent name, the more she risks getting in trouble herself: "My [public] housing contract—that's considered fraud [because my name is incorrect]. And if you commit fraud, you lose your job. So it's like, damn, I'm not even going to get into this. You know, I probably could fight it and beat it because I had no knowledge of what my mother has done. And if they look through all my records, all through the years, I've been working under [her maiden name]. I've never used [my father's name] for anything. But what [my aunt] might have used [my father's name] for, I have no idea."

It takes these kinds of "fixes" to get by in many poor households, and while most people realize it's a form of cheating, they don't see it as a major immoral act.[11] You hustle, you "fix" things, you work at legitimate jobs, you avoid paying the utility bill in order to make the rent, you help your neighbors and relatives, and only after all of these work-arounds are in play can you manage to make it from one end of the month to another.

The trickiest and most emotionally fraught forms of money management involve the taxes that coresident relatives place on one another for goods and services. When Kyesha lived with Dana, she paid the phone bill, Dana paid the rent (after the subsidy was figured in), another relative paid for the cable bill, and the uncle Kyesha and Dana looked after (who didn't live in their house at all) covered the gas and electric. Balancing the contributions of all of these parties is a delicate business, and it rarely works smoothly. Kyesha resents her eldest sister's freeloading and the fact that she dropped out of school and has no skills she can parlay in the job market. Her complaint is more pragmatic than moralistic: if Irene can't get a decent job and spends her time loafing with a boyfriend, she is a parasite on the extended household system whose leisure is coming out of Kyesha's hide, among others. Kyesha contemplates the day that she becomes the matriarch of this clan—a day that may not be too far off, since Dana has been diagnosed with cancer: "I already told my mother that if something happens to her, Irene is getting kicked out of the house because the rent won't be [a Section 8–subsidized] $220 no more. I have an income—that rent's gonna be $690 a month. 'You and your man ain't going to be laying up in that house sleeping, not paying shit. I don't care if you *offered* me money. I don't like your lifestyle. I don't like that you blame everybody for you not getting a job because *you* dropped out in the eighth f——ing grade.' No, I'm not tolerating that shit."

Kyesha doesn't understand why Dana puts up with Irene's antics in the first place. Their half sister, Jimona, works hard in school and is determined to go to college. Jimona, now fourteen, is the one Kyesha is most proud of. She has made Jimona the beneficiary of her own life insurance policy, after her own son, in recognition of her achievements. But Irene is another story. Indeed, Kyesha has let it be known that the day their mother is laid to rest, some drastic changes will be in the offing. Blood may be thicker than water, but it isn't thick enough to cushion Irene. Kyesha has her mother's power of attorney and a plan for what she will do with it: "I told [my sisters and brother] 'I love all of y'all, but if Ma ever die, the hell with you all. I'm not kissing none of your asses. Irene, you and boyfriend better find an apartment soon because . . . if my mother ever got to the point where she was in a hospital and god knows there's no point for her? I'm going to literally tell you, 'You have to leave the house. You're not living with me. . . . You have nasty ways and I don't like it.'"

Irene got the message and tried to strike a deal. "Just give me $1,000," she told her mother, "and I'll leave." Dana wasn't buying. Irene and her boyfriend are still there.

There is more than sibling rivalry at work; distinct cultural systems are in play. From Kyesha's perspective, a competent adult is someone who works for a living, pulls her own weight, and does what she can for others in the family. She embraces this mainstream model so thoroughly that even Dana comes in for a load of criticism for her many years on welfare. Kyesha doesn't respect people who sit on their rear ends and collect public aid, and she doesn't appreciate the tax deductions out of her paycheck that go toward making such a life possible. Never mind that Dana's availability as a child minder has made it possible for Kyesha to stay in the workforce. The matriarch has fallen short of credible adulthood, and her daughter looks down on her for it. Irene is even worse, for she doesn't even make the effort to hustle the way Dana does. She isn't out there hooking people up with jobs as Dana has done for Kyesha; she isn't helping out with child care or braiding hair for some pocket change. Instead, she is sucking her relatives dry and bringing a dependent man into the house in the bargain. Structural arguments about changing labor markets do not cut it with Kyesha; even when she allows that decent jobs are harder to find, she is not ready to let anybody in her family off the hook. She cleaned urine off of elevator walls and wore a Burger Barn uniform that neighbors disrespected. Jimona studies hard. If they can do the right thing, Kyesha muttered to herself, why the hell can't the rest of the family? The values debate goes on in her head and spills out of her mouth. She can't wait to make her virtues stick.

Yet Kyesha wasn't about to sit around waiting for her mother to die. Living under the same roof with Irene was getting on her nerves, and Dana's high-handed ways with Anthony were bothering her too. She redoubled her efforts to earn more money, hoping that she could save enough to move out on her own. Not only did Kyesha field two legitimate jobs, she also worked up a couple of entrepreneurial prospects on the side: "I would take $1,000 or so out of my pocket, give a party, sell tickets for $10 a head, have 300 people. Right there, that's three grand! And if they're buying drinks for $2 or $3, I was getting like $7,000. . . . But the place I liked to give the parties . . . banned it because the DJ punched this girl in the face, knocked her unconscious, and the f——ing ambulance had to come and get her."

Kyesha had rented the recreation room in her own housing project for these parties, and because she was a resident, the management charged her only $250 to use the space. Shut down in Malcolm X, she turned to another project for a party location, but there she was asked to pay the full fee of $800. That was the end of that money-making scheme.

Another opportunity presented itself when public housing finally came through with an apartment for her in another Harlem neighborhood, way uptown near the Dominican enclave of Washington Heights. Initially Kyesha was delirious at the idea of having her own place. Finally, she could get out from under her mother and live life on her own terms. Financial needs argued against it, though. Although the rent was only $481 a month, that was a big chunk of her earnings. Instead, she offered the place to her uncle, a harmless, semifunctional military veteran who gave her $600 a month for it. He also handed over an ATM card that gave her access to an account she could withdraw money from to pay for his necessities. One day Kyesha walked into that Washington Heights apartment and found her uncle kneeling against the bed in a prayer position, naked from the waist down—and dead.

Several weeks later, as the family settled his affairs, Kyesha discovered that her uncle had stashed away nearly $90,000 in a savings account in Banco Hispania. Evidently he had let his military pension pile up year after year, living frugally and apparently oblivious to his own wealth. Because no will could be found, his next of kin, a sister who had ignored him for the previous decade at least, got the windfall, while Kyesha and her mother, who *had* actually cared for him, were left with zero. Incensed by this injustice, Kyesha took the few thousand left in the ATM account to which he had given her access, kept half of it and gave half to Dana.

This helped to cushion Kyesha a bit, but it all seemed to evaporate in short order under the pressure of bills. What she needed was a job that paid better than Burger Barn. Having put in four or five summers cleaning up around the Malcolm X Project, she caught the eye of one of the supervisors, who encouraged her to put in an application for a proper (not part-time) job as a janitor. After years of applying for city jobs, Kyesha didn't hold out that much hope. To her amazement, however, she landed the job, which instantly boosted her salary, gave her the health insurance she needed, and opened the door to the wonderful world of overtime pay. With a decent salary in hand, she and Anthony moved into the apartment her uncle left behind when he died.

It is not paradise, but it is, at least, hers. Anthony claims the only proper bedroom, which is furnished with a heavy wooden bunk bed. The other bunk, he explains, is for his sibling, whenever he gets one. Kyesha's bedroom occupies what would otherwise be a living room; a large queen-size bed dominates the space, and a small kitchen leads off from it. A confessed TV addict, Kyesha indulged herself in a large-screen monitor and has a huge collection of DVDs, stored in racks around the walls and on top of the mirrored dresser opposite the foot of her bed. The apartments in the postwar building have low ceilings and long corridors that let in only a modest amount of light, so Kyesha brightened the atmosphere with liberal amounts of rose and orange paint, blotted on with sponges to achieve a textured effect.

It seems to suit Ramsey, her live-in boyfriend, a Puerto Rican man also in his late twenties, who spends a lot of time at home with Kyesha. It's an on-and-off-again bond, as most of Kyesha's relationships with men have been since the years when she was Juan's steady girl. Ramsey grew up in the Malcolm X Project where Kyesha lived until she got her own place, and where she works at the moment. They have circled around each other for quite some time. Ramsey has been in and out of jail several times on drug charges, which cooled Kyesha's ardor a bit and sent her looking around for other company. She found it in Henry, a married man and blue-collar construction worker who had some assignments around the project where she works. She has had her disappointments in both relationships:

Me and Ramsey been intimate off and on for, like, three years. . . . He just got out of jail, but I didn't know that. . . . He had told me, like, six months later. He was like, "Look, you're a really nice girl. You work hard and you got a lot of stuff going for you . . . and, to be honest with you, I'm not ready to settle down. I just got out of jail. I need to sew my wild oats, which means instead of making you just another piece of ass, let's just be friends. We can hang out, whatever."

So I was hurt by that, of course, because I had dated him for six months. So I started seeing this other guy named Henry. Been through a terrible divorce with his ex-wife. . . . His [current] wife had [cheated on him and] had a kid by somebody else, while making him believe it was his. He didn't find out until after the kid was five.

Henry had been so distraught about his wife's affair that he'd had a vasectomy so that she couldn't fool him again. He withheld this little bit of information from Kyesha, who had told him she was looking to have another child. Between that betrayal and his generally controlling behavior, Kyesha dumped Henry. He promptly took up with another woman and later married her, something he had refused to consider with Kyesha.

On the rebound, Kyesha ran into Ramsey once again. One night he was so hung over that she gave him a key and told him to let himself out when he woke up in the morning. The key never came back. He moved in and stayed. On one level, this pleases Kyesha no end. She has been longing for a real man for years, and most of the eligible prospects have either used her as a short-stay girlfriend, turned out to be married when they assured her they weren't, or were down on their financial luck and looking for a free ride. Kyesha doesn't meet many "good" men living and working in the projects. She rarely runs into men who make as good a living as she does. She fantasizes about hooking up with such a man, imagines that she'll dress up in a slick outfit and go clubbing in the financial district, where she might run into her dream date. But the probabilities are against Kyesha, as she well knows.

For the moment, then, she settles for Ramsey, but not without reservation. She worries about his attraction to the drug trade, especially since Ramsey's legitimate job, as a processor at a large bakery, pays very little. Given his prison record, this job is about the best he can hope for, although the pay is so meager that Ramsey maintains a steady hand in the drug business to supplement it.[12] "Three-time felon, one more time, twenty-five to life he gets," Kyesha notes with a worried tone. "I'm like f——this. I'm not getting involved." But the fact is, she has gotten involved—in his life, not his trade. She doesn't ask too many questions about what he does during the day when she is at work. When it becomes clear as day that he is selling weed to augment his paycheck, she unloads: "I told him I don't want his dirty money. He can take it and shove it. . . . And he gets mad. Like, 'What the f——[is the matter with you]?' [I tell him] 'I don't want your dirty money.' So he'll do something like buy sodas. Pepsi, bread. He'll buy groceries because he know I ain't going to take it from his hand. Because the first thing a man who sells drugs [says] when he get caught, 'Oh, I was doing it for *us*.'"

Ramsey wants to assume something approximating a traditional relationship and doesn't care for the way he is beholden to Kyesha. She understands the complication, but when it gets in the way of having a good time, she loses patience. If she can afford to treat them both, why not? "I'll ask him to come out with me and go to the movies and he'll tell me no. And I go, 'Why?' He'll say, 'Well, when we go out, I want to pay for it. If I can't pay for it, then we're not going out.' So I think he has a thing about me making more money than he does."

During his high-dealing days Ramsey netted nearly $2,000 a week. Runners did the dealing for him, while he accrued the benefits.[13] Ramsey could throw a lot of cash around in those days, which is why he chafes at the idea that he no longer has money to spend on his woman.

This is the first time in her life Kyesha has lived with a man who is dealing drugs. She worries about the consequences of "Ramsey's baggage." Dangerous strangers, legal vulnerability, and the poor example that illegal activity sets for her ten-year-old son—these are the occupational hazards that trouble Kyesha. Convinced that kids take note of their surroundings and mimic what they see, she worries about the lessons Anthony is absorbing from Ramsey: "When kids see you do shit, they just wind up doing it. It just generates over. . . . They see their father or the grandmother allowing these type of people [in the house] and they going to get hooked on the bullshit. You know, it's like a 90 percent chance because you're putting them in that environment and that's all they know."

Why, then, did she let Ramsey into her life? "I got to the point of being so lonely," she confessed, "that I was like, maybe my standards are too high. . . . Let me go for somebody just for liking them. That's what I did." But she was right to worry, she now realizes, because the more time he

spends in her house, the scarier the consequences: "I care about him a lot
. . . I do. I can't say I don't. But I don't know what I'm going to do with that
man. I tell him, 'You're not gonna smoke that shit in my house; don't bring
your shit to my house. You want to stay on the street, you keep the street
over there in the projects where our parents live. And you let your mother
be OK with that shit, but when you come up here . . .'"

How does Ramsey deal with these demands? "[He stays] quiet. Quiet."
Kyesha pays the rent, the phone bill, and brings home the food. Ramsey is
a kept man, and he knows it. All he can throw into the power equation is
affection, constancy, or the absence of either. This defines the struggle between them: "I say I want to do this in life: I want to get married. I want to
have another kid. [He responds,] 'Well, my financial situation ain't right.'
[I say,] 'Well, when the hell is it going to get right? When are you going to
make it right?'" Silence.

Middle-class women are not unfamiliar with this struggle. Getting their
men to commit and settle down is hard. But Kyesha finds that her options
in the marriage market are limited to men like Ramsey, and time is passing.[14] She would like to fill that second bunk bed in Anthony's room; she
would like to have a husband to rely on. Wild as she can be on Saturday
night, there is another Kyesha lurking within, one that would like some
degree of dependability in her life. She wonders whether that will ever
come to pass. Like many black women, she worries that she will not have
that option or that she will find herself forever limited to losers.[15]

Although Kyesha thinks about the implications of her romantic life for
her son, she rests a little easier knowing that his father is so much a part of
his life. Juan keeps his son three days a week, makes an effort to take him
to museums or the New York Aquarium, which is several hours away by
public transit. Once a Burger Barn worker but now a born-again Christian
working as a file clerk, Juan is hopeful that he can give Anthony the kind of
stability, affection, and extra-classroom education that he did not have
himself. If Anthony emerges out of his childhood with a stock of "cultural
capital," it will probably be his "absent" father's doing.

This is not to say that Kyesha's own upward mobility has been of no
consequence for Anthony. He does not have to worry about being evicted
from the home he knows. His mother can and does provide for him, especially the sneakers and clothes that early adolescents live and die for.
Most of all, now that Kyesha can afford their own apartment, Anthony is

no longer the object of struggle between his mother and grandmother. There is less conflict in his immediate world, though he is aware that Ramsey and his mother have their differences. How much Anthony knows about Ramsey's drug business is anyone's guess, but thus far Kyesha's worry that he will imitate his elders has not been realized.

There are other potential benefits for Anthony if his mother keeps her grip on the civil service. Some day, she might be able to help him get a decent job too. Kyesha has observed that this is one of the few routes that are open to people like her and, by extension, some day to Anthony. Other routes, in her judgment, are closed: "Skilled trades—carpenter, plumber, brick-layer, glazer—is a predominantly white field. And that's guaranteed. You could count the blacks or Hispanics in that field throughout the five boroughs. To get those jobs, you don't come from where I come from, like a janitor. All you have to do is have five years' experience on the job [to get a job in the building trades]. Your father's a glazer and you've been working with your dad for five years and he own a company, he can put that down on a reference for you and then they'll snatch your application to get the job."

The difficulty of securing the high-paying, unionized jobs in the skilled trades makes the civil service that much more appealing to African Americans, who have trained their eyes on these occupations for decades. These jobs are among the few prospects for steady work with benefits, like health insurance, pensions, disability, and overtime. Now that Kyesha has been blessed with just such an opportunity, she goes the extra mile to try to pull her friends and family members along with her. The minute the grapevine carries word of an opening, she is on the phone, badgering one of her "partners" to get an application in. Not all of them qualify, of course, because a high school diploma is required. But those who do will hear from Kyesha if they look like reliable material. She refuses to use her stock of brownie points for total losers. But for those who might be able to cut it, Kyesha has become a kingpin, a person worth knowing. She is the "go to" girl for friends back at the Barn or from the projects who are looking for an opportunity.

Alas, few of her long-time friends can play the same role in her life. Because she has outstripped them in the race toward the top, they possess little information that would be valuable to Kyesha. New people that she has met on the job are another story. A couple of Italian American men who

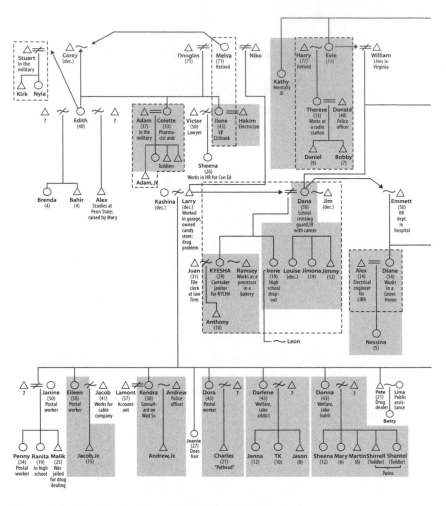

Figure 1.1   Kyesha's family tree, 2002. Art by Robert Levers.

are higher up in the hierarchy of the Housing Authority have taken a liking to Kyesha. One in particular has become something of a mentor, urg-
ing her to study for the periodic exams for managerial jobs, clueing her in
to the story on raises and promotions. Even though union rules make
many of these things public and transparent, informal knowledge is still
important. For example, the fact that the classes are less valuable than the
manual in preparing for the managerial exams is something one learns
from friends in the know. Without this informal coaching, Kyesha proba-

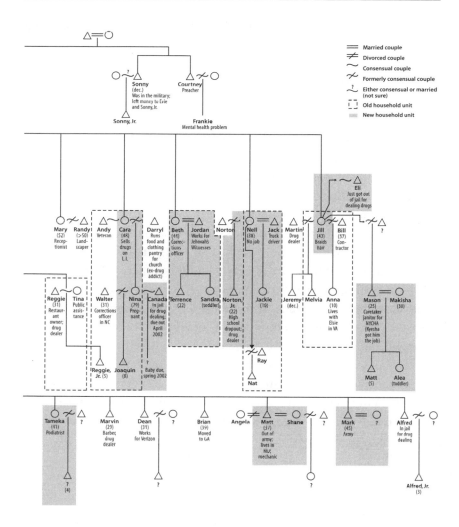

bly would be unaware of the opportunities for heating and plant technicians. She wouldn't have paid attention to the notices that come from the downtown office.

It would be a blessing if Kyesha could translate her occupational mobility into real financial security, perhaps buying an apartment of her own. Gazing out of the window of her rental in the projects, she is not too happy with what she sees. It's a tough neighborhood that has more serious crime problems than the Malcolm X Project, where she works. Kyesha would like nothing more than to beat it out of there and find a place in a

safer enclave. Despite earnings that exceed the wildest dreams she had
when I first met her in 1994, such a move seems unlikely. She estimates
she would need to double her earnings before she could afford even a
modest one-bedroom apartment, unless she finds a dependable man to
share the burden. Ramsey does not seem like a promising candidate. He is
not wedded to the drug trade by choice; a man with a prison record like his
does not impress many legitimate employers as the trustworthy type. But
one shouldn't count on Ramsey pulling his weight with the household
finances. So Kyesha appears to be stuck, and she has found few ways to
stockpile savings that could translate into real assets.

Yet, considering the circumstances of her own upbringing, and the fortunes of other family members in the same generation—siblings and cousins aplenty—she is not doing too badly. Her family tree (Figure 1.1) tells a
complicated story of lives that run the gamut from success stories like her
half-brother Alex, who works as an electrical engineer for the Long Island
Railroad, to her sister, Irene, who dropped out of school and is unemployed. Kyesha has uncles who work for local hospitals and the police department, and cousins who are drug dealers who have been in and out of
jail. Her aunt Cara sells drugs out on Long Island while her ex-husband
runs a food and clothing pantry for his church. Kendra, her cousin who
works on Wall Street as a consultant, lives with Andrew, who is a police officer. Two of Kyesha's triplet cousins developed serious cocaine habits, but
the third is a life-long postal worker. A number of her male cousins work
for AT&T.

Problem cases outnumber the triumphs in her family constellation, but
there are examples of upstanding citizens who have done well for themselves. Few of Kyesha's more privileged relatives have made a mark in
the private sector. Instead "city jobs," or positions with the public utilities, are the holy grail of the job seekers among them. Steady work at
good wages, with medical and retirement benefits—that is what everyone
has been after, from her grandmother on down. Since Kyesha made this
breakthrough, she has conscientiously tried to foster others whom she
felt were reliable into the ranks of the Housing Authority, like her cousin
Mason.

Like the other successful people in her network, Kyesha has learned that
one has to be judicious in choosing those who can make good use of an
opportunity and shut out the people who abuse her trust. She learned

that lesson long ago, through the example of her grandmother Evie, who opened her doors to her grown children when they were needy and ended up taking in so many of them that she sold her house to her daughter Beth and moved into an apartment. Evie figured she could "just say no" if she lacked the space for them to move into, but she was only partially successful. As the kinship chart in Figure 1.1 shows, in 1995 Evie had a three-generation household consisting of her common-law husband, Harry, their grown daughter, Therese, and son-in-law, Donald, and their two sons, Daniel and Bobby. Therese and Donald had fallen on hard times; neither one had a job, though Donald was training as a truck driver. By 2002, the same people were still under Evie's roof, though by then Donald had found a job as a police officer and Therese was working as a gofer at a radio station. Despite her best efforts, Evie has not been able to outrun her family obligations, and now she hopes that her kin will help her as she reaches her mid-70s.[16] Fortunately, they are indeed better positioned to support the matriarch of the clan.

Kyesha is not looking to repeat her grandmother's example in her own home, though it is not hard to imagine her in years to come with multiple generations under her roof. She takes after Evie in her willingness to help others, albeit from a distance, and her constant monitoring of her kin. If you want to know how someone is doing in the extended clan, it is a sure bet that Kyesha will know. Those social graces have stood her in good stead in her life as a worker, both at Burger Barn and now in the Housing Authority. Her generosity attracts the positive attention of fellow workers, who know that she has a certain soft spot for the people she spends her days with. She displays none of that sullen front, familiar to many New Yorkers who have to contend with public housing bureaucrats. Kyesha puts people at the center of her world, and they return the favor.

The Story of Carmen and Sal

Piled high in Carmen's double closet is a treasure chest of lamps, dishes, cooking pots, silverware, curtains, sheets, towels, and home decorations—all neatly packed in their original boxes, awaiting the day when Carmen and Salvador move into their first house. The microwave oven in her apartment kitchen broke down two months ago, but Carmen steadfastly refuses to open the brand new one that is stuffed onto a high shelf in the treasure closet. Its debut must also await the day they head for the suburbs and wave good-bye to the teeming city streets and Spanglish cacophony that mark her Washington Heights enclave.

"This neighborhood is nauseating," Carmen snorts. "I hate it!" It's not like Carmen to be so irritated, but she is particularly upset because that day her neighbor had torn down the clothesline the building super had strung between their two fourth-floor apartments. Carmen had paid good money for that line, but her neighbor was hogging the space and, with two little kids, Carmen has a lot of laundry. After several heated arguments, Carmen declared that she was the proper owner of the clothesline and demanded that Rosita stop using it. An hour later, Rosita bellowed out the window and when Carmen appeared to see what the ruckus was all about, Rosita waved a knife in the air and cut the line down before Carmen's eyes. Until the line can be restrung—to a different neighbor's window—laundry is stretched out over every surface in Carmen's tiny kitchen, which doubles as the family's only eating space. "It's gonna cost me seventy dollars to fix the damn laundry line," she groused.

Jorge, the Dominican super, drops by to fix Carmen's bathtub, which has been backed up and spewing hair balls for the past week. She barely has time to remind him about the leaking radiator in the living room because she is elbow-deep in *habiculelas* (beans), which must be sifted and cleaned by hand, rinsed in water over and over, and finally cooked in a large pot, a ritual familiar to any Dominican housewife. Carmen calls the corner grocery store to order a fresh chicken from the live poultry market. "Miguel [the store owner] buys from the live market once or twice a week," she explains over her shoulder, "and I only buy from him on those days." Salvador will be home by 5:00 and he expects to see dinner on the table, so Carmen is in a hurry to make everything right.

Karina, Carmen's seven-year-old daughter, has the week off from school and finally struggles out of bed at 11:00 AM and wakens her little sister, Gina, a three-year-old whose dark, curly hair frames a pair of cherubic cheeks. Ordinarily they would both be shaken out of their slumbers at 5:30 AM so that Carmen could brush their hair, feed them breakfast, and bundle them up for the daily walk to school and the day care center. The morning ritual leaves Carmen just enough time to hop the subway to Midtown Manhattan, where she works the early shift at Lord and Taylor. But today they can rest up and try to distract their mother from her chores.

Karina wanders into the living room, the largest of the four rooms in the family's one-bedroom apartment, and snuggles into the plastic-covered sofa, her favorite blanket wrapped around her shoulders. She likes to fiddle with the decorative birdcage that hangs over the couch, though Carmen shoos her away from it. Karina extracts permission to watch TV, bundles the blanket around her waist and waddles back into the bedroom she shares with Gina. Their twin beds are covered in bright quilts and puffy pillows, which they use to prop themselves up before the large TV and VCR in the corner. Dolls and stuffed animals cram every corner, spilling out onto the floor. Looking out into the airshaft at the offending clotheslines snapping in the wind, Karina figures she can probably go outside after her favorite cartoons.

Now that the beans are cooking and the chicken is on the way, Carmen sets about straightening up the room that she and Salvador share, a dining room converted into their own little palace. Proud of her decorative touch, she dusts the scented candles and artificial flowers that grace their dresser. A queen-size bed, an entertainment center, and a desk with a computer fill up the modest room, giving it that overstuffed feeling: too many things jammed into too small a space. It's the story of their lives.

What Carmen really longs for on a day like this is a green lawn and a quiet street where Karina and Gina can ride their bikes. She wouldn't say no to a clean park with smooth wooden benches (rather than the splintered ones in the run-down park at the end of the block, with its broken swings and glass-strewn pavement.) Carmen would like to be able to send the kids outside on their own, rather than feeling obliged to hover over them so that they don't get hurt. She knows that Karina wants to enjoy the kinds of things that suburban kids can do so easily. "Karina wants to have a yard," Carmen sighs. "She wants to play outside, ride her bike, have a dog, rabbits, and birds."

Perhaps even more than these amenities, Carmen longs for the kind of community she grew up with in the Dominican Republic, even if it was poorer than Washington Heights. Everyone in her neighborhood knew her and her extended family; no one was ever alone. "In my country," she explains, "people help you if you fail. They want to know if you are OK." Not so in the big city, where everyone is in a rush and no one knows your name or your history. "Here, if you fall, people will walk over you. Here life is quick," she says rapping her knuckles on the counter. "I don't like that about the city. If you don't know your next-door neighbor, he may pass you by and won't even say good day."

This lament has grown stronger since Carmen and Salvador visited Grand Rapids, Michigan, where most of Carmen's extended family has now moved. Drawn to New York along with thousands of other Dominican immigrants in the 1970s, Carmen's aunts and uncles later joined a secondary stream that has begun to change the face of the Midwest and the American South, now the destination of choice for many first-time immigrants as well as seasoned veterans like Carmen. In the 1980s, when the auto factories and the steel mills were shedding jobs at a record pace, immigrants stayed put in the gateway cities of Los Angeles, New York, and Miami. But the prosperity of the 1990s revived the auto plants in the Midwest and the prospect of good wages in the packing houses of Kansas.[17] Carmen's relations found good fortune in Michigan:

> My aunt Bella was the first. Her husband wanted to live there because all of his family lives there. He works in a food processing plant and Bella works at a hospital. My grandmother followed Bella there because Bella is her favorite daughter. Grandma takes care of all of her grandchildren. After that, Uncle Leonis left. He's an accountant. Then Imelda left; she has a beauty salon. Then Belinda [followed], and she works in the hospital too. Belinda's husband has a beauty salon too. After Belinda, Anastasia went; she also works in the hospital. When my grandmother left, she took my father and Nardo, his brother. Gimela was the last to leave, in 1999.

The chain migration pulled nearly twenty of Carmen's family members to Grand Rapids, leaving only Carmen and her sister behind, a little remnant of the nuclear family. Some of these Michigan newcomers are working-class hospital employees who do maintenance (Bella and Belinda); others are entrepreneurs; and still others are skilled workers: Gimela is a nurse. Collectively, they help one another find jobs, housing, and child care, and just as they did in New York, they patch together a safety net that prevents anyone from falling on hard times. Since wages are high in Grand Rapids and housing is cheap, some relatives have been able to buy houses and build up some equity. In the space of two generations, they have found a degree of security that would have been impossible to grasp in the Dominican Republic. Carmen is tempted to move, and every phone call from the Midwest ends with the plea, "Come, join us!" Much as their lives (and especially their houses) appeal to her, Carmen looks on from the distance of the big city and places the idea on the back burner.

In part, her reluctance to move stems from the upward mobility that she and Salvador have experienced in New York. Much as she may complain, the fact is that New York City has been good to them both. When we met in 1993, Carmen was making change at Burger Barn, and Salvador, then her *novio* rather than her husband, had only recently left the Barn for a slightly better job stocking shelves on the night shift for a pharmacy chain. Eight years later, Sal was pulling in nearly $46,000 a year as the manager of a video shop. When Carmen works, they have a combined income of more than $60,000 a year, which is respectably middle class, although it doesn't stretch as far in New York as it might elsewhere.

The pathway from Burger Barn to their current jobs was far from straightforward. It was full of blind alleys and exploitative bosses, as well as opportunities that boosted their prospects higher than they had ever thought possible. Hard work and drive have paid off for them, but networks and contacts were essential to making those virtues matter. Family supports were critical, particularly once Carmen and Sal had kids of their own. It is a saga of zigs and zags rather than a straight line to success, and even though they have done well relative to their starting point, they cannot afford anything larger than a one-bedroom apartment, especially if they want to save.

After their wedding celebration in 1994, Carmen and Salvador moved into a tiny apartment in the heart of New York's Dominican community. Back then, Carmen's grandmother, aunts, uncles, and cousins were still living in the same building; their homes had adjoining doors. The little ones in this entourage whizzed through the apartments, while Grandmother held court. Spanish-language cable TV hummed all day in the background, but silence ruled when the soap operas beloved back home were on the air.

Living cheek by jowl had its downside, of course. The newlyweds had no privacy. Yet since they also had no money, the upside was clear: Carmen could eat with her relatives and Salvador could go visit his when the food budget got too tight. And tight it was. Even with two minimum-wage paychecks, the rent took up nearly 80 percent of their earnings. Carmen was in charge of the household accounts, and she began to hide the bad news from her twenty-two-year-old husband. In September she would pay the phone bill and stiff Con Edison; in October she switched her loyalties and sent a check to the utilities company and let Verizon wait for a month.

Financial pressures grew to almost unbearable levels when Carmen's pregnancy (little Karina on the way) turned out to be problematic. Without health insurance or the cash to pay a doctor, she went without prenatal care for as long as she could. But in the middle of our fieldwork period Carmen developed a high fever, could not hold food down, and began a downward spiral of weight loss—not a good sign. Carmen's aunt took her aside and lectured her until she relented and signed up for public assistance, hoping to lay claim to a Medicaid card. A sympathetic caseworker rushed the paperwork through, and Carmen was able to see a physician regularly after that. He assured her that the virus had not hurt the baby. Karina was born without incident several months later.

The family needed more money to make ends meet, so Sal took a second job in a food pantry. He worked all night in the pharmacy, came home to catch a few hours' rest, and then headed to his church to hand out hot meals to the homeless for a modest salary. It wasn't enough to keep the family afloat, though, and his absence only made Carmen more anxious to find a way to get out of the house. After all, with her grandmother on deck to help take care of Karina, she reasoned she could manage part-time hours at the very least.

In 1996, when the baby had grown into a toddler, Salvador finally relented, grudgingly, and Carmen went back to Burger Barn to recapture her job as a hostess, handling organized birthday parties for hyper-excited children. The fast-food restaurant is in the heart of her Dominican neighborhood, and so everyone who frequents the place speaks Spanish. Carmen is still more comfortable in her native tongue, and in her corner of Manhattan nothing else is really required. A hard-working, efficient, organized, and bright woman, Carmen was always a valued asset at Burger Barn. The daughter of a teacher in the Dominican Republic, Carmen has completed several years of college, and she easily mastered the managerial tasks thrust in her direction. Had she wanted to stay with Burger Barn, it seems clear she could have been a general manager in a short period of time. Indeed, rival Burger Barns in the area bid for her and she moved back and forth between them, increasing her salary a marginal amount each time.

By January 1998, Carmen had had enough of the Barn. "I was pregnant [with Gina], but I didn't quit only because I was pregnant. I had worked for six days in a row; the last day I worked [at the Barn] was supposed to be my day off. They called [New Year's Day]. They were going to open at 10:00 AM and nobody else wanted to work. I was the only crazy one who picked up the phone that day, the unlucky one." The general manager told Carmen she had no choice. She protested, "It's my day off!" He cajoled her into coming into work, promising her that she would be able to leave at noon when the other swing manager arrived. "It was 1:00, 2:00, 3:00, 4:00, 5:00 PM, and no one else was there. At about 5:20, the owner arrived. He said that no one else was coming and that I had to stay and work until 7:00. I told him, 'You know what? I don't think so.' I got my things and left. He called me the following day and wanted to know if I was going back. I said, 'No I'm not! I'm tired of you.'" Carmen has her pride, and after nearly five years of hard work on behalf of Burger Barn, she determined that it was the end of the road for fast-food jobs.

Carmen returned to school to continue working toward a degree in psychology and promptly landed a work-study job at Bronx Community College, courtesy of Karina's godmother, Marisela. She worked the help desk in the computer center, assisting students who had no experience with the technology so that they could spell-check their papers, print their work, or do research on the Web. Marisela had put in a word with the Puerto Rican manager of the operation. Carmen, an Ecuadorean immigrant they called Dona Elvira, the "great-grandmother" of the help desk, and three African American students collectively comprised the *viejitas*, the "little old ladies" of the computer center. "It was always fun because you would do your homework there. I didn't have to worry about getting home to watch Karina and do my homework because I got it done there. When someone needed help [on the computers], they would raise their hand and then I'd help them. And when you didn't have homework, you hung out, talked about our husbands, married life, and all that."

Apart from providing Carmen with a lot of free marital counseling, the job opened her eyes to the possibility that teaching might be just the ticket. It seemed she had a gift for it, and since her mother is a teacher, she was familiar with the profession and eager to try it. Carmen and three coworkers trooped down to the New York City Board of Education together to apply for jobs as teachers' aides. Mountains of paperwork and civil service exams awaited them, which they duly completed. "They told us we qualified for the jobs," Carmen recalled, "but that there were many ahead of us. Nothing [happened]." They waited and then waited some more, in

vain, as it happened, for none of the *viejitas* was called in for a job. When
work-study ran out at the end of the spring semester, Carmen opted for
temporary retirement and waited for baby Gina to arrive in the middle of a
steamy August.

Carmen took a semester off from school to take care of her infant,
something the family could almost afford because, by now, Salvador was
making more money. After two years of working as a stock boy on the
night shift, he had moved up to the assistant manager slot. As good as that
sounded, it netted Sal a modest raise of only fifty dollars a week. When he
caught the next brass ring, the more coveted general manager slot, he
stepped up to $300 a week in salary, or slightly under the poverty line for a
family of four. Sal figured he could do better, especially with more experience under his belt, so he jumped ship to a rival drugstore chain and
boosted his take-home pay by almost $200 a week. The extra money was
more than welcome, but it came at a price: Salvador was working seventy-
hour weeks and Carmen was starved for his company, once again. "Look,
if you continue there, you gonna die," she lectured him. "He left home at
8:00 A.M. and got back at 10:00 at night. I would tell him, 'You only want
to be in retail? Do you think you can do something else?' And he would
say, 'That's my life, retail.'"

Salvador's father, a chef, emigrated to the United States when he was
twelve, and his mother works in a food factory. Sal grew up in a working-
class household that needed his income. Education was something other
people could afford; Sal was sent to work as soon as he could legally leave
school. In a society where the mantra of advanced education has grown
louder every year, Sal's trajectory led him to question his own intelligence.
He tried the GED exam several times and failed. Even though he missed a
passing score by only two points, he has given up on the goal of a high
school diploma.

Yet there are niches in the retail world where formal education does not
matter much, and fortunately for Carmen and her family, Sal finally stumbled on one of them: a managerial job in a video store. With a salary of
$46,000 a year, Sal has come a long way from where we found him only
eight years before, flipping burgers for the minimum wage.

They could move closer to their dream of a real house if Salvador were
more accommodating of Carmen's desire to work full-time. He encour-
ages her to go to school and is proud of her educational accomplishments.
Sal thinks Carmen should go to the Fashion Institute of Technology be-

cause she likes clothes and stores. Never mind the tuition, which they cannot afford; if he was denied an education, she should have hers. But when Carmen wants to get a real job that pays decent money, so she won't have to ask Sal for a domestic allowance, he balks. Carmen responds with a tantrum. She threatens to walk out on their marriage if he doesn't capitulate, berating him for the undeserved jealousies he hints at when she works alongside other men. Waving her hands in the air, she blows these complaints off and tells him that she doesn't want to beg him for every dime. In the end, Carmen sneaks out and lands a job before Sal knows what has hit him, and he adapts fairly quickly to the increased household income, as well as to her happier state of mind.

That is more or less how Carmen ended up running a Laundromat for her uncle Jorge, who had observed that his industrious niece was going crazy with nothing to do all day but tending to kids and looking at magazines. "Since you like to work so much," he said with a slight challenge in his voice, "I have an offer for you." Jorge had hired a contractor to set up Laundromats in several Spanish-speaking neighborhoods, and he needed people he could trust to run them during the day. The shop he had in mind for Carmen was in Brooklyn, an hour's subway commute from her home, but she jumped at the chance to get out of the house. On the days she worked, she would have to leave Karina, then age four, and Gina, only three months, in her aunt's care, having carefully prepared their food and clothes the night before. Even in the dead of winter, Carmen struggled out of bed at 5:30 AM and made her way to Brooklyn, where she spent the day bending her back: "I earned forty dollars a day. That place was huge. It had nineteen machines in the back and fifteen in front. They were huge machines, twenty-pound loads in each. There were twenty-something dryers. When I arrived, I said, 'Good morning.' I didn't ask what my job was; I picked up a rag and began to clean. I cleaned the outside of the machines. I cleaned the tables. I bought paper towels. I swept and mopped."

By the end of the first day, she thought to herself, "I'm gonna be dead by the end of the week." But she wasn't. In fact, Carmen did such a fine job that her uncle asked if she could move to a different Laundromat and help get it off the ground. "Look," he told her, "I really like that, on your first day, you took the initiative. I didn't have to tell you what to do, and I like that." Initially skeptical of his motives, Carmen relented after she saw the second store. It was much smaller—only ten washers and ten dryers—and she thought she could take her kids there with her. What's more, she reasoned, if she kept the kids with her for the morning, in the afternoon she could leave them with her aunt and go to school.

From then on, she woke up at 5:30, bathed and dressed her daughters, and boarded the subway with them by 7:00. "I'd brush my babies' hair on the train; the youngest would fall asleep. When we go to the Laundromat—we had a large window with a cement block below it—I would blow up an inflatable bed and let the girls sleep there, with a sheet over them. They slept there until noon. My husband went to the McDonald's that was two blocks away to get breakfast."

When her workday was over, Carmen took the subway back to Washington Heights, dropped the kids off, and scurried off to Bronx Community College and the degree program she had left behind when Gina was born. She stuck with the schedule for sixth months, quitting the job only when she found that she was failing in school as a consequence: "No one would come to relieve me at work. One week, the manager had me work the afternoon shift all week. I started at noon and left at midnight. That week I didn't go to school at all . . . If you miss class three times, it's terrible. Imagine, I was absent eleven times!"

The last straw was the day Anthony, the store manager, promised to relieve her in time to make a final exam. "No problem," he assured her. Carmen was uneasy. "I know how you are," she lectured him. "You get caught in traffic and don't make it." No, no, Anthony promised, "I'll be there early." She called at 2:00 to remind him, "It's my final!" Nervous, Carmen took the girls outside to catch a breath of fresh air and let Gina try her new trick: walking a few steps and plopping on the sidewalk. Carmen chatted with the woman next door, owner of the beauty parlor on the corner. "I hope he gets here on time," the neighbor commented, shaking her head. "I don't think it's fair for you to be losing classes." The lady across the street who ran a dry cleaning business concurred. "Why are you working here? You should be dedicating yourself to your schoolwork."

Carmen listened to them and fidgeted with her cell phone. Anthony wasn't answering. As 4:00 PM rolled around, she called again and caught him. "I'm stuck in traffic, but I'll be there in twenty minutes." Stomping with frustration, Carmen gave up, flipped the "Be Back in Five Minutes" sign on the door, and ran off to drop her daughters at her aunt's house. "My aunt said she needed to go out and couldn't watch the girls. She told me to leave them with her daughter, but my cousin hates kids and treats them bad. So I called my sister. She says, 'Sure, bring them here.' It was already 5:50. I dropped them off, walked six blocks and got into a cab. When I got to the university it was 6:40. The teacher refused to let me in."

If Carmen hadn't missed so many classes, the professor explained patiently, she could have taken a make-up exam. But with eleven absences, she would have to repeat the whole course. To make matters worse, Anthony left twenty-five messages on her home phone complaining that Carmen had left the store locked and unattended. "You told me you would be there in ten minutes, so the store wasn't closed that long, right?" Wrong. Anthony hadn't arrived until 10:00 PM. She hung up on him and never went back.

When the fall semester rolled around and Carmen was back in school, Salvador's hours at the pharmacy were still running late into the evening. She would get out of school at 4:00, pick up her daughters, and then sit at home without any adult company. Three months passed, and once again Carmen was restless. When a friend landed a job at a Lord and Taylor department store, the two women decided to see if they could secure a second position for Carmen. This time she did ask Sal if he had any objection. He did. "They filled your head with ideas!" Sal argued. "Stay home! Take care of your daughters. As long as your daddy [Sal] gives you money, you don't have to go anywhere."

"No, Sal," she explained. "It's not the same for me to earn my own money. When I earn my own, I feel important. And I can help with our household expenses."

Exasperated by her stubbornness, Sal relented. Carmen skipped down to Lord and Taylor and took the requisite drug tests, and after two weeks of training, she started the best job she has had to date: as a member of the "flying squad."

Today's department stores are run like collections of specialized boutiques. Each designer—from Tommy Hilfiger to Polo—has its own space and its own crew. At Lord and Taylor, few of the stock people who straighten up the clothes racks and place new items on the floor work for the store; instead, they are employees of the fashion design firms. Carmen was assigned to work with the clothing line DKNY, and she took to the job with gusto. Always a clothes maniac, she loves to arrange outfits with striking colors and jazzy styles. From 7:00 in the morning until 3:00 in the afternoon, Carmen creates order out of chaos:

I organize the front racks first because that's the first thing the customers see. Then I fix the center and finally the back. I figure out

what's needed on the floor, what merchandise was sold. Then I go to
the stockroom, grab the clothes I need, . . . scan the clothes to see
what has been marked down. . . . Now if I have new merchandise, I
have to make room for it. I move the old stock back and put the new
stuff up front. I change the fixtures so that everything looks different.
Colorful—you have to make the colors work. You can't have solid
with solid. And you have to mix and match when you change the
mannequins.

Though she was new to retail, Carmen took to it with alacrity and
quickly absorbed the importance of her role in the marketing process. "It's
up to us to make the customer feel good and buy our clothes. . . . We want
to see the sales go up, that way the vendors . . . will know that the person
who is working for them is doing a good job." She sees her work as a creative contribution to the sales mission. "Every time I create my wall and
front desk and change my floor and see that the clothes sell, I say [to my-
self], 'Man, I made it work.' I made the colors match. The clothes don't
come the way you see it displayed. No, it all comes separated. I dress the
mannequins. You try to mix and match so that people can see how they can
use a pair of pants."

Among the many jobs Carmen has held in the time I have known her,
this one gave her the greatest license to use her head, to make decisions on
her own. And because she is responsible for replenishing the inventory,
she can monitor the impact of her work. She can measure in a rough way
whether her artful designs are producing results, and that is a satisfying
feeling. In this respect, the job is like the work-study position she held in
the computer center, where the gratitude of her student customers signaled that she had made a difference. For while Carmen likes the income,
she also wants to feel she has achieved something for her trouble.

Most of her working life had been devoted to jobs that were less rewarding, largely because they were scripted and left only modest room for her
to exercise her own judgment. Were those years at Burger Barn helpful in
any respect in preparing her for Lord and Taylor? "Yes," she explained,
"because [in fast food] you deal with customers every day. As a cashier,
you're challenged, 'cause if you don't take care of your customer, they'll
yell at you [or] complain to the manager." Carmen noted that she had
started as a cashier and moved up to a hostess, where she had to master
more people skills, learn to figure out their needs, and control her temper

in the face of a hot-headed customer. "If I had gotten the job at Lord and Taylor before [Burger Barn]," she explained, "I don't think I could have put up with it." The Barn helped her come out of her own immigrant shell: "I used to be very timid. I think that working at Burger Barn helped me evolve into a sociable person. I'm not afraid to approach people or to be approached. Now I talk to the tourists. I ask them about their countries and even recommend clothes for them to buy, you see."

Her years of work experience and general tendency to assume responsibility lead Carmen to go beyond the call of duty. Like the other vendors with boutiques inside Lord and Taylor, DKNY shares its employees with the store. For the first two hours of their shift, they are supposed to straighten up clothes that do not belong to the specialty vendors and mark down sales items in areas other than their own. "In other words," Carmen explains, "Lord and Taylor gets free workers." They are paid by the vendors to do the work that is properly the responsibility of the store itself. If the night shift gets bogged down responding to the demands of the store, the day shift—Carmen and her co-workers—ends up with an overload. "When Marisa and William don't have time to organize their shops at night, we have to fix them in the morning. That's not right, [but] if their shops are disorganized, I have to organize them. I always organize William's shop because it's right next to mine—he's got the men's clothes. If I don't fix his area, it makes my area look bad. If Marisa's area is unorganized—she does infants—it makes William's area look bad, so I have to fix her area too, after I do my floor first."

These problems do not escape the attention of the vendors, who resent having to pay for work that is not properly theirs. Their representatives quiz Carmen about what the night-shift workers left behind, about whose work they actually accomplished on the payroll of Polo or Hilfiger. "If they can't do their job," the reps warn, "they'll be taken off the payroll." Carmen is valued for going the extra mile, and she is loyal to her fellow stock clerks and covers for them when they are press-ganged into doing something they shouldn't have to do.

Her job at the department store placed Carmen in the thick of the multicultural arena that is the New York City labor market. Carmen's floor managers are from Trinidad, while the night manager is Italian American. Her co-workers seem to hail from just about everywhere. "We're Dominicans, Boriquas [Puerto Ricans], from Trinidad, Jamaica, Saint Martin," Carmen explains. "What else? Americans, Polish, Russian,

Hindi." The diversity of Carmen's work world takes her out of the monocultural neighborhood that is her daily experience in Washington Heights. On her block, in the local park, in the poultry market and the corner store, everyone hails from the Dominican Republic. On the job, it's a different story. This is one of the many reasons why engagement in the labor market matters. It moves people who live under conditions of ethnic or racial segregation into an environment where their common identity as workers comes to the fore. And while they do not forget their own heritage, on the shop floor they tend not to dwell on the social divisions that often flare on the street.

While these friendships rarely transcend the barrier between home and work, they matter to Carmen in an emotional way. September 11 brought that truth home to her. The Midtown area was brought to its knees by the attack on the World Trade Center, in part because it is a stone's throw from the Empire State Building, which was rumored to be the target of bombs in the days that followed the attack. Penn Station, the main artery of the subway system on the West Side of Manhattan, was evacuated and closed for a period of time because of its proximity to the Empire State Building. Jittery workers in the tall towers in the surrounding blocks were afraid of being trapped in elevators. On September 13, Carmen was scheduled to go to work for her regular morning shift. Reporting for duty with her heart pounding unusually hard, Carmen did her best to calm down. She was riding up the escalator when the fire alarms sounded. Carmen scrambled to find Annie, her manager, terrified that another attack was in progress, and asked, "What happened?"

"Don't ask," Annie yelled over her shoulder, "Just go! Let's go! Go to the ground floor!" Hundreds of shop assistants cascaded down the escalators, but Carmen ran in the other direction, up to the floor where her fellow "flyers" were working: "No one told the flyers what had happened. The store was empty [that early in the morning] but no one told the people in that office what was happening. So I went to the ninth floor—I work on the seventh—and told the people there we had a bomb threat and they had to evacuate. Well, you know those Chinese women, and Gloria—she's American—they ran out of there yelling, 'Oh my God!'"

In an emergency, workers know, they are supposed to avoid the elevators, but the department store's escalators are so narrow that they could not bear the traffic of employees stampeding out of the ten-story building. Carmen broke the rules and led her party to the elevators. "Close the door, close the door!" they hollered, but Carmen prevented the elevator from moving.

"No," she insisted, "we're missing Jill." Jill, the Irish American manager on the ninth floor, walks with a cane and was hobbling as fast as she could in their direction. With her safely inside, the elevator finally started its descent at what seemed to the panicky workers too fast a speed. Ultimately, though, they made it, just in time to see the whole elevator system shut down, forcing the remaining staff onto the stairs. Once outside on the sidewalk, Carmen's crew could take inventory of who was missing:

> We all started to cry because we didn't see Annie anywhere. . . . The sixteenth, seventeenth, and eighteenth floors all panicked. That's where the white people work, the ones in the executive offices. We call them *los blanquitos* [the little white ones]. I couldn't find Yanella—she lives next door—I couldn't find her. I saw Susan and said, "Where is Yanita?" She tells me, "I don't know, she was last with me in the cellar." So I began to cry, "Oh Yanita, she's gonna die."
>
> We finally moved when the police and bomb squad arrived. They moved us two blocks down. The Gap store was already closed; the people from the Empire State Building were running toward us. And we were yelling, "Annie, Annie!" It turned out she had stayed inside to make sure all of her people were out of the store. Yanella had exited out on the Sixth Avenue side of the store.

Carmen was entirely undone by the terror and stayed home from work the next day, trying to get a grip on her nerves. She paced the floor of her apartment, held onto Karina and Gina, baked up a storm, and periodically flopped onto the living room couch, staring into space.

Sunday was her day off, but she went into work anyway. By then, she just wanted to see her work friends face to face, to congregate with the fellow traumatized. "That day," she remembered a year later, "we told Annie that she shouldn't scare us again like that; that she shouldn't have waited for us to come out. You know what she told us? She said, 'I don't have anyone. I don't have dogs, cats, or anyone to care for.' She has no kids. She's forty years old. She says, 'If I die, don't cry for me.'" But what Annie really meant, Carmen realized, was that Yanita, Gloria, Jill, and the rest *are* Annie's family. Even if Carmen never sees Annie on her block, there is a bond there, and both of them feel it.

Carmen appreciates her work most of all because it makes her feel like a real adult who moves around in the world, rather than a housewife with no options. She understands that her need to mix with other workers disturbs her husband, and her own upbringing in the Dominican Republic has led her to share some of his values. It is not as though she thinks Sal is wrong on this count; Carmen is not happy about having to jerk her kids out of bed so early, and she has her misgivings about their child care. Yet the American experience has taught her another set of values, about what an adult woman should expect, about the importance of autonomy and her obligation to contribute to her household and her own development. The two perspectives are not easily reconciled, and her flip-flop pattern of staying home, then going to work, then retreating to the house, then stepping out into the labor market once more reflects the complexities of her thinking. Still, the struggle is worth it. "I like to feel the excitement of being in a hurry in the morning," Carmen insists. "It's a responsibility; you have to have motivation to [go to work]. . . . If it's your job, you have to go, you can't stay home, otherwise you'll get fired. . . . I don't like being locked up within four walls. If I'm [confined] I'll get fat, ugly, bored. When a woman is out in the street, working, going to school, she has to get dressed, look nice. That makes a man feel good because they say, 'Oh look at my wife! She looks so good when she goes out.'"

If all that mattered in retail was the motivation of workers like Carmen, she would have a future of upward mobility to look forward to. Yet because it is a bureaucratic environment loaded with rules—about punching in, the length of bathroom breaks, the half-hour lunch period—it is a system that even the most diligent can cross. Carmen discovered this unhappy fact one day when she was called on the carpet by Lord and Taylor's internal security department. It seems that Carmen had opened a Lord and Taylor Express Credit account in Sal's name. The employee handbook, she was lectured severely, prohibits "doing any transactions for co-workers, family members or friends." "I know that about transactions," Carmen told security, "but it didn't say anything about Express Credit." Carmen had taken an application home to Sal, who completed the form and gave it to her to bring it back to work, thus avoiding the long wait a mail-in application would require. Carmen had checked with various co-workers at the time she clocked the credit application in and was told that it wouldn't be a problem. Even the office manager had shrugged it off. "If anything was wrong," he explained, "you would get a slip that says 'Denied.'" Nothing of that description had ever come their way, so Carmen had assumed all was well and used the credit card to buy things in the store.

Carmen's employee ID was whisked away and she was suspended for two weeks for this violation of company policy. She was humiliated and embarrassed. "I felt awful," she said sadly. "If I had been fired for stealing something, then I would accept it. . . . But I couldn't do anything about Sal's card after the account was opened. The only thing I could do was tell my manager, and I did. So I felt bad because I did something without being aware of it. And if what I did was so bad, why didn't they say something?"

Ten months had elapsed between the issuance of Sal's card and Carmen's suspension. Annie was distraught on Carmen's behalf and upset about losing a dedicated, hard-working employee whose services she depended on. "She was crying," Carmen recalled. "She said, 'This is some bullshit, I can't believe this.'" Then Carmen said Annie lowered her voice and said, "I'm not supposed to tell you, but you need to get help from the union."

Carmen thought about it but then just gave up. She was embarrassed and humiliated, afraid to tell Sal (who would say he told her so, since he hadn't wanted her to take the job in the first place). "What hurts me most is my hard work, my daughters. My daughters have suffered because of my stubbornness to want to work. . . . I was getting my daughters up at 4:30 AM to dress them, comb them, make breakfast, make lunch, and make breakfast for my husband. I had to take the girls downstairs to the babysitter's apartment, and on many occasions they had to stay with my babysitter's boarder. Too many times, my daughters have been sick, and still I have gone to work because I didn't want to be absent."

Carmen had gone to work even when Gina was hospitalized for an intestinal blockage. The little one had to wear an oxygen mask; Carmen slept by her side in the hospital, then ran home in the morning to take Karina to the babysitter. She got so frantic she asked for a brief of leave of absence, but it was denied because too many other people were on vacation. Carmen had shouldered this burden and clocked in at Lord and Taylor. She had put in so many hours—without clocking in so that she would not rack up unauthorized overtime—that her manager had complained she would get fired for letting Carmen work when she wasn't supposed to. To work with that level of dedication and have it end in a cloud of suspicion put Carmen into a psychological tailspin.

"I can't stop thinking about [the suspension]," she says. "I lie in bed thinking about it until I fall asleep. I think about when they called me. I felt so humiliated; I felt stomped on. . . . Sal is happy. He's happy to see me at home. He likes to call home and find me there. But . . . I don't know. I'm not a housewife. I feel like an imprisoned bird at home."

Her co-workers call her to say that her station on the floor looks terrible without her. Her manager tried to intervene and get her reinstated, but Carmen was too crushed to pursue it any further. "I feel so angry," she laments, more in frustration than fury, "I wanted to set [that store] on fire." But nothing has changed her mind.

Carmen was unsure if she would ever find another job like the one she lost. Just as our fieldwork ended, she heard of an opportunity from Karina's godfather, Sal's best friend, who had once worked alongside both of them at Burger Barn. Their two families attended a baptism together, and Carmen told him of the debacle at work. "Don't let [those people] get to you," he said. "Come work for me." He runs the shoe section at an Old Navy store. Sal was livid, but as usual Carmen was ready to get back to work.

PART I

Chutes and Ladders

2

The Best-Case Scenario

❦

The economic context for *Chutes and Ladders* was one of extremely weak labor markets that gave way to unprecedented growth, which pushed unemployment down and encouraged firms to hire among groups that are routinely at the end of the queue. That prosperity did not last. Yet the expansion continued long enough for us to examine what happens to the working poor and their families when the economy improves around them. Were workers like Jamal, who labored at the bottom of the market, able to take advantage of opportunity, or did low skills and weak educational background hold them back? Were the pessimists who sounded alarm bells about the fate of working mothers like Kyesha and her unemployed sisters coming off of welfare correct—that they would remain buried in poverty, even if they did land jobs? Or were the conservatives who argued optimistically that any job is better than no job right in thinking that a getting a foot in the door would pay off over time?

These are critical questions for scholars, policymakers, and the concerned public, who once dwelled mainly on the size of the welfare rolls. Men and women who are able to move up from entry-level jobs may find themselves leaving hardship behind. Those who cannot are likely to be sucked below that critical poverty line, even when they work full-time and year-round. While transfer programs like the Earned Income Tax Credit (EITC) make a significant difference by putting more earned dollars in the hands of low-wage workers, by themselves they do not rescue families from poverty.[1] What matters, then, given the current rules of the game, is what kind of opportunity the labor market offers to poor workers, and who among them is positioned to seize it.

In this chapter we examine two essential background questions. First, what were the trends in employment and poverty nationally and locally in New York over the eight-year period during which we tracked the fortunes of this inner-city labor force? Second, why did economists concerned about poverty believe that workers like Kyesha and Jamal—the poorly educated and low-skilled—would remain mired in bad jobs? After considering these issues, we turn to the data from our three waves of interviews to find out what actually happened to the Burger Barn labor force.

The Economic Landscape

Economic growth in the 1990s was unprecedented. Beginning in April 1991, the economy grew for 120 consecutive months—the longest expansion in U.S. history.[2] In 1993, when the research for this book began, the national unemployment rate stood at 6.9 percent. By December 2000 it had dropped to 3.9 percent—its lowest level in thirty years.[3]

New York City routinely posts higher levels of unemployment than the nation as a whole, and, indeed, at the end of the 1991 recession the city's unemployment rate was nearly 2 percentage points higher than the national average (Figure 2.1). In fact the employment situation actually got worse in the Big Apple during the first years of the national expansion, so that by 1993 New York's annual rate of unemployment stood at a gloomy 10.4 percent. Hence when I first ventured into the Burger Barn restaurants to find Jamal, Kyesha, and Carmen, the lines of job seekers stretched out the door and around the block, even when the only thing going was low-status, minimum-wage slots. For every fortunate applicant who landed a job at Burger Barn, thirteen job seekers were turned away—and these were the lowest-skilled entry-level positions on offer.

It took time for the national expansion to register in the New York region, but by the year 2000 it had. At the turn of the millennium, the annual rate of unemployment dropped to 5.3 percent in the city.[4] Robust expansion, tight labor markets, and low interest rates created opportunities for traditionally disadvantaged groups such as women, African Americans, and Latinos. Millions flooded into the labor market and landed jobs.

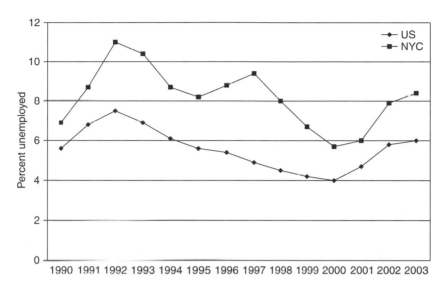

Figure 2.1   U.S. and New York City annual unemployment rates, 1990–2003.
Source: U.S. Bureau of Labor Statistics *(www.bls.gov)*, ID:
LNU04000000.

Unfortunately, what went up did come down, and the next recession, which began in March 2001, saw unemployment rates rise nationally and locally. At first the impact was modest: in 2001, the unemployment rate in New York City rose at a slower rate than in the nation at large. However, the picture worsened in the city as the general economic slowdown and the consequences of the attack on the World Trade Center took their toll, pushing unemployment back up to 8.2 percent by 2003.

Wage Growth and the Profile of Poverty

What impact did these employment figures have on the wages of American workers nationally and locally? It took time for the long period of stagnant wage growth to break, but by 1995 the upturn began to register in workers' pocketbooks.[5] Even so, three more years passed before the median hourly wage of middle-wage earners reached its 1979 level.[6] Rising wages helped to pull many—including the least advantaged—out of poverty. As Figure 2.2 shows, the overall poverty rate of 15 percent in 1993 was reduced to a low of 11.3 percent in 2000—a level not seen in twenty years.[7] African Americans, who have long fared the worst in the labor mar-

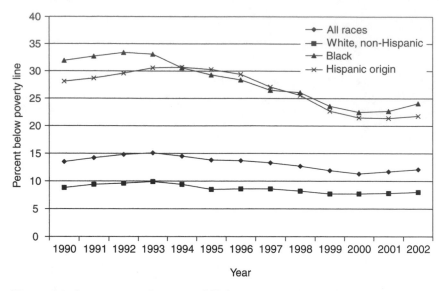

Figure 2.2   Poverty status by race and Hispanic origin, 1990–2002. *Source:* U.S.
Census Bureau, *http://www.census.gov/hhes/poverty/histpov/hstpov2.html.*

ket, saw their poverty rate drop sharply. The gap between black and non-
Hispanic white poverty rates narrowed dramatically, and Hispanic poverty
declined to levels not seen since 1978.[8] The rising tide of economic
growth genuinely did lift millions of boats across the country.

New York City has long suffered from high rates of poverty compared
with the rest of the country, hence it typically takes longer for the national
economic climate to have an impact on New York's poorer citizens. In
1993, when this longitudinal research began, poverty stood at 27 percent
in the Big Apple. By the peak of the business cycle in 2000, it had plunged
to 19.8 percent (Figure 2.3).

This was a historic rate of improvement, but to put the achievement in
perspective, the poverty rate in 2000 was still akin to that of the late
1980s.[9] Moreover, not everyone shared equally in the recovery. The gap
between blacks and whites shrank nationally, but the disparity between
them actually widened in New York City because whites did even better in
reducing poverty in their ranks.[10] The real action, though, was with people
like Carmen and Sal. In 1994, Hispanic New Yorkers were mired in poverty to the tune of 45 percent. By 2000 that number had dropped to 29
percent—still a sizable proportion, but a remarkable decline nonetheless
(Figure 2.4).

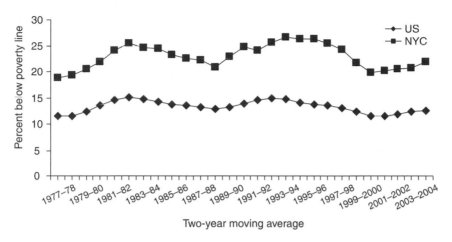

Figure 2.3 Poverty rates in New York City and the United States. *Source:* Community Service Society tabulations from the Current Population Survey.

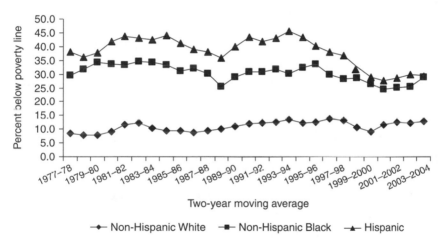

Figure 2.4 Poverty Rates in New York City by race/ethnicity. *Source:* Community Service Society tabulations from the Current Population Survey.

For residents of central Harlem—home to three of the four Burger Barn restaurants where our subjects were working when they were first recruited—high poverty rates remained a fact of life during the early part of the 1990s.[11] Thereafter, though, the economic landscape improved.[12] The household poverty rate went down by 5 points over the course of the decade.[13] Going into the next millennium, the positive trend continued: the number of households under the poverty line declined to 26 percent in 2002 from its 1990 high of 38 percent, a welcome change that rivaled the magnitude of improvement seen during the postwar boom years of the past century.[14] The percent of the central Harlem population receiving some form of government income support declined sharply as well.[15] In 1994 nearly 35,000 central Harlem residents received public assistance—either Aid to Families with Dependent Children (AFDC) or Home Relief. By 2000 this number had dropped by two-thirds.[16]

What drove this shift? The changing composition of Harlem's population—especially the increase in the number of high earners who live there—was clearly part of the story. Over the course of the 1990s, central Harlem's population grew by more than 7 percent, gaining residents earning incomes above the poverty level while holding steady in households below the poverty line, including those in extreme poverty (Figure 2.5).[17]

We cannot tell whether these figures represent upward mobility among those formerly below the poverty line or the arrival of new, more affluent residents in Harlem.[18] Most likely, both trends had an effect. Certainly the influx of new residents fleeing the overheated real estate market in the rest of Manhattan brought new wealth to the community. Yet gentrification was not the only force in play. The economic boom, in combination with welfare reform, also pulled many Harlem residents out of poverty.

Given declining unemployment in the city during the 1990s, we might assume the picture brightened for Harlem workers. Unfortunately, tracking unemployment rates at the neighborhood level is difficult. What we can look at is the employment-population ratio—the proportion of the working-age population that is employed, including discouraged workers (those who may want to work but have given up looking for a job).[19] Looking at this ratio, the dire employment picture showed little sign of improvement: half of Harlem's working-age population was still jobless in 1999 (Figure 2.6). The gap between central Harlem and the city as a whole narrowed, but this was largely because job holding went down in New York City.[20]

How does this stagnant employment picture square with the significant improvement in Harlem's poverty level? The employment-population ratio has remained the same, but the composition of the jobless population may have shifted. It includes students, parents raising children, and others

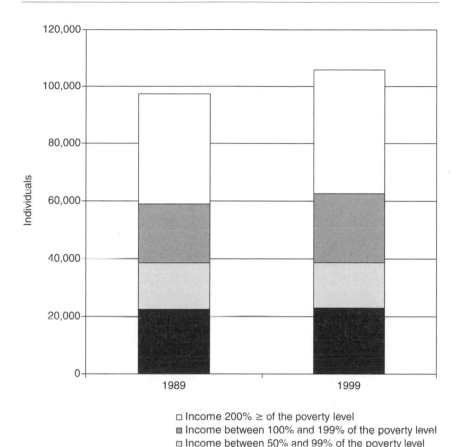

Figure 2.5   Central Harlem (Community District 10) poverty status, 1989 and
            1999. *Source:* New York City Department of City Planning Commu-
            nity District Profile, Community District 10, December 2004.

who voluntarily opt out of the labor market. While we should not ignore
the problems faced by many Harlem job seekers even in best of times, the
neighborhood's improving poverty profile suggests that the composition
of the jobless population may be changing.

It seems safe to say that the United States came as close to full employment in the late 1990s as it will for the foreseeable future. Much of what
policymakers expect full employment to do for the working poor came to
pass: people returned to work, welfare caseloads were reduced, poverty
rates dropped, wages rose, and economic inequality began to shrink.

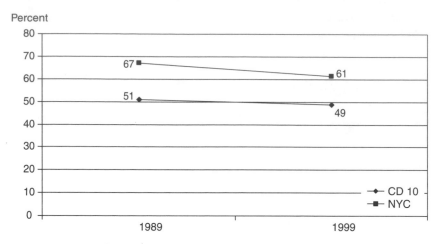

Figure 2.6   Central Harlem (CD 10) and New York City (NYC) employment-
population ratios, 1989 and 1999. *Source:* U.S. Census Bureau.

Expecting the Worst

What kind of future might we have anticipated for Jamal or Kyesha or
Carmen when we left them at the end of the *No Shame* project in 1995? I
was quite pessimistic about their prospects, for three reasons. First, like
their compatriots at the Harlem Burger Barns we studied, they had put
a lot of effort into looking for better jobs. Jamal applied everywhere he
could think of. Kyesha trooped downtown to take the civil service exams,
hoping to follow in the footsteps of her grandmother Evie, the postal
worker. Nothing came of it. Carmen was always able to find a job, but
her wages hardly budged. They were long-time veterans of the fast-food
world, and it appeared—after nearly two years of observation—that their
future would look a lot like their past.

My second reason for expecting stagnation was that the looming flood
of new entrants to the labor market, spurred by welfare reform and the immigration of low-skilled workers from countries such as Mexico, promised
increased pressure on the supply side.[21] The swollen ranks of job seekers
would, I thought, only depress wages by extending the already long job
lines in Harlem, making it difficult for the working poor already in place
to garner wage increases.

Finally, the literature on the career patterns of low-skilled workers, such
as it was, did not offer much encouragement. Economists trying to predict

what former welfare recipients would encounter when their time limits expired turned to surveys like the National Longitudinal Study of Youth (NLSY) and the Panel Study of Income Dynamics (PSID), or studies that examine the fate of job-training graduates.[22] They concluded that those who went off welfare were likely to share the same fate as the working poor: their jobs would pay poorly, provide few benefits, and offer only modest opportunities for advancement.[23]

A more recent wave of research has shifted away from the specific—and often politically charged—question of what happens to women leaving welfare to a broader concern with the nature of low-wage work in America. The unprecedented growth in income inequality that began in the mid-1970s, and continues virtually unabated even now, has left a large segment of the workforce behind—especially low-skilled minorities and immigrants—while simultaneously providing advantages to the best educated.[24] Concern about this issue is voiced not only by advocates and researchers who focus on the working poor. Leaders in the business community and economic policymakers have increasingly emphasized the threat to economic performance created by the mismatch between the needs of employers and the skill level of the American workforce.[25]

Structural transformations in the U.S. economy—globalization, revolutions in information technology, deregulation, and changes in financial markets—have rewritten the rules for employers concerned about profitability, and have made the 1990s look like a positive respite in a longer-term downward trend.[26] To remain competitive, firms often adopt cost-cutting strategies such as freezing compensation levels, increasing workloads, using temporary workers, and shifting frontline jobs to lower-cost locations or contractors. Computers are pressed into service to automate repetitive tasks once done by low-wage workers.[27] New technologies have also changed the methods employers use to recruit and screen employees. On aggregate, this may translate into "up-skilling" among those who are still on the job, since the jobs lost are disproportionately the ones at the bottom of the skill pyramid. But that is little comfort to the workers who used to hold those positions—especially those with only a high school degree or less education—and who are no longer needed now that machines can do their jobs more efficiently.[28]

Unless they had the good fortune to find jobs with innovative employers committed to "high-road" labor practices, or in the few sectors of the economy where wages were stable or growing, workers like Jamal would not be able to land jobs that would pull them out of the ranks of the working poor, or so the literature suggested. "Even the extremely tight 1990s labor markets, which resulted in the lowest unemployment rates in thirty years," Applebaum, Bernhardt, and Murnane point out, "did not allow the real earnings of male high school graduates to return to their 1970s level."[29]

The Demand-Side Question

As the economy began to grow at a more rapid rate in the late 1990s, we might have expected concerns over employment to diminish. Not so. Even under more favorable conditions, it was not clear that there was sufficient demand to absorb the new supply. In Illinois, for example, estimates showed that in 1997, there were "at least twenty-five job seekers for every job that pays at least poverty wages and seventy-four workers for every job that pays at least 150 percent of the poverty line."[30]

Unemployment rates do not capture discouraged workers, those who are not actively looking for work but would take a job if one were offered, or part-timers who want full-time work. Even when the official unemployment rate dropped to 4 percent in 2000, the rate of labor underutilization was 7 percent (Figure 2.7).

National unemployment or even underemployment statistics in the peak years of the boom made it hard to see some of the underlying shifts in the demand for labor. According to some economists, the significant increase in return to education during the 1980s indicated that "the demand for labor [had] shifted against the low-skilled worker."[31] In an era of technological advance in the workplace, those without education and training were particularly out of luck in the labor market.[32] Holzer's research confirmed that this was the case for the least-skilled job seekers.[33]

Low-skill workers—those who have received welfare for years and those who would not dream of asking for government help—are not an undifferentiated population. There are numerous gradations at the bottom of the labor market. In a weak labor market these distinctions are difficult to see. The difference between a high school dropout and a graduate may amount to very little if unemployment is high enough and neither can get a foot in the door. When this study first began in 1993, Harlem's fast-food restaurants were staffed not by teenagers looking for pocket change but by men and women in their twenties and thirties trying to raise families or pay for

Figure 2.7 Rates of labor underutilization. This graph shows the unemployed, discouraged workers (those who want a job but think no work is available, those who cannot find work, and those who lack schooling and training), employees working part-time for economic reasons, and marginally attached workers (those who want a job but did not actively look for work in the preceding four weeks because of child care and transportation problems). *Source:* Current Population Survey 2004, Series ID: LNS13327709, seasonally adjusted.

their own schooling. Tight labor markets brought into relief the distinctions among low-wage workers because it opened up opportunity for some and failed to do so for others.[34]

What characteristics matter? Low levels of human capital (education, skills, and training) lead to poor career trajectories, especially for male workers in poor urban areas.[35] Between 1991 and 1995, more than half of America's high school dropouts who were in their thirties experienced a bout of unemployment. In contrast, only a quarter of college graduates of the same age found themselves out of work.

Human capital corresponds to the *quality* of the jobs workers can expect to land, as well. By definition, good jobs have high wages, offer job security, and present opportunities for advancement. Bad jobs, in contrast, are marked by low wages, high turnover, poor working conditions, and little if any chance for promotion.[36] Who secures the good jobs? Three-quarters of young women spend time in a "good" job, but their likelihood of securing one is quite variable.[37] Less than half of women without a high school degree were in a good job from age eighteen to twenty-five, and only 17 percent were found to be in good jobs by age twenty-six to twenty-seven.[38] In contrast, nearly 90 percent of women with some postsecondary schooling have had a good job at some point, and 61 percent work primarily in a good job by the time they are twenty-seven. Women with children are clearly disadvantaged. Mothers are less likely than their childless peers to have had a good job or to be working primarily in a good job by their late twenties, and they take a significant wage hit, to boot.[39] For every additional child she has, a low-skilled woman's wages will suffer "above and beyond their effect on work experience and job tenure."[40]

Does this situation improve over time for men or women? That is, does more experience on the job pay off for workers who start their career at the bottom? The existing research—which has focused especially on welfare leavers—says no. Low-skilled workers who start out in jobs that pay poorly see little wage growth.[41] Either low-skilled workers bring less work experience to the table or they reap lower returns on their experience than others do. While workers in the primary labor market (characterized by high wages, job security, and mobility) are rewarded for accumulating additional human capital, denizens of the secondary labor market see little compensation for the same investment.[42] It appears that the most powerful determinant of upward mobility is the quality of the initial job taken, rather than the skill set of the worker.[43] Where we do see evidence of improvement, economists argued, the picture is somewhat illusory: workers are putting in more hours and therefore garnering more earnings, but they are not seeing increases in their wages.[44]

Jumping Ship

Long-term low earners work for firms that pay low wages. For them, the path to a better living lies not in internal promotion but in changing employers, in the hope of landing a job at a higher-wage firm. Job changers are more likely than "loyalists" to escape low earnings.[45] Does this imply that the best strategy is to move from job to job as often as possible? It depends: wage gains result from moving to better firms and better jobs, but it is best to move early and then accumulate some seniority and skills.

Unfortunately, the career pathways of low-wage workers rarely develop this way. Between 40 percent and 68 percent of those who enroll in training programs for the low skilled leave their low-wage jobs within six

months, and the majority had changed jobs within the past two years.[46]
But the kind of moves they make see them cycle from one low-wage employer to the next. When Jamal shifted from Burger Barn to the pastry and
coffee shop C'est Bon and back again, he saw no improvement in his fortunes. His job pattern is typical of young workers who churn through positions at the entry level. Paul Osterman has argued that this is not a catastrophe, for youth workers need to try on different kinds of employment in
order to settle into desirable niches.[47] When the same strategy is pursued
by adult workers, however, it can scar them with the appearance of unreli-
ability. A vicious circle develops in which jobs that offer little opportunity
promote job-hopping, and churning through jobs makes job seekers less
attractive to employers.[48]

Even with additional job training, progress is slow for low-wage workers. After welfare reform, a mania for training programs swept the land,
but it is sobering to learn how little progress they have yielded. One study
found that two-thirds of individuals who left a low-wage service job for a
job training program returned to a similar position. After a second training stint, the results remained the same. If anything, these individuals
seemed not to be on a "job track" but on a "training track."[49]

Wages are not the only form of reward workers seek. Benefits are of
great importance as well, and low-wage jobs are generally devoid of them.
Among welfare leavers who searched for work, approximately 60 percent
found a job. Moreover, most landed work that paid more than the minimum wage. Yet it was the rare job that also provided benefits. Fewer than
half had paid sick leave, a crucial benefit for low-wage families.[50] Since kids
get sick often, their working mothers develop unstable patterns of work
attendance and become vulnerable to losing their jobs. On average, more
than seven in ten former welfare recipients worked at some point during
the first year after going off the dole, but only four in ten worked consistently.[51] The same problem afflicted low-wage workers who were not
caught up in Temporary Assistance for Needy Families (TANF). Reformers anticipated this problem and tried to address it by providing the
benefits that would help to sustain labor force attachment, but for reasons
that are still obscure, only modest numbers of workers took advantage of
the child care subsidies, food stamps, and health insurance programs that
help the working poor make ends meet.[52]

Most of the studies discussed here draw on data collected during the
early 1990s, when unemployment was relatively high. They yield pessi-

mistic projections for workers like those at the heart of *Chutes and Ladders*. For the women among them, the forecast is especially bleak, since the cost of child care and the increased responsibility of motherhood exposes them to economic burdens, interrupted labor force participation, and the skepticism of employers, who worry about increased absence from the shop floor. For both men and women who were already part of the low-wage world before welfare reform was instituted, this research was not particularly comforting either. It suggested that their long-term fate was dismal and that they were about to be joined by millions of similarly situated sisters, who would stagnate with them at the rocky end of the labor market.

Such were the convictions of many economists, sociologists, journalists, and policymakers when our research began. Little did anyone know that welfare reform would roll out in the midst of one of the great economic booms of the twentieth century. With low interest rates, high growth, and unprecedented declines in unemployment, labor markets tightened and opportunities opened. It was, without question, a sustained period of prosperity.

Burger Barn Workers over the Long Run

Our initial studies of Harlem's Burger Barn labor force were not designed to answer longitudinal questions, but they were a place to begin, and with some modification they have become a window through which we may view the long-run career patterns of low-wage workers. This research commenced in 1993 with a wave of interviews with two hundred individuals employed in these fast-food restaurants in Harlem and Washington Heights; in 1995 we added interviews with nearly one hundred job seekers who had applied for Burger Barn jobs in 1994 but had been rejected. The demographic composition of the original sample is described in Appendix A. The lax labor markets of the early 1990s meant employers could be choosy, and they tended to go for older applicants over the traditional teenage labor force that the fast-food industry was built for. Hence, while there were teens in our study population, they composed only 35 percent of the original sample of workers and job seekers; about 65 percent were adults. Indeed, more than half were well into their adult careers, since they were over the age of twenty-five when we conducted the first wave of interviews.

Two waves of follow-up interviews were conducted for *Chutes and Lad-*

Table 2.1 Study sample comparison, 1993 and 1997

	1993	1997
Race		
African American	190 (65%)	70 (68%)
Dominican	47 (17%)	14 (14%)
Other Latino	39 (13%)	19 (18%)
Other	16 (5%)	0 (0%)
Sex		
Female	155 (53%)	64 (62%)
Male	139 (47%)	39 (38%)
Highest degree completed in 1993		
Did not finish high school	158 (54%)	62 (60%)
High school diploma	88 (30%)	28 (27%)
GED	11 (4%)	2 (2%)
Some college/no degree	29 (10%)	10 (10%)
Job training/tech/vocational degree	1 (0%)	0 (0%)
Associate degree	0 (0%)	0 (0%)
B.A./B.S.	5 (2%)	1 (1%)
Beyond B.A./B.S.	2 (1%)	0 (0%)
Independent household in 1993		
Yes	129 (44%)	37 (36%)
No	165 (56%)	66 (64%)
N	294	103

ders. In 1997 (wave 2), we went back to our study population four years after the first contact point and covered a random sample of slightly more than a hundred of the original subjects. Then in 2002 (wave 3), we conducted a very modest follow-up with a representative sample of forty of the workers and job seekers.[53] In most of the ways we can measure, the 1997 follow-up sample looked a lot like the people we began with, as Table 2.1 suggests.[54]

Though the follow-up samples in 1997 and 2002 were representative of the initial sample from 1993, the resources available to help us find the subjects were modest, particularly at the final contact point. Attrition was high. Hence, the findings must be treated with caution. Small *n*, nonrandom studies of this kind cannot generate definitive conclusions about the pathways taken by this population as a whole. For that, we need a much larger and more representative sample. Chapter 5 takes on that challenge. For now, though, we turn to the findings on Harlem workers.

Broadly speaking, the sample did well from 1993 to 1997. When we found them for the follow-up interviews, 73 percent were employed. Most surprising to us, these Harlem workers had completed more schooling and training. In 1993, 60 percent of the sample was over the age of twenty-one and therefore already beyond the age when one might expect significant investment in education, especially for low-wage workers. By 1997, 78 percent had a high school degree or general equivalency diploma (GED)—only 42 percent had this degree in 1993—and 29 percent had some college education, compared with only 9 percent in 1993. This continued educational advance is impressive for what it suggests about attachment to schooling among these inner-city residents.[55]

Wage Patterns

Some workers had been on the job for a long period of time, while others were relative newcomers, but both the experienced workers and the neophytes were taking home very modest pay. In 1993, the median wage of the employed persons in the sample was $4.25 an hour (in 1993 dollars).[56] Four years later, the median wage of those people who were working had increased substantially, to $7.49 an hour (again in 1993 dollars).[57] The wage gains for those who were working at both points in time are represented graphically in Figure 2.8.[58]

The pattern was surprising. In 1993 these Harlem residents were poorly educated workers or job seekers, less than half of whom had completed high school, even though 90 percent were over age eighteen. Yet by 1997 most had stayed even with inflation, and more than a third had experienced significant wage growth.

In dissecting their wage experience, it is helpful to consider the origins and destinations of different wage groups (Table 2.2). Among those who were unemployed in 1993, more than half were once again without work in 1997–98. However, the remaining 43 percent had found work by the time of the follow-up.[59] The next group in this table, workers who were receiving the minimum wage in 1993, had variable outcomes as well. More than one-fourth were unemployed in 1997. Ten percent were still stuck at the minimum wage, which is a near guarantee of poverty unless they live with other earners. For the majority of people who earned the minimum wage in 1993, though, the news was positive: 65 percent were above the minimum wage and one-third had added more than $2.00 per hour in real wages in four years.

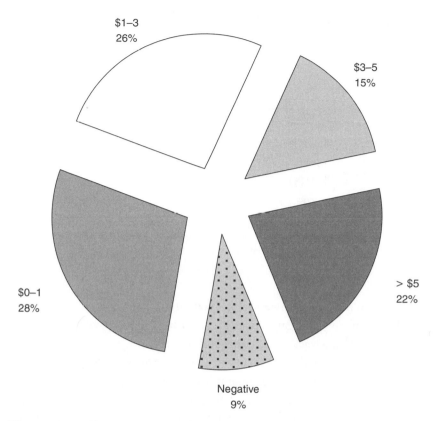

Figure 2.8 Real hourly wage growth among those employed in 1993 and 1997.

When we look at the middle income earners, those who earned between $4.26 and $9.99 in 1993, we see more upward mobility. True, 15 percent were unemployed four years later, and a little more than half were stuck at approximately the same real wage. But 27 percent were "high flyers" by 1997, making in excess of $10.00 per hour, a real hourly wage gain of more than $1.25 per year. The most advantaged wage group in Table 2.2, nonmanagerial workers who were already earning more than $10.00 an hour in 1993, is too small to serve as a basis for any systematic observations.

What kinds of jobs do these 1997 wage destinations represent, and what kinds of demographic patterns map onto these outcomes? The unemployed in 1997 were far more likely to have started out in 1993 as rejected applicants to Burger Barn. Sixty percent of them were not working in 1993–94. A slim majority of the unemployed were women, but 45 percent were men. They were among the older people in the follow-up study. This

Table 2.2 1997 wage "destinations" of 1993 wage groups (all in 1993 dollars)

1993 wage groups	1997 wages				
	Unemployed	1997–98 min. wage ($4.66)	$4.67–$9.99	$10+	*Total*
Unemployed	20 (57%)	2 (6%)	12 (34%)	1 (3%)	35 (100%)
1993 min. wage ($4.25)	8 (26%)	3 (10%)	17 (55%)	3 (10%)	31 (100%)
$4.26–$9.99	4 (15%)	1 (4%)	14 (54%)	7 (27%)	26 (100%)
$10+	1 (50%)	0	0	1 (50%)	2 (100%)
Total	33 (35%)	6 (6%)	43 (46%)	12 (13%)	94 (100%)

Note: In 1997 the minimum wage increased to $5.15. In 1993 dollars this is $4.66.

is a group in trouble: they were employed only episodically during the first four years of our study and most are well into their twenties (or older) without much of a track record on which to rely.

Francine is an apt illustration of this pattern. She was rejected by Burger Barn in 1994 and by 1997 was unemployed and living with her boyfriend, who worked as a messenger. She had been on AFDC/TANF since 1994 and had neither worked nor gone to school during this period. She applied for a number of jobs in the year immediately preceding our follow-up but was not hired. She manages on food stamps, welfare payments, and money from other family members.

Sixteen percent of the workers we reconnected with in 1997 had jobs paying at or close to the minimum wage.[60] Most of them were women (77 percent), and almost 80 percent were African American.[61] They worked as kitchen staff, cashiers, security guards, housekeepers, and teacher's aide interns (in New York City schools this is more of a custodial function than an instructional position, and in some schools it is a workfare placement). These are essentially entry-level jobs for which the qualifications are minimal. This group experienced little or no wage mobility or occupational upgrading, but they had been employed most of the time.

Florida is a case in point. She is twenty-eight years old, a mother of five, three of whom live with her (the other two live with their grandparents on her ex-husband's side of the family). She is a high school dropout and was working at Burger Barn in 1993, but she quit when she suffered a burn on the job. As of 1997, Florida was working as a security guard for five dollars an hour. Between those earnings, TANF benefits, and food stamps, Florida was barely making it, but she was not on the unemployment lines.

Of the people we connected with in 1997, 33 percent were working at jobs that paid at least a dollar above the minimum wage (but less than ten dollars an hour).[62] The average age of these workers was twenty-five, and a high proportion of them were women. What kinds of jobs did they have? We found fast-food swing managers, salespersons, stock clerks, secretaries, telemarketers, bookkeepers, and laborers. These are the kinds of jobs that the entry-level workers in Burger Barn aspired to move up to in 1993, because on the whole these jobs were regarded as cleaner (less greasy) and less stigmatized. A large group of them have been able to do just that, and though the quality of their jobs improved, their wages were another story.

Tonia, twenty-five, was born in Belize and had lived in the United States for ten years. Her aunt, who works as a secretary, holds the lease on the apartment where Tonia and her two children—ages three and five—had lived for the past several years. She began working at Burger Barn for $4.75 an hour in 1993 and by 1997 had been promoted to a first assistant manager position, which paid $7.50 an hour. Tonia had applied for only one other job in the four years since we first interviewed her. The Gap had turned her down. She made do with her salary, food stamps, some alimony payments, welfare for her children, and the cost sharing she had worked out with her aunt.

The most impressive success stories over the first four years, the high flyers who moved up into jobs paying ten dollars an hour or more, had landed a variety of jobs. They were managers in Burger Barn, unionized hospital attendants, mail carriers, janitors, payroll clerks for the city, and porters. The various routes they took to reach this nirvana are described in detail in Chapter 3. It will suffice to say at this juncture that it was more than what most people from poor households in segregated, high-poverty neighborhoods expected to experience. These are the Kyeshas and Jamals of this world. And while Carmen herself had not seen wage growth or occupational mobility of this kind personally, her husband Sal certainly had.

Unemployment Spells

Employment stability is another dimension along which our sample fanned out into trouble cases and success stories. During the period from

1993 to 1997, 50 percent of the sample had at least one spell of unemployment. But the higher the earnings category, the less frequent were brushes with joblessness. High- and middle-wage earners who were out of work at any point during the four-year period spent far less time unemployed than those in any of the other earner categories. Not only did they earn more when they worked but they also worked more continuously than the low earners. Only 6 percent of the high earners experienced any unemployment; three times that many low-wage workers had at least one spell of unemployment. Although this comparison is consistent with the literature, it bears notice that more than 80 percent of the low-wage earners were employed continuously and yet remained at the bottom of the earnings heap.

What can we conclude about the trajectories of Harlem's Burger Barn labor force at the midway point in our research, in 1997? First, averages tell us very little. It is the dispersion—the fanning out into pathways up and down—that matters. By 1997, three groups had formed out of what was in 1993 mainly an undifferentiated group of minimum-wage earners and job seekers: a bottom group that was only episodically employed and remained dependent on the largesse of others, including public assistance; a middle group that had remained steadily employed and held its own against inflation; and a set of high flyers who saw significant wage gains and improvements in their working conditions.

The Last Roundup

Between 1997 and 2001 the economy continued its roaring growth, and something unseen in decades—worker shortages—began to crop up in various parts of the country, even in some Rust Belt zones that had been dormant for many years. The downturn that emerged in the spring of 2001—which deepened after the terrorist attacks of 9/11—lasted only until November, but economic revival was slow and anemic.

Unfortunately, our sample is too small and cuts out too early to capture many of the negative effects of this "jobless recovery."[63] Nonetheless I wanted to know how the Harlem workers we had studied were faring eight years after they were first interviewed. For the third and final phase of our research, we had the resources to track down and interview only forty people out of the three hundred we began with.[64] We chose these subjects according to the outcomes we knew they had attained by 1997, and we divided the final follow-up group into thirds: a top group sampled from among those who had been high flyers in 1997, a middle group who had seen more modest wage gains and only slight improvement in the prestige of their jobs, and a bottom group that had done poorly. We went back to find and interview these forty subjects in 2002.

We collected information from them about their experiences in the labor market, any additional education they had received, and changes in their households (particularly among their children). We asked them a series of more subjective questions aimed at discovering how their worldview had changed over time, if indeed it had. These last questions were repeats of queries posed in each wave of the study, and they made it possible to examine whether our respondents thought differently about the world—about economic opportunity, about their personal prospects or the destinations of their children—as a consequence of their divergent experiences in the world of work. These issues are discussed in detail in Part 2 of the book, and they were in many respects the raison d'être of the third wave of the study.

We convey what we learned about the employment experiences of these forty people in terms of percentages to give the reader a sense of the diversity of their destinations, but these data should not be interpreted as hard numerical findings. The sample is simply too small for precision. Our account of their outcomes in 2002 describes the different paths these Harlem residents traveled over the eight years that we knew them.

Getting a Job

Finding a job was not much of an issue in the low-unemployment years that marked the second term of the Clinton administration. When we caught up with our forty subjects again in 2002, 15 percent were still at the same job they had had in 1997, and 12.5 percent of those employed in 2002 had switched jobs only once. Another 30 percent of the sample had held just two different jobs over the five-year period from 1997 to 2002. The rest of the group had switched jobs three or more times. As the analysis of the Survey of Income and Program Participation (SIPP) data in Chapter 5 shows, switching jobs is crucial to getting higher wages. In lax labor markets, this is true because employers are not under pressure. In tight labor markets there is the potential for wage gains from both internal promotion and job-hopping (Table 2.3).

Table 2.3 Number of jobs held by wave 3 respondents, 1997–2002

Number of jobs held	Frequency	Percentage
No employment	1	2.5
At same job from wave 2	6	15.0
1	5	12.5
2	12	30.0
3	6	15.0
4	4	10.0
5	3	7.5
6	2	5.0
7	1	2.5
Total	40	100.0

Table 2.4 Unemployment among wave 3 respondents, 1997–2002

Unemployment spells	Frequency	Percentage
None	19	47.5
1	11	27.5
2+	10	25.0
Total	40	100.0

Of course, the number of jobs held does not necessarily tell us about how much time this group spent employed. The news here was good (Table 2.4). Nearly half the workers in the final follow-up—48 percent—had been continuously employed since 1997. Just under 30 percent had experienced only one spell of unemployment. In some cases these unemployment spells reflected time away from work to care for a newborn. In others, they reflected the fact that, with access to better jobs, many were now in a position to collect unemployment insurance for the first time. Of course, even one month of lost wages can have dramatically negative consequences on a family budget.

In 2002, about one-fourth of our sample was not employed. Even though they were living close to the poverty line, family obligations or educational plans took these workers out of the labor force. Patty, a thirty-seven-year-old African American, started out at the minimum wage and then climbed the ladder to management at Burger Barn. By 2002, though, Patty had decided to go back to school. Her partner provided enough income to support the family. Deanna was also successful on the job, but she quit working when she fell afoul of a co-worker, reasoning that, anyway, she was only two months away from delivering her first child. Marisa took time off after the birth of a new child and a move to a new city to help her family settle in, but planned to be back at work soon. In all of these cases, husbands or partners stepped in to cover the bills in a pattern that would be familiar to middle-class two-earner families.

At the other end of the spectrum are those who were involuntarily unemployed—people who would still be at their jobs if they had the choice. Richard had a good run making storage lockers but was fired over a disagreement. Rather than jump at the first job that came his way, John took advantage of unemployment insurance while waiting for a decent job to turn up. Sabrina worked a short while in food service downtown but lost her job after 9/11. Disabilities prevented some from working full-time, and others in this involuntarily unemployed group have intermittent work histories and substance abuse problems that have impeded their attachment to the labor force.

Show Them the Money

It is one thing to find a job; it is another to land one that pays enough to support a family. Among the people we contacted in 2002 who were employed, the average hourly wage was $15.45 and the median hourly wage was $14.49. Of course, averages can be deceptive. To better understand how the improved labor market of the late 1990s affected these workers, we might begin ranking the sample by multiples of the minimum wage (Table 2.5).

Only a few of the workers were stuck in jobs paying the minimum wage or anything close to it. Most had jobs that paid above 200 percent of this threshold, and more than 20 percent had risen above 300 percent of the minimum wage. (Given the decreasing value of the minimum wage over the past thirty years, though, even 300 percent above it provides limited buying power.) Fifteen percent of those in our sample were in a household whose income was below the federal poverty line.[65] Yet virtually all of those subjects were out of labor force. Those who were working had climbed above the poverty line through a combination of their own earnings and the wages of others in their household.[66]

The cost of living in a city like New York is so high that exceeding the

Table 2.5 Distribution of hourly wages, 2002

Hourly wage	Frequency	Percentage
Unemployed/not in labor force	12	30.0
$5.15–$10.30	3	7.5
(min. wage to 200% of min. wage)		
$10.31–$15.45	16	40.0
(200% to 300% of min. wage)		
$15.46 and over	9	22.5
(>300% min. wage)		
Total	40	100.0

federal poverty standard still signals a fairly meager standard of living; this national standard does not acknowledge regional differences in the cost of living.[67] The federal poverty line is so low that it would stretch to cover only food and housing in New York, with nothing left over.[68] An individual earning the minimum wage would have to work 131 hours per week to afford an average one-bedroom apartment in New York City; to afford a typical two-bedroom apartment, he or she would have to make $19.10 an hour.[69] The self-sufficiency standard—which offers a far more complex calculation of the costs of basic goods and services in the local community for different family configurations—is arguably more appropriate for measuring the progress of the Burger Barn workers in moving out of poverty. Using that yardstick, 42.5 percent of the group failed to earn enough to cover their basic needs in 2002. Nonetheless, even with this more conservative standard, 58 percent were self-sufficient.

How did the individuals in our final wave get to their place in this wage distribution? Their pathways were quite variable. About one-third were working at all three waves of interviews, in 1993, 1997, and 2002, and for them we can assemble a picture of wage changes that helps us trace their progress. Two patterns seem apparent in this small sample: one group (Figure 2.9) experienced a significant jump between 1993 and 1997, capitalizing on the education and skill they could bring to the table in what was, for most, their first leap beyond entry-level jobs. However, they were not able to sustain this ascent and in the second wave, from 1997 to 2002, their wage gains were much smaller, suggesting that they had hit a plateau.

Of course very few workers—including those who are highly educated—see exponential wage gains year after year. Most workers hit a point where the credentials they have to offer and the networks that facili-

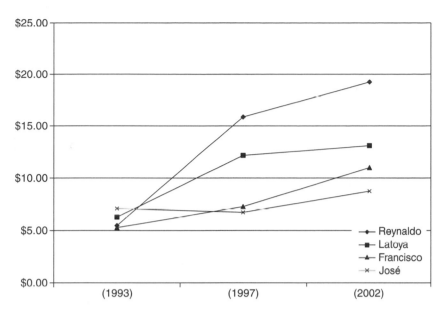

Figure 2.9 Decreasing or modest rate of wage change.

tate their mobility will not pay off any further. From there, they are likely
to stay even with inflation unless dramatic changes open up opportunities
because of worker shortages or the floor drops out from below them as
gluts in the labor market make them more expendable. Wage increases for
these folks will be relatively fixed, reflecting the wage patterns of their particular firm and industry.

The same may be true of the workers in Figure 2.10, who saw significant increases in their wages in the period from 1997 to 2000. There is
no guarantee that they will continue on this "up escalator"; indeed, since
they are all well into adulthood, it is unlikely. However, their big wage
jump came later than it did for the group in Figure 2.9 and the leveling-off
process was not yet visible as of 2002, when we last interviewed them. The
substantial gains made post-1997 were typically the result of landing a job
in a higher-paying industry, not climbing a wage ladder in the same industry or firm. Nadine, Larry, Cassandra, Mike, Jamal, and Kyesha all benefited from moving out of a low-wage industry like fast food, where the rate
of pay increases was minimal, to jobs in industries—transport, municipal
employment, manufacturing, and retail management—where the levels of
pay are far higher, even on the lower-rung jobs.

The experience of the working poor is far from monolithic, and there

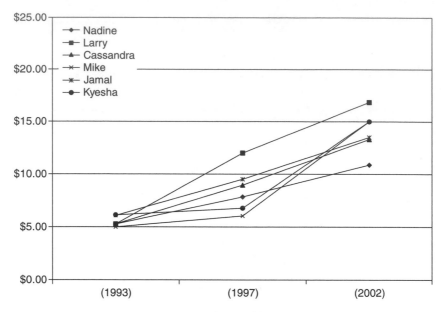

Figure 2.10 Increasing or steady rate of wage change.

are many paths to follow out of poverty. A booming economy is no guarantee that every worker will move up in the ranks—but it does make visible the peaks and valleys of the terrain that Jamal, Kyesha, and Carmen
faced as they worked to improve their lot.

It is tempting to celebrate the real progress encouraged by sustained low
rates of unemployment, but since that situation does not last indefinitely,
we should remain mindful of the underlying trends that may make it hard
for people to continue an upward ascent. The problem is particularly critical for low-skilled men. Over the past several decades, the sectors of the
economy that have had the largest declines in employment—manufacturing, finance, and professional services—are industries with a majority-
male workforce (72 percent).[70] In contrast, educational and health services,
the only sector in New York City to see substantial growth, has a majority
of female employees and accounts for almost 20 percent of the city's jobs.[71]
These trends have hit young black and Hispanic men the hardest. New
York's employment-population ratios—measures of the working-age population with paid employment—collapsed for this age group between 2000
and 2003. The job-holding rate for New York City's workers age sixteen to
twenty-four shrank eleven points, to 35 percent. For black men the rate

dropped twelve points, to 51.8 percent, and for Hispanic men there was a seven-point drop, to 66 percent.[72]

The national picture is also cause for concern. Wages for low-skilled men and women have diverged not because women are doing so well but because low-skilled men are doing poorly. Absolute wages for low-skilled workers of both genders fell between 1971 and 1997, but the ratio of female to male wages increased, from .65 at the beginning of the period to .76 at the end.[73] Economist Rebecca Blank tells us why: the real wages of the least educated men plummeted.[74] From 1979 to 1993 male high school dropouts lost 22.5 percent in wages, while females with the same level of education suffered only a 6.3 percent decrease.

Given this sobering trend, is there any value in examining a period of time when the economy was so strong that it gave a lift to so many boats? Yes. Taking a close look at the mobility patterns of people who emerged out of high-poverty, racially segregated neighborhoods, burdened by high levels of unemployment, tells us something about why opportunity matters. Moreover, as we will learn in more detail in Chapter 5, approximately the same rate of wage gain develops in "troughs" when the economy is not so healthy. Upward mobility is possible, then, in good times and in bad.

3

High Flyers, Low Riders, and the "Up but Not Out" Club

❧

The wage patterns described in Chapter 2 do not give us much of a feeling for how these Harlem workers traveled along the mobility paths open to them. For that, we turn to the life histories of workers drawn from the final follow-up interviews conducted in 2002. Our final forty subjects can be divided into three categories: the high flyers, who made it into the ranks of stable working-class or middle-class employment; the "up but not outs," who remained ahead of inflation and moved up from the bottom of the wage scale but had not found real economic security; and the low riders, who remained stuck in dead-end work or had no work at all.

How do we define the boundaries between these groups? One important measure of wage mobility is the rate of wage increases. Workers who increase their pay on average every year—either through promotions and raises on the job or by switching to higher-paying jobs—are on an upward trajectory. The high flyers had seen average hourly wage gains over the eight years of this study ranging from $1.00 to $2.75 per year in real dollars. This healthy rate of growth means that everyone in this category was in a job paying at least $15.00 an hour by 2002, which translates into a yearly income of about $30,000. The most successful of the high flyers were earning $50,000 to $60,000 per year. Most of these workers had also been continuously attached to the labor market.

When we look at the workers who are up but not out in 2002, we see smaller rates of wage growth, lower levels of pay in their current jobs, and more time spent out of the labor market. For this group, real wage increases were under $1.00 a year, and 2002 wages were in the range of $12.50 to $15.00 per hour. The households in this "club" were doing better or worse depending on the relationships our subjects had built with partners who might be contributing (or not); our subjects could not rest easy on account of their own trajectories in the labor market.

Finally, the low-rider group was bumping along the bottom in jobs paying less than $12.00 per hour, seeing paltry or negative real wage gains, experiencing significant spells of unemployment, and moving on and off of welfare—when they could access it.

It is important to remember that everyone discussed here started out in a bad job, in a poor neighborhood, and at a time when the economy was in a "bust" phase. From this low point in 1993–94, how, then, did the boom years play out in the lives of these workers? Of course, some would have been upwardly mobile—and some would have remained low riders—no matter what the conditions of the larger economy. In a sample this size, we cannot easily tease apart the different, sometimes contradictory effects of structural forces and individual behavior. Yet by looking at how people fared during this exceptional economic period, we can learn something about the many ways people can make the transition out of minimum-wage jobs and examine the differences among the people who remained among the ranks of the nation's working poor.

High Flyers

How did the high flyers earn their wings? They found three main routes to upward mobility. The first involved internal promotion in a growing firm that paid good wages. The second path took them down the "human capital" road, which required stepping out of the labor market long enough to acquire more education or specialized training, and was available only to those with relatives or partners able to take up the slack and earn a living. It was also available to the fortunate few whose firms support educational advance through tuition subsidies, time off for schooling, or both. Finally, the third route was one familiar to our informants because it was the path traveled by their most successful relatives: landing a union job.

Internal Ladders

Among those workers who were earning more than ten dollars an hour, the most common job category was a store manager at Burger Barn, a fact that reflects the importance of internal promotion for low-wage workers in the fast-food industry. In 2002, 20 percent of the high earners were managers in the firm where we originally found them (though not necessarily in the same restaurant). The fast-food business is known to recruit management off the shop floor. Moreover, inner-city communities are still growth areas for this industry, which has largely saturated more affluent communities and now turns to poor neighborhoods and to overseas locations for expansion. Bad jobs are not all created equal. Low-wage positions in firms that are growing may offer more upward mobility to entry-level workers than the same kind of job in a business that is shrinking.

If anyone had told Jamal back in 1994 that he was going to end up making $32,500 a year, when he was earning the minimum wage and could not afford to pay the rent on a tenement room, he would have been astounded. Back then, churning through a series of entry-level, low-wage jobs in a lax labor market, he had no prospects for the kind of life he now leads, and the frustration was eating him up inside. He knew he needed more education, but he had no time for it. He wanted to find better jobs, but he couldn't demonstrate any real skills. Jamal was stuck, or at least that is how it seemed to him, and to me, more than a decade ago. How, then, did he become a high flyer, this most unlikely candidate for good fortune?

Jamal stumbled on an industry that still pays good wages and provides internal ladders for people who can learn on the job. The lumber business is not particularly attuned to formal educational credentials. What Jamal's bosses care about is whether he can figure out how to hoist a load of wood without dropping it. Few applicants walk in the door of the laminating factory knowing how to do that. Most have never seen the pressure gauges and the thermometers Jamal has to monitor so that the wood doesn't snap in pieces or overbake. All the company wants to know is that their entry-level workers are teachable, and they have learned, through experience, that a high school diploma doesn't necessarily tell them who can do the job and who will make a mess out of a pile of wood. The man who can master those tasks and earn a modicum of respect can move from the graveyard shift to the day job, from the labor pool to a more specialized role, and even from the shop floor into a spot as a crew chief.

A job in the manufacturing sector was once the ticket to a lifetime of job security and income advancement.[1] The rise of the service sector—and the decline of firm size—has put an end to career ladders of the kind that were typical in manufacturing.[2] In its upper ranks, the service sector provides high-pay, high-skill jobs, but its low-skill, low-pay jobs on the bottom lead to relatively few middle-rung positions and hence have fewer ladders on which to climb upward.[3] As Edward Peña's experience demonstrates, it is no small challenge to find the internal ladders—such as they are—in the service sector.

In many respects, Edward's story is similar to Jamal's. A twenty-five-year-old Dominican who grew up in northern Manhattan, Edward did not graduate from high school and has been working since he was a teen. Along the way he had a child with one girlfriend, but he is now married to someone else. Unlike Jamal, Edward has family in New York, and until he moved into his wife's apartment, he was living with his mother, grandmother, and siblings. He was one of the people in the study who had applied unsuccessfully in 1993 for work at Burger Barn. By the time we interviewed him in 1994, Edward had landed a job at a Burger Barn in another part of the city. After that job, he worked for two years as a messenger for a delivery service but still earned only the minimum wage of $4.25. Looking for more money, Edward went back to Burger Barn, where he took a maintenance job that paid $4.50 an hour. Realizing that he had a better shot at higher pay in a different industry, he took a job as a security supervisor at $6.00 per hour. After eight months he was able to make another switch to a different security guard slot that paid $8.00 per hour.

What Edward learned was that the pathway to more pay was a credential: in this case, the certification to carry a weapon. With this in hand, he was able to land a job as an armored-truck guard. At first the pay was only fifty cents an hour better than at his previous job, but he was finally in a position where time on the job would translate into higher wages. Over the course of the next three years, his hourly pay went up to $11.30, and he was also receiving benefits. From this job Edward moved to his current position as a guard at Federal Plaza in Lower Manhattan. It is not a government job; the security services he provides are contracted out to the company he works for. But the job does pay more than $15.00 per hour, with employer-provided health insurance and vacation pay. Edward is glad to have made it as far as he has working as a security guard, but he harbors no illusions that there are any rungs left for him to climb. His income may go up, but there are no chances for promotion: "I'm not looking forward to moving up over there because the only thing I look forward to is my check to go up, that's about it. And when I made this decision for security [it] was because, like I said, [with] my education level right now, this is the only place I could go right now [where] I could make the type of money I've made since I left high school. And I feel that I've done pretty well. But one day there is going to be an end to that."

Edward's experience is a latter-day version of the internal ladder. His climb has been internal not within a firm but within a labor market niche where he has been able to build up the track record and basic credentials that gain some degree of advancement. In comparison with Jamal's experience, this path seems a lot less orderly, but this is the only kind of ladder that many workers are going to find.

The Human Capital Strategy

Movement up the occupational ladder often depends on acquiring educational credentials.[4] Employers rely on diplomas to indicate whether the applicant can read, write, and do simple mathematics. They use the sheepskin as an indirect way of sorting out people who can stick to tasks, follow orders, and learn new things. This kind of human capital, then, is a mixture of hard skills and the capacity to develop new ones.[5] Employers may also look upon degrees as indicators of soft skills: the capacity to work within an organizational context, to get along with co-workers and customers, to discern the rules of interaction.[6]

The middle-class model of human capital accumulation, which depends on many years of formal education that qualify their bearers for higher-order jobs, operates at the bottom of the labor market too. Lauren Cravette is an example of someone who understood the value of credentials during the years when it was still possible to go to college in order to fulfill the requirements of the AFDC system. Without the support she received for her education and training, she would almost certainly be stuck in a low-wage job, scrambling to look after her child on a single income.

In 1993 Lauren was living in Harlem, where she applied—and was rejected—for a job at a local Burger Barn. Today, the twenty-six-year-old African American lives in Bedford-Stuyvesant—once a community synonymous with crime and poverty but now gentrifying as the exodus from Manhattan raises the income of new "Bed-Sty" residents. Lauren has a pleasant apartment she found through Harlem's local paper, the *Amster-dam News*. She lives with her daughter, Jane, who commutes with Lauren into Manhattan to a good public school on the East Side, close to Lauren's job. Lauren works in a building in one of New York City's most affluent neighborhoods, in the accounting department of a prominent non-profit foundation. Plush carpets, elegant lunches, courteous co-workers, and generous benefits make this a real dream come true for Lauren, who was on welfare when we first met. When we found her again in 2002, she was earning about $30,000 per year and could claim tuition reimburse-ment for any further education she wanted to pursue.

Her salary does not put her in "fat city." She still has to watch her pen-nies, even though Jane's father reliably contributes $240 a month to the support of his daughter. Rent—even in a former ghetto neighborhood in Brooklyn—takes almost a quarter of her income. Nonetheless, Lauren has two invaluable assets: a secure job that she can hold onto until something even better comes her way, and a work environment that she enjoys.

Lauren's pathway to this fortunate outcome began with a summer stint in a public job program for teens:[7]

I worked for summer youth since I was fourteen, and then they started a [Yes] program. So I also did tutoring and stuff through another pro-gram called [North End Youth]. I knew the director there so I asked her about any [intern] programs for the fall. She mentioned the [Yes] program, and she gave us an interview. We went, and it was for seven weeks. I did an excellent job, better than all the other kids. People who were there called me back to do part-time work as a clerk and then the full-time clerk for accounting left and they asked me if I wanted to do the job. I had no accounting experience, so they trained me. I caught it quick. They couldn't believe how I caught on so fast.

Lauren stood out from the crowd and also learned that she liked fiddling with numbers. When she got pregnant and had to go on welfare, she figured out that she could go back to school to fulfill her AFDC work requirements, a policy that has since been eliminated.[8] She used the time wisely to get some formal training in accounting, to complement what she had learned on the job. But Lauren found that combining schooling, motherhood, and the burdensome oversight requirements of welfare was frustrating, so much so that she left the rolls of her own accord. Coincidentally, and fortunately, the part-time summer job she had held in a hospital accounting department became a full-time opening, and she jumped at the chance. From then on, as she explained with relief, "Everything started getting better for me."

The spread of the Internet as a job-search tool eased the burden of looking around for new opportunities.[9] One particular ad caught Lauren's eye, she said, because she knew the location was classy. She contacted the placement firm listed on the Web, and before she knew it, she had made her own great leap forward: "Careerpath.com . . . had a lot of listings for jobs, but it had Kelly Services [a well-known job placement firm] so I decided to call. They asked me to fax in a résumé, then they called me in for an interview. They liked what they saw. Everything was basically the same description for this job that I [already had], but just making more money, which is great. If I could do the same thing at another job and make more money, I want to go for it."

The job interview taught Lauren that her instincts about the value of education were right on target. Her résumé signaled to the hiring manager that Lauren was a good fit for a foundation that funds research: "The vice president . . . looked at my résumé and said, 'I see you have your associate's degree in social science. You did child psychology, and I see the different courses that you took in school for your degree.' So she said, 'That's why we picked you.' She said, 'We have a lot of candidates, but since you have your degree that's more with the social sciences, we felt like you would be a good candidate for the job.' And then she said, 'We noticed that you were saying you wanted to finish college and continue on for more education.' They do a lot of early childhood education, social sciences, and stuff like that."

Working at the foundation introduced her to the novel idea that a workplace can be a support to her family rather than a commitment that competes unduly for her time and loyalty. She discovered this the hard way, when illness forced her to take some time away from work. Had this happened when she was at Burger Barn, she would have been shown the door. At the foundation, just the opposite was the case:

> My daughter had surgery in June. Everyone [at the foundation] was so supportive and making sure that she was OK. They were OK about me taking those days. Jane had to stay out for about five to eleven days of school. They were very understanding.
>
> Just recently, I was sick all week last week. Jane had a virus and I got

it. So she was sick, but I think I got it worse. But they were so supportive. I came in, like, three days last week. Every day they would say
on those two days, go home Lauren. . . .

I think it's about the people. [There are] people who are kind-
hearted, and then . . . people who are cold-hearted. . . . You have a
child, that's your problem. You have a job. We need you here. Then
you have those who had kids, who may be in college now, but remember when they were young, so they understand.

It proved possible for a number of our high flyers to move up internal
job ladders by accumulating experience and skill (like Jamal and Edward
did). For others, educational credentials attained during stints of low-wage
work qualified them for better jobs later (like Lauren). However, a "fu-
sion" pattern was also evident, in which a worker entered the labor force at
the lowest entry level and, in fits and starts, piled up educational credentials that made possible new occupations or opportunities for internal advancement. David Lamont, a Haitian immigrant in his mid-twenties,
added to his stock of human capital by spending his fast-food wages on a
trade certificate in refrigeration and air conditioning installation and repair. With its price tag of $4,000, the trade school would have been out of
reach had it not been for the generosity of David's aunt and uncle, who
took him in and covered his living expenses. They run a livery service for
fellow Haitians out of their home on Long Island and have enough space
that they could put a roof over David's head, too.

For three years, David dragged himself to evening classes where he
learned how to read wiring diagrams, run exhaust pipes through walls, and
recognize the tell-tale signs that a fan is burning out. There were days
when he was so tired after putting in an eight-hour shift at Burger Barn
and then commuting for another hour to the trade school that he would
nod off in class. Yet when the three years were up, David had a credential
that was worth something, and within six months he landed a job, with
benefits, that paid three times the amount he had been earning at the grill.
Most Burger Barn workers knew they could do better in the labor market
if they could go back to school, but few were able to follow through. Their
families' immediate needs took up every dime they earned.

While David had to fund his own training, some low-wage workers
get lucky and land in firms that are ready to invest in them.[10] Helena
Menardo, a twenty-six-year-old of Dominican descent, was able to pile up
her credentials on company time. She has her bachelor's degree, is married

with two children, and her full-time job as the manager of a call center at a large insurance company pays more than $60,000 a year with benefits.

Helena's first experience in the corporate sector began not after college but as a high school intern at a large insurance company. Although she interspersed her unpaid internship time with stints at Burger Barn, she set her sights on a real job and landed one as an entry-level administrative assistant in the insurance firm. With a firm grasp on the lower rungs of a big corporate ladder, Helena could peer up to see an internal pathway that promised increasing wages and more responsibility on the job. While racking up seniority, security, and skills, she worked on her educational profile on the company's tab. She completed her associate's degree at the Borough of Manhattan Community College, one of City University's junior colleges, and then advanced to City College for her bachelor's in public administration. Helena's employer got a more skilled (or at least credentialed) worker who could be promoted, and Helena ended up with a much better résumé than she could ever have hoped for if she had had to cover the educational costs herself.

Bridget Warner is another high flyer who parlayed her way up the career path by gaining skills and credentials that put her in line for better jobs. Bridget understood early on that, as a young black mother without a high school diploma, she was going to end her days over a hot french fry vat if she didn't distinguish herself from the pack. The evidence for that conclusion was all around her. By 1997, she was twenty-four years old, living in a three-generation household consisting of her mother, who was unemployed; her father, who worked as a cook; her sister, who had landed a job as a customer service representative; and Bridget's own first child. Her work history consisted mainly of entry-level jobs at the minimum wage, like the one she held when we first met in 1994 at Burger Barn, and like the cashier's job she had in a supermarket in 1997. Those jobs tended to last only a few months at a time, and then Bridget would move on to something that looked more promising. She found a temporary position working as an administrative assistant for one of Manhattan's community boards, which paid two dollars an hour above the minimum wage, but it lasted only four months, leaving her no option but to return to the supermarket cashier's job. When she got pregnant again, she dropped that position and bided her time until another temp job came her way that paid a good wage (eight dollars an hour), in the payroll department of a large bank.

But Bridget was laying the groundwork for a better future, studying in her spare time for her GED. She had also taken the initiative to acquire a certificate of completion from the for-profit business academy Drake Business School.[11] Subway riders in New York City are familiar with Drake, for it advertises its program in colorful panels that rest just above the heads of the straphangers. Bridget paid dearly to acquire the skills she needed for low-level white-collar jobs, but she felt it was worth it. "When I went to Drake and got the skills, it helped. So, when I was working at Chase, I didn't have those skills. I didn't have the computer skills, the Microsoft and things like that. When I went to Drake and I picked up those skills, I was able to get jobs like that [temp one at the bank]."

Once she had that business certificate in her hands, Bridget stopped applying for fast-food jobs and put herself in line for white-collar positions at the lower levels. She knew that she didn't have a fully recognized diploma, but that was out of the question anyhow. What Bridget did was land the next best thing: "I didn't have the time to do a four-year college like I had planned on originally, because I had children. My time is kind of limited to things that I have to do, so I needed, for myself, to get something—get some type of school. . . . So the business certificate, even though it's not a degree, it's like more or less my basically saying that I did something. . . . It's not a degree, it's not the best thing, but it says, 'OK, you've got this skill.' It will make it much easier for me to obtain the type of job that I want as far as the business world is concerned."

Her theory was proved when she finally landed a job through a temp firm in 2001 that pays more than fifteen dollars an hour, with benefits. Since her new employer provides educational subsidies, Bridget can look forward to better possibilities in the future when she completes a bachelor's degree.

Forging a link with a solid firm that pays well is clearly a good move, as a recent study shows.[12] Once inside this charmed circle, even interns, like Helena, and temps who become hires, like Bridget, can gain access to the advantages these firms provide to continue their education, start their family, and sweeten their pay.

The Union Label and the High Road

Many of the high earners in the study were working in jobs that were not particularly skilled or high up in the organizational chart. Instead, they had found the holy grail: a union position or a nonunion job in a sector with high levels of unionization. A significant union presence in a job sector means better working conditions and wages at the firms that are organized, and it also means competing firms are pushed to pay comparable wages to attract employees.[13] Hospital attendants, mail carriers, janitors, city payroll clerks, and unionized porters in an apartment building are all represented among the high flyers in our group. Collective bargaining has clearly been a critical element in their good fortune.

Reynaldo found a job as a porter in a unionized high-rise, where he is responsible for garbage collection and cleaning up around the property. That work may well be deemed more skilled than a job running a french fry station, but the difference is probably not enough to account for the wage differential of nearly eight dollars an hour. That is the union difference at work.

Reynaldo was ensconced in a summer job flipping burgers when we first interviewed him in 1993, but he left a month later to go back to a continuation high school, from which he graduated at the age of twenty. In 1997, when we interviewed him in the first follow-up, he had held a variety of jobs since Burger Barn, working as a cashier in a toy store and as an odd-job repairman doing under-the-table electrical and plumbing work (which he learned at his father's side) in the Dominican neighborhoods of the far Upper West Side. Reynaldo spent some time in junior college, but when his girlfriend became pregnant, he dropped out of school to look for a good job to support the family. In 2000, a friend of his father recommended him for the position as a porter in an East Side apartment building, a job he had held for just over a year when we found him in the final follow-up study. Rey was now living with the mother of his child, earning fourteen dollars an hour with full benefits, and anticipating his partner's return to her job as a cashier. Together they were making good money. His job is essentially a manual labor position, but because it falls under collective bargaining, the position pays well and is rich in benefits.

Belinda, a thirty-year-old African American woman, exemplifies a related pattern. She, too, has been the beneficiary of a union job, but unlike Rey, Belinda qualified for it after she made a significant investment in education and job training. Belinda started out in Burger Barn when she was a part-time student at a community college; her earnings paid for her college expenses. She dropped out of that school, later enrolled at Long Island University for a short time, and dropped out again.[14] During this period, she applied for jobs as an operating room technician and a data analyst at one of the city's major hospitals, but did not get either position. Eventually she found a job as a nurse's aide, a position that paid fourteen dollars an hour. Even though she did not complete the schooling she began, her coursework in health science positioned her for a position at the bottom of the hospital hierarchy, in a union job. Her wages have only grown since then.

Adam, a thirty-six-year-old African American who left school after the tenth grade, is another person who took the union path to upward mobility. When we reconnected with him, Adam had been working for four years as a driver for an express delivery firm. He was earning $70,000 a year with full benefits. A well-respected and reliable driver, Adam had been offered opportunities to move into management, but he turned them down flat. Supervisors are often fired, he explained, which is why Adam prefers the protection of the union.[15] Through his job, he met a client with a screen printing business, and Adam created a second job for himself running a T-shirt printing company out of his home. T-shirts turn out to be profitable; Adam and his new (third) wife are bringing in another $30,000 a year with that business. He needs the extra income because he now has custody of his two kids—a thirteen-year-old girl and a six-year-old boy. The family rents in the Bronx, but they have set their hearts on having a home of their own and are in the process of building one in North Carolina, near where Adam's family lives.[16] North Carolina beckons as well because there are better schools there for his children than the ones they attend in the Bronx. With a teenage girl in the house, Adam has become more aware of the pitfalls of raising a child in the Bronx. Having sent his daughter down South for occasional summers, he has come to believe that it would be a less risky place for her to get through adolescence.

To get from here to there, Adam will have to find a way to bring his good fortune in the working world with him. Despite his steady track record with the delivery firm, the transfer is proving more problematic than he expected. In North Carolina his firm pays comparable wage rates, but it does not pay benefits. Adam would get to keep his high salary, but he would be paying out of pocket for health insurance and retirement contributions. "I was at least hoping that they had the benefits for us," Adam laments, "which they don't have. That is what surprised me, because I thought at least everyone should have some type of coverage, but they don't have that."

Pedro is another example of someone without a high school diploma who became a high flyer. His first big break was a job with the New York City Board of Education as a unionized kitchen worker. "I was working for a deli," Pedro remembered, "and [my friend], she was the cashier. She asked me if I was interested in the Board of Education because she had a friend on the inside that could help me get a job, and that is how that happened." But even at a good hourly wage, the part-time hours did not add up to enough money to make ends meet.[17]

Pedro set himself the task of finding a second job, and in the course of his search, he stumbled on the big-box retail chain Costco. The "Wal-Martization" of the economy has been a big worry in many American communities. All those cheap consumer goods bring with them low-wage, no-benefit retail jobs. Yet not all big-box retailers have taken the "low road." Costco has opted for a very different workforce model than the one Wal-Mart follows. At Costco, employees receive higher wages and benefits, they have opportunities to develop new skills, and they have access to internal job ladders.[18]

Pedro recognized the main chance when it came his way, and he jumped at it. He has since made good use of what Costco has to offer. "After my three-month probation," he reported, "I was promoted to full-time. I got my benefits, vacation time, and sick time. [At that time I was a stocker] and I did that for about a year, and they liked my detail and [stocker] skills and stuff like that. So they approached me and said they wanted to promote me to a driver! I have been a driver for about ten to eleven months, and now they are talking to me about promoting me to a supervisor. So now I am in the process of following that."

Pedro's job brings in $15.65 per hour with benefits (he makes approximately $32,000 to 35,000 per year with lots of overtime). With that kind of money, Pedro was able to realize his life-long ambition of becoming a home owner. In 2002 he purchased a house on Staten Island (for $197,000) and moved out of Brooklyn for good, along with his wife, their new daughter, and his wife's daughter from a previous marriage.

Adam and Pedro succeeded by landing jobs in firms that have taken the high road in the way they treat their workers.[19] Their policies are exceptions amid the larger trends of deunionization and low-road employment practices that are typical of the service industry. Adam and Pedro's experience reminds us that the pathways to upward mobility are historically contingent. If organized labor continues to shrink—as it has for decades now—the door may be left ajar just a crack, rather than sitting wide open for the working poor.

While union jobs represent a holy grail for workers in the inner city, they are mostly associated with the public sector in the minds of African Americans. Many have elderly relatives who were fortunate to be working as the equal-opportunity programs of the post–World War II years grew, when the federal government led the way in opening the civil service to minority applicants. When you talk union with most Harlem residents, it is the "city job" that comes to mind, long before positions at Costco or Federal Express.

By 1997 Larry, a twenty-nine-year-old immigrant from the Caribbean, had finished high school and about two years of college. He was already two years into his dream job as a computer technician for the New York City Planning Commission. Although he was still technically a part-time employee, Larry worked forty hours a week, and his responsibilities grew year by year until, in 2002, he became a team leader, one step down from manager. Making a salary of $35,000 per year with full benefits, Larry was living well when we found him again, especially since he was single and had no family to support. In fact he was still living with his mom and his three siblings, contributing a nominal sum of $40 toward the monthly rent, although that arrangement was to end soon because, at long last, Larry had found his own place, and he could now well afford it.

Occasionally, Larry says, he is tempted by the thought of a private-sector job because those salaries reach higher levels. But when he thinks seriously about it, he realizes that he couldn't really entertain a shift out of the public sector. The seven years he has been in the saddle of a city job have taught him the value of his niche: "Private, they can just fire you at any given second," he reminds himself. "You're not guaranteed a job tomorrow. I'm not saying that you are [safe in the civil service]— knock on wood—but I'm a lot safer than I am with private. With private you can make a lot more money, but they don't offer the same benefits or security."

High Flyers: Up and Down

Wage growth doesn't necessarily follow a straight line, particularly for those who start out in the ranks of the working poor. Careers are interrupted when people go back to school or have children or need to take care of sick or elderly relatives.[20] High flyers may come face to face with downward mobility either by choice or through the vicissitudes of the market.[21] Losing a job can be the spur to a "voluntary" step backward: the decision to take a lower-paying job in order to sort out options and plot a strategy for moving forward. Miguel and Francisco know all about this pattern.

In 1997, Miguel—or Mike, as he calls himself now—was still working toward high school graduation, but he never finished. He had a son in 1998, and that put pressure on Mike to stay on the job and forget about school. He was working in a P. J. Richards electronics store, where he remained until May 2000, when he called it quits. By that time Mike had worked his way up to management and was earning close to $40,000 a year and full benefits. But the hassle of managing employees, ensuring that the store was fully staffed, and dealing with demanding customers was more than Mike had bargained for. Constant stress and anxiety were wearing him out. Mike decided to opt out of the managerial rat race and took a less responsible sales position at another electronics shop. He said he was much happier: "To be honest, I just don't like working hard," he explained. "My father was in construction, and that's not me. He used to come home every night and his back's hurting. I don't like strenuous work. What I do, I think it's relaxed, laid back. You get to talk to people. Listen to music."

Francisco Ramirez had also seen his wages go way up and then down. A twenty-seven-year-old Puerto Rican, in 2002 Francisco was working as a supervisor/assistant manager in a high-end candy shop and café on Manhattan's East Side. The pay was eleven dollars an hour with no benefits. This job was a long way down the ladder from the best job he ever had, as an operations manager for a well-known Internet startup company—we'll call it City Express—that promised to deliver almost anything to New York's city dwellers within one hour.

Francisco's is something of a Cinderella story, via the dot-com bubble. After dropping out of college, he churned through a series of dead-end jobs as a security guard, and then found himself a little better off working as a dispatcher for a courier company that carried letters and documents around the city. Although dot-coms were sprouting in Manhattan's "Silicon Alley," Francisco never gave them a second thought because he had no computer skills. Nonetheless, there was one place where his experience as a dispatcher met the mania for just-in-time delivery, and he seized the opportunity. "I saw an ad in the *Village Voice* for dispatchers," he remembered:

I have experience in dispatching, but my title was the boss of a dispatcher. So I said, you know what? They're probably going to need somebody to manage these guys. And so I just submitted my résumé, and the guy called me back actually on a Sunday morning. . . . I was just really surprised [but] it turns out he worked for this big brokerage house, the [same] company I was servicing [at the time]. He was just taken by my résumé and the experience that I had, and he wanted to hire me that day. He basically told me, "We are going to need people to do this. But right now, we need you basically to do whatever. Kind of come in and just grab everything." So that's how it started. And the money was just so much better. The money was just on the table, and a sign-on bonus. "Come on, we really want you to be a part of this." And stock options—they really made me feel like this was not going to be [another] dot-com. . . . "You're going to be one of the persons who, if we succeed, if we do . . ." The idea of being rich!

City Express clocked in orders to move everything from sandwiches to legal documents around Manhattan, guaranteeing delivery in under an hour. Francisco was quick to realize that his skills were a key—if under-appreciated—part of the business model: "They stressed time. If you ordered something at 11:59 PM or AM, we had to get it to you by 12:59. And so when it was all said and done, I had the most important job. I was responsible for getting it to you, because it defeated the purpose if we got it to you in over an hour. . . . I had all the input when it came to the delivery aspect."

Francisco seized the opportunity to develop a whole new set of managerial and analytical skills. The job also exposed him to the supreme frustration of living through a firm's growth pains and then its downturn:

In the beginning, it was just about maybe a handful of people making this work with their ideas. At the end, it was over a hundred people with their ideas. . . . You lost touch with the original people. Because you had all this excess money, you brought in people with these titles . . . who really didn't know too much about what was going on. . . . But [with] their titles and their histories and stuff like that, you brought them in, paid them so much money, and you actually put them above the people who had these great ideas and who were making it work. Basically, you lost touch with what you started with. You were a part of this huge company and you were making it work from the bottom up. Then to see it just crumble, and at the very end nothing comes out of it. It was a little painful.

When City Express closed down for good, Francisco left the dot-com whirlwind for the calmer atmosphere of a traditional courier firm. Even that turned out to be more pressure than he wanted, though, so he stepped back from the delivery business altogether and elected to take a "filler" job in retail, working in the candy store. He is free of the responsibility he had in his earlier jobs, but he has also had to adapt to being lower down in the hierarchy. Francisco has more on the ball than his current job lets him show.

It's been hard in the beginning because I came in as an associate. I kind of had to take orders and listen to higher-ups, which I don't have a problem with, but it was just, coming from a level where I was above that level . . . it was like, "Wow, I'm usually on the same page as them or maybe a couple of pages ahead of them." It was like I was always doing things, and when they would say, "Did you do it?" I would turn and say, "That's done already." It's like, "I'm way ahead of you. You really don't have to worry about it. Go focus somewhere else."

Francisco is tempted to go back to the courier industry, where he could earn more, but for now he's happy to work in a pressure-free situation. As his work biography shows, the pathway to a high-flying income may be punctuated by ups and downs, with better jobs slowly replacing worse ones in a graduated ascent. Yet arrival in the ranks of high wage earners does not guarantee permanent residence. Francisco's hourly wage at the candy store and café is considerably lower than the rate he claimed in 2000.

Abandoning stressful jobs for greater peace can lead to big financial losses. But sometimes it can lead to good fortune. For Vicente Moreno, trading a warehouse management position for a job driving a livery car translated into a wage increase. Moreno is a thirty-one-year-old Dominican American who was born in New York. He dropped out of high school and took a series of blue-collar jobs. In 1997 he landed a spot as a packer in a warehouse in Pinebrook, New Jersey, where his aptitude caught the owner's eye. This led to a sweet promotion to the position of warehouse manager.

Proud as he was of his success, Vicente was also worn out by his long commute from New York, so in July 1998 he quit working at the warehouse and, following in his father's footsteps, became a livery driver. His clients include lawyers from the big downtown firms and brokerage houses. Moreno works around the clock as a driver, but he still finds it less stressful than his old management job, and makes a tidy sum—$1,400 per week, or about $73,000 a year. He has no benefits, which is a problem, but the wages are glorious, so he has no intention of leaving the road. Vicente's dream future involves working a few more years as a driver and then retiring to the Dominican Republic, where he hopes to open a tire shop.

The pathways that led our high flyers from Burger Barn to the good jobs they enjoyed when we interviewed them again in 2002 offer snapshots of both the past and the future of the labor market. On the one hand, there are the trajectories that were once common routes to upward mobility: unions and internal promotions. There is no denying that unions are losing ground, and the length of internal job ladders is shrinking in many firms. These changes have left many other potential high flyers looking for another way up, moving through loosely organized labor markets where temp firms play a key role, playing the field in search of good jobs in high-road firms.

Of course, some high flyers earned their wings through the practice followed by middle-class families: piling up educational credentials that permit movement into the upper reaches of the labor market. In the past twenty years, the greatest prizes in the wage sweepstakes have tended to go to the most educated workers. However, this was not the predominant route to upward mobility for the former Burger Barn workers we followed. Although their stories do reveal a significant increase in years of schooling, few have managed to complete a college degree.

Instead, it is the group below the high flyers—the up but not outs—who are most committed to the human-capital route. However, this choice has not taken them as far up from the bottom of the labor market as they would have hoped. To understand why, we need to look more closely at their experiences over the past eight years.

Up but Not Out

In some ways distinct—and in other ways almost indistinguishable—from the high flyers are the workers who landed in the middle of the income distribution in our study. More generic clerical skills tend to be essential for the middle-range positions they held when we met up with them in 2002, so it comes as little surprise that temporary-employment agencies played a crucial role in connecting these folks to their jobs.[22] Midrange earners switch from job to job more often than high flyers. There is a lot of value in finding the "better" version of these jobs, at firms that offer greater flexibility and better benefits.

Many in the up-but-not-out group are still pursuing a bachelor degree or an associate degree. Completing an education can take many years, and the payoffs to their investment may not be evident for years to come. Now in their mid- to late twenties, these workers may well be in their thirties before they reap the full benefits of their human capital investment.[23] They may ultimately fly higher than the positions they occupied in 2002, but this will depend on their capacity to stick with higher education, a feat that gets harder as they get older and family responsibilities impede their ability to stay in school.

Climbing a Short Ladder

Just as internal job chains and human capital accumulation produce high flyers, so too do these strategies create upward movement for those in the Up but Not Out Club. However, there are some clear limits to what even the savviest worker in this group can achieve. Latoya is a case in point. When we first met, Latoya was an entry-level worker in a Harlem Burger Barn who had been on the job for about one year.[24] She was promoted to a swing manager position (which paid approximately fifty cents more per hour than the entry-level job) about a year later. By 1997, when we caught up with her for the first formal follow-up study, Latoya had become a salaried store manager, earning nearly $25,000 per year. Opportunity knocked on Latoya's door when the owner of the Burger Barn where she had started acquired two new restaurants and began promoting his shift managers up the chain of vacant slots. Before this chance came Latoya's way, she had applied for other jobs outside the fast-food industry but had found little success. In the end, internal promotion was her ticket. In 2003, when I last saw her, she was still at her managerial job.

However, Latoya had topped out at Burger Barn, and while $25,000 was a great deal more than she was earning in 1993, when she was close to the minimum wage, it was not sufficient to free her from significant financial constraints. She was no longer officially poor, but she was not very far above that magic line, in part because she has four children to care for on her income. More important, though, Latoya is not likely to see great improvement in her situation in the future. She does not have enough education to qualify for jobs that are dramatically different, and it shows. Her literacy skills are weak, and her dialect is nonstandard. Yet she is hard working, efficient, and very personable. Latoya can motivate the people who report to her and her boss knows it, which is why she has been promoted about as high as this firm can take her, short of a major change in her skills. At Burger Barn, these limits impose an earnings ceiling that is much lower than, for example, what Francisco earned at City Express, or even what Jamal made in the laminating factory.

School and Work

Ebony McAdam will probably do better than Latoya in the long run. A twenty-five-year-old African American who lives by herself, when we interviewed Ebony in 2002 she had been working for a year as the desk receptionist at a corporate law firm located near New York's Grand Central Station. She was earning $28,500 and getting full benefits.[25] Between 1997 and 2002, Ebony had completed her associate degree at a community college, and when we last met she was enrolled part-time at City University, working toward a bachelor of arts in political science. Her goal is to get a law degree, and her firm has a tuition reimbursement program for law school. Ebony would like to be an entertainment lawyer—a glamorous career, and one that might not be out of reach if she gets her JD. It would certainly represent a huge step up the prestige ladder, considering where we found her in 1993, working behind the counter in a Burger Barn while trying to finish high school.

It has taken enormous determination for Ebony to find her way into the white-collar world while balancing a daunting burden of family responsibilities. She was raised by her grandparents, who are both dead now. The city took her home away after they passed, having determined that the public-housing apartment was too large for Ebony alone. She was moved into a smaller place in the same building that she rents for $525 per month. While that is not an enormous sum for a New York City apartment, it consumes about one-fourth of her monthly salary. With her mother now dead as well, Ebony needs to stretch her resources to take care of her fifteen-year-old brother and also have enough left over to assist her sister, who had recently had a baby.

A temp agency played a crucial role in Ebony's path through the labor market, offering a helping hand that millions of other workers have also grasped. Temporary-employment firms are used by half of all private employers in the United States and by almost three-fourths of those who employ more than 500 workers.[26] The main attraction of these employment brokers is that they provide flexibility to employers, who can avoid the commitment and cost of hiring full-time employees to meet their labor requirements. Because the temp industry has made it easier for firms to fill jobs with workers who receive lower wages and fewer benefits than the permanent employees they have replaced, we don't often think of the world of temporary work as an opportunity for individual income growth. However, in tight labor markets firms often turn to temp agencies for new workers, with the expectation that they will hire permanently from this pool rather than spit out the workers when they are no longer required.

While Ebony wasn't looking for temp work, a temp agency caught hold of her résumé and placed her in the cushy spot in a downtown law firm that became a permanent job: "I sent my résumé thinking that it was a job. It wasn't a job. It was [a temp] agency, and when I got there, she said, 'I like your look. I think they will like you.' She sent me here. I interviewed with the office manager that was the senior partner. They liked me. They hired me. That was it. So I really didn't go through the temp agency. I just kind of went straight from them to here. They hired me the same day and that was it, and then I started working about a week later." No doubt temp agencies care about skills, but in a labor market in which many people are reasonably proficient in the basic language and math skills needed for secretarial work, factors such as "looks" and "likability" play a key role in determining who gets hired.[27]

Workers have many motivations for temping. Some really want short-term employment, while others are shopping for permanent opportunities.[28] Ebony was clearly in the latter category, and her strategy paid off. Although the job at the law firm has not put her on easy street, it is considerably better in quality and pay than the Burger Barn jobs she held in earlier years. And if she can find her way to the law degree she hopes for, she may see an even better job in the future.

Then again, not every degree comes with a guarantee of economic security. Tamara Jones is a twenty-seven-year-old African American who had just graduated with a bachelor's degree from Truro College when we caught up with her in 1997. By 2002 she had a full-time job as a social worker and was earning about $26,000 per year with full benefits. She had

four children (ages eleven, eight, five, and one and a half) and was separated from her husband. Social work had seemed like an important profession when Tamara was thinking about careers, but when she was last interviewed she was no longer confident it was the right choice. She runs into
lots of people who lack respect for social workers.[29] "Even though I graduated with a bachelor's degree, I did not expect to be a social worker. And
now I am. I thought so high of it when I wasn't one. And now I realize that
people actually think very low of social workers. It doesn't have an effect,
but sometimes I really wish that somebody could spend a day with us and,
just . . . like, we could have TV program, 'a day in the life of a social
worker,' so they can see how [hard] the job is. You know?"

Moving up the ranks into a managerial position might be one way for
Tamara to deal with these frustrations, but as a single parent of four kids,
she knows she cannot take the time to get the master's degree that would
allow her to advance: "When you get your master's degree, you get the opportunity to move up to a supervisor. And I had tried before to go back to
school for my master's, but at that time it was very stressful in my job, and
I just abandoned it. I said, 'I can't do this,' you know? So there is opportunity to go up if you get your master's degree."

Entry-level social workers are required to meet professional standards,
but they are paid wages that are barely comparable to nonprofessional jobs
in other fields. That is why, despite her white-collar identity, Tamara remains in the Up but Not Out Club.

Determining the right balance of education versus work experience is a
problem that many workers in this wage group confront. Every year out of
the labor force costs them, and for those who cannot turn to partners, parents, or adult children to help support their household, piling up credentials can be difficult even when the motivation is there. Others have the
option to go to school but aren't sure the payoff will really justify the
opportunity costs, in part because the employers they encounter value
experience on the job more than they do credentials.[30] Amy Watson, a
twenty-six-year-old African American, had been in and out of temp jobs,
mostly in medical offices. In 2002 she was working for an ob-gyn practice
on Manhattan's East Side, earning $28,000 and full benefits. She had re-
cently returned to school at the College of New Rochelle to get her bachelor's degree (she was going part-time). She was still unmarried and living
with her son, now seven, in a subsidized apartment in Far Rockaway.

Amy took her first job after she completed a training program, because she needed to get some experience, but she soon realized the price she would have to pay to gain a toehold in the medical field: "I had just finished the medical assistant's school, and I wanted a job, and it was basically as if I had to prove myself. So I had to . . . do things at the job in order to build up my experience so I could be able to go out and find a better job."

Her first employer offered a low salary of ten dollars an hour and reneged on an initial promise to pay her benefits. Amy was putting in her time, though, in the hope that the track record she created would make it possible for her to find a better version of this job in the future.

Though their pay was modest, the positions that Ebony and Amy secured were actually better than many of the jobs taken by the others in the up-but-not-out group. Both women had become repositories of information that it would take time for their employers to replace if they left. Thus, slowing employee turnover by providing decent working conditions was more of a priority in these firms than in many we encountered at this level.

Cassandra Simon is all too familiar with the other end of this continuum.[31] In 1993 we found her at Burger Barn earning the minimum wage. In 1997 she had earned her GED, but she has had no further education since. She had problems in the past with drug addiction but has been clean for many years now. Still, with this stock of human capital, she cannot compete for a job like Amy's and has to settle for something that is not dramatically different in wages but is far less rewarded and more pressured. She works as a customer service rep for one of New York's largest health insurance firms.[32] The pay is $26,000 per year, with full benefits and a union. It is clearly a step up from fast food, but she is still living close to the edge, especially since she has a teenage son for whom college is now looming.

Cassandra takes some pride in knowing that her work helps people settle their insurance claims, and it certainly matters that she has a union job. Yet her working conditions telegraph "low status," and she bridles under the surveillance the firm employs as it monitors workers for errors and complains that the training they receive is insufficient to avoid mistakes:

> When I started the job initially, I was having extreme difficulty with the [data entry] system. . . . I felt I wasn't trained long enough. . . . It was only six days. [There were] days that I actually had to get up and find a corner and just vent. And then you don't get that support.

When you go for assistance, it's not with compassion. It's, "OK, this is A, B, C, and D. Do you understand it now?" But [that's] not simplifying it. It [could] be simplified so that I can comprehend it and perform my job better. . . . It can be overwhelming.

Not only are you dealing with providers and physicians, you're also dealing with four supervisors. The Quality Care System [the firm's billing system] alone . . . is very stressful. . . . You have to be very strong willed, very determined, self-sufficient, and independent . . . to stay with a company like this, because it's very demanding. There's no room for errors. You have to be accurate. You have to be on cue. You just have to be, like, totally 100 percent functional in all areas. . . . I don't feel that I get support enough. I feel like it's more of a cutthroat type of environment than anything. There's no unity with the supervisors and the employees. There's no foundation. . . . I work for these people and I'm sorry to bad mouth my company. . . . They really suck.

Cassandra would like to work in a firm where co-workers and supervisors value her effort, invest in her knowledge base, and support her family commitments, but that is not the kind of job she has now. Her firm is not particularly interested in improving the skills of its telephone workers, and it does not appreciate her life as a mother. The relationship is instrumental, not affective: "[They] don't know what's going on in a person's life. . . . If you have that added stress from home-related problems, it's a lot. . . . Your job is your job and your problems are your problems. The two can't go together. So there's no unity there in that company at all. I don't feel like there's support," Cassandra says.

In all these small ways, Cassandra's experience diverges sharply from that of high flyers like Lauren, the accountant for a nonprofit foundation. Lauren's income is not dramatically different—she makes only a few thousand more per year—but her manager not only cares about her as a person and supports her when she has a sick child, she also provides a great deal of personal training that has made Lauren confident about her ability to do the job. Cassandra has experienced the sharp end of the globalization stick. If she can't figure out how to do this job with a minimal amount of training, chances are somebody in India will be able to do it instead, at a fraction of the cost. The firm doesn't feel the need to be attentive to her training needs because she would be fairly easily replaced. Not all customer services jobs are like this. One of Cassandra's previous jobs—a holiday-season job at a company I will call giftcertificate.com—involved the same kind of work but in a much different climate, with much less pressure: "I wasn't stressed. I didn't have those extra eyes on me. I was more relaxed. I could perform my job. The atmosphere was . . . so calm and peaceful and tranquil that it just made your job so fabulous. And the people that I worked with, we were like a family. . . . You could hear yourself think. . . . I was really devastated when it was over."

The workers we followed in the up-but-not-out group are clearly better off than they were in the entry-level jobs they had when we found them. They have seen significant wage gains; they are more likely to be white-collar workers, free from the grease and heat of the grill; their jobs are respectable, rarely require uniforms, and do not cause them to cringe with embarrassment. Yet unlike the high flyers, they are still financially stressed, particularly those who have children. Rent takes up a significant amount of their income, and they do not earn enough to contemplate home ownership in the near future. Those who have benefits are far better off than those who do not, and the majority have access to health insurance, at least. Their income—not counting the contributions of their partners—is well above the poverty line. But New York City is an expensive place to live, and even more costly when you are raising children. Their jobs do not pay as well as the high flyers' jobs and, more important, they do not have a lot of potential for further advancement.

Those Up but Not Out Club members who are still in motion, still on the long march through the higher-education system, might leave these midlevel jobs behind altogether someday and take their place among the high flyers. Indeed, their futures are tied more closely to the credentials they can compile than is true for blue-collar union workers like Jamal. If Jamal can demonstrate reliability and continue to master the on-the-job skills that the laminating factory needs, he will be able to earn more and perhaps graduate into the ranks of the foremen—and stay there. But for Ebony, who works at the law firm, a major move upward will depend on her securing that law degree, because only then will she be in the running for jobs that are of a higher caliber.

Low Riders

Even in tight labor markets, people tumble through the cracks. Among those we followed, a few had relapsed onto public assistance and were watching the time limit on their benefits tick away. Others were relying on the kindness of boyfriends or relatives to keep them afloat. These workers, who had very little education—especially women who were high school dropouts—were the low riders in our study, those who circulated in and out of the labor market, usually in minimum-wage jobs. And even those who had more education could find themselves in this bind if they lacked access to child care and therefore became branded as an unreliable worker.

Some of these folks were among the "hardest to employ," a group who, even the staunchest critics of welfare admit, will require public support for the long term.[33] For others the problem lay not in their lack of attachment to the labor market but with the sectors they were employed in and the types of jobs available to them. These informants were in their late twenties and working in jobs that paid less than twelve dollars an hour—wages typical for less experienced workers, not those who had been in the labor market for close to a decade.

After leaving school in the tenth grade, Jesús—a twenty-nine-year-old Puerto Rican—worked at a series of porter jobs (for a tire company and for the retailer Brooks Brothers). In 2002 he had recently landed a position as a technician in a veterinarian's office (paying $11.50 an hour and full benefits). Jesús was still living in his mom's rent-controlled apartment. His girlfriend and a sibling lived there too. He contributed $200 to $300 toward the rent of $650 every month.

From one perspective, Jesús's situation was not all that unusual. Like many people looking to build a career, he could take a job for low pay because he was still living at home and his housing costs were modest. "I could survive with the pay right now with the predicament I'm in, I could survive," he says. "I'm good with this." But Jesús is twenty-nine, not nineteen, and he has basically been living at home since he dropped out of high school. He has also been working, but without a high school degree or on-the-job skills, Jesús is stuck in the lower levels of the pay scale. Jesús is confident that if he keeps his position as a vet tech he will be able to earn more. "Easily" twenty dollars an hour, he says. "I would like to enroll back into school," he notes, but knows this isn't very likely, because he is "so busy with paying rent and all this catching up."

Kevin Ames, a twenty-five-year-old African American, was in a similar state of limbo. He had more education than Jesús—two years of college classes—but no credentials to show for it. Kevin was working in child care for a public agency, a job that he didn't like very much. It paid $9.50 per hour, and he thought of it as just temporary, "to pay the bills," but the job was conveniently located near his apartment. Unlike Jesús, low wages had not kept Kevin from setting up his own home, because he had some savings from a death benefit that came to him after his father passed away. But that cushion wouldn't last for long. Lacking both credentials and connections to get the kind of job he hoped to land, Kevin was likely to stay among the ranks of low earners.

The best job Kevin had ever held was working for the Metropolitan Transportation Authority (MTA) as a toll collector on the Triborough Bridge. He wasn't a permanent hire, and at the time he'd had a bad attitude toward the job. As low man on the totem pole, he had always had to stay late on his shift. "I kick myself now," he says ruefully. He would have had it made if he had landed a permanent job with the MTA.

Jesús and Kevin have changed jobs with some regularity but on the whole have remained attached to the labor force. Their ascent from the ranks of low-wage work was stalled by a lack of credentials and connections, and it was not clear that they were going to clear this bar. Yet there was nothing particularly crushing that was holding them back.

Women with children who find themselves in a similar situation, with the same kind of human capital liabilities, are less likely to pull ahead because there *are* real structural barriers before them. Vanessa Burges, a twenty-eight-year-old African American, lived with her two children in subsidized housing. In 1997 Vanessa was enrolled at Borough of Manhattan Community College, but she had to drop out to support her family. She then returned to school at Truro College. Her mom helped out with some of the child care, and that burden was diminished once her eldest child began attending Family Academy (a choice public school) and the younger child was placed in a subsidized day care program.

Vanessa was living on the dole but "got tired of being on public assistance—it wasn't enough for me," so she got a campus work-study job in the admissions office. "A girl that I went to class with," Vanessa remembered, "introduced me to my boss and told me that there were work-study positions open. I went [to the office] and met [the boss]. . . . He told me to come back when I was registered, so I got registered and I came back to him [for] an interview. The first thing he said to me, 'If your grades slip beyond 3.0, you're fired.'[34] He didn't want to hear any ifs, ands, buts, no excuses. He was going to fire me. So I maintained my required GPA, and I have been working there ever since."

Vanessa knew from previous experience that work-study jobs are often of little value, and she had had her share of campus positions that were really make-work jobs. This one was different, in part because her supervisor was more serious and professional about giving her opportunities to learn new skills. Vanessa said to herself, "This might be a real ticket." Vanessa's new attitude was also a reflection of the difficult financial situation she found herself in. "I appreciated [this job] more because I was broke. . . . It was a breakthrough for me, because I was really struggling at the time. I'd never been used to not having money. And so when I had to totally rely on public assistance, it was depressing for me. . . . I had two kids, and $109 is not enough to split between two kids plus yourself. Every two weeks."

When the welfare authorities came after her, insisting that she drop out of school and work full-time for her benefits, she was furious: "They wanted me to work in a park. Here I am, I have a college education, I'm almost finished, and you want me to work in a park. That was very degrading to me. If they would've told me, 'We have this office position for you' or 'We have a position to help you,' I would have taken it. But you're telling me you want me to work in a park? I've worked in a park before. I've seen the job that must be done. To me, it wasn't fair."

Fortunately, an alternative opened up: a permanent job in the admissions office. Vanessa was first in line, since her work-study job had given her the necessary experience. She said good-bye to welfare and joined the ranks of the full-time labor force, albeit in a job that pays too little to guarantee self-sufficiency.

Bumping along the Bottom

If Vanessa can accrue more experience and parlay that job into management, she can look forward to a better day. For others earning low wages, there is no reason to think the future will be any different. José Ramon, a twenty-eight-year-old Dominican who has been in the United States for fifteen years, is a case in point. José had worked in many of the traditional positions open to immigrants with limited skills and limited English-language proficiency such as stockperson, security guard, and loader. But they had led nowhere.

"I got my job through some friends of mine," José explained when we reconnected with him in 2002. "I worked with them before in Brooklyn. When I ran into them I asked them if they were hiring, they said yes. I told them I need a job, so I went and spoke with the owner—he already knew me from before. I asked him and he said yes, that I should report the next day." José was earning seventy dollars a day working in the loading bay of a warehouse. After one and a half years on the job he had yet to receive a raise.

"They don't want to give me a pay raise, they don't want to give me . . . my rights," he complained. Yet José hesitated to push very hard, because the softness of the post-9/11 economy had convinced him that he could lose what he had. "I've wanted to ask for the past two months," he laments, "but I always back off. I don't know . . . I . . . I'm afraid that they'll say no. I don't know what I would do. I might feel uncomfortable. . . . They should give me a raise without me asking for it. They're a large company. It's their duty to give raises every six months or every year."

Like many immigrants, José's dream is to own a small business. "I plan to go to school," he says wistfully. "I want to get my GED and then study something—business. I want to have a hair salon . . . I taught myself. When I was young, about sixteen, I use to cut my friends' hair." José has arthritis in his hands; his hands ache in the wintertime when he is lifting heavy boxes in the loading bay. So he dreams of being the brains, not the hands, behind the beauty shop: "I'll be the businessman; I won't have to cut hair. I'll have a lot of people there. . . . Yeah, it's my dream. I want to own a business."

Only if José can find some capital and learn how to use it will this dream rescue him from the loading docks. One problem José does not face is mustering the work ethic. He has been on the job since he was a young teenager, and he does not expect anyone else to provide for him. José faces no barriers—other than his physical limits—in committing himself to a job day in and day out.

Down and Out

For others at the bottom of the wage barrel, serious personal problems were an issue. Sabrina, a thirty-five-year-old African American, had had a fledgling career in the food services industry, but she had also waged a long-term battle with drug addiction that had taken its toll.

Sabrina first found work through a drug-treatment program she was required to take in order to beat a drug rap.[35] Cocaine addicts are not promising material for employers, and Sabrina had no reason to see herself in a more positive light until she encountered people in treatment who had pulled themselves together. "I started seeing a lot of people taking advantage of the training and doing different things with their lives," she explains. "I'm going to take advantage of it [too]," she told herself. At the time, she was pregnant, and after her baby was born she told her social worker that she wanted training to become a cook or a chef. Miraculously, "everything fell into place."

Sabrina's entry into the legitimate labor market was a credit to the rehab program. With the help of its instructors, she landed her first real job in a food service firm that catered to Wall Street brokerage houses. As luck would have it, though, her first and best job went up in smoke when the World Financial Center, which housed the brokerage firm for which she cooked, came down on September 11. The experience knocked the wind out of Sabrina's sails, and when we met in 2002 it was not clear that they would fill again.

Sabrina was unemployed and so was her partner. Together they had a three-year-old child, and her partner's two sons from a previous marriage—ages fifteen and eleven—lived with them as well. Sabrina's two older girls were living with their great-grandmother. Her family lived a cramped existence in a small, subsidized apartment for which she paid a very low rent. In 2002, six months after the 9/11 terrorist attacks, Sabrina said she was contemplating going back to work and hoped to land a job as a prep chef through a temp agency that specialized in the catering industry. She knew she couldn't expect anything long lasting, at least not at first: "You have to grab whatever they offer you to start out with," she explained. "Usually most jobs they have can last for two weeks . . . any time up to three months. And sometimes when you stay on these jobs, if they like you, they'll hire you. It's a start."

Sabrina's confidence in the possibilities for the future reflected the success she'd had pre-9/11, working for Sodexho, a large corporate catering firm. "My record was superb. My chefs felt that I was reaching a certain level in the company, that I deserved to move up." She hopes they will remember this track record after her hiatus. When we spoke, though, Sabrina was taking a few months off from work: "Well, the money I had gotten from the disaster [unit] and the money I got from my taxes, I've been able to live off that and relax and enjoy for a little while. I feel like I've worked so hard over the past four or five years, trying to get my life back in order, I just felt I needed a break for a little while." That little break could cost Sabrina dearly, but the prospect did not bother her much.

While most of the workers at the bottom of the wage distribution had gotten the message long ago about looming time limits on public assistance, some resisted the news. Nolita's application to work at Burger Barn had been rejected in 1995. She was not working when we interviewed her again in 1997, nor in 2002. Nolita had held retail jobs for periodic stints, but in 2002, at age twenty-six, she was on public assistance and was taking care of her five-month-old son, Malik. She also had a five-year-old daughter. She lived in subsidized housing with her new boyfriend, in an apartment building on Manhattan's Lower East Side. She has only a ninth-grade education and has never been able to make it out of the low-wage labor market, when she works at all.

As Nolita sees it, welfare authorities ignore her responsibilities as a mother.[36] "Right now my caseworker trying to get me to work," she explains, "and child care is hard for me to find. . . . They're insisting that I find child care as if it's easy, as if it's out there somewhere. So basically they're telling me if I don't find child care, I get nothing. And I could see if it was from a lack of trying and that they knew that there was help. But they know themselves there's no help. So how can you force me to find something that's not [there to be found]?"

After-school care for her elder daughter is a problem as well. "They don't provide bus services to go from the school to the after-school program," Nolita reminds us. "[So] if I do find [an] after-school program, it still leaves me stranded." Thousands of other single mothers confront the same problems and have the same worries about their children's safety. Nolita is likely to be forced to make an unsavory choice.

For those low riders who had a criminal record, the options were even more constrained.[37] Randy Hodges, who had been rejected as an applicant to Burger Barn in 1994, was a forty-three-year-old African American with a past addiction problem and a prison record. He was not working in 2002, and he had not been working when we interviewed him in 1997 either. Randy had worked a few stints as an ambulette driver, but that had been the extent of his working life. Most of the income in his family derived from his wife's work, food stamps, and the public assistance benefits they received for taking in their two grandchildren. Randy had never finished high school, and he did not make any attempt to get more education over the eight-year period of our research. He had his dreams, mainly of a city job with benefits, but they were not realistic. Instead, Randy was able to make ends meet because the family paid a low rent ($183 per month) in the housing projects and because his wife had a more stable employment history, which included a stint working for the police department in a town in New Jersey. Absent their low-income rent subsidy and his wife's pay, Randy could not have sustained his on-again, off-again work trajectory. Then again, with his prison record and lack of diploma, it was not clear that he could have done much better even if he were more motivated.

"I've now been out of trouble for sixteen, seventeen years," he explains. "But it still follows me. Every time I go and fill out an application, they'll just send me back a notice saying that 'Sorry, we chose someone else.'" When asked who these employers were hiring instead, Randy was quick to point to the main source of competition. "Mexicans," Randy notes. "I've lived in [my neighborhood] for twenty-seven years. When I first moved there, there was only blacks and Hispanics [being hired] and now, they're hiring—I see a lot of Mexicans. . . . I know they're hard workers. They're very hardworking people and reliable." He didn't resent the Mexicans for succeeding where he had failed, but it didn't escape his notice, either, that their reputation for hard work was giving employers a lot of alternatives to hiring a black man with a prison record.

Trajectories through Time

If ever there was a difficult place from which to launch a career, it was Harlem's fast-food restaurants in 1993 and 1994. Hopeful job seekers were lined up out the door and around the corner; they went home empty-handed. Employers simply stuffed back-room filing cabinets with their applications. The fortunate minority who bested the competition were paid the minimum wage and had to stifle their own embarrassment in the face of peers who sneered at their uniforms. When they tried to find better jobs, they often met blank stares or rejection letters.

By the late 1990s, it was the employers' turn to search high and low for workers. Although central Harlem never saw the record tight labor markets that the rest of the country enjoyed, even in this epicenter of poverty, jobs were on offer and better opportunities opened up for those who had survived the bad times in the ranks of the working poor. Workers in other parts of the country zoomed ahead at an even faster pace. For high flyers like Jamal and Adam, the pathway up to the end of our study really was paved with gold. In 2002 they were earning salaries that would have been simply inconceivable to them in their early twenties. For the 20 percent of our sample who followed similar upward trajectories—by gaining more work experience or education, by climbing the rungs of job ladders that opened up as firms expanded their ranks, by finding those firms that still paid high wages for blue-collar jobs, or by landing precious union jobs—the late 1990s and the early part of this decade were truly the glory days.

The Up but Not Out Club did fairly well for itself but could not wave good-bye to financial worries. In an expensive, high-taxing city like New York, earners who had topped out at $26,000 a year or thereabouts still had to watch their pennies, live in less expensive neighborhoods, and often commute long hours to their jobs. Their jobs, in sectors like customer service or telemarketing, often offered little in the way of advancement prospects. Breaking out of the club generally requires a lucky break—a union connection, a jump to a high-paying firm—or new skills, like a completed degree. Some club members are likely to make that transition because their children are getting older or because they have married and now have another earner to pay the bills while they go back to school. Given the gendered division of labor, the fate of women in the club depends much more on finding such a partner than is generally true for the men.

Finally, we come to the low riders. This is the group that welfare-reform skeptics were worried about, and with good reason. These workers had moved in and out of the labor market and hence had not compiled the kind of work record that employers look for. Even in a period of low unemployment, their fortunes had been rocky. As in any group, there were some individuals who were probably only temporarily down on their luck (like Vanessa) and others who were in more permanent trouble (like Randy and Nolita). The latter predominate among the low riders, which is why this is a category that deserves attention. Without the backstop of the welfare system, their fate and their children's fortunes depend almost entirely on what their relatives and partners are willing to do for them. And in most instances, that backstop has its limits.

In a sample as small as the one we followed over the course of eight years, patterns are instructive but hardly conclusive. While the trajectories that led people into our three outcome groups are probably fairly representative, we cannot tell from these data whether the proportions are. For that, we need bigger numbers and a sample that is not restricted to one geographical area, as this one was. In Chapter 5 we will return to these questions with the best data we have.

4

All in the Family

✿

When economists think about what propels a worker through the labor market, skills, education, and work experience come readily to mind as the qualities that matter. These are the forms of human capital a job seeker lays out on the employer's table, in hopes of being pulled from the stack of applicants. The fortunate few end up where they do because they can demonstrate that they are superior to the competition.

Yet our sojourn with Harlem's fast-food labor force tells us that human capital and even social connections take a person only so far. Family is critical to the equation, as both a spur to greater achievement in the labor market sweepstakes and, at times, a barrier to mobility. No account of the employment pathways of workers who start out at the bottom would be complete without an exploration of how family relations—between adolescent workers and their parents, adult employees and their partners, working parents and their children—shape their trajectories.

It would be convenient to be able to tell a causal tale here, and of course the statistics that show us that single mothers are at greater risk for poverty than their married counterparts point toward the association between family status and labor market success. But all of the usual problems of selection bias interfere with the desire to explain this connection: single mothers or unmarried fathers may be different in many respects from those who marry or do not have children. Those "unmeasured" qualities may be responsible for the association of poverty and family status. Be that as it may, the statistics tell us that something is going on here, that family does matter in the development of labor market pathways. Hence we need to explore the way family demands create "push factors" that propel the effort to move ahead in the work world. Even more important, perhaps: we need to understand how families create burdens that hinder mobility, or create supports that enable it. From this vantage point, one's livelihood turns out to be more than the expression of personal attributes. Careers are also collective projects, undertaken by individuals on behalf of intimates whose well-being depends on their success.

For many Burger Barn employees, family was the most important reason for seeking or holding on to a job in the first place. Parents may be able to put bread on the table but need to ask their teenagers to help with the rent or the phone bill. Single moms tell their sons that the Nikes they want will have to come from their own earnings. Once they hit early adolescence, poor teens often first contribute to the household economy by babysitting their siblings or young neighbors, and then by venturing out into the formal labor market. The majority of the Harlem workers chronicled here took their first job when they were thirteen to fifteen years old. They bagged groceries in local stores, made deliveries for flower shops on Valentine's Day, ran errands for the man at the corner newsstand, and flattened the boxes no longer needed by the local drugstore. They were paid off the books and under the counter, and their earnings often relieved the pressure on their families to provide for their teenage "extras." Slowly these sons and daughters begin to provide for most of their own needs, and as their earning power increases, they are expected to contribute serious money to their mother's household. From the parent's perspective, what started out as a passel of liabilities—children who need to be supported—can emerge, in late adolescence, as a mainstay of household finance, earners whom no one wants to see move out and take their income with them.[1]

From the young adult's perspective, the family is a powerful spur to a greater work effort because reaching adulthood in mama's house has its frustrations. Throughout the postindustrial world, the transition time from adolescence to adulthood is lengthening, but even the most elastic conception of youth reaches a breaking point.[2] Thirty-year-olds who are still homebound elicit raised eyebrows, at least in the United States.[3] Between the ages of twenty-two and thirty, though, lies an uncomfortable gray zone peopled by young adults pushing for greater autonomy and parents trying to lead households with a sudden surplus of opinionated grown-ups.

The ethnographic evidence of intergenerational tension is abundant throughout our field notes. That this represents a pattern rather than an exception becomes clear when we compare national data with our sample of Harlem workers. In 2002, 11 percent of Americans age twenty-five to thirty-four lived at home (Table 4.1). We cannot tell from this information whether they had been living continuously with their parents; many may have moved out and then returned—the so-called boomerang children. What we do know is that about one-tenth of those in this age group were not living independently. When we look at the data from Harlem, we see how poverty and family responsibilities delay the onset of independence (Table 4.2). As our Harlem workers have aged, they have clearly continued to transition out of their parents' nests. Nonetheless, the most positive figures in Table 4.2 still show more than twice the proportion of these adults living with their natal families than is true among their agemates nationwide.

Living under the parental roof can be awkward at the best of times. When the household grows to include the third generation, as it did in Kyesha's case when her son was born, the strain ratchets up a notch.[4] Under these circumstances, the role of the family ricochets back and forth between that of a valuable buffer against hardship and a galvanizing push that spurs young adults like Kyesha to find a job that pays enough to liberate them, once and for all, from the natal family.

For adults who have finally crossed that threshold and found their way to autonomy, family continues to be both a ball and chain and a resource, depending on the relationships within those domestic walls. Having a young child imposes demands on low-income parents that can easily derail their work lives, particularly if they have no extended kin living nearby or willing to help. If illness strikes, particularly chronic conditions like asthma, which is now at record rates in communities like central Harlem, a working mother will be forced out of the labor market.[5] But it does not take a medical nightmare to make a consistent work record hard to assemble. Lacking reliable, affordable child care is enough, as many studies have already shown.[6]

Cohabiting couples of long standing and those who are married are in the most advantageous position in the labor market, for they have

Table 4.1 Percentage of young adults living at home in 2002

	Age 18–24	Age 25–34
Total	51%	11%
Male	55%	14%
Female	46%	8%

Source: U.S. Bureau of the Census, *http://www.census.gov/population/socdemo/hh-fam/tabAD-1.pdf.*

Table 4.2 Burger Barn adults age 25–34 living at home, 1994–2001

Independent household	Wave 1	Wave 2	Wave 3
Yes	100 (34%)	59 (57%)	30 (75%)
No	194 (66%)	44 (43%)	10 (25%)
Total	294	103	40

more reliable shock absorbers to cushion workers from the impact of family demands. Backing each other up on a daily basis, they counteract the destabilizing forces that so many single parents must contend with on their own.

To capture the key roles that family structure plays in the career pathways of low-wage workers, we will explore three life stories that exemplify distinctive patterns we observed in the eight years we followed the Burger Barn workers. In the first instance, Kyesha pulls herself out of the fast-food industry and finds a job that is good enough to allow her to establish herself without any help from a partner, much as she might desire that companionship for its own sake. In the second, Kyesha's good friend and former co-worker Latoya marries and finds that the help of a mate makes it possible for both of them to move up in ways that were almost impossible before. Finally, we turn to Latoya's half sister, Natasha, who is essentially standing still. With her mother's help, Natasha maintains her steady work record and finds jobs that are less stigmatized, though only marginally better paid, than the one she held when we met her. Yet she foresees no real prospects for upward mobility.

Along the way we encountered variations on these themes, but the important point is to see beyond the human capital questions. Workers who started out at Burger Barn making the minimum wage are three-dimensional subjects who have made complex trade-offs in the attempt to make family and work possible, not unlike their more affluent counterparts in the white-collar world.[7]

Moving Up, Alone

When I first met Kyesha Smith, more than a decade ago, she was a single mother of a round-eyed eighteen-month-old baby, Anthony, madly in love with the one man she knew who had the wherewithal to rescue her from her mother's household. Kevin, the manager of the drugstore down the street from the Burger Barn where she worked at the time, was just about the best-looking and most prosperous man to come her way. In the daily diary she kept for me throughout the first six months of 1994, she wrote her name alongside his countless times. Mrs. Kevin Jackson. Kyesha Jackson. Kevin and Kyesha, circled in hearts. She fretted constantly about the overbearing authority of her mother, Dana, and fell into fits of frustration about how she couldn't really do without her mother's help if she was going to stay on the job and still take care of her son. Kevin looked like the only ticket out of that morass, as well as the best prospect for a real marriage.

In Kyesha's world, family responsibilities extend far beyond the nuclear model that middle-class Americans are familiar with. Enmeshed in a complicated web created by kinship ties, and called to action by periodic catastrophes—lost jobs, poor health, drug addiction, the sudden departure of a parent who is sent to jail or who must go down South to care for an elderly relative—Kyesha's relatives have always stepped up to the plate to do what needs to be done for one another. Dana's sister took in her adult children when they fell on hard times. Kyesha's paternal grandmother, Melva, lived for a time with one of Kyesha's cousins. The cousin's daughter was married for a time, got divorced, and then moved in with Grandma Melva, even though she earned enough to live on her own as an employee of Con Edison. When Ilene, Melva's daughter, developed a drug addiction, Melva raised Ilene's son; she tried to gain custody of the child from the Department of Social Services but was refused on account of her advanced age. It is characteristic of Kyesha's extended family that personal problems are not private. They are the business of the extended family, particularly the women, who are its linchpins, and whoever has the resources—however meager—to attend to the needs of those who cannot care for themselves is on the line to do so.

As Carol Stack pointed out more than thirty years ago in her classic monograph, *All Our Kin*, private safety nets of this kind are both virtuous and durable. They also curb the upward mobility of their members. Those who can count on a steady flow of resources, so much so that they do not foresee needing the help of their kin (fictive and real), can afford to cut those ties and keep their income or time to themselves, but they must be very sure they won't need to rely on the kindness of family again. Working poor people are rarely in such a position. Even those who have come upon good fortune, or have worked impossibly hard to create their own, know that they can hit a pothole and lose what they have struggled for.[8]

Against this backdrop of expectations, Kyesha looked for the middle ground. She wanted to be a married woman living in her own space, and she knew that meant keeping more of her resources to herself. While she had no intention of abandoning Dana or her siblings, she wanted out from under them, and she wanted the opportunity to make a life with Kevin outside the deadening milieu of the projects in which so many members of her family live. Kevin's managerial income had made it possible for him to become a homeowner; he had bought a flat in a beautiful old brownstone in a once prosperous Harlem neighborhood that had become a drug zone. New owners moving into the area were determined to turn it around and had begun calling on the police to drive the dealers out. Kyesha watched with admiration and longing as Kevin transformed what was once a run-down building into a home that was almost stately, with its mahogany staircase and original hardwood floors. For a girl accustomed to urine-stained elevators, leaky plumbing, ceilings that disintegrate, and graffiti throughout the halls, Kevin's home was the other side of the moon.

Kevin's daughter by an earlier relationship visited most weekends and Kyesha grew fond of her. She braided the little girl's hair and picked out her clothes. Together, the threesome cuddled on the couch to watch videos. Little Anthony spent Saturdays and Sundays with his own father, but Kyesha could picture him sitting next to Kevin's daughter, eating popcorn. She was looking for the family life she had never known, rather than the one she knew all too well.

Kevin had other ideas. He didn't see Kyesha as wifely material. She wasn't ambitious enough, or sufficiently educated. Kevin wasn't a snob, exactly. He had grown up in a group home, himself, and been rescued by his grandmother. Yet he had worked his way into his managerial job in the drugstore and was proud of his modest prosperity. If he wanted a wife at all—a decision that was none too clear to begin with—he thought she should be someone slightly more refined. A loose association with Kyesha was enough for Kevin; she was not the woman of his dreams.

Lying on her bed in Dana's house, Kyesha would wait for the phone to ring and the sound of Kevin's voice. But in her head, the doubts began to gather: "I fell in love with an older man who knew exactly which right buttons to press in my time of need. And now, even today, I think I fell a little too hard because I still don't understand why sometime when he treats me like shit, I still love him the same as when I met him. I know I could change him, but I just gotta figure out how. I really wanna marry this man, but he just scared or he just really don't take me serious enough to commit to me, that's all" (diary entry, January 24, 1994).

Occasionally Kevin would call to invite her over, but as the months went by, Kyesha took to calling him herself. Once in awhile he relented, and occasionally he even acted upset if she let some distance creep in between them. "Where was you at all weekend?" he would demand.

"I was chillin'," she would answer as nonchalantly as she could. "Remember," Kyesha reported telling him, "you had a attitude so I left you alone to think why you feel this way."

Plucking her heartstrings, Kevin told her he "couldn't sleep cause [he] was worried."

"Was you really worried?" Kyesha asked. Speaking to her diary, she put her finger on the impossible situation she was sliding into. "He makes me feel so insecure about myself," she wrote, "that I feel f——ed up. When a younger girl dates an older guy, if he dis her, she gets devastated. Because if an older man throws you away, you think something's wrong and no younger man will want you either."

Kyesha spent most of 1994 yo-yoing back and forth between complete infatuation with Kevin and volcanic anger. By the end of that year, it was all over between them. Then began a fruitless search for another man to fill Kevin's shoes. As the account of her life in Chapter 1 makes painfully clear, that search has borne little fruit. Kyesha has ricocheted from one loser to another, some married, some on the rebound, some in trouble with the law. Her relationships have lasted a few months and then withered. Somewhere along the line, Kyesha recognized that she was going to have to chart a path largely on her own. There would be no rescue from dependence on her mother if she didn't achieve it herself.

Kyesha has had her share of loneliness and depression, but she pushes past it and finds ways to fill her life. Like many single mothers, she has lots of women friends, as well as cousins and workmates, to socialize with. As Anthony has gotten older (he was ten when we last met), Kyesha has been able to relax about the once-vexing subject of child care. She no longer needs Dana night and day as she did in her days of working rolling shifts at Burger Barn.

This daughter of a long-time welfare mother and a father who skipped out when she was young has found herself a little rock of stability. What she has not found is someone to share it with.[9] As her romantic biography shows all too clearly, she has never had the kind of steady relationship she craves, and the prospects seem to grow dimmer as she advances in the world of work. There is an irony here: a man who earns more money becomes a more desirable husband. A black woman in the Harlem projects who is doing as well as Kyesha quickly exhausts the attractive possibilities for partners in her own community. Men who are her equal are in modest supply and many have long since been "reserved," as they are the object of ferocious competition. The men who are left, Kyesha says with resignation, are a lot like Ramsey.

What, then, is the relationship between family and labor market trajectory in Kyesha's case? Clearly, the in-kind support she received from her mother—who put a roof over her head and watched over Anthony when he was a baby—coupled with the help she continues to get from her grandmother, have been instrumental in her ability to move up in the world of work. She would not have known how to secure her job as a caretaker and repair chief at the Malcolm X Housing Project—and hence would not be among our high flyers—had it not been for Dana. It was Dana who maneuvered Kyesha into line for this job, leaning on her own contacts in the housing projects, where she is a veteran. While now Kyesha could pay someone else for the services she receives from her grandmother, she rests easier about Anthony's safety because she knows Melva is a responsible, caring person. Anthony's father, Juan, remains a fixture in his son's life and provides Kyesha with a welcome gust of free time most weekends. He contributes to Anthony's support, takes his son to museums, and ensures that his son knows the meaning of church. When Juan's mother was alive, she also helped out by looking after Anthony on those weekends when she and Juan together had charge of the little boy. The extended kinship network that surrounds Anthony had enabled Kyesha to create a steady track record at work, unbroken for nearly fifteen years, thanks to reliable child care arrangements of the kind that elude so many single mothers.

Kyesha's upward mobility has delivered her into an enviably secure, well-paid job that she landed on her merits and has retained because of her performance. Much as she would like a husband, she did not need one to get to this destination, nor does she require a partner in order to stay there. Having only one child makes a big difference in this equation. Kyesha has been pregnant three times in her life—once at sixteen, once at eighteen, and again when she was twenty—but only once did she permit the pregnancy to come to term, the one time she thought she was bound for marriage. The loss of that relationship was a sobering comedown, and as much as she loves Anthony, she recognizes that having another baby as a single mother would make it almost impossible for her to hold down the job she has now. Indeed, she need only look at her own mother, who gave birth to another daughter who is younger than Anthony, to see what a perpetual stream of little ones means for one's work prospects. The best job that Dana has ever been able to hold was a workfare job as a school crossing guard. Kyesha has come much farther than that in her own life, and she does not intend to jeopardize her success. If she cannot find a real husband who will help to raise his child, she says, she will learn to be content with Anthony and the New York City Housing Authority.

If Kyesha's were a lone success story, the one single mother who made it into the ranks of high flyers on her own, we could hardly deem her trajectory an example of a common pathway. But she wasn't alone. For another case in point, we turn to the story of Jamilla, a fellow Burger Barn veteran who should win the award for the most remarkable turnaround story of the lot. When we left Jamilla in 1994, she was working in the kitchen at Burger Barn, having been deemed insufficiently attractive to sit at the cash registers. She was a high school dropout, earning the minimum wage. It was clear even then, though, that Jamilla had it in her to do better. She was thoughtful and well-spoken, and Jamilla's favorite pastime was reading for pleasure. Yet by the time of our first follow-up, in 1997, she had had enough of Burger Barn and was on welfare, taking care of her children full-time.

Not long thereafter, Jamilla had an epiphany of sorts and decided it was time to finish her GED. Her GED instructor helped her with more than the test. He taught Jamilla and her fellow students how to pay bills, find jobs, and think about the future. Jamilla took the class to heart, and when it was over, she passed the GED exam and found a job in a department store in Times Square. With her finances in somewhat better shape, she did some serious thinking about what kind of career she wanted. "I love to

cook," she thought, "so why not train to be a chef?" She took out a loan
and enrolled in a culinary school that included in the curriculum an unpaid
internship. Jamilla lucked out when her placement turned out to be in an
elegant restaurant in one of the Midtown tourist hotels.

She stuck to her schooling, her internship, and her part-time job at the
department store, which paid only eighty dollars a week, but she began to
buckle under the financial strain. Paying the rent and feeding her kids
proved impossible on that salary, and she started to run out of steam. One
morning she called it quits all the way around and failed to show up at the
restaurant for her 5:00 AM shift. The chief chef called her and begged her
to come in because he really needed her help. Jamilla couldn't turn him
down, and she has not missed a day of work since. Feeling that her work
was critical to the operation was all the motivation she needed.

Jamilla's impossible schedule continued for a year, until she completed
her culinary training and landed a real job in a restaurant in Saks Fifth Avenue, where she earned far more than ever before. Within the first month
at Saks, Jamilla paid her back rent and bought her kids their first new
clothes in months. Her skills were especially valued in the restaurant's
high-volume setting. When we last met with her, she was a sous-chef,
which means she both cooks and supervises other cooks. She has her own
set of cooking knives, avidly reads books by famous chefs, and watches the
cooking channel on television so often that her kids complain she's hogging the tube.

This one-time welfare mother is now a stylish professional. She is play-
ful with her workmates and glows with satisfaction and confidence. She
has several boyfriends but is not particularly serious about them. Her focus
is on the job and on her kids, who are now teenagers trying to master the
complexities of New York's subway system. Jamilla's daughter has graduated from high school and has been studying at a fashion design institute
while working as a tutor in a school. Her son is on target to get his high
school diploma as well, and she has taken in a nephew to raise as her own.
Like Kyesha, Jamilla has pulled herself up—and her children—without a
partner, having tugged on her own set of bootstraps.

Jamilla's ascent occurred only after her youngest child was well into
school. It would not have been possible when the children were younger,
for (unlike Kyesha) Jamilla did not have a strong kin network to turn to in
managing her kids. When they were young, the family was quite poor and
struggling. It took years of hard work for Jamilla to find better options, but
it also took a period of time for her kids to grow older and more self-suf-

ficient, and for the New York City school system to assume some of the responsibility for their daytime hours. As her example shows, it is possible to climb out of poverty without the kind of private safety net Kyesha had, but it is not a simple matter. And in Jamilla's case, as in many others, it was the combination of her own drive, the supportive assistance of one teacher, and the cooperation of her children—who are proud of her achievements and let her know it—that spurred her on.

The Marrying Kind

Today I have to be at work at 7 AM. I hate getting up at 5 AM. I was at work when I start think about the good time I had with Jason and the bad time. He made me cry a lot. I could not even work for the tear felling down my face. I will be glad when this is all over. . . . If it was not for my best friend, Natasha and [Natasha's sister] Stephanie . . . tell me that it will be OK and that I can make it . . . I hope that Jason don't make it hard for me. (Latoya's diary, October 17, 1993)[10]

When I got home from work, Donna [Jason's daughter, who lives with Latoya] said that her father want me to get Jason Jr. [from his home] and want to talk to me, so I wait. Then when I went up stair, I knot on the door. Donna open and said come. But I told her that I would wait outside of his house. She come back with Jason Jr. I start to get him dress. His father come to the door and told me to come inside and get him dress. I did. He start to yell about he had been a fool about me and him. I did not say nothing. He start to get mad and madder, so I left and told Donna to bring Jason Jr. hear. Her daddy said, "You get him" and start saing real bad thing about me. I do not let him get me mad. When he seen that I was not going to fight with him, he want to talk about thing we should have talk about a long time ago like how he feel about me. I told him that I need to know that he love me. I aways let him know how I feel about him. If he could do the same for me. We got a lot of thing of our chest. (Latoya's diary, November 3, 1994)

Latoya Dayton started her family life very young. Married at seventeen to Elvin, a good-looking neighborhood charmer who turned out to be worse than no good, Latoya had three children by the time she was twenty-two.

Shaquina, her eldest daughter, Ellie, next in line, and Keena, bringing up the rear, twined themselves around their mother's legs and pulled her to the park or to McDonald's on 125th Street, Harlem's main boulevard, during the years when most of her friends were finishing high school and finding their way into the labor force. It was Elvin's trip to the state penitentiary that sent Latoya looking for work. She needed the money; welfare did not provide enough to keep her young family afloat. Besides, Latoya was bored at home with no adult company. When her three daughters were in public school, she reasoned that she had time for at least a part-time job. Her seventeen-year-old (childless) stepsister, Natasha, came to the same conclusion just about that time, and the two of them took to job hunting together. At first it was just a lark, a way to pass a little extra time in the Midtown stores where the sisters liked to shop.

With little experience to their names, apart from Latoya's brief under-the-counter stint in a candy store when she was fifteen, neither sister had a lot to offer the employers they approached. Natasha's diction and grammar are conventional, but she was not yet a high school graduate. Latoya's speech style marked her as a poor black girl from the projects, and she was a high school dropout to boot. After several weekends spent dropping by the human resources departments of the Gap, Macy's, Old Navy, and the like, Latoya and Natasha took the plunge and headed to the one place known around town for employing any warm body: Burger Barn. They were hired instantly and began working side by side. Eventually, though, they rearranged their shifts so that Natasha could take the morning child care shift with Latoya's children while their mother worked. Natasha's mother, Lizzie, took over late-afternoon child care responsibilities, and Latoya beat it home to handle the evenings. With the twenty-four-hour clock covered, virtually everyone in the extended family could hold a job. Indeed, when Natasha became a single mother herself in 1995, little B.K. simply joined the crowd, and Lizzie's apartment began to look more like a child care center than a home.

Into this complex picture waltzed Jason, the first man Latoya really fell for after her disastrous marriage to Elvin. Jason was a different kind of guy, a working man with skills that could command a good wage. Somewhere along the line, Jason had learned to lay down wood and linoleum flooring, expertise that was worth something in the construction trades, so much so that Jason could practically pick and choose when he went to work. In 1993 he was earning more than fifteen dollars an hour, nearly four times the minimum wage. A hefty blue-collar man, Jason put in his time and brought home a handsome paycheck, with which he wooed Latoya. She thought she had "died and gone to heaven." Jason was dependable and willing to help put a stronger foundation under the family. Still, given her bad experience with Elvin, Latoya was not about to assume that she could rely on any man to earn a living for the family, so she kept her job and kept her Jason, at least for a few years.

Jason had been around the block a few times as well. A neighborhood tough as a young man, he had had a number of relationships with women who lived in the same neighborhood as Latoya, including one with Wakita, the mother of his daughter, Donna, then ten years old. Donna was just getting to the age where she didn't get along with her mother when Latoya came into her father's life, and she ended up moving in with the new couple. Thus, by 1992 there were four children in Latoya's house, but because Jason was living there as well, for once there was more than one adult to shoulder the burden. Between the two of them, and with the continued assistance of Latoya's stepmother and siblings, the household ran with admirable efficiency and had a financial cushion it had never enjoyed before. Latoya was careful not to lean too hard on Jason's earnings and allowed as if she never expected money from him, but he assumed the role of man of the house and on his own volition contributed to its support.

The birth of Jason Junior cemented their bond and made them into a real family. He was only a year old when our fieldwork began and was, as the firstborn son amid a bevy of daughters, the sweetheart of the whole household. Latoya took a couple of weeks off when she had little Jason, but her around-the-clock child care system remained intact and she rarely skipped a beat at Burger Barn. Jason Senior picked up the slack when Latoya needed help with the kids and was an anchor in Latoya's life. After years of being without male company, Latoya was about as happy as she could remember. Indeed, it was during this time that she moved up a step to the bottom rung of the managerial structure at Burger Barn, accepting more and more responsibility for overseeing cash in the till, personnel, waste reduction, and the daytime crews. Jason's presence meant that she could focus more attention on the shop floor, rarely had to take time off to take kids to the doctor, and could—for the first time—be an entirely reliable worker.

This stability began to falter when their relationship hit the skids. Jason cheated on Latoya with one of his old girlfriends, and Latoya threw him out. Once again Latoya was on her own, but now she had five children to support: her own three daughters, Donna (Jason's daughter), and Jason Junior, now five years old. The tense moments recorded in her diary, quoted at the beginning of this section, took an enormous toll on Latoya's peace of mind. She couldn't sleep; she was exhausted all the time; and she worried incessantly. It fell to her to manage the homework regimes of her children, the increasing workload at Burger Barn, and her own depression caused by the failure of her relationship. To compound the trouble, her finances were in bad shape. Although Jason continued to help with the cost of taking care of his two children, it simply wasn't enough. Because her private troubles coincided with the onset of welfare reform, Latoya found herself on the receiving end of benefit cuts that took her right over the edge into insolvency. "Gust when I thou that it could not get eney worst," she noted in her diary, "I got a letter from public assistace saying that I make to much money and that they would cut my Medicaid and the little food stamp that they was giving me. Now what I'm going to do? How will I make it? It look like when I try to do better for me and my kid something or someone want to hold me back. Then I call the worker. He said that there nothing he could do. Now tell me how five people going to live off $220 a week plus rent, light and gas?"

Latoya pored over her bank accounts and scribbled numbers on pieces of paper all night long, trying to see her way clear to covering the bills. If she stiffed the gas company in February so that she could pay the phone bill, and then reversed the order in March, she could just barely get by when she did have food stamps. Without that help, she had no choice but to look for a second job. "I don't spend that much time with my kids now," she confided to her diary. "What am I going to do? I really need some help. Who will be with my kids? I can't ask my sister and friend to rays my kids. Christmas is right around the corner. I know what it is like to get up on Christmas day and your tree is empty. How can I look in to those big eyes and tell them that Christmas is [off]? They say that they help the poor, [which is] what I am."

Latoya arranged to take the afternoon shift at Burger Barn so that she could clear the morning for a second job. Over the succeeding weeks, she took overnight shifts at the Barn and worked even when she came down with a lousy cold. Her search for another position took her to the downtown stores where she thought they would be hiring for the holiday season.

Before she could get very far with that project, trouble surfaced at the Barn. "I was at work at 5:30 AM," she remembered. "When I got to work, it was not the same. Something was wrong. Patty had worked last night. I ask her if she know what had happen. She say yes. So I got the store ready for 7:00 AM [shift]. At 7:00, Kyesha came in. I ask her if she know. She say nothin'. Patty say that she lie. Then when Bob [the general manager] came in, he did not say much at all. Then Phillip say, 'Bob want to see you.'"

Ninety dollars was missing from the till. Bob, the general manager, gave Latoya the ninth degree. Latoya protested her innocence, but Bob remained suspicious. After heated denials and counterquestions, Bob told Latoya that he had no choice: the store owner wanted her sent home for a two-week suspension without pay. She could come back when she was ready to replace the missing money. After nearly five years on the job and several promotions, Latoya took this news like a slug in the guts. "They are treating me like a common criminal," she fumed. "I could not believe that they think I took the money! All this time I have been here, and they think that I did this." She made it as far as home, where Natasha was babysitting her kids, collapsed on the couch, and flooded into tears. Not since Elvin had been sent to jail had she felt so hopeless. No man, no job, and five kids—one not her own—to look after, with Christmas just around the corner.

Fast-forward eight years, to the fall of 2002. As her kinship chart shows, Latoya is now the mother of six children, three of them Jason's (Figure 4.1). Latoya and Jason got married in 1998. The family moved from central Harlem to a gigantic housing development hard by the edge of the Harlem River, in the shadow of Yankee Stadium. The five buildings form a J shape around a concrete plaza, and stretch twenty-five stories high. Most hours of the day the plaza is in the shadows, but the state park that runs along the river offers the children space to run in the open. The open side of the plaza—which is strewn with litter and smells of garbage—is bounded by a multilevel parking lot (where Latoya and Jason leave their car), a Laundromat, and a bustling Pathmark grocery store.

Visitors to Stadium Towers must pass through a guarded security gate and check in with a second guard sitting behind a high desk inside the lobby. What with the high gates, the sheer size of the buildings, and the barren plaza, the feeling of the housing project is fairly foreboding. The atmosphere is little improved by the pit bulls that snarl and tug on their heavy chain leashes while their owners grab a smoke on the plaza. In the

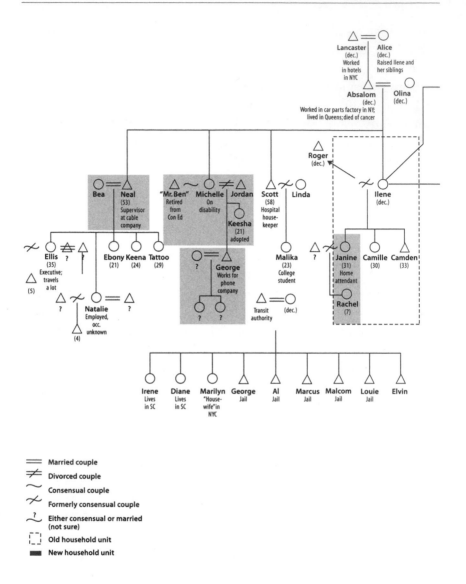

Figure 4.1 Latoya's family tree, 2002. Art by Robert Levers.

wintertime the area is quite desolate, but in the summer, Latoya notes, people congregate on the plaza. Jason and Latoya have a bit more space in their new apartment than they had in their Harlem days, but the neighborhood itself is no safer. Latoya can see the drug dealers when she looks out her window, and she isn't too fond of the drunks who hang out all day.

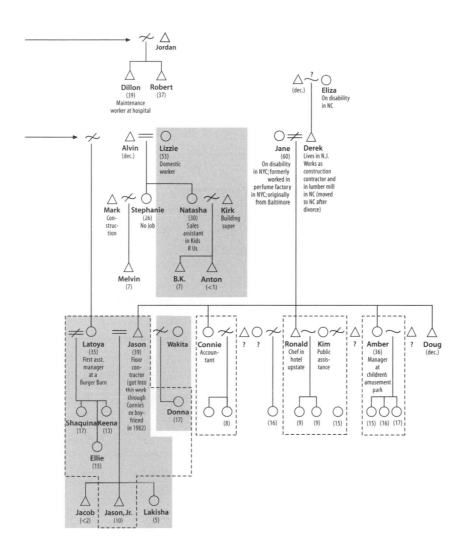

Keena, her thirteen-year-old daughter, explains that the cops make regular drug raids but never arrest anyone because people scatter and disappear into the buildings. The "town crier," a neighbor who seems to know all the gossip, warns Latoya when something bad is about to happen, and that triggers a curfew in the house. All the children must be upstairs by 9:00 PM. Danger comes from all sides, from cops and criminals. The police are known to shoot without provocation and occasionally to hit a child. Gang members simply don't care about the lives of project residents; for them, Stadium Towers is just a convenient drug market. Gunfire at night is routine, but still unnerving.

Graffiti marks the hallways on the fifteenth floor of building ten, where Latoya and Jason make their home. Fluorescent lights flicker as they die out overhead. "People on this floor get along," she says, and her immediate neighbor is especially friendly. The children beg to differ. Keena and Shaquina remember a feud with kids down the hall who poured ammonia on the doorstep when their baby brother, Jacob, was born. Latoya says she was comparing their floor's relative tranquility to the open fights that make other floors so dangerous. Still, she monitors the goings-on in other buildings and warns her stepsister Stephanie not to consider a move to building thirty or forty, since most of the trouble seems to emanate from over there.

Whatever the public atmosphere, inside Latoya and Jason's two-bedroom apartment, the scene really is tranquil. A long table in the vestibule holds a large white Bible, surrounded by unlit candles. Pictures of the children adorn the walls and conceal the places where the paint is mottled and peeling, the aftermath of various water leaks. The family keeps rags on the floor of both bathrooms to soak up the water that runs constantly from the faucet and leaks from the toilet pipes. Their monthly rent of $900 does not guarantee them much attention from the super. But the soft yellow color of the living room, with its floral trim, makes for an inviting place. A desk holds the family's computer and several biblical texts, which they keep at the ready. Near the dining table is a set of narrow shelves encased in glass, where Latoya proudly displays the photographs and mementos from their wedding.

"We've grown so close," she marvels, "it's unbelievable." Latoya speaks of her wedding as if she were a newlywed, even though by 2002 she and Jason have been married for several years. Natasha, Latoya's half sister, helped her pick out the sleeveless, baby blue, floor-length gown, and they borrowed a veil from the wife of Bishop Percy, the man who married the couple. The bride and her maid of honor cried all the way through their manicures and hairdressing appointments, and on through the dinner reception that followed the ceremony. "I was bawling as I walked down the aisle," Latoya remembers with a smile.

Bishop Percy was a central figure in their lives. He died in 2000, but the largest and most prominent photo in the family's apartment is one of the bishop and his wife, whom the children call Grandma. Grandma Carol was the office manager for the floor contracting business where Jason worked for years. It was only natural for Grandma to coax Jason into the church. In the late 1990s, when Jason first heard the bishop call to the Lord in his small Harlem storefront church, the sermon struck him with such force that he decided to devote his own life to the service of God. A changed man, Jason gave up drinking and hanging out with his buddies on Friday nights. He married Latoya and brought her to church as well. Together they have become devout believers; Latoya teaches Sunday school classes for the youngest children. They have returned to their roots. Lizzie, Latoya's stepmother, has been trying to drag her daughters to Sunday services their entire lives. Now, to her amazement, Latoya's family fairly revolves around the church.

When Bishop Percy took sick, Jason stepped into his pastoral shoes, leading the Sunday service and running the church. Even the church falls on hard times, and when the rent on the storefront space zoomed skyward, the church gave in to the landlord's pressure and began searching for a new place for its congregation. Jason now devotes most of his hours to working on behalf of the church and spending time with his family, and little on flooring. The family's income now derives largely from Latoya's earnings, though Jason takes on a construction job or two when the demand is high. But Jason and Latoya are of the view that church work comes first, and since their family life has become more central to Jason as a consequence, they believe that the Lord will provide.

Latoya now has what she dreamed of for years: a stable marriage, a devoted husband, and prospects for a future of constancy, if not comfort. Their apartment is no larger than the one she lived in when she was on her own, but more space is not her highest priority. What Jason's presence means for the family is that Latoya has an emotional bedrock to rely on, a second (somewhat sporadic) income to help with the family's expenses, and an additional pair of shoulders to bear the weight of raising the children. Her own work life reflects that stability. Except for a nine-month leave of absence Latoya took when she tried her hand at Starbucks and spent time at home taking care of her young son Jacob, she has been employed by the same Burger Barn owner for more than a decade. Today she is the first assistant manager in one of his restaurants in the center of Harlem. She is responsible for hiring, firing, and counseling workers, tracking inventory, purchasing supplies, bookkeeping, working with the general manager, and filling in at the register when the need arises. She is a salaried worker and in 2002 was earning about $27,000 a year with full health benefits for herself and a modest amount of paid vacation. Higher management knows that it can depend on Latoya, and she is secure in the knowledge that she can lean on Jason. The whole package works, and that has made her promotion material, which is no small achievement for a high school dropout whose literacy skills are limited.

While it's considerably more than she earned when we first met, Latoya's income cannot really stretch to cover the expenses involved in supporting her new family. Jason's contributions, which are more modest now that he makes his money working for the church rather than in floor construction, brings them up to an annual income of about $35,000 in a good year. Though the family does not receive public assistance—and has not for all of Latoya's working years—she still requires Medicaid for the children and occasionally avails herself of a few items from the church's food bank. A modest monthly disability check comes to Latoya because Jacob, her youngest, is severely asthmatic and has been in and out of hospitals since he was three months old. His grandmother—Latoya's mother—died of asthma five years before Jacob was born. It is hard for Latoya to still the panic she feels inside when Jacob begins to wheeze, and the feeling gets worse when emergency room doctors don't believe her when she explains that the boy needs immediate treatment. They take their time, and that could be fatal.

Despite the regular care that their Medicaid coverage makes possible, Jacob's chronic condition frequently flares into full-blown attacks that come without warning. At nearly two years old, he is a veteran of children's hospitals, having been in and out of intensive care units several times in his short life for asthma attacks that have come close to killing him. The little boy's medical needs have forced Latoya to cut back to part-time work on occasion, as she feels compelled to stay with him in the hospital, even when Jason can be there as well. This would spell the end of work for many mothers in Latoya's neighborhood.[11] Bob, the manager at work, values Latoya so much that he tells her to take whatever time she needs to care for her son. Latoya's many years of service, the hard work she puts in year-round, and the maturity she brings to her work have engendered a loyalty that translates into important benefits. Burger Barn employees are not officially given sick pay, and crew members—entry-level workers—are simply dismissed if they are absent from the job. For Latoya, though, an exception is in order. Nevertheless her earnings take a hit when she has to be gone from work for too long, and having Jason with her helps both because he steps in to help with Jacob and because he can cover some of the earnings losses that Latoya incurs.

Perhaps the most important consequence of the marriage and the move to their new home, though, was the improvement the children in the family experienced in the schools they attend. When the family lived in Harlem, Shaquina (now seventeen), Ellie (fifteen), and Keena (thirteen) attended overcrowded, rundown schools where their classmates were often out of control. When they moved to the Bronx, they landed in a better school where teachers seem to be on the lookout for them.

In the summer of her fifth-grade year, Ellie was chosen for a special nature expedition that took her to Portland, Oregon, where she met the famed primate specialist Jane Goodall. On the recommendation of several of her middle-school teachers, Ellie attended a two-week summer program between the seventh and eighth grades that is designed to identify promising students for exam-based public and private high schools. Held on the campus of a venerable New England boarding school, the summer program introduced Ellie to a world entirely different from the Harlem streets she knew. She was motivated to pursue a scholarship placement at the school, and although her test scores were not brilliant, the admissions staff admired her perseverance and motivation. Ellie was admitted, and the annual tuition of $34,000 was covered by a full scholarship, a stroke of amazing good fortune that was orchestrated by Mr. Gaines, the social studies teacher at her Bronx middle school. She works full-time at Latoya's Burger Barn during her Christmas and summer vacations to earn enough money to pay for extras, and Ellie is headed toward successful graduation from her prestigious boarding school. With luck she will not repeat her mother's life experience.

Mr. Gaines is of the opinion that Keena should also head for boarding school, since she too has been getting good grades through the fifth and sixth grades. More of a homebody than her older sister, Keena isn't comfortable with the idea of going so far away. Latoya is more protective of Keena because she suffered from seizures when she was a small child and sometimes seems in fragile health. Mr. Gaines has tapped Keena for City Prep, a city-based organization that offers children courses to prepare for the standardized entrance exams to elite high schools.

Ellie and Keena are recognized as being smart, polite, and hardworking. They get their drive and devotion from their mother, whose own literacy skills are quite limited, as the excerpts from her diary show. Latoya was a member of the working poor for most of her life, well into her twenties, and while her father had had a decent income as a truck driver when he was working, his alcohol problems had interfered with his staying on the job. Her stepmother, Lizzie, to whom she is very close, is a God-fearing, spunky woman who has worked her entire life as a domestic, never earning enough to move from her very modest apartment near Spanish Harlem. Latoya's parents were poorly educated, and she has not gone far in school herself, although she has improved her work skills by taking internal management courses at Burger Barn. Neither Latoya nor Jason could give the children much help with their homework, and they are not particularly keen on doing things like going to museums. What they could do, for those kids who would listen to them, was to sermonize on the subject of education and then provide the stable household, loving attention, and structured environment that made it possible for Ellie and Keena to prosper. They will surely break the cycle of poverty in this family.

That their successful future was not foreordained is clear enough when we cast an eye toward others in their family tree. Donna, Jason's daughter by his first wife, Wakita, has become a wild one. Jason's erratic relationship with Latoya during Donna's adolescence sent her into something of a tailspin. By the time Jason decided he was a religious man and a responsible father, it was too late. Donna had her own ideas about how to have a good time. Tall, slender, and very beautiful, at seventeen, Donna was attracting the attention of boys and was not in the mood for rules. When Latoya and Jason put their four feet down and insisted that she observe a curfew, study in school, and behave with more decorum, a nasty fight broke out. Jason either slapped Donna in the face or, as Donna alleged in a complaint to Child Protective Services, hit her in the eye. Whatever the case may be, a restraining order was placed against Jason, and he and Latoya were restricted from working with children for many years to come. Donna bolted for her mother's house, figuring that she would find a more lenient atmosphere there, and she is no longer a fixture in the family household.

Latoya's daughter Shaquina, also seventeen, has led a troubled life. Like Donna, Shaquina came into her teen years when Latoya's household was barely hanging on financially and Jason was seeing other women. Latoya was not as vigilant with Quina as she is now with her younger children; she didn't have the stamina to deal with teenage tantrums.

Quina got involved with a group of girls who beat up a neighborhood teen and stole her necklace. The victim pressed charges, and though she told the judge that Shaquina had tried to break up the assault and eventually the charges were dropped anyway, the girls were all told to report to probation officers. About this time, Shaquina decided she, too, had had enough of Jason and Latoya's "house rules." She wanted to stay out late and hang with people who were up to no good. Her parents lectured her: "If you want to stay in our home, you have to live by our rules." Shaquina split, taking refuge with one friend after another. Although her family warned her that she was headed for trouble, Shaquina refused to come home. In November 2001 a judge sent her to live in a group home on Staten Island. Right up to that moment, Quina had been the picture of a stoic, but when that sentence came down her bravado expired. She cried, screamed, and begged not to go.

Nonetheless, the experience seems to have had a calming effect. Latoya visits Shaquina once or twice a month on Sundays and calls her every day. Shaquina is attending school and getting good grades. Because she has behaved herself, Shaquina qualified for early release under probation, but she will be on a short leash, and the courts can remand her to the group home if she rebels or mixes with the wrong people. Comparing the experiences of Donna and Shaquina, the eldest and most troubled children in the household, with the positive trajectories of Ellie and Keena, we see how much family structure and neighborhood can affect the pathways that shape the lives of adolescent children in working-poor households.[12] Superficially, these siblings are all part of the same household.[13] Sociologically, they come from quite different families and communities.

In their formative years, Donna and Shaquina were raised by a single mother who was financially stressed and whose on-and-off-again husband was a source of conflict and sorrow. Their schools were overcrowded, full of kids who were hard to manage, and generally chaotic. At the same age, Ellie and Keena are living in a stable, two-parent household that, while not enormously better off, has a reliable financial base composed of two contributors, one of whom has ascended to a responsible managerial job with benefits. The schools they attend employ teachers who are on the lookout for bright kids from poor minority families and are positioned to foster their ascent into high-quality schools that will put them on an entirely different trajectory than the one experienced by their elder siblings. Except for the fact that the characters are the same, there is almost no comparison between the environments that produced the elder and younger children in this household.

Though Latoya managed her responsibilities with enormous grace despite the hardship of her first marriage to a prison-bound husband and the emotional turbulence of her early years with Jason, during those periods of instability she was just trying to keep her head above water. With Jason reliably by her side, she has been able to focus on taking care of a very sickly baby, raising her younger kids to be responsible and hardworking, and moving up in the managerial structure of Burger Barn. Despite continuing financial worries, Latoya is genuinely happy and optimistic for her family. She believes that Shaquina will straighten out, hopes that Donna will come back into the fold, and is proud enough to burst over the accomplishments of Ellie and Keena. She worries about little Jacob's asthma but does not feel defeated by the burdens it places on her. Latoya has learned to be resilient in the face of troubles that might destroy others. Her credo, learned from Bob—her manager at Burger Barn—is to focus on what she can do to improve her life. "People sometime point the finger at others when things go wrong," she noted sagely. "But I always remember what Bob told me. Whenever you point your finger at others, there are always three fingers pointed back at yourself." Demonstrating with her own hand, she pointed her index finger at Jason, her thumb up at God, and bent her three other fingers toward herself.

With a sample so small, it is not possible to determine whether marriage or cohabitation creates the conditions for a positive employment situation, or whether the causal force runs in the other direction. What is clear is that the association between high earnings and living as a couple is strong. Echoing the observations in studies by Edin and Kefalas, I found that the high earners in my study were one and a half to three times more likely to be residing with their spouses or partners than were low earners. While many of these cohabiting couples were not formally married, as Latoya's example suggests, marriages do take place, often many years after the couples began living together.[14] Researchers interested in poor households may have overemphasized the importance of formal marriage. Resources are pooled—at least partially—in cohabiting families, and joint decisions on labor force participation are common. Childbearing and raising children are tasks undertaken as a unit, and the relationships can be quite durable. The average length of time that high- and middle-earning workers in our study had lived with a partner was more than four years. Yet tying the knot does matter emotionally and may well predict the real staying power of couples.[15] Being a "Mrs." certainly mattered to Latoya, and Jason's decision to become a married man signaled a far more serious commitment on his part as well.

For earlier generations of women, getting married actually hurt their prospects in the labor market, and the same can still hold true for women today. It may spell the end to their holding a job, particularly if they marry a man who can afford to support them. When the fairy tale unfolds this way, it may also mean mobility for the family—an upturn in income and standard of living—even if it leads to unemployment for the wife. This is not the ending I would have imagined for Ana Perez-Maldonado's story. Stylish and attractive, Ana looks a little like J-Lo. She was twenty-two when we met, a newly arrived immigrant from Ecuador who had come to join her aunt and uncle in New York.[16]

Taking advantage of the fact that her legal guardian—Uncle Guillermo—was now a legal U.S. resident, Ana moved in with his family. Ana had barely set foot in the door when she was saddled with the care of her five-year-old cousin during the hours he was out of school, put on a strict regime of house rules, charged with paying the household phone bill and some of the furniture costs, and told she had to ask her uncle's permission to take English language classes, which were held in a rundown classroom near Penn Station. Everyone in Guillermo's house over the age of sixteen—including Ana and an older cousin—was expected to work. Guillermo and his wife held four jobs between them. Ana thought this was a fair bargain at first, but when she could not complete her English classes and found it hard to find a job like the one she had left behind in Ecuador, she began to sink into a depression. She had a good degree from a Ecuadorean high school and work experience as a secretary in a law firm, but without a better command of English, she was locked out of the white-collar world.

When we met, Ana had finally found a job working for Burger Barn as a hostess (the position given to all the pretty girls), in a Dominican neighborhood where English is virtually useless. I say "virtually" because, while most of the customers are Spanish speakers, some are not, and those who spoke only English often gave Ana a hard time when she did not understand their requests. Many days she would cry on the shoulder of her manager, who would coax her back to work, telling her it would be all right in the end. She was mortified and angry that the bosses had put her in a position where her language problem magnified the difficulty of the fast-paced job.

No doubt Ana would have adapted in time, but trouble at home made trouble at work harder to cope with. Like many immigrants driven to make it in a new country, her aunt and uncle worked around the clock, and they expected a complete commitment to the household from everyone who was of an age to contribute.[17] They were irritated that Ana was not turning over more of her income and incensed that she was not willing to shoulder more of the child care burden. Never lacking for male attention, Ana wanted to go out on dates instead. She and her aunt and uncle were on a collision course, and by the spring of 1994 the conflict came to a head.

The catalyst for the confrontation was Ana's new boyfriend, a good-looking young man who was born in the Dominican Republic but had been a long-time New York resident. "I was hosting a party [for children] at Burger Barn," she remembered, "and I turned and saw him. I was very attracted to him! He saw me as well. We kept looking at each other. . . . He sat in the restaurant and waited for me to get off work. That's how we met. He continued to visit [Burger Barn] and we got to know each other. He then invited me to his house and I invited him to mine. [Manuel] wanted to formalize our relationship. The only problem was my uncle."

Uncle Guillermo was not fond of Dominicans. "They are below us," he thundered at Ana.

"Every time we watched the news," Ana said, "a Dominican was being accused of killing someone, or accused of selling drugs, or taking drugs. This made everything worse for me. . . . My aunt and uncle would tell me that [Manuel] was no good for me, that I should focus on work and school. That I should think about dating in the future. But I was already twenty-three years old! I was doing everything right; I wasn't causing them any problems. But they just didn't understand me."

Guillermo threatened to send Ana back to Ecuador to protect her from predatory Dominicans. He was a little late. Only days before, a friend and customer from Burger Barn had taken Ana to a clinic near the restaurant, and the pregnancy test she had taken had come out positive. Manuel took the news in stride, announcing to Ana that they were getting married.

Ana had the baby in a New York hospital with her new husband's uncle and younger sister by her side. Manuel had enlisted in the army and was by then in boot camp in Oklahoma. Their infant daughter made her first trip to the Dominican Republic at the age of two months, to stay with Manuel's mother while Ana searched for a home for the family in North Carolina, where Manuel was posted after boot camp. When their new home was ready, little Carlita came back from her short stay with Manuel's mother, and the family settled down.

At the time of our last interview, Manuel and Ana had been married for seven years. Carlita was in the first grade and had a four-year-old sister, and Ana was heavy with her third pregnancy. Where marriage had made it easier for Latoya to work full-time, the ring on Ana's finger had authorized her to stay at home.

Manuel is a highly skilled airplane mechanic, having completed three years of community college and a year of aviation school at the army's expense. They live in a modest suburb south of Boston. In 2002 they were living temporarily on the first floor of a single-family house that belongs to Manuel's sister and brother-in-law while they awaited approval of a home mortgage. They had saved assiduously throughout their marriage and had managed to buy an apartment in Tennessee, where Manuel was posted with the military for awhile. Although he was earning only $24,000 a year, the mortgage on their apartment was just $330 a month, far less than rent. Over time it had appreciated in value, and their equity would help them buy their new home in Massachusetts.

With the training Manuel received in the military, he has been able to land excellent, well-paid civilian jobs. In fact, he has three of them. He works the midnight shift as an airplane mechanic for US Airways, he holds a part-time construction job, and he has the occasional side jobs in construction that he and his brothers hire out for. Manuel and Ana do not get to spend a lot of time together because he is always on the job, and this bothers her, but it also enables her to do what they both feel is necessary: stay home and take care of the children. Unlike Carmen, who chafed at the housewife role, Ana revels in it. Indeed, even during her advanced pregnancy she was cooking meals from scratch for the entire family—her in-laws and her own kids. Along with her sister-in-law, another immigrant from the Dominican Republic, she also does all the cleaning and washing for the six people who live in the house.

Ana's family is not rich. The week we visited to catch up with her life, both of her daughters were feeling sick, which meant a doctor's visit was in order. Ana and Manuel took them to a clinic for low-income families, where a rundown office serves as the waiting room. Ana has a Mass Health insurance card that entitles her to public health benefits; she also receives government benefits through the Women, Infants and Children (WIC) program.[18]

When Ana gets up to take her daughters into the doctor's examining room, Manuel relaxes a bit and notes with relief that, with the three jobs he has, they can now go food shopping without having to worry too much about their budget. He is worried that they will not qualify for the mortgage they have applied for but hopes for the best. All in all, things are looking up for this family.

That is not because Ana's own labor market position has improved; on the contrary, she no longer has one. Relative to the days when she did hold a job, though, her family is upwardly mobile. Ana might be a low rider herself, but Manuel is a hardworking high flyer. Together they have a modest but stable lower-middle-class life. Of course, Ana's situation depends on that marriage holding steady. Fortunately Manuel is a devoted husband, and they rarely fight with each other. She would like to see him more often and feels lonely when her sister-in-law is not around. But Ana is a happy woman, and she does not have a burning desire to get a paying job, partly because her unpaid job as wife, mother, chief cook, and bottle washer is so demanding, and partly because—by custom—she feels her place is in the home. Marriage and family brought an end to her work career, at least for now, but they replaced her earning power with the superior wages of her husband.

Stuck in Position

Moving up in the world is an objective that most of the Burger Barn workers were willing to sacrifice for, but it is not important to everyone. For some, getting by is enough. Stability rather than mobility is the goal. Unlike many of her friends and kin, Natasha has never expressed a desire to have much more or to live anywhere else. A cousin to Jamilla and half sister to Latoya, Natasha was thirty years old in 2002 and the mother of two boys, B.K. (age seven) and Anton (one). She and her children were living with Lizzie, Natasha's mother, and her spunky poodle, Ricky, in a three-bedroom apartment in Spanish Harlem.

It is the same apartment Lizzie has lived in for twenty years, and it looks much the same as it did when we first saw it in 1993. The couches and chairs in the living room are covered with faded, worn fabric. Knockoff Persian rugs cover the floor, and plants, knickknacks, and stuffed animals are arrayed around the edges of the room. Against one wall is a bright red padded bar. Lizzie's room is off the living room and faces the street; Natasha and Anton sleep in the second bedroom down the hall. B.K. bunks in the living room on a sofa bed, and the third bedroom—the one Natasha grew up in—is piled high with the belongings of Natasha's somewhat itinerant sister, Stephanie.

Natasha has had relationships with several men, including Kirk, the father of her two sons, but she has no desire to find anyone special at this point, or to have more kids. "I don't know," she says, thinking, "I guess because—this 'death do us part,' I'm not ready to commit like that. I really don't see myself going into a marriage and then getting a divorce maybe a year later. I don't want to go through that. It's just not one of my things. Like [Kyesha's] a fanatic. She wants to be married. And it's not, like, in my interest at all. . . . And then it's like she don't care who it's to. Like with anybody she dates, 'I want to be married.'" Natasha laughs. "I never felt that way."

Natasha was happy when her parents, Lizzie and Alvin, finally married—after more than thirty years of on-again, off-again living together—but she didn't think marriage changed anything very fundamental. After Jason and Latoya got married, the whole extended kin network had turned to Alvin and Lizzie and simply announced that it was "their turn," and that was that. Sadly, almost a year later to the day, Alvin died of a heart attack and Lizzie went from being a newlywed to being a widow. She remained the head of Natasha's household, though, and life resumed its premarital configuration.

Natasha did live on her own for three years, from 1997 to 2000, in an apartment in the Bronx when B.K. was her only child. A fellow Burger Barn worker sublet the place to her, and eventually Natasha took over the lease. She is a somewhat solitary person who enjoys quiet and privacy. Living in her own place afforded her the kind of peace she craves. At $580 a month, she could just barely manage the rent when she was working full-time. When the clothing store she worked for at the time cut her hours back—from thirty-eight to no more than twenty—her short-term independence came to an abrupt end and she returned to her mother's apartment. Natasha was disappointed by this setback, but she has since recognized the advantages of living with Lizzie, now that she has another son and the need, once again, for her mother's help with child care.

Lizzie's house is very crowded, with both of her daughters and her three grandsons—B.K. and Anton, plus Melvin, Stephanie's boy (age seven)—living in the modest apartment. It doesn't help that the sisters don't get along very well. Natasha doesn't approve of Stephanie's lifestyle, since she seems intent on going out to clubs and hanging with friends rather than caring for her son. Like Latoya's youngest, Melvin has asthma, and it requires vigilant management. Stephanie seems oblivious. "I've seen [Mel] when he comes in the house," Natasha confides in a distressed voice, "and he's like, 'I can't breathe all day. I've been wheezing all day.' And that scares me. And Stephanie can just get in the tub, daydreaming. I walk into the bathroom and am like, 'He can't breathe! If you don't get out of that tub—!' I'm panicking because I don't like to see that. It looks like it hurts. And you can tell when he's sick, because Melvin's a very busy guy. He's always doing something. He's always doing something, into something, looking for attention, always. Making you have to yell at him for whatever reason, or talk to him. And it's like when he's sick you feel so sorry for him, because he's laying there. You ask him, 'What's wrong? You OK?' It's like the worst."

Natasha is proud of her devotion to her own children and thinks Stephanie is making a big mistake with hers. Although she worked long hours when B.K. was little, she took care to find a good child care program for him and kept watch over his development as he headed toward elementary school. The contrast with Stephanie's more laissez-faire approach is clear. Natasha is determined to oversee B.K.'s academic preparation and believes that nothing should be left to chance. "I would bring him home and I would go, 'What you did today in school?' 'Oh, we played this, we played that.' And it was like really no lessons learned. [But it turned out] there was actually lessons going on; when I got the book back, I was like, 'You were doing something!' You know. They had the date on it. I'm like, 'Don't tell me you didn't do anything.' But during the summer I taught him how to sound out words. He started asking me, 'What does that say?' So I told him how to sound out words, and he reads so good. I just love it."

Disagreements over how to raise their children made the interaction between the sisters a bit edgy in such close quarters. Fortunately, Stephanie was none too keen on doubling up with her intrusive sister, and several months after Natasha arrived, she and Melvin moved out to live with a long-time friend of Stephanie's who needed help with her rent in the Bronx. Stephanie works as a bus matron for children with disabilities, and with her help, her roommate got a job at Burger Barn. This left Natasha, her two sons, and Lizzie to themselves.

Natasha's earnings have improved slightly since we first met in 1994. Back then, she was earning the minimum wage. By 2002 she was making $10.88 an hour, but more important (especially to her), she had moved out of Burger Barn into a "cleaner" job as a sales associate for a children's clothing store, Kids R Us (KRU for short). She landed this job through an old Burger Barn contact who had moved on to KRU and knew the store was hiring. At the time, Natasha was reluctant to quit the Barn. Her stepsisters and closest friends all worked there, and that made the day fly by. It was the lousy wage that finally drove her out. Despite a promotion to first assistant manager, she never got more than a twenty-five-cent raise. Though she willingly took on more and more responsibility, she was never paid for it. Eventually she threw up her hands in the face of the owner and left in disgust. KRU was only too happy to have her.

Her salary jumped from $7.50 an hour to $9.50, but then the uptick in her earnings stopped. Because she is a good saleswoman, Natasha often qualifies for the firm's monthly bonuses—a $50 gift certificate—and semi-annual rewards ($300 certificates). She has won the big bonus four times and has one of the best sales records in all the KRU stores in the New York area. These extras help to push up the value of her take-home pay, since she can make good use of those certificates for her two children. Through this job, Natasha qualified for a good medical plan, but she has to pay for it: almost $100 a week to cover her family. When she was working full-time, this was manageable. When the store cut her back to part-time, the insurance payments cut more deeply into her resources, and this contributed to her decision to give up her own apartment.

The KRU job was a welcome relief from the more stigmatized work at Burger Barn. Yet Natasha misses the responsibility she had at the Barn, where she was on the management track. Customers at KRU sometimes mistake her for a manager and other salespeople look up to her, asking her advice rather than turning to a supervisor. Some of the management people feel threatened by her natural air of authority, and that worries her. In any case, she is not likely to be promoted because the store is top-heavy with supervisors. They have offered her a job as a desk monitor, answering phones and handling customer service, which is in a sense a more responsible job, but after discussing the prospect with an assistant to the president, Natasha concluded that she couldn't afford to take a job that would take her out of the running for those essential bonuses.

Natasha works on Manhattan's East Side, in the middle of the "Gucci belt," and most of her customers are white and rich. Occasionally she encounters a snob, like the guy who comes in and expects everyone to drop what they are doing to watch over the Jaguar he parks in front of the store. Yet most of her patrons are more respectful than the people she used to serve across the counter at Burger Barn. Shoppers looking for children's clothes often need assistance, and they rely on Natasha for her expertise in sizing or finding the right bib to go with an infant's shirt. They seem to respect her knowledge and certainly do not act superior. Her conventional diction probably eases these interactions and may be one reason why KRU was eager to place her in this store. Natasha is completely unable to use slang. She always employs proper English. Anything less formal sounds forced, she thinks. "I remember Stephanie calling me at the store and telling me that it sounded like a white cracker when I answered." Her ex-partner, Kirk, the father of her two sons, always says that she "sounds white" when he calls her at the store. "That doesn't bother me," Natasha notes with amusement.

Though KRU has been a good place to work, in the spring of 2002 Natasha had started thinking about searching for a new job. Her part-time hours were not enough to keep a family of three afloat, even with her mother's low rent. How would she go about finding a new job? She had no idea. "I'll probably look at the newspaper want ads," she said after thinking about it. What Natasha would really like is a job like Kyesha's, with the Housing Authority, and she knows a guy down the street from Lizzie's house who works for the same agency and claims they are hiring. She'd be willing to take a job like that, even cleaning elevators (as Kyesha does), because the pay and hours are better than at KRU. Plus, she wouldn't mind the job security. When the post office listed openings in the newspaper, she also duly noted that down. For now, though, Natasha is going to wait until Anton is admitted to the family day care center where he is on the waiting list. And if nothing better than KRU turns up, she will manage. She has never lacked for work and knows that she can find a new job.

One reason for Natasha's confidence is the fact that Kirk maintains a steady presence in their sons' lives. He takes care of B.K. every weekend, and the two of them spend a lot of their time bike racing in New York and

New Jersey. B.K. has been the proud owner of four bikes already, and his room is lined with trophies from his racing victories. Kirk takes care of this expense entirely. He buys B.K.'s clothes and shoes, and takes him out to movies and restaurants. When Kirk went to Kansas to visit his family for Thanksgiving, B.K. got to go along. From his earnings as a building superintendent, Kirk gives Natasha sixty dollars in child support every two weeks, and he is unfailingly reliable. If she needs to buy something special, Natasha feels comfortable asking Kirk for help. For that matter, her mother relies on Kirk from time to time as well.

Kirk has been steadfast in his support for his sons, even though he and Natasha broke up for the first time when B.K. was only a year old. They reunited when he was three but split up again in 1999, just before Natasha discovered she was pregnant with Anton. Despite this on-again, off-again history as a couple, they are constants are parents. Indeed, Natasha is close to Kirk's mother, who lives near Boston and often invites her to bring the boys for a visit.

The stability of his family life has obviously made a difference in B.K.'s life. He is a well-spoken boy who enjoys school when many of his peers do not. We had dinner together several years after the formal conclusion of our fieldwork, and he explained that he and one other boy in his second-grade class pay attention to the teacher, and that it is hard to concentrate because of the wild behavior of their classmates. B.K. is especially annoyed by a girl in his class who specializes in writing curse words on the board just to get a rise out of her classmates. Natasha was beaming over B.K.'s report card and the news that his teacher thinks he is one of her best students. If he maintains this trajectory, B.K. may well develop into the kind of star student that his cousins, Latoya's daughters Ellie and Keena, have become. Family stability can come in many different packages, not just the married variety that Latoya finally achieved.[19] The child who knows that his parents love him and will look after him can prosper even if Mom and Dad have never lived under the same roof.

Moreover, it is quite possible for a three-generation family like Natasha's to create a loving home and a stable configuration of adults who look after the children and provide for one another from the earnings they share. The more conventional version—the nuclear family—may even be a less predictable bet, in this age of high divorce, than the form that has evolved in Natasha's life. Yet because single mothers like Natasha and her mother, Lizzie, are at much greater risk for poverty, their stability is always at risk.

Subsidized housing has cushioned the impact of their low income on the family's standard of living. Lizzie pays $185 a month for her modest apartment, and the rent has not gone up in years. In 2001, though, major leaks broke through in the living room, kitchen, and bathroom ceilings; huge chunks of plaster rained down onto the floors. Housing officials trooped through the building to check on the damage, and one finally persuaded Natasha that it was time for them to apply for Section 8 vouchers and get out. Miraculously, given the cuts in federal funds for Section 8 housing subsidies, Natasha and Lizzie received their certificates and began the search for a new home. Their hope was to find separate apartments near each other so that Lizzie could continue to help Natasha with her boys.

Finding affordable housing in Harlem has become a nearly impossible task since the real estate market in the rest of Manhattan heated up and drove thousands of more affluent New Yorkers uptown from the swankier parts of the city to this cheaper district.[20] Rents are low no more, and this has put pressure on old-timers like Lizzie when they are forced out into the market. Together with her daughters, Lizzie searched high and low, through local newspapers, rental offices, and van tours organized by the Section 8 housing office. Nothing. Though she had been warned against it, she signed up with a housing search agency, which turned out to be a fraud. Lizzie paid $125 to be shown a nice, affordable apartment in Harlem and thought the place was hers for the asking, but she was never contacted again by the "landlord," who was supposed to produce a lease. Natasha later realized that the con artist was the no-good brother of the boyfriend she had had when we first met in the early 1990s. The last time she had seen the guy, he was hooked on drugs and in trouble with the law. Evidently he had found a new trade, scamming apartment hunters who hardly have any cash to spare.

Despite the upward pressure on rents, the neighborhood has scarcely improved in the years Natasha has lived there. When the city constructed a new police precinct building at the end of her block a few years ago, crime seemed to die down at first. But for reasons that are unclear, once the station was actually up and running, the drug dealing revived. When cops were making regular raids on the dealers, life was better for the majority of residents who are law-abiding citizens. When the raids stopped—and no one knows why they did—gunfire returned to the night. The most notorious and scary characters have slunk back to their regular corners. With them back on the street, the whole community has to watch its back, which is a source of great frustration for Natasha and Lizzie. Nonetheless Harlem is home, and they don't want to move to a foreign land like Brooklyn, even though the Section 8 van driver told Natasha that you seldom hear about crime and violence there, compared with the south Bronx or Harlem.

As Latoya's experience makes clear, a move out of the old neighborhood does not always land the family in much safer surroundings. Latoya still has some of the same problems to contend with in Stadium Towers, but even Natasha would agree that it's better than the area where she lives. That's one reason why both Natasha and Stephanie considered moving to the Towers themselves. Stephanie actually followed through on applying for a place there, but her application was rejected because her earnings were too low. The same would be true for Natasha and Lizzie, so the Stadium Towers option disappeared. Indeed, the last time we saw them, most of their housing options had run out and they seemed resigned to staying in the old leak-prone apartment.

Lacking Kyesha's high income, or Latoya's two-income household (and management job), Natasha's prospects are more dubious than theirs. A good mother, a responsible daughter, a calm—steadily employed—presence in her own neighborhood, Natasha is in many respects doing well. But her standard of living is low and her career has stalled out in ways that do not bode well for the future. Natasha is treading water. That is better than sinking, of course, and there are plenty of examples of Burger Barn workers who have done worse than she has, especially those who do not have family to turn to as Natasha does. Yet at nearly thirty years of age, Natasha has an annual income of $11,000 (in 2002 dollars), which is well below the poverty line. Without her very low rent and the resources (monetary, space, and in-kind help) provided by her mother and Kirk, she would be in serious trouble. Unless she gets lucky someday and lands a job like Kyesha's that will make it possible for her to live autonomously, or she changes her mind about marrying and finds someone who can help to shoulder the burdens of raising two sons, it may be necessary for her to stay with Lizzie for many years to come.

❧ In the winter of 2005, journalist Judith Warner published a best-selling tale of woe titled *Perfect Madness: Motherhood in the Age of Anxiety.* In it she laments the "arms race" among perfectionist mothers who drive themselves to distraction trying to produce the perfect child. As Warner acknowledges many times over, hers is the rant of a privileged class that has too much of a good thing. Wives released from the drudgery of the work world by their high-earning husbands jump instead into the high-stakes tournament of child rearing, while working mothers who earn enough to hire nannies still feel pressured to achieve the elusive balance between work, family, and self.

Problems like these are hundreds of times more serious for the working poor. The difference between living a lifetime below the poverty line and managing to rise above it often turns on the configuration of the households formed by the nation's poor workers and the division of labor (and earnings) they are able to arrange. We do see exceptions—people like Kyesha and Jamilla, who manage to do it, if not on their own, then with the help of a mother who lends a hand when the children are young, instead of a steady partner who is in it for the long haul. The most advantaged workers are those—male and female—who find wives, husbands, or long-term cohabiting partners who can contribute additional income and be available to share the burdens that work and family impose on all of us. Without these critical supports, many working poor people will end up like Natasha. There is no dishonor in her station, but there isn't much mobility in it either.

What we learn from these stories is that mobility through the labor market is largely contingent on household and family configurations that are obscured by an exclusive focus on skills or education. Human capital is a necessary but not sufficient prerequisite for upward mobility; if it is not backed up by support from a kin network, it cannot easily be deployed, at least not in a society where the raising of children is largely a private matter. Family support can come in unconventional forms and may involve multiple households in a common economic orbit of resource distribution, in-kind exchanges, and intergenerational sharing. The objective is to improve the picture for the extended network by fostering the labor market mobility of some members, who are able to lean on a support structure manned by others.

5

The National Picture

The view that poverty is a trap with few ways out has been used by both conservatives and liberals to advance their political agendas. To conservatives, the lack of upward mobility is a sign of a "culture of poverty" that can be changed only by instilling a work ethic among those who fail to take responsibility for their own plight. On the other side are the traditional liberals, who say the lack of mobility signals the need for large-scale public intervention to compensate for the lack of opportunity. While their policy prescriptions differ, the premise is the same: mobility is rare.

Kyesha would chuckle to hear these pessimistic predictions; so would Jamal. Their lives stand in sharp contrast to such dour expectations—and they are not alone. Twenty-two percent of the people we began following in 1993 realized wage gains in excess of five dollars per hour in real terms by the time of our first follow-up in 1997. The upward trajectory continued into the new millennium for many. However, high flyers were not in the majority. Indeed, most of the low-skilled workers whose lives were first chronicled in *No Shame in My Game* made only modest gains over the eight years we followed them, and nearly 9 percent suffered wage losses.

How generalizable are these findings? Do they mirror the experiences of other fast-food workers in different cities, or in different times with weaker economic conditions? Are these experiences typical of workers in other jobs? Would the same picture emerge if whites and the rural poor were included?

These types of questions arise naturally in any discussion of case studies. By design, the data for *Chutes and Ladders* are drawn from a small, nonrandom sample. The primary objective was not to get precise estimates that could be used to generalize to broader populations. Rather, the sample design reflected the priority of getting a rich ethnographic profile of the 300 workers who self-selected into in the fast-food labor market in Harlem. Moreover, in focusing on low-skilled workers in high-poverty, high-unemployment neighborhoods, the Harlem study was something of an acid test for the future mobility of the working poor. If minority workers in poor, racially segregated neighborhoods can "make it" when the economy improves, then presumably a focus on the impact of tightening job markets is warranted for understanding working poor Americans more generally.

We need to identify those "winners" in groups such as ours and ask what makes it possible for them to pull away from the pack. If we can figure out which structural supports make a difference, perhaps we can extend more of those resources to other potential high flyers. If, on the other hand, very few escape poverty wages even when a rising tide begins to seep into poor neighborhoods, then more concerted intervention may be needed. Either way, it is important to establish how generalizable the findings presented in Chapter 2 are for low-wage workers in poor families and the extent to which the individuals in our case studies are representative of a larger population.

This chapter deals with the questions of both precision and representativeness by drawing on the Survey of Income and Program Participation (SIPP), a large, nationally representative data set covering the period from 1985 to 2000.[1] Specifically, we address two questions. First, do the same general wage and employment histories found in the Harlem Burger Barn sample emerge when we try to replicate this sample with the SIPP? And second, are the optimistic patterns found in the Harlem sample during the late 1990s generalizable to other periods and populations? Specifically, we explore what happens when we include workers from low-income households who work in other types of jobs, or who started in those jobs when economic conditions were weaker.

The SIPP Survey

The government's Survey of Income and Program Participation was designed to provide comprehensive data on assets and liabilities that are integral to eligibility guidelines for federal assistance programs.[2] The structure of the survey and the data it provides on employers, wages, earnings, and households make it particularly useful in answering our key questions. The SIPP data set is a nationally representative sample of people over the age of fifteen in the civilian population who are not institutionalized.[3] The target respondents, and everyone who lives with them at each contact point, are interviewed once every four months during their participation in the survey; they are assigned to panels that last for two to four years. Because they are contacted at four-month intervals, the hazards of memory are less serious and the data are more reliable.

The first panel commenced in October 1983 with sample members in nearly twenty thousand households; the second got under way in February 1985. Thereafter, panels were initiated every February, but they lasted for different periods of time, depending on available funding. Their sizes differed as well, for the same reason. These complexities led to a redesign of the SIPP in 1996. Since that point, the panels were extended to last for four years, and overlapping panels are no longer used. The initial sample size was increased to more than forty thousand, and an oversampling of households from high-poverty areas was built in.

We rely primarily on the 1996 panel, which follows respondents from December 1995 through February 2000. This time span allows us to track individuals during the strongest labor markets in recent history, including waves 1 and 2 of the *Chutes and Ladders* sample (1993 through 2000). We also use the 1986 through 1992 panels to explore the effects of generally weaker economic conditions.[4] In particular, this allows us to see whether the results discussed in Chapter 2 can be generalized to periods of weaker economic growth.

At each interview, SIPP respondents are asked to identify their employer and to report their earnings and hours worked during each month. With this information, we can construct job histories that show when respondents move to new employment and the wages they receive during each month of the job.

We begin our analysis by replicating the sample of Harlem workers developed for *Chutes and Ladders* as closely as possible.[5] To be included in this base sample, an individual had to be black or Hispanic and to have been surveyed by SIPP in a nonmanagerial job paying an hourly wage in the food service industry.[6] At some point while in such a job, the person had to have been between the ages of eighteen and forty, living in a metropolitan area, and in a family with an income less than 1.5 times the poverty line.[7]

To replicate the time period of the Harlem study as closely as possible, we start by using only the 1996 panel. The individuals who "qualify" for observation are then followed through the remainder of the panel, including their movement into new jobs and periods when their family income exceeds the poverty threshold. It is important to remember, though, that *all* the respondents in this sample were living in low-income households, either officially poor or "near poor" when they were first selected for this analysis. All of them are black or Hispanic, and they live in cities. These qualifications guard us against picking up teenagers from affluent households in the suburbs who take entry-level jobs for pocket money. Kids from these more privileged backgrounds are likely to experience wage growth over time, but they are different in many ways from the working poor we are interested in, thus we have taken care to eliminate them from this analysis.

In addition to the first group, the base sample, we look at the experience of three additional groups, to see if this narrow sample is representative of a wider population of disadvantaged workers. For our second sample, we add black and Hispanic workers from poor households who hold nonmanagerial jobs *in other industries* than food service. This sample allows us to see if the first set of results is unique to jobs in the food industry. In the third sample, we include all ethnic groups, to see if the results are particular to blacks and Hispanics. Finally, in the fourth sample, we include residents of nonmetropolitan areas, to see if results are generalizable to people facing very different labor markets than those in the inner city, where our inquiry began. (See Appendix B for a thorough breakdown of the occupations and locations in the sample groups. Appendix C shows jobs ranked according to their prestige scores, and summary statistics for the four samples are presented in Appendix D.)

The Harlem replication, or base sample, includes 140 males and 145 females. Adding all nonmanagerial jobs to the sample increases the sample size to 2,006 males and 2,260 females. After adding whites and persons living in nonmetropolitan areas, the sample size increases to 6,617 males and 7,285 females.

The demographic characteristics of these four samples suggest that members of our base sample have considerably less education than members of the three broader samples, even though members of all samples are in their mid- to late twenties and come from poor households. Fifty-eight percent of males and 45 percent of females in our base sample had less than a high school degree.[8] At the top of the educational distribution, only 9 percent of the males and 18 percent of the females in our base sample had more than a high school degree at the time they were first observed.[9] When *all* nonmanagerial jobs are included, the proportion with more than a high school education increases to 23 percent for males and 31 percent for females.[10] Thus, limiting the analysis to workers in food services leads to a disproportionate number of less-educated workers, even after controlling for being in a poor or near-poor household.

The educational composition of our base sample corresponds closely to the educational distribution of applicants hired by Burger Barn. In that sample, 53 percent were high school dropouts and 9 percent had more than a high school degree. The close correspondence in the educational distributions suggests that the SIPP base sample is quite similar in terms of human capital to the Harlem sample.

Replication of the Harlem Sample

We first use our base sample to explore the longitudinal findings described in Chapter 2, which show that substantial upward mobility is possible even for workers who start out in what might be thought of as dead-end jobs. We use the 1996 panel of the SIPP to examine the distribution of wage changes, to see if large wage gains are possible, or even common, in a sample with the same age and race composition as the Harlem sample. These SIPP respondents were working in food-related occupations and living in families at or below 1.5 times the poverty level. While the geographic area is broader than in the Harlem sample and the occupational classification includes more than fast-food workers, the correspondence between these two samples is fairly good.[11]

Before turning to wage growth, we first examine the distribution of initial wages. Initial wages in food-sector jobs averaged $6.65 an hour for males and $5.75 for females, in constant 2000 dollars.[12] While there is some dispersion around this mean, even the top end is not very high, with only 10 percent of males making more than $9.04 an hour. For females, the ninetieth percentile is $6.87.

For those hired by Burger Barn, the mean starting wage was $5.98 for males and $5.58 for females.[13] Since the starting wages for both samples— the original Burger Barn workers and the SIPP base sample—are so close, we conclude that these are very similar populations, in spite of the fact that the former covers only a single firm (with multiple establishments) in Harlem, while the SIPP replication covers a broader set of jobs and a wider geographic area.

We now turn to our primary object of interest: the distribution of wage growth. We begin by using the SIPP as if we had information at two points in time. Since the SIPP panels are too short to observe people four years after they first enter a food-related occupation, we start by comparing wages one year after the person is first observed in a food-related occupation.[14] This limits our sample size to eighty males and seventy-two females.

Our analysis confirms the popular stereotype: the typical worker experiences only modest wage gains.[15] The average wage increase was $0.27, or 3.8 percent, for males and $0.25, or 2.9 percent, for females. While the mean absolute wage growth is moderate for workers who started in food-related occupations, we find a great deal of heterogeneity here. Fully 30 percent of males and females experienced a decline in real wages. This does not mean that there were no success stories. Ten percent of men had yearly wage gains greater than $1.73, or 28.3 percent. For women, the corresponding wage gain was $1.42, or almost 24 percent. Clearly, a subset of people living in poor households and working in food-related occupations do experience upward wage mobility. This supports the qualitative conclusion reached in Chapter 2, that substantial upward mobility is possible even for workers in jobs that have been dismissed as "dead-end."

Thus far we have looked at one-year wage gains for our SIPP sample. These gains may not be representative of long-term wage growth. They could overstate wage growth if wages initially increased rapidly but then leveled off. Alternatively, it may take more than a year for a worker to be recognized as a good employee or for a worker to move to a better-paying job. In that case, initial wage gains would understate long-term gains.

To maintain a sufficiently large sample, while also looking at multiple-year wage growth, we drop the requirement that a worker has to be employed one year after we first observe him or her in a food service job. For each worker, we calculate the average monthly wage growth over all months in which the person is observed working and translate this monthly growth rate into an annual growth rate.[16]

Fully 40 percent of males and females experience declines in real wages.[17] However, this is offset by substantial wage growth at the top of the distribution. Those in the ninetieth percentile of the wage growth distribution see an increase of $1.82 (29.5 percent). For males, the mean wage change is substantially higher than in the more limited sample. Men see an average increase in wages of $.58, or 6 percent. While 40 percent of the sample has a decline in real wages, the top 10 percent gain more than $1.52, or 18.4 percent. This confirms once again that substantial upward mobility is possible, if uncommon.

To see if wage growth is larger for those we observe for a longer time period, we then consider only those individuals who remain in the sample for at least eighteen months after they are first observed in a food-sector job.[18] Mean wage growth for males observed over the longer time period is somewhat lower than for the whole sample, and those at the tails show greater changes. Females show a lower mean wage growth when observed for a longer period, but the lowest and highest wage gains are similar across groups.

While these data are consistent with the qualitative conclusion that some workers in seemingly dead-end jobs are high flyers, the SIPP data suggest that nationally there are fewer success stories of this kind—individuals with real wage gains of greater than $5.00 an hour over a four-year period, or an increase in wages of $1.25 per year. Only 11 percent of males and 13 percent of females in the SIPP sample reached this very high standard, which is smaller than the 22 percent reported in Chapter 2.[19]

While we can only speculate about the reason for the differences between these two samples, three explanations are at least plausible. The first is that the process of landing a job at Burger Barn in 1993–94 screened out all but the most motivated workers. The fact that only one out of fourteen applicants got a job at that time is a good indication of how selective employers could be. As a result, those who succeeded in getting a Burger Barn job may have been more likely to become high flyers than those found in a random sample in which employers have fewer good choices.

The second potential explanation is that it may have been easier to follow high flyers than less successful Burger Barn workers. Attrition is always a problem in longitudinal studies, and it takes substantial resources to follow up with people who move frequently. If the less successful are more likely to drop out of a survey and the SIPP is better able to follow such people, then it will show fewer high flyers.

The third potential explanation for the differences between the SIPP and Harlem samples is measurement error. People often have trouble

remembering their wages exactly, particularly if asked to recall the information many months after the fact. While ethnographic information helps
us verify whether reported wages roughly correspond to the jobs held by
the respondents, there is always measurement error in self-reported wage
rates, and this could have pushed some of the Harlem study subjects over
the line into the category of high flyers.[20] This is far less of an issue for the
SIPP because the data are collected every four months.

Finally, we note that despite our best efforts to constrain the Harlem
replication in the SIPP so that it matches the original sample, the former
is a more heterogeneous group than the latter.[21] The range of employers
represented in the replication group is more varied than the one-firm limitation of Chutes and Ladders, and the SIPP occupation codes include a
wider range of workers than the entry-level, minimum-wage workers who
are the sole focus of this book.[22]

In any case, we can conclude from this evidence that the SIPP confirms
that high flyers exist, even among food service workers. The qualitative
conclusion that there are success stories is clearly borne out, even in the
nationally representative data set. Our quantitative conclusion is that the
estimate of the proportion of workers who are high flyers in Chapter 2 is
somewhat higher than in the nationally representative data set. When the
very demanding criterion that wages grow by $1.25 per year is applied to
wages measured in 2000 dollars, we find that 11 to 13 percent are high
flyers compared with the Harlem sample, which yields an estimate of 22
percent. The reason for the discrepancy is not clear, but we suspect that
attrition of less successful Burger Barn workers is at least part of the story.
We cannot be entirely sure, though, because the longitudinal follow-up of
the Harlem sample located a larger number of participants who were
down in the dumps than those who were succeeding beyond their wildest
dreams. In any case, there are bound to be unmeasured sources of varia-
tion, particularly in a small, nonrandom sample.

How Representative Are Food Service Workers?

One would like to use information in Chutes and Ladders to draw conclusions about a broader set of workers than blacks and Hispanics who start in
the food service industries in metropolitan areas. Do the results we find in
the Harlem sample and the SIPP base sample carry over to the larger population of workers from poor and near-poor households? To answer this

question, we augment the sample incrementally. First we add persons observed in other nonmanagerial jobs, then persons of other races, and, finally, persons not living in metropolitan areas, to see the effects of each change. Throughout, we continue to impose the same age criteria and the restriction that the workers have to be living in a household with income below 1.5 times the family poverty line at some point while holding a nonmanagerial job.

As before, we begin by looking at the distribution of initial wages. Not surprisingly, wages are lower in the base sample than in the sample that includes persons who were observed in any nonmanagerial job.[23] Men's wages increase from an average of $6.65 an hour to $7.99 when we add other nonmanagerial jobs. Women's wages increase from $5.75 to $7.10. This indicates that the average food service worker received roughly $1.35 less per hour than workers in other nonmanagerial jobs. It tells us, in fact, what Harlem job seekers already know so well: fast-food jobs don't pay.[24]

What happens when we add whites to the base sample of blacks and Hispanics living in metropolitan areas, and include workers living outside metropolitan areas?[25] Given what we know about the relationship between race and wages, we should not be surprised to find that the addition of whites increases starting wages—but, it turns out, not by very much. Initial wages in the ninetieth percentile increase from $12.53 to $13.75 for males and from $10.15 to $10.39 for females. Adding nonmetropolitan residents reduces the mean starting wage, but this change also has a small effect. The size of these effects probably reflects the fact that we continue to require that sample members are living in a poor or near-poor household when first observed in their nonmanagerial jobs. This family-income criterion reduces the impact of race and metropolitan area.

Requiring SIPP sample members to be in food service jobs clearly reduces starting wages, a finding that comports with our observation that entry-level food industry jobs are poorly paid compared with the general types of jobs held by workers from poor and near-poor households.

We now turn to our main object of interest: wage growth. Given that starting wages are lower in the food services than in other nonmanagerial occupations, one might expect that wage growth would be higher for food service employees, since they start nearer the bottom. If so, the findings described in Chapter 2 would tend to overstate the extent of growth for persons starting in other nonmanagerial jobs.

This seems to be the case, as our inspection of mean wage growth for our different samples shows.[26] For men, the mean wage growth is 6.0 percent for the base sample, which is roughly 1.5 times as much as we see in the other samples. Women in the base sample had a mean wage growth rate of 4.0 percent, while the expanded samples experienced wage growth ranging from 5.1 to 6.2 percent. What we learn from this is that, in low-wage jobs, it is indeed easier to garner a large *percentage* increase in wages, because the dollar amount required to achieve it is much lower.[27]

At the end of the day, what we really want to know (to compare the Burger Barn workers' trajectories with those of their national counterparts) is the proportion of individuals with wage gains sufficient to reach the five-dollar real wage increase over four years. Those are the people we deem high flyers. Since high flyers are defined in terms of a dollar cutoff, this threshold is easier to reach in jobs with higher initial wages, since even small percentage changes in wages can lead to larger dollar changes if the wage level is high. While 11 percent of males and 13 percent of females in the base sample reached this $1.25-per-year threshold, the proportions increase to 19 percent for males and 16 percent for females in the sample that includes all races and all nonmanagerial jobs in both metropolitan and nonmetropolitan areas.[28]

The base sample reveals high wage growth for a subset of the population one might have previously considered to be stuck in dead-end jobs. We conclude that the decision to use food service workers to make inferences about a broader population does not distort the picture. If anything, we find that this population has dollar wage growth that is lower, or comparable to, the broader sample of persons working in all nonmanagerial jobs and living in poor or near-poor households.

Differences by Period

Thus far we have focused on patterns of wage growth among low-income individuals during the mid- to late 1990s, a period marked by sustained economic expansion that raised the wages of those at the bottom of the labor market. This stands in contrast to the prior decade, which saw rising inequality and ended with a major recession. Did the workers we studied who achieved high rates of growth fare especially well because of the favorable economic conditions for the less skilled? One way to address this question is to use the SIPP to compare wage growth in the 1996 panel, which follows workers during the last half of the 1990s, with wage growth recorded during the prior years, which were characterized by rising inequality and a sharp economic downturn.

To do this, we compare the wage growth recorded in the SIPP for the period from October 1985 to April 1995 with wage growth for the period from December 1995 to February 2000.[29] For both time frames, we look at the base sample (replicating the Harlem sample) and our broadest sample (persons of all races observed in nonmanagerial jobs in metropolitan or nonmetropolitan areas while living in families with income below 1.5 times the poverty line).

What do we learn about wage increases in good times and bad? We find that changes in mean wages and changes at the top of the distribution were similar in the latter half of the 1990s and the earlier period, though there were some exceptions.[30] For example, the mean increase in real wages for men in our broadest sample between 1985 and 1995 was $.34 per year, which is not much less in percentage terms than the $.45 increase between 1996 and 2000. Likewise, the ninetieth percentile of the wage growth distribution in both periods was $2.44. Mean wage growth for women was substantially higher in the later expansionary period. They saw average wage gains of $.56, or 5.6 percent, in the late 1990s, compared with $.30, or 3.4 percent, in the earlier recessionary period.

If we use the criterion that defines high flyers—$1.25 per year in real wage growth—we find that the two periods look very similar.[31] The proportion of male high flyers in the most inclusive sample is 19 percent in the period covered by the 1996 panel, while 18 percent of men reached this high standard in the earlier period.[32] For women, we see a small increase, from 14 to 16 percent, between the two periods.[33]

Our analysis of the SIPP data therefore implies that the period covered by the *Chutes and Ladders* study was not atypical for the population being studied. This result was somewhat unexpected and should be interpreted carefully. It should be noted that our finding that wage growth after 1996 was similar to that during the prior ten years in no way implies that economic expansions don't matter for the least skilled. Lower unemployment rates clearly help low-skilled workers find jobs, and this increases their earnings and, thus, family income. This increase in hours is important even if the expansion has no effect on the wage rate. The distinction between employment (hours worked) and wages is crucial in interpreting our findings.

By now it is well established that economic expansions have a large effect on hours worked but modest effects, at most, on average wages.[34] What is more surprising is that those at the bottom of the wage distribution are not more likely to move into higher paying jobs during expansions than during weak economic conditions. Our finding that upward mobility is not cyclically sensitive is certainly credible. If less-skilled workers are always anxious to move into the next job up the job ladder, even at the wage offered during a recession, employers will always find enough workers willing to take these jobs and will not have to increase the wage premium during expansions. If, however, expansions lead to a shortage of workers willing to take these jobs, then one would expect greater upward mobility during recoveries.

Two other studies have examined the impact of cyclical conditions on wage growth, and both find positive but modest effects. Based on the Longitudinal Employer-Household Dynamics (LEHD) file from the U.S. Census Bureau, the first study examines earnings mobility of low earners in the 1990s, drawing on data from five states and including workers of all races and ethnicities, from metropolitan and nonmetropolitan areas, and from all industries.[35] This research uses definitions of low earnings and transitions out of low earnings that are different from our own. "Low earners" are prime-age workers (age twenty-five to fifty-four) who "earned $12,000 per year or less for each of three years during the period 1993 to 1995." Transitions out of low-earnings status are divided into "partial" transitions (the individual experienced periods when earnings dipped under $15,000 per year) and "complete" transitions (the individual consistently made more than $15,000 per year).

Because this research focuses on annual earnings rather than hourly wage rates, it cannot separate the impact of increased hours during an expansion from the effects of increased wages. The authors find that most workers experienced an increase in earnings, but only 8 percent of the initial low earners made complete transitions out of low-earning status over a three-year nonrecessionary period.[36] Examining year-by-year changes in earnings leads the authors to conclude that the economic boom of the latter half of the 1990s and the increases in the federal minimum wage in 1996 and 1997 did not have a dramatic impact on rates of annual earnings growth, though the recession year of 2001 appeared to dampen earnings growth considerably. They conclude that business-cycle conditions have small effects on the probability of making a complete transition out of low-earning status.

In comparing racial and gender groups, the authors conclude that male workers had higher average earnings growth and were more likely to escape low-earning status than female workers within each racial or ethnic group, and white males had higher rates of escape and earnings growth than any other group.[37] They find that the primary route to higher earnings is to change firms early on and then stay in the new firm. These job transitions often lead to immediate increases in earnings and sometimes to higher earnings growth in the new firm.[38]

The other study that focuses on the impact of unemployment on wage growth looks at differences in the average wage growth in twelve different sectors.[39] The assumption that workers who change sectors experience this average wage growth brings the authors to the conclusion that improved cyclical conditions do lead to increased wage growth, especially for workers in the bottom half of the wage distribution. The positive effect of economic expansions on wage growth is, however, very small.

Our overall conclusion is that the period covered by the *Chutes and Ladders* study may have been a particularly good period for wage growth. But if it was atypical, the impact of the difference between the booming post-1996 period and the decade of higher unemployment rates is not likely to be large. This implies that the findings reported in Chapter 2 are not limited to periods of strong economic recovery.

Changes in Characteristics

What kinds of changes accompany wage growth? Were high flyers more likely to increase the hours they worked? Did they change jobs more often than other sample members? If so, is there anything systematic about the types of jobs they obtained? Did their higher wages translate into significant changes in poverty status? Did their personal situations change?

In addressing these questions, we begin with a caution. The data we draw on here are purely descriptive and cannot be used to draw conclusions about the causes or consequences of becoming a high flyer. For example, we may discover that high flyers were more likely to get married than low riders. Yet we cannot determine whether they got married as a result of obtaining a better job, or whether they obtained a better job because they had greater responsibilities as part of a married couple.

We see no increases in educational attainment for the nine high flyers observed over the eighteen-month period in the SIPP, but small increases for other sample members.[40] Two of the four male high flyers took classes beyond high school. Two years later, this remained unchanged. Other men in the sample increased their high school graduation rate from 37 to 44 percent. The proportion of high school graduates among women who were high flyers was 60 percent (three of five). In the following eighteen-month period, there was no change. For other females in the sample, educational attainment increased marginally. Increases in educational attainment, therefore, are not common occurrences for either these high flyers or other sample members. This stands in contrast to the findings of the Harlem study, where we recorded significant gains in education and training. The differences here may be attributable to the time period of observation. Although the Harlem sample was studied over an eight-year period, findings on education were most closely observed during the first four years, 1993 to 1997. The SIPP study follows workers for only eighteen months past the first observation. We know that it takes longer than that for poor workers to make major progress toward higher education.

Interestingly, piling up schooling may make a greater difference for those who are in the middle wage groups than it does for the high flyers. In the Harlem study, Adam, the Burger Barn worker who was by the end earning $70,000 a year working for a package courier, had not had time to finish working toward his high school diploma, and his incentive for doing so was low. For Lauren, the accountant in a nonprofit foundation, more education was the ticket out of welfare and low-wage work; her incentives were powerful.

Turning to other demographic characteristics, we find small increases in the marriage rate for all groups in the SIPP sample but a substantial increase for male high flyers. The marriage rate stayed constant for women who experienced large wage increases, and it jumped from 16 to 21 percent for other females in the sample. In contrast, the marriage rate for the male high flyers increased from 0 to 25 percent (one of the four high flyers got married during the observation period). For other men in the sample, there was only a 2 percent increase in marriage (from 32 to 34 percent). As a result, the marriage rate of male high flyers was significantly higher than that of other males in the sample in the second period.

Thus far we have focused on the growth in hourly wages. Earnings may also grow, however, because of an increase in the number of hours worked. In fact, the increase in earnings for female high flyers came less from wage increases and more from an increase in the number of hours they worked.

Female high flyers increased the hours they worked by 12.0 hours in the eighteen-month observation period, while other women increased their hours by only 2.5. For male high flyers, the opposite is true. Male high flyers *decreased* their weekly hours worked by 3.8 hours, while other men were working 2.2 more hours per week at the end of the eighteen-month period. Among high flyers, the number of weeks worked for females increased from 2.6 to 4.2. Male high flyers worked an additional 3.5 weeks. All others increased the number of weeks worked by just over half a week. Thus, female high flyers gained from both working more hours per week and working more weeks each month. Males benefited from a significant increase in the number of weeks worked while cutting back slightly on the number of hours worked each week. Both realized an increase in wages.

One potential route to higher wages is to move into a managerial job. By definition, none of the high flyers started in a managerial position.[41] Eighteen months after first observing these workers in qualifying jobs, two of the five high-flying females held a managerial position, while none of the four high-flying males did. Around 5 percent of the other sample members were in managerial positions. While this did contribute to higher wages, it should be noted that not all managerial jobs pay well, as exemplified by the proportion of sample members who were not high flyers but who, nevertheless, were in managerial jobs. Indeed, at Burger Barn the lowest rung of management typically earns just $.25 to $.50 more per hour than entry level line workers. It may be stretching the category to call these positions management at all, though they do have responsibility for coordinating fellow workers on the shift, which is why they bear the title. In any case, the rewards to this step on the job ladder are quite minimal.

While we are interested in wages by themselves, we also want to know how these wage increases add up in terms of household income. Here the news is good for high flyers: men saw an increase in household income of $458 per month over the eighteen-month period, which is a whopping 62 percent change in the right direction.[42] Female high flyers did even better, increasing their income by $2,104 per month—almost double their household income at the first observation. For the comparison group—those who were not high flyers—income grew by $925 per month for men and $286 per month for women, or 56 percent and 20 percent, respectively.[43]

Nevertheless, while high flyers experienced substantial economic growth, their incomes are still close to the poverty line. All of the high-flying men and 20 percent of the women are still poor in the second year of observation. When the cutoff is raised to 1.5 times the poverty line, we find an additional 20 percent of high-flying women have incomes under this threshold. It should not be surprising that many high flyers remain poor, since these workers are still earning relatively low wages.

While high flyers have relatively low incomes, they receive little public assistance. In fact, none of the high flyers in the SIPP sample was receiving AFDC or TANF benefits at the eighteen-month observation. Thus, while this population is still poor, it is not dependent. At the same time, however, they are likely to be living in public housing. They rely on subsidized rents, which permit them to stretch the income they do have farther, in many cases, than they would be able to stretch it if they had to pay market-rate housing costs.

We are interested in learning what kinds of movements the high flyers had to make in the labor market to achieve the progress they show. Did they change jobs or stick to their original station?[44] While some of these workers remained in the same occupation or were promoted, the majority of the high flyers switched occupations. Some of the jobs that high flyers held eighteen months after first being observed were jobs that required specialized training or certification (for example, in hairdressing or accounting), suggesting that some of those who are high flyers do invest in training in order to move ahead.

An alternative way of comparing jobs is to classify each job on the basis of its socioeconomic index (SEI), which is a standard measurement of occupational prestige.[45] Since individuals who qualified for the sample started in very similar positions, the SEI scores for high flyers and other sample members were similar in the first observation of the qualifying job (around 18). Eighteen months later, the mean SEI score had increased more for high flyers, especially for females. One high flyer held a position with an SEI score of 65, and a few had moved to jobs with an SEI score of 47.[46] The increase in SEI among high flyers is considerably higher than for other sample members.

❧ The main objective in this chapter has been to see if the conclusions presented in Chapter 2 for the Harlem study may be generalized to different populations and time periods. Specifically, are the experiences of a small, nonrandom sample of black and Hispanic workers hired by fast-food restaurants in Harlem in the mid-1990s representative of the wider set of workers from poor and near-poor households?

Our analysis of the Survey of Income and Program Participation leads us to three major conclusions. First, the qualitative conclusion that a subset of food service workers from poor and near-poor households experience substantial upward mobility is confirmed in the national data set. Even by the very high standard used in *Chutes and Ladders* (five dollars per hour in real wage growth over four years), the fact remains that substantial growth is possible for a nonnegligible subset of the population. Second, focusing on food service workers in a large city does not seem to bias the results. When we broaden the sample to include other workers in poor and near-poor households, we find similar results. If anything, the broader samples show more wage growth. Third, the fact that the Harlem study was undertaken during strong economic conditions does not seem to overstate the extent of upward mobility. When we replicate the analysis for an earlier period marked by weaker labor markets for less-skilled workers, we find substantially the same results. At the same time, other researchers have found evidence that high levels of economic growth do matter, mainly because they provide employees with more work hours and, to some degree, better wages or opportunities for upward mobility.

While our findings indicate that upward mobility is possible for a sizable minority of workers in jobs that might be considered dead-end, it should be kept in mind that these high flyers started off with very low wages. A worker who starts at five dollars per hour and experiences an increase of five dollars per hour over a four-year period has indeed doubled her hourly wage in four years. This sizable increase, however, does not land her solidly in the middle class. She and her sisters, who are making much less impressive gains in the labor market, remain vulnerable to poverty and hardship.

PART II

The Inside View

6

Streetwise Economics

❧

Salvador and Carmen are learning how the game is played. Salvador is now a store manager for a nationwide chain of video rental outlets. Carmen worked until recently at Lord and Taylor. They've long since traded in their cheery Burger Barn uniforms for more elegant attire, their federally mandated minimum wages for heftier paychecks. One recent winter the Dominican couple comes to the conclusion that they do not want their two young daughters to grow up in the cramped quarters and polluted air of New York City. Salvador puts in for a transfer with his company (let's call it Movies America). He wants to relocate to one of the stores in Michigan, where Carmen's aunts and uncles moved a few years back, drawn by the high wages in a region that is reviving after years of economic erosion. Carmen and Sal are attracted by the idea of living in a house and of reconnecting with her extended family in Grand Rapids.

Little does Salvador know that he's a valuable asset at Movies America— one of those rare managers who can keep the staff hustling, the inventory in order, and the customers happy. The district office in New York won't let him go; the request is denied. "Why don't you stick around for a while?" they say. Sal waits around, and then several months later he asks again. He'll leave even if they don't permit the transfer, Sal threatens.

That's when things get interesting. Salvador, the valued employee, starts receiving generous offers from the district manager. They'll give him a fat raise. They'll move him to a posh store. Sal takes a weeklong vacation to mull things over, but the phone doesn't stop ringing. What was he thinking about the offers? Had he made a decision? The higher-ups want to take Salvador out to some of the other stores, show him the fiefdom that could be his. Back at home, Carmen's phone rings. It's the Movies America district manager, hoping to persuade the loyal wife that what is good for Sal's career is good for Sal's family. Carmen is skeptical. "If you are so sure that he is so good, and . . . if you are so happy for him and glad that he's learned so much, and he's one of your best guys, why don't you let him go?" she asks.

"If you own a company and you have twenty good managers, and out of twenty, three are best, would you let go of one of your top people?" the supervisor asks.

"Of course. It's for his own good," Carmen snaps back.

"You're a liar. You wouldn't want to lose one of your good guys."

Carmen hits her boiling point ("I have a temper that you cannot imagine," she confesses). "So, you're calling me a liar . . . because I'm trying to get something good for my family," she says. "I'm trying to get him to get out of here. To become somebody, have a house. You probably have a house. You don't care about nobody. You can't care about him. You just care about [Movies America]. You have your own house, maybe you have a limo that picks you up every morning or whatever. Your kids don't have to worry about getting financial aid . . . because they probably don't need that. So don't tell me that you know what is good for me and my family, because you don't know." Carmen pauses, catches her breath.

"I'm sorry you feel that way," the woman says.

"You're going to lose him," Carmen tells her. Click.

A few days later, Salvador announces he's sticking with Movies America in New York and tells Carmen to forget about Michigan. The hook was a $2,000 pay raise. He likes the store he has been deeded, too—it's in bad shape, with flabby sales and a muddled inventory, but he knows he can turn it around. "Come on, Carmen, work with me," he pleads.

Carmen listens to the angel nagging on her shoulder and finally relents. "I thought about it and I'm right beside you. I'm gonna support you, don't worry."

When Salvador arrives at the new store for his first week of work, he fills out the necessary paperwork and makes sure to tack on his $2,000 raise. His boss looks over the numbers and is puzzled. "What is this?" she says.

"The $2,000 you offered me," Salvador replies. "You did say it."

"Oh yeah, I did say it. I thought you hadn't heard me." She signs the papers.

It was a promotion that Salvador and Carmen had stumbled upon, almost unwittingly, but in hindsight it made sense. Salvador was an experienced manager, having been the boss at two different drugstores before moving to the video chain. Movies America was short on qualified staff. The labor market had tightened up, and qualified employees were getting harder to find. Salvador, the skilled worker, was cashing in.

Over the past several years, Sal and Carmen have been sussing out the rules that govern this most treacherous of playing fields, the labor market. They've learned that a worker needs to show the boss that he's valuable, that she can't be easily replaced. They've learned that labor relations are a constant give and take, and that you can't be passive if you're looking for a raise. And they've learned that you always seek the higher-paying job. Move with the momentum of the market. Loyalty is for dead-end proletarians. Salvador savors the challenge of his current job, but he's not tied down—and never has been. When Salvador was working at Discount Drugs, a new drugstore—PharmaMart—opened up in the area, and Salvador applied and got the job. As Sal worked his way up the ladder at PharmaMart, several Movie America shops sprouted up nearby, and Salvador applied and got that job too. "So, every time a new business opens, you're going to leave your job?" Carmen once asked him.

"If they're going to pay me better, oh yes, I will," he assured her.

Economics has taken on the mantle of a hard science, with all the attendant models, equations, and variables. But it represents more than just theories woven in cloistered academies; it is an everyday reality that ordinary individuals must reckon with.[1] Lack of education does not insulate them from the tug of supply and demand, and many realize it. Though they may never have taken an economics course, and may never use terms like *elasticity* and *market share*, American workers understand, to a lesser or greater extent, how the market—their market—works. They have a sense of what it takes to work their way up the job chain. They have some understanding of what employers are looking for, how competition works, why education and social networks are important. The understanding is far from perfect, and at times workers seem quite irrational in their behavior, especially when it comes to the long-term impact of the educational or financial decisions they make today. Nevertheless, American workers—including low-wage workers—have picked up quite a few Economics 101 concepts from that most severe of instructors, personal experience.

This might surprise students of urban poverty. Sociologists have argued that concentrated poverty emerged in neighborhoods like those where Carmen and Salvador live mainly because more economically mobile families picked up and left.[2] What followed them in this exodus weren't just intact families, job networks, and sources of neighborhood stability, but knowledge. Social-isolation theory suggested that impoverishment "by subtraction" stripped these communities of people who understood what Carmen—a one-time Burger Barn worker—appears to know quite well: the rules of the game.

This chapter will consider the folk knowledge that low-wage workers have of labor economics—what the workers themselves might call a simple matter of common sense. We will look at the views workers have of their employers and of how hiring and promotion decisions are made. We will examine their street-level understanding of human capital and social networks. The objective here is not just to describe their beliefs but also to provide a sense of where, in the universe of an individual's experience and learning, they come from.

Playing the Man's Game

After years of leapfrogging from job to job, Jamal has learned what makes an employer tick. When the six-foot-tall, 250-pound African American walks through that office door and sits down for a job interview, he knows what kind of personality he needs to exude: competent and confident. That self-assurance can backfire—he can appear to be quite intimidating—but when he sports his earnest demeanor, Jamal manages to impress potential employers time after time. He has some experience, yes, but he doesn't just list it on a résumé and let it go at that. Jamal also knows how to sell himself. When he drops by to inquire about openings, he doesn't waste his time talking to receptionists or administrative assistants. He makes a beeline for the hiring manager and states his case. Quite often he is successful: Jamal has been working consistently ever since he was fourteen, when he bagged groceries for some under-the-table cash. His first employer, a Jewish man who owned a small store, was nice to Jamal and tried to give him advice about how to approach a job properly. Jamal admits he didn't listen: he has lost a number of the jobs he's had over the years, through lateness and general disinterest. But he keeps getting more work. The skills and intelligence that Jamal possesses are telegraphed by his manner, and these help to catch an employer's eye where his formal credentials (he's a high school dropout) might not.

High flyers like Jamal recognize that the only way to be successful in the labor market is to convince employers that you're special, that you are a notch above everyone else who is clamoring for the job. Economists have a word for this: "signaling." (This concept continues to draw interest in economics circles: just a few years ago, Stanford economist A. Michael Spence received the Nobel Prize in Economic Sciences in part for his work on job-market signaling.)[3] In a competitive market, individuals need to find ways to telegraph the impression that they are the superior candidate. Low-wage workers who seek something better learn these tricks on their way up the ladder.

Putting on a good show demands more than just bravado, of course. Job seekers also need to consider the little details—for instance, the ways that they dress and talk. While most of the people we followed stressed skill and experience, many recognized that physical appearance and communication skills were paramount.[4] For example, Bridget knows that being a black woman from Harlem puts her at a disadvantage in the job market, but she also realizes that if she speaks in standard English, dresses in a professional fashion, and keeps her cool at all times, she won't be identified as "that type of person."[5] "The way I carry myself, and the way I talk, and the way I present myself is how a person's going to perceive [me]. So, if you come out, 'Hey, what's going on? Wuzzup? Wuzzup?' they're going to treat you . . . the way you present yourself. It's all about presentation. . . . Yes, I come from Harlem, and, yes, I come from a neighborhood, and, yes, I'm black, but that doesn't mean I'm that type of person. You understand? I'm not, you know [a loser]."

At the age of twenty-eight, Bridget hasn't yet attained her dream job (as a nurse), but she's managed to find a position in the white-collar promised land, working in the bursar's office at a local college. Proper speech and dress are requirements in professional circles, but these lessons aren't absorbed by all of her peers, Bridget notes. They'll speak in black slang; they'll dress to impress a different crowd. As for Bridget, she has learned over the years to respect how important "impression management" is to winning over employers.[6] She even insists—with some vehemence—that presentation and performance are *all* that matter; that race has no effect on a person's chances in the job market. "I do have friends that believe, 'I [won't] get this job because I'm black and the person that was interviewing me was white,'" she says.

> I said, "But you know what? Whether they're white, Chinese, it doesn't matter. Everybody's the same, regardless, and I don't believe there's a person that's actually racist. They're not racist. It's the way you present yourself. They see you like people we see on TV. 'I don't like that black person because that's how all black people act, and you make all black people look bad.'" And then, you have some black people that say the same thing. Black people say, "I don't like that white person because they are that way," but in actuality, they're—all people are the same. So, I love everybody. It's not, you know, it's not a big difference.

Bridget says that she has run into some "ignorant" people before, but she maintains that she's never personally experienced racism. "I've seen it done, but then I've also seen the reason why you had that experience done to you," she says, with an arched eyebrow.[7]

For racial and ethnic minorities, fitting in at the office may mean more than just wearing the right clothes and speaking with the right diction: it also can entail bottling up completely justified fury when others—who think they are being funny—make those borderline racist remarks, or crack off-color jokes that happen to be about your culture. Lanice McPherson remembers applying for jobs and getting enthusiastic responses from employers she talked to over the phone. But when she showed up for the interviews, she was met with surprised looks: how was it that a "McPherson" was black? "McPherson is an Irish name," the employer would point out—as if this were news to Lanice. "Yes, I know," she'd reply calmly. "Don't worry, we're all family. I have it in the blood. It's OK." Riffing off her Irish-sounding name is a good icebreaker, Lanice says, "for someone like me," but not all people would respond to such an incident with good humor. "If someone told that to one of my cousins, they would lose it," Lanice says, "because they would be, like, 'Why does it always have to be about a race issue?'"

For all the workers like Lanice who have been successful at landing good jobs, there are many more who continue to get rejected. It's one thing when this happens to someone who has a mental or physical disability. What bothers Ebony is the fact that more-fortunate others, who have the intelligence and ability to do better, don't make the effort. Ebony grew up in the projects, surrounded by people with this attitude—kids who seemed to have no purpose in life except to "run around acting stupid." These days the twenty-five-year-old works as a receptionist, making $28,500 a year with benefits, while some of her childhood friends remain unemployed, still living the wild life. They find the fact that she works "hilarious," she says. "[They're] like, 'You have a job? Who are you working for? Don't you want to have stories to tell your kids when you turn, like, thirty and forty?'"

Ebony—the kid who was considered "odd" because she liked to read—continues to see things differently from her peers. They defend their choice not to pursue a career by attacking Ebony for being too straight. She, in turn, questions whether they can survive without a steady income. "I would like to live to see thirty and forty," she tells them, "and I don't know that you are going to." Ebony didn't care for the dangers and uncertainties of street life back when she was a kid, and she hasn't changed her mind. She doesn't understand why her friends won't grow up, find respectable jobs, and make something of themselves.

Yet even Ebony has trouble making the game work for her. She thinks she should be doing better than $28,500 a year. All she has to do, she tells herself, is impress the right employer—with the same polished "look" that she used to win over the office manager at the law firm where she now works. But to meet the right employer, she first needs to know the right people, and Ebony doesn't possess such contacts. She doesn't have the social status that would yield them. She can't turn to her friends for assistance—they're too busy trying to extend their teens into their late twenties. Even her friends with jobs haven't been much help to her. True, they make decent money, but "they work for transit or they are teachers or they drive busses," Ebony points out. They don't hobnob with the sorts of people who could sign her up as a paralegal or a model/actress, the two jobs she really wants. Ebony was able to land her current job through a temp agency, but she knows that things would be much easier if she had friends in the right places. She knows this but can't do anything about it, and the realization is intensely frustrating for her.

Once the corporate gatekeepers decide to let a job candidate through the front door, there's no guarantee that the newbie will succeed. In fact, the same signaling skills that served the job seeker well may not always help the promotion candidate. This is the lesson Jamal learned at his latest workplace. When he got the job at the lumber mill out in California's hinterlands in 1996, Jamal started off hauling stacks of wood off the conveyor belt and soon moved up to a position driving one of the loaders. But Jamal soon realized that the assertiveness that had gotten him the job could be a liability on the shop floor. The first problem arose when Jamal requested not to work with a certain other driver because the two didn't get along. Jamal claims that his supervisor, who didn't care much for Jamal, used the request as an excuse to demote him.

Especially in the low-wage sector, workers need to have a high degree of patience to survive on the job, patience that to some workers might seem suspiciously like acquiescence. They must learn to endure—with a smile—heavy-handed supervision, disrespect, and, at the very bottom of the labor market, the indignity of exploitation. Some never do, and they pay the price for being unwilling to buckle. When we first met her, Anita was working at Burger Barn. She was eventually promoted to manager—the only black manager at the store. The owner was African American, but she preferred to hire Hispanics, Anita says, because they would "work for cheap." "She didn't want to pay them," Anita says. "She had a whole Spanish staff that was just running the store on the wing. When I came in there I was like, 'No, this is done this way, this is done this way. This is the right way to do it. I know the Burger Barn book from A to Z. You can't tell me nothing.'" Anita was unhappy that her boss was taking for granted all her experience and hard work and hiring other workers with no qualifications except a high tolerance for low pay. "That's right, you're going to have to pay me for your services if you want your store ran correctly. That's it. You got these people up there working this register, taking in all this money every day, and you don't pay them nothing and they don't speak up for themselves. . . . Am I supposed to be training your general manager, [even though] she's over me? No. That's your job. I'm not going to train her. That's not my job. I'm not going to do her job, either."

Anita decided to leave. The owner told her that she should stay, "being that you're the only black person in the store." Anita was steamed. Just because both she and her boss happened to be black women, did that mean Anita ought to forgive all the mistreatment and disrespect she had endured on the job? She would not put up with that guilt trip. "If you want a black person in your store, you could have one," she snapped back. "So don't try to pin it on me, because I'm leaving. . . . I don't want to hear that."

What her boss wanted—what all bosses want, Anita says—was someone who will not complain, someone who will just do what the manager tells them. "If it's just labor, I think they look at someone they can train and use until somebody else better comes in," the twenty-seven-year-old African American told us in 1997, after finding a new job as a food and beverage assistant at an upscale New York hotel. "And they get all the work out of them, and move on." Although she now had a job with somewhat more pay and prestige, she still chafed under the arbitrary rule of the boss. "Even food service—I mean, if somebody don't like you, they'll hold you back because they don't like you. It can be personal, or they just don't like you, or you're not doing what they're asking of you."

Put up or shut up—that is what workers have to do at Burger Barn, a fast-paced, low-margin business where turnover is high and even a high school dropout with no experience can land a job. Anita recognized that, in other industries, employers couldn't just hire warm bodies to staff their offices; they had to find "the best person possible" for the job. When we met up with her again in 2002, Anita was the co-owner of her own small business. She continued to insist that the employer-employee relationship boiled down to, as she put it, "my way or the highway." Yet as a business-woman in the position of hiring her own people, Anita had a greater appreciation for the boss's perspective. She recognized that employers are looking for more than a decent résumé: they want "somebody who wants to work. Somebody who is motivated and wants the same thing that they want. Somebody who wants to learn and doesn't know it all." Just five years earlier, Anita had been the worker who thought she knew it all; now she is a boss herself, working hard to keep a pint-size company in the black—and she's not about to let anyone tell her how to run her own business.

Social scientists have studied what employers look for in new hires.[8] They find that smarts and technical expertise are important, yes, but so are "soft" skills: "abilities and traits that pertain to personality, attitude, and behavior rather than to formal or technical knowledge."[9] These soft skills include things like enthusiasm, reliability, and willingness to learn. (Our respondents appeared to recognize their value in the labor market: seven out of ten of the entire sample—and every one of the high flyers—mentioned a strong work ethic, dependability, or motivation as traits that employers look for in new hires.)[10] Different soft skills matter in each industry. In a fast-food restaurant, workers who accept low wages and don't complain—the pliable employee Anita couldn't be—are telling employers that they are playing the game. The same premise applies, to some extent, in the white-collar business world. It's summed up in the choice words of advice that Lanice's boss once gave her: "Understand, I'm not here to try to build relationships, build friendships and all of that. All I want is someone that can come in here and do the job. That's it."

Nevertheless, there's a tension between what the typical employer wants—obedience—and what workers need to do to prove that they are worth a raise or promotion. Moving up is all about sticking out, Bridget notes. Only a few people at a time can climb up the corporate ladder, so you have to give your boss a reason to choose you for a place in that queue. When you act timid, you're just asking for the boss to ignore you. "Some employers might say, 'It's good of you to stay at your desk and be quiet,'" Bridget says. "[But] that's not necessarily true. You're not going to get anywhere sitting at the same desk if you don't speak up." The way that a worker shows she's a worthy prospect for promotion, Bridget says, is by doing her work efficiently; being responsible on the job; showing promptness, neatness, and personality; and, most important, speaking her mind—tactfully but firmly. "You have to know how to speak up and voice yourself," she says. "If you're not going to voice yourself, don't expect to be at this particular job."

Bridget describes her experience working in the payroll department of a Manhattan bank, where she became frustrated that most workers just did their work from eight to four and shut their mouths, even though secretly they hated their working conditions.

"You sit at a desk with a whole bunch of other employees, your other peers, and everybody will say the same thing. . . . 'I'm tired of this job.' And you say to yourself, 'Why am I sitting here saying I hate this job, when I've got to get up and come to this job every day?' Either leave or ask for a raise or, you know, voice your opinion on what it is that you don't like. We have monthly meetings. [When] you go to your monthly meeting, raise your hand and say, 'Listen, I'm not too comfortable with this and this and that going on.' You've got to let someone know."

Of course, timing is everything. When the economy is in the tank and employers are hacking away at labor costs, it is risky to let your true feelings show, and workers at the bottom know this all too well. This was the situation throughout much of the 1990s in New York: a slack labor market with unemployment levels shooting above 10 percent. During this downturn, even Bridget appeared less eager to wrangle with an employer. Compare her aggressive comments in 2002 with her words in 1997, when Bridget was unemployed and getting rejected even for sanitation jobs. Back then, Bridget was concerned mostly about pleasing the boss: "They [employers] look for personality. They look for skills. They look for a lot of things, but I know the main things is usually their skills and your personality, because . . . an employer doesn't like to have an employee working on their job and they're gloomy and sad all the time."

Three years later, the unemployment rate in New York dipped below 6 percent. Bridget took classes at a business academy and picked up some computer skills. She landed a temp job at a local college, and eventually parlayed it into full-time employment. When we last talked to her, she was feeling better about her future prospects. She wasn't worrying about getting or keeping a job. Instead, Bridget was thinking about branching out into a new profession—as a home health aide. "I'll be up to where . . . my standards are, and in a different atmosphere, a different field," she says. "Not the keypunching job [where] everybody tends to say, 'Oh, I'm so sick and tired.'"

Through experience, low-wage workers also learn the importance of gaining leverage in the workplace—what we might call a good market position. It's a lesson that every labor organizer puts into play when the time comes to call a strike: the essential, hard-to-replace people—from the press operators at a newspaper to the electricians in a factory—won't get fired or demoted. So go after them, if you're an organizer; or be them, if you're a worker. Adam has learned how to stay clear of the boss's recession-time hatchet after several years of working in the courier business. He laid claim to a key credential—a commercial driver's license—which makes him much in demand within his industry. "Everything, if you look around, no matter where you at, even down in the South, it was driven there, you see?" Adam says. "Up in the city, even your grass and trees were driven here. . . . The longer you have the [license], the more you use it, the more you have a chance of making more money."

The other factor in Adam's favor is the strong union at his company—an advantage that has become increasingly rare for American workers.[11] Adam, a self-described Republican, admits that he is "bittersweet" about unions. It's an old-boy's club, he notes, and the boys better like you if you want to stay in the workers' ranks. Brownnose enough, and you'll make your way up the wage scale quickly; but don't expect the union to save you when the corporate higher-ups really want your head—and decide to slip the union bosses some cash for their cooperation. "There are some people that get fired and the company just wants to get rid of this person, and they talk to the union, and the union looks the other way," Adam explains. "They say, 'I can't help [you].' They come out to do their job because the guy paid their union dues, but they do a half job and don't really push the issue of trying to get his job back and all of this. I've seen that."

That said, Adam recognizes that union membership does translate into high wages and job security for those savvy enough to play the game. "I'm still not at top pay yet," he points out. "Top pay is almost close to, like, $90,000 a year." After September 11, when corporations around the country were slicing fat from their payrolls, Adam's union was able to protect his job. "If it wasn't for the union, with my wages that I'm making, I'm quite sure that I would have been the first one to go." He laughs. "But because of it I had job security."

In fact, Adam declined an offer to become a supervisor at the company's local airport operations center because a management job would have meant forgoing the shelter of the union contract.

> They did offer me that, to become a supervisor, but I don't like the way they treat their supervisors. It's here today, gone tomorrow. They don't like what you do, you're out the door. . . . With the supervisors, you've got so many people underneath you that you have to be in charge of, and if someone messes up it reflects on the supervisor. Especially now where we're going through a lot of turmoil as far as supervisors are concerned, their job is more on the line. Because if something goes wrong, they can't fire a courier or even customer service, because union is there to back them up. So the next one to get their head chopped off is the supervisor.

In his study of a unionized chemical plant, sociologist David Halle found much the same attitude among the factory workers: more than half of those who were offered positions in management declined them, mainly because they feared losing the protection of the union. "So long as they remain within the range of jobs entailing union membership men will be fired only for blatant violations of company rules. The union contests every firing in arbitration, and the company knows it must build an overwhelming case to be successful. But supervisors can be fired at management's whim."[12]

Adam is reluctant to risk his well-compensated job for a shot at a big management title. He and his fellow union members have some real power in their workplace; if they don't like the way a supervisor is treating them, they can tell that person off. Adam sums up their attitude this way: "We was here before you. We're going to be [here] after you go. So it's not your way, it's still our way. You may be in charge, but as long as we do our job according to what [our company] said in the contract, you can't do jack diddly to us." ("The managers hated that," Adam adds.) So long as Adam's fellow workers stick together, they can stick it to the boss. After almost a decade at the company, Adam has learned these and other lessons about power in the workplace. Rank-and-file workers like him can seek shelter in the union contract, but they had better be chums with the union bosses once the layoffs begin. The old-boy's club works for Adam because he knows the clubhouse rules.

Not all workers, of course, are fortunate enough to find a job high up in the production chain, much less one with a strong union to back it up. And even workers who are valuable to their employers are easily cowed into thinking they are not. Experience may eventually teach them to recognize and exploit their worth, but many low-wage workers—perhaps buying into the mainstream perception that they are unskilled and expendable—have difficulty learning basic lessons about power dynamics in the workplace. Bob, a veteran Burger Barn manager, talks about how Latoya doesn't act with enough confidence in the workplace. "Latoya will call me crying, 'Ray [one of her supervisors] was here talking [trash] to me,' and I'm [asking myself], 'Why is he treating her like that?'" Bob says. "He only treats people [poorly] that he knows that they have nowhere to go. That's how I see it. And I told Latoya, I said, 'Latoya . . . you . . . go out and market yourself. Make them think you've got somewhere you can go, and he'll start treating you [better].'" Latoya has been a loyal employee at Burger Barn for ten years, and while she finally reaped some rewards for it—promotion into general management, for example—she has also been taken for granted and assumed to be immobile. People without choices are often taken advantage of.

The thing is, Latoya has tried to leave Burger Barn before, and the ex-

perience was a painful one. The years she had spent in the fast-food industry, Latoya quickly learned, did not provide leverage in another workplace.
In 2001, when Latoya's youngest son, Jacob, developed severe asthma,
Latoya decided she needed to quit her job at Burger Barn and take care of
him. Latoya stayed at home for a while, but soon she got it in her head that
she was becoming soft and lazy. One day she stopped by a Starbuck's in the
Bronx to see if they needed part-time help. They liked her management
experience and offered her a job as a shift supervisor. After graduating
from the company's barista school, she started work at a store on
Manhattan's Upper West Side, and soon she was transferred to another,
more troubled coffeehouse in the same neighborhood.

Latoya quickly diagnosed the problem: the manager, a friendly but woe-
fully inexperienced woman in her midtwenties, was scheduling her inexperienced workers for the morning shift, believing that they would train
faster that way. That didn't make any sense to Latoya, who knew that the
morning hours were their busiest time—a time when they should have
their best workers behind the counter. "With my knowledge, I was like,
'Well, anybody could be a store manager here. Duh. It don't take rocket
science.' And, true, it's less work than Burger Barn, but it all boils down to
the same customer service—you know, inventories, managing your labor,
dah, dah, dah, dah. . . . Starbuck's is the place where you got to get friendly
with your customers. They want you to get to know the customers by
name—same as Burger Barn. The customers in the morning do not want
you to stop and have to wait on a long line. They want fast service. They
want to be in and out."

Tensions began to flare in the mornings. The coffeehouse was near a
hotel, and tourists would often mill around inside, contemplating what
kind of muffin to have with their Mocha Frappuccino. Latoya's manager
would put two greenhorns on the shift, to train them, leaving the two veteran baristas to help them rather than serving customers themselves.
Meanwhile, Latoya recalled, the regulars waiting impatiently in line were
ready to explode. "They're like, 'Look, I got to go to work, OK? So, what,
you're on vacation? Hello? Reality is I need to be [getting out of here].'
While they wasting time helping them, customers are going out the door,"
she explains. "The DM [district manager] was like, 'Well, how come
you're losing so much sales?'"

That wasn't the only problem at the store. The manager also had a habit
of disappearing for the entire day, saying she needed to take care of paperwork. "They showed me how to do the paperwork," Latoya recalls. "The

paperwork takes an hour's time. Maybe two hours at the most. She would take all day doing paperwork, and we would have a line going like this," she says, spreading out her hands. Latoya was quite annoyed. It was simply bad management: "One thing Burger Barn teach you is that you can't make money if you're the leader and you're in the back."

Latoya tried to tell her boss what was going wrong. Ninety percent of their business came from the morning coffee sales, Latoya pointed out—if they continued to put inexperienced workers on that shift, they would keep losing customers. But the manager wouldn't listen to any of Latoya's advice. "She was like, 'Yeah, well, you worked at Burger Barn.'. . . That was her attitude. 'Oh, you worked at Burger Barn. Burger Barn is whack, and they don't pay you no money. Here at Starbuck's, I make this much money.'" It wasn't just Latoya's manager; everyone seemed to think that management experience at Burger Barn might as well have been time served on Mars. "A lot of times they [would] say, 'Well, you come from fast food, so you don't know nothing about coffee,'" Latoya says. "So, my experience at how customers want to be treated—they undermined that because of my background, where I had worked. But they hired me because of my background. Isn't that so stupid?"

Latoya had more than a decade behind her in the restaurant business. She knew how to manage a store, how to make the customers happy. She didn't understand why her new bosses could not get past their prejudice against Burger Barn. "If you take the time and listen, don't look at where my background came from, don't. Then again . . . look at it, because a lot of people take Burger Barn employees because we teach people quality, we teach people customer service, and it's a lot of—friendliness. So if you look and say, 'Well, Burger Barn underpays, and that's why you're not there.' No, don't look at that. Look at what I have gained from Burger Barn to help you."

Working at Burger Barn had taught Latoya a great deal about making it in the restaurant business, but she still had much to learn about making it in the labor market. Yes, her experience was valuable—it was valuable enough to get her a job, in this case. But it wasn't enough to win her respect from her new bosses. In the upscale, Upper West Side neighborhood where she worked, in the latté-and-chai extravagance of the coffee business, the many years that Latoya had put into her career at Burger Barn didn't amount to much—just some time on training wheels before she rode with the big boys.

Underestimating one's capacity to do better than the status quo is a problem for many workers who start out at the bottom of the labor market and lack confidence that they can expect anything better. Lauren, the single mother who works at the social service foundation, spent several years in an accounting job at a hospital before she made the move to this job. She wanted something better, but she was hesitant: Was she qualified? "It's weird," she says from her current vantage point, "but no, I didn't think [I had the skills to get this job]."

Her co-workers at the hospital didn't think so either. They were surprised that she—a single, African American mother from the 'hood—could get a job at such an upscale operation. "It was like, 'You're leaving? How did you get that job?' So many questions were getting thrown my way," Lauren recalled. They were sucked into low opinions of themselves and, by extension, of Lauren, because people were hardly ever promoted in their department and nobody encouraged them to gain new skills or look for better opportunities.

Lauren rebelled against the attitude at her old workplace—that she couldn't do better, that she had a secure job and she should just be satisfied with it. She seemed to understand how the world, according to economists, worked: that toiling for companies without steep internal ladders would get her nowhere.[13] "I didn't feel like there was room for me to grow," she says of her old job. "They weren't trying to promote anyone. It was just like you sat in that one position. And me, I'm the type of person that likes to learn different things. I felt like I was just doing the same thing day to day." Partly through luck and partly through perseverance, Lauren was able to find a more fulfilling job that will position her for later growth (in her case, a dream career in academia). "They're not afraid to let you do things here. No one is hiding their position from you to show you new steps."

Through their day-to-day experiences on the job, workers like Lauren learn that loyalty to a mediocre employer is foolish. They learn to leave the labor market's blind alleys for jobs with more room to grow. At times, frustration with all the running to stand still inspires them to take radical steps. Anita chose to leave a steady job in a toy store to start her own business. "I got tired of not moving up," she says. "It was like, I can only do this. Your brain starts to get numb because you go into circles. [Any] sister can do this job. Going out there to find a box of Monopoly. Here you go." For Anita, the misery of her co-workers provided a constant reminder that she didn't want to follow their path to nowhere. "I been in companies where people worked fifteen, sixteen years and never got to the point where they want to be," she told us. For a person of color like Anita, discrimination presented additional worries: a particular employer could "hold you back" if they didn't like your kind, she says. "Maybe . . . she don't talk correct English or she can't speak Spanish. Or we don't like Jamaicans. Or whatever, you know." Anita wanted nothing of the kind. Her solution? To break out of the salaried ranks altogether and become her own boss.

As for Latoya, she quit Starbucks and went back to the Burger Barn in Harlem. She wants to be in an environment where people listen to her opinion, where higher-ups are willing to confront problems rather than hiding out in back. Latoya knows how the market works, how to make a profit; she doesn't need someone a decade younger than her telling her that her experience just doesn't apply. Anyway, she doesn't mind working alongside Bob again, her old boss and compadre. "He's still good. He's still 100 percent Bob." But Bob needs her, she adds, beaming. "I'm like his strong arm."

"I'm Working Clean"

After eight years, most of the fast-food workers we followed had taken off their Burger Barn caps and uniforms for good. Even if they hate their current job, they don't ever want to go back to working the fry machine. It's not just about the low pay. There is a hierarchy of jobs in our society, and with time, even low-wage workers expect to see themselves moving up to the more desirable, more prestigious positions that have better working conditions. Work that requires them to get "dirty"—to dunk fries, flip burgers, mop floors, throw out trash—is at the bottom of that ranking, and no one wants to stay there for too long.[14] That's why Reynaldo is pleased with his job working as a "hall man" for an upscale co-op. For $42,000 per year, plus benefits, he watches over the control panel in the lobby, sends tenants up the elevators, and signs off on deliveries. "I don't have to deal with garbage," he says. "I'm clean. I'm working clean." (This is a view known all too well by the untouchables of India, whose status is defined by the dirty, socially defiling jobs they must take: handling dung, caring for the dead.)[15]

How physical a job is, however, is only one criterion among the many that workers use to judge its desirability. Generally speaking, they see the labor market as divided into various spheres of good and bad: clean and dirty, varied and monotonous, autonomous and closely supervised, creative and deadening, respected and stigmatized. There may be benefits to doing certain types of physical labor when they provide an escape from jobs that are frustrating and ego-killing in other ways. Reynaldo, for instance, spends his mornings working for himself, doing remodeling work for extra cash. In the basement of a building he owns, he keeps ladders, wooden planks, electrical wires, pipes, and two dozen trashcans full of construction scrap (acquired by bribing city trash collectors). It's Reynaldo's own little kingdom, walled in with neatly stacked paint cans. Sure, the work is physically demanding, but when Reynaldo goes out on a construction job, he rarely has to deal with personality conflicts.

That is not the case at the co-op where he works in the late afternoons and evenings. The tenants there are extremely wealthy, and 95 percent of them (according to Reynaldo) are Jewish; the rest are non-Jewish but white. The staff, on the other hand, is predominantly Hispanic, with a few African Americans and one Russian, whom Reynaldo says is grossly favored. ("The building sees him as the only white person working there, so they want to keep him, even though he's pissy drunk, or smoking crack cocaine, or whatever; they won't get rid of him.") Customer service, the bane of many low-level workers' existence, is not Reynaldo's strong point. Management recently sent him a warning letter, complaining that unnamed tenants found him uncooperative and rude. (Reynaldo dismisses the letter as maneuvering on the part of management, which he claims wants to bump him from the payroll so they can hire a newbie for two-thirds his salary.) He says that most of the co-op's residents are "OK," though he has had run-ins with some of the more cantankerous ones:

> They watch you, like, strange, you know what I mean? They watch you funny, like you are a piece of shit, you know. I don't know if it's the money or if it's racial, but I think it's racial. But sometimes I think that it's because they're so wealthy, they think you're like nothing, you know. Let's say the tenants leave and you say, "Good morning." They don't say anything to you, they just go right past you and give you a nasty look—you know, like that. There's nothing you can do about that, you're there to perform a service and that's it. That's why I try to keep it straightforward, I don't get too personal.

The ethnic divide at Reynaldo's co-op has created such a charged atmosphere that even unintended slights are understood as deliberate. Though his job at the co-op doesn't require him to get his hands dirty, Reynaldo dislikes it because he has to put up with other people's attitudes. He sums up the merits of his two professions this way: the hall-man job is "less work, more stress," while the repair job is "more work, less stress." "You feel like you're always under surveillance, and you're under pressure, and you have to watch what you say. Even though you want to say something you can't say it because, you know, you have to watch yourself. It's like, you're under pressure a lot, I feel. And then if you have conflicts with your fellow employees, it's another stress."

Some people might find this aversion to stress on the job to be mere grumbling, but recent research seems to support Reynaldo's intuition. Studies show that having a job with high demands but a low degree of control increases the risk of cardiovascular disease and other ailments.[16]

Of course, there are different kinds of stress, some "good" and some "bad." Francisco may complain incessantly about the stress he suffered as the operations manager for a startup courier company, where every day was a "bunch of chaos." ("One day I would do payroll, and the next day I would do this, that, and the other.") Compared with that position, his new job as a supervisor at an upscale candy shop and café feels like a vacation. At the same time, Francisco clearly gets excited when he talks about his dot-com days. Last time we spoke with him, he mentioned that he was considering returning to his old job—the company kept asking him back. "A lot of ideas came from you," Francisco says of his previous job. "You had a lot of input. A cool atmosphere. I mean, the pressure's on when the pressure's on, but the pressure's not on constantly."

Workers like Francisco are willing to accept stress on the job so long as it means real responsibility or a variety of engaging challenges. Epidemiologist Michael Marmot has gone so far as to argue that "stress" is not a very useful way to describe the emotional strain that people experience on the job—if it's true that "stress for one person is stimulation for another," he points out, we should instead focus on more specific conditions. "Whether or not biological stress pathways are activated has much to do with the degree to which circumstances are controllable," Marmot writes. "The man or woman with all the e-mails, the city lawyer who works through the night making megabucks for his client (and himself) has high demands. If he or she has a high degree of control over work, it is less stressful and will have less impact on health." On the other hand, when workers have little control over their situation at work, a job with exceedingly low demands is no boon. The reality of many jobs, Marmot points out, is that they are "monotonous, boring, soul-destroying"; they involve work that, even if it cannot be called "stressful," leaves the employees drained at the end of the day.[17]

The Burger Barn workers we talked to recognized the importance of autonomy in the workplace. Always having to defer to clueless customers, they pointed out, meant not just sucking in their pride but also spending their days in a boiling pot of negativity. In addition, the tedium and repetitiveness of the work became too much for many to bear. When we last caught up with Karen in 2002, she didn't have a job and told us that she'd take anything "except for [fast food] which was too easy for me. I like challenge. I have to have something that's making me think that, like, I'm making a difference by doing something."

Anita, the former Burger Barn manager, had fled from that end of the labor market as quickly as she could. "You go in every day and do the same thing. You're talking to people about menus. . . . You showing people how to wash forks." Since then, Anita has worked at some upscale restaurants, and she points out that they are no utopia, either. "It's hard work and . . . what you get tipped is part of your salary, and it's too unpredictable—[I] can't do that."

As they grow older, the more successful workers come to the conclusion that they deserve to graduate from the ranks of menial labor. If at all possible, they steer clear of the kind of "unclean" jobs they once held. "Right now, I feel like I'm overqualified for those positions," says Lauren. "I mean, if I needed it as a second job for extra money, maybe I would do it. I don't know." A moment later, she adds, "I'll work in a sneaker store or a clothing store. That's fine." Anyone who is still stuck in a Burger Barn job past the age of twenty-five is looked upon as damaged.

That said, not all workers are interested in high-powered, high-stress jobs. Kyesha, for instance, tells us—half in jest—that she'd enjoy a job with zero responsibility and zero worry—as she puts it, getting paid good money just "to fix shit." In a different way, Carmen also has little inclination to shift her career into high gear. Though her parents were teachers and she herself has an associate's degree, Carmen had found herself content working the clothing racks at Lord and Taylor, a job that she readily admitted didn't require much education but nevertheless allowed her to express her artistic side. Carmen enjoyed dressing the mannequins and laying out the merchandise. She was thrilled whenever she felt her day's work had actually made an impact on sales.

Carmen had looked up to her boss, a kind woman who treated the floor workers like family. At the same time, she was content with the level of responsibility and creativity she had as just a member of the crew. She couldn't help but notice that her boss—forty-two years old, graying hair, without a family of her own—didn't have a life outside the store. ("She can sleep at Lord and Taylor if she wants to.") Carmen didn't see herself as a housewife ("I feel like an imprisoned bird at home"), but she also knew she had an identity beyond the one she wore to work from 7:00 to 3:30, as the doting mother of two children, a devoted (if feisty) wife—and an aspiring poet. When she was working at Lord and Taylor, she did her job and did it well, but she wasn't tied down to the demands of her workplace. In fact, Carmen is quick to point out that she doesn't really need to work. Salvador is willing to support her, and to make extra cash Carmen runs a bustling business of her own making foam cake toppers (sold for up to fifteen dollars apiece) and other assorted domestic decorations, à la Martha Stewart. "Nice thing, too, is that the decorations never go out of style," she notes.

The workers we interviewed have developed their own criteria for an acceptable job. For one thing, they say, it has to pay a respectable wage. "To go out and get a job, I can't settle for anything under five dollars," Bridget told us in 1997, at a time when the twenty-four-year-old was shuffling from one low-paid temp job to another. "Five dollars? Only thing five dollars can do is keep you going back and forth to work. That's it. Five dollars can't even get food on the table. It can't even buy you fast food nowadays, you know." But a low-wage job may turn out to be worth it if it comes with benefits. Even low-skilled workers can do the math. "I will take six dollars, five dollars an hour, if I have full benefits with, you know, package and all that," says Randy, the forty-three-year-old recovering drug addict. "That's the most important." Adam, too, underscores how crucial benefits are: he left his previous job at a department store because, after his daughter was born, he needed a good health plan. Recently, he has contemplated leaving his current courier company for another one because it offers much better benefits. "I would probably apply for anything as long as it had benefits with it," Adam says. A good wage is important, he adds, but "the wage usually comes, with time."

By 2002, Anita had left her dull days of clocking in for a paycheck behind her: she and her sister were running a small business screen printing T-shirts, hats, buttons, balloons, and other novelty items. Sales were good, the costs were low ("all you're paying for is paint"), and Anita no longer had to worry about putting on a good show for the boss. "I think I'm more creative when I work on my own and I don't have to answer [to someone else]. I can work. If I get a thought at twelve o'clock at night . . . I can jot the idea down. If I'm working for somebody, I'm not getting up at twelve o'clock to write an idea down."

Lauren still has to answer to a boss but, like Anita, she has found a workplace where creative thinking and personal initiative are appreciated. Though she may be at the bottom of the white-collar ladder, she was pleasantly surprised by the fact that the foundation's president routinely sits down with her and other low-level office workers for lunch. "In a lot of big companies, it's rare that you get to see the president. And since we see him every day, he has lunch with us. He'll sit at the table and we'll have a normal conversation with him. You forget that he's the president of this foundation. You get the assistant president . . . and she's great, too. She comes and she has lunch with us. And in the meetings in the beginning, they always tell us that if you want, you can step outside your job description to help everyone here and there. It's pretty cool."

The Credential Question

Getting a college education has been a long, arduous journey for Ebony. The daughter of drug-addicted parents, she was raised by her grandparents in an East Harlem housing project, and she paid her own expenses throughout high school by working a shift at Burger Barn. No one in her family had ever graduated from college, but in her early twenties Ebony decided to take classes at a community college. At the time, she was working forty to forty-five hours every week as a personal assistant at a small ad agency. Things got ugly after Ebony got into a spat with her boss over an internship she wanted to take, and Ebony felt she needed to leave. But without a paying job, she couldn't afford college.

Ebony left anyway. She took a vacation to mull over her options. "I took a month or so to myself," she says. "I went away. I have some family in Florida, and I went to visit them. I came back and I said, 'I have to get a job, this is what I have to do.' I am not very religious but I do believe in

God. So I prayed on it and I said, 'Whatever comes to me, this is what I am going to take because I am supposed to.'" She immediately found a job as a desk receptionist at a corporate law firm in Manhattan. Her new employer encouraged her to continue her studies, so Ebony returned to school. She received her associate's degree in 2000, and now, at twenty-five, she is enrolled at another local college for a bachelor's degree in political science—as a full-time student, even as she continues to put in forty hours a week at her law-firm job.

Compared with her peers, Ebony has done well: she has a decent-paying job and is on track to attain her dream of becoming an entertainment lawyer. Yet, after all her efforts to advance her education, these days Ebony is unsure about whether the struggle will pay off. On the one hand, she knows that education is important—everyone says so. On the other hand, she looks at friends—one woman who got an associate's degree in accounting and now makes an ample salary at a firm in Chinatown, another who got a two-year degree in nursing and now works as a registered nurse—and she doubts whether her own degree in political science will be worth as much once she graduates. Before, Ebony thought that a bachelor's degree would open up doors to new avenues of employment. "But it doesn't. It really doesn't," Ebony insists. She's learned a hard lesson: "[What] it is about now is knowing the right people and getting in the right place. . . . What they teach you in school, you basically don't use it in the office. [You] start all over. And it is so sad that we don't know these things, and those of us who do try and better ourselves go into it blind. And by the time you figure it out, well you wasted about two, three years of your life sitting there trying to go to school."

Ebony worries that studying hard and graduating with honors may not pay off the way she thought it might. What she really needs to do is mingle with the right people, worm her way into the right clique. "You can get Cs and Ds on your transcript, but if you know the right people, we are going to get you in," she says. "And it is a bad thing, because it doesn't really happen too often with kids from the inner city. You don't know people like that, and then the people you do know who probably can help you, they don't. They are too busy worrying about how they are going to do something to better themselves."

Ebony and other low-wage workers can't be blamed for being confused about the value of an education in today's economy. Research shows that more years of education lead to better long-term earning prospects.[18] But this kind of analysis groups highly compensated MBAs, JDs, and PhDs with the rest of the working world. In Ebony's circles, it's not always so clear that more education pays off. Will the salary that Ebony can fetch with a bachelor's degree in political science match that of her friend who decided to go to nursing school? Comparing all graduates of four-year colleges with all graduates of two-year colleges, the answer is plain, but when you break down the categories, the results become muddier. Fields of study make a big difference: individuals with bachelor's degrees in the humanities or education see lower returns on their educational investment, whereas an associate's degree in a field like engineering or computers (for men) and health (for women) tends to be associated with higher incomes.[19]

In his 1979 book *The Credential Society*, Randall Collins noted that schools often don't teach workers the skills they will use in the workplace. "Job skills of all sorts," he observed, "are actually acquired in the work situation rather than in a formal training institution."[20] Latoya is a case in point. She has never finished high school, and her lack of formal learning sometimes shows. She doesn't read well; she stumbles over sentences. Her grammar is nonstandard, and she has trouble writing complete sentences. Nevertheless, she is a competent manager who is greatly valued by her employer. Burger Barn put her through classes—on operations, on management—but mostly she learned on the job, under the tutelage of the general manager, Bob.

Years of experience taught her the fundamentals of business economics. After she finally landed a position as an assistant to Bob, the restaurant's owner declared that no one on the payroll was going to get a raise until Bob and Latoya brought food costs down and controlled labor costs. "The food percentages was 31 percent," Latoya says. "Thirty-one percent of the money that we brung in paid for the food. It's not supposed to be that." Workers were giving food to their friends and running up the food bill. Latoya and Bob cracked down. They kept an eye on the cash registers at all times, making sure no one slipped even a single apple pie across the counter without a receipt. The food costs gradually ticked downward. "We went down from 31 to 29," Latoya says. "Twenty-nine to 27. Still wasn't happy. Twenty-seven to 25. We have 25 now." Latoya, the high school dropout, has learned enough about costs, revenues, and (as she puts it) "profitabilities" to run a successful business.

There are several examples in our study sample of people who have done exceedingly well without higher education. Though she has only a high school degree, Lanice found a steady job as an administrative assistant at an entertainment conglomerate in New York. Thanks to a supportive boss, she is poised to scale the corporate ladder. It's not that Lanice dismisses the importance of education, but she insists that, for her, the lack of those credentials hasn't been an impediment:

> Don't get me wrong, I am an advocate for education. I think it's very important. My sister just got accepted at [a] university—full scholarship, great person, honor student, lovely. Go for it. But for me, I can't say that [lacking a degree] has stunted my growth. And maybe if it was hard for me to find a job at any given point in my life, I might feel differently, and it might have made me say, "OK, maybe I got to go and just get some kind of degree on paper." But because every time I went out for a job I got one, it was not a big deal. . . . People in my family who have had education and have, you know, maybe not the bachelor but at least associate degrees, they still come to me like, "Can you do my résumé? Can you tell me what to say?" And I'm like, "Sure," and that's only because they know that even though I might not have the education, I do get the job, and every job I get I make sure that it's paying more than the last.

People don't just acquire skills and credentials in school. Just as important is the opportunity for exposure to and mastery of behaviors and codes that minimize the transaction costs of bringing new employees into the workplace. In other words, schools are crucibles of cultural capital.[21] Yet they are not the only way of molding young workers into work-ready material.

Lanice's experience suggests that on-the-job mastery of these codes is, in and of itself, what counts. So long as employers are convinced that workers understand what is expected, they don't necessarily demand educational credentials. Lanice's account of one of her job interviews underlines the point:

> [An interviewer] was looking over my résumé, and . . . he said, "You didn't put your college education on there." And I was like, "Oh, I didn't. I didn't feel the need to do the college thing." I said, however, "I am very qualified to do this job, and things that I do not know, I learn very quickly." And he was like, "Well, you know, you should just

put it on there anyway . . . because just from talking to you, no one would ever know that you didn't have the traditional [degree]. And," he said, "quite frankly, I probably shouldn't be telling you this, but not many people are checking that hard to see if you went, and because of the way that you carry yourself and the way that you talk, you can definitely put a college on there and nobody will question it." And I was like, "Oh, all right," and that was pretty much the end of that.

Most low-wage workers, however, are not so dismissive of the value of a college degree. Immersed in a culture that emphasizes the importance of education, they have internalized the centrality of diplomas to their own success. Roughly a third of the workers in our sample obtained a college degree or took some college courses during the course of the study—half of them when they were in their midtwenties or older. They may agree that educational credentials are not an accurate barometer of aptitude, but they also recognize that employers often use them in this way.[22] Helena is one example. When we met up with her in 1997, she was twenty-one years old, already married, and the mother of a two-year-old son; she and her husband both worked, and Helena attended classes at a local community college. By 2002 she had two sons, but she had nonetheless managed to get a bachelor's degree in public administration. She persevered partly because of her Dominican immigrant mother—who had harassed her constantly about schooling—and partly because she knew that it was prerequisite to upward mobility in her workplace.

Today Helena oversees thirteen people and makes $62,000 with full benefits. She admits that her college degree doesn't really help her on the job: "For me, it's just a piece of paper." When she hires new people in her unit, education is not her "number one thing," she says. Helena looks instead at a person's experience in the customer service field. She learned what she needed to know mostly from experience, sometimes from common sense—but never from the college courses that got her that diploma. "But I have it," she adds. Helena knows she wouldn't have gotten her last promotion without the sheepskin.

Even workers who delayed going back to school—or have found it impossible to do so—eventually see that securing credentials is crucial for landing a job in a better paying industry. A single mother of three, Bridget has not yet been able to follow through on her plans to attend a four-year college. She regrets not going, and is reminded of this fact every time she shows up for work at the college bursar's office. At the age of twenty-eight, she has to put up with condescending twenty-one-year-olds who think they're smarter than she is: "They're trying to telling *you* something that you've been trained to know . . . and they're cussing at you and everything." In spite of the barriers she faces, Bridget continues to persevere academically. Recently she picked up some additional computer skills in a vocational program that ensures, she hopes, that employers will "look at [her] different."

Bridget is quick to separate the credentials from the knowledge that credentials are supposed to represent. It's not that she doesn't have skills; it's that she needs a piece of paper to prove it. "I know they [employers] see people that have high school diplomas and they automatically say, 'Well, you don't have any skills because you didn't go to college.' And that's not necessarily true because there's a lot of people that have college degrees and still don't know much." Nevertheless, she insists that her future depends on getting more education—on getting the kind of credentials that could signal to employers that she really is worth hiring. Bridget's need to support her children (a five-year-old son, three-year-old daughter, and newborn infant) may mean that she will always have to prioritize the short-term goal of pulling a steady paycheck over the long-term goal of finishing college. Her current job is "not enough to maintain a family of four," she laments, and she is determined to improve her chances in the labor market.

The Burger Barn workers we met who had not finished school tend, like Bridget, to regret that failure deeply. For some, this regret is a realistic acknowledgment of the fact that they may never be "successful," at least in conventional terms. "Without an education, you can't get but so far," Marilyn says matter-of-factly. The last time we saw her, in 2002, she was twenty-nine years old, living with her unemployed girlfriend, and still without her GED. She had just gotten out of prison after serving an eighteen-month sentence for selling drugs. In prison she had taken courses for the GED, but she did not get her degree because, she says, she did not have enough time to prepare for the exam before she was released. Marilyn was doing maintenance work at a courthouse, making $5.25 an hour, and though she had applied for a number of jobs—in construction, as a security guard, at another fast-food restaurant—she was pessimistic that anyone better would ever hire her, an ex-felon with no high school diploma.[23]

Even workers who have finished high school—and have clean records—have found their way up blocked by the words "college degree required." Larry, a twenty-nine-year-old Puerto Rican, works as a computer technician at a city agency. Though he is technically part-time, Larry works a full forty-hour week and has been promoted to "team leader," just one step away from manager. Nevertheless, he sees few prospects for further advancement because he doesn't have a college degree. "Not having a degree, it held me back," he says. "Even though they know I'm capable of doing the work, that's where the politics comes in. So I have to have that. At least if I had my [associate's degree]—that's enough, because I have experience and the time in there to cover any of the other things."

It is intriguing that a number of the high flyers have such strong regrets about not going to school, given that their own experience would seem to belie the assumption that education matters. At the age of thirty-six, Adam is making $70,000 a year with full benefits as a deliveryman for Air Express. He's one of the most affluent people in our sample, with a paycheck that far outstrips those of almost all the college graduates. "Honestly, I never—not in my wildest dreams did I ever expect to be where I'm at today," Adam admits.

> I always seen myself just living check to check, just getting by, not really making—I was looking to make like $30,000, not no $70,000. That was shocking, to see that three years ago, when that first W-2 came and I realized, boy, I made $68,000 last year. I had to go back and recalculate, and I'm like, "I didn't see it." I know why I didn't see it, because all I did was go back and pay all the bills I owed within that first year. But after that, my five-year-old son, he's very quick to say, "Daddy, I want." We have got just about everything there is. I mean, everybody has got their own computers, everybody has got their own things, and it's amazing. It really is. God is great.

Even though he's a high school dropout who has made it big, Adam still subscribes to the conventional wisdom that getting an education will get you further than working. "Now I can provide more for my kids," Adam admits, "but for them to get anything from me, I do do one thing: I stress education out of them. 'You want something? I want you to come home with a high school diploma.'"

Like many parents, Adam is almost obsessive about the quality of his children's education. He aims to move down to North Carolina, where his mother lives and where the schools, he says, are better: "Just about all the teachers have at least a bachelor's degree, which is good, being that you know your child is really going to learn." He laments that his thirteen-year-old daughter is failing some of her classes; he speaks with relish about getting his son interested in reading through Hooked on Phonics. At the same time, Adam confesses that, in his industry, "it's not that big [a deal] to have an education." He'll continue to make wages that many college graduates would kill for, all thanks to a strong union and the relative scarcity of experienced couriers who have a commercial driver's license.

Adam recognizes the trade-offs between school and work. On the one hand, lack of education has "closed some doors": he had meant to stay in the courier business for only two years and then get a government job, but for most government work you need a high school diploma. At the moment, Adam is also trying to expand the T-shirt printing business he and his wife run out of their home, and he's pushing his wife to get her MBA so she will have the necessary skills to take their company to the next level. On the other hand, Adam realizes that the main reason that he is making so much money is that he has spent many years in the courier business and has worked his way up the union ladder. The top union-scale salary where he works ($90,000 a year) can be reached after about a decade on the job; it's likely that Adam wouldn't be making nearly as much if he had used the past several years to finish high school and go to college. And even if he loses this job, he shouldn't have any difficulty finding a new one, he notes, given his commercial driver's license and his experience.

Like Adam, Vicente never finished high school, but he is still raking in some serious cash—about $73,000 a year—as a livery driver. It's quite a leap up the wage scale for someone who, in the early nineties, was rejected for entry-level employment at Burger Barn. Back then, Vicente, his mother, and his younger sister were living off of food stamps and AFDC checks. In 2002 Vicente still lives with them in a rent-controlled apartment in Harlem, but he finally has a stable job—stable enough to consider bringing over his wife and two-year-old son from the Dominican Republic. He doesn't receive benefits, but then again he doesn't have a supervisor, and he doesn't have to punch a timecard. "If I don't want to work that day, I don't work," says the thirty-one-year-old. "If I want to work three hours, I work three hours. . . . I love my job." Like Adam, Vicente has made up for limited education by seeking out an industry with good wages—and obtaining the credentials he needed (in Vicente's case, a $300 taxi license) to gain entry. In spite of his success, however, Vicente is quick to point out that not having a formal education has limited his opportunities. Once, he says, he applied for a job in the mailroom of a city hospital; they wouldn't hire him because he didn't have a high school degree. "I've done well, better than what I expected. . . . Without having a high school diploma, you don't know where you're going."

Individuals like Lanice, Vicente, and Adam, who have overcome their educational deficiencies, are unusual—and will likely become even more so, given the current trend away from unionized work and toward a high-skilled, knowledge-based economy. That said, anecdotal evidence indicates that even high school dropouts can land that dream job—one that fits their personality, matches their skills, and offers the protection of a union (or, lacking that, the high-flying wages of a growth industry).

Yet the success these individuals achieve in spite of their lack of education does not sever the cultural link between education and success. They hear society's mantras loud and clear, and that leaves even our success stories with a raft of "what if" questions. If he had finished high school, could Adam have found an even better career match? If he had gone to college, would Vicente be enjoying a posh office job? Or are their present jobs more than they could have ever hoped to accomplish, high education or not?

Getting and Giving Back

In *The Truly Disadvantaged*, his classic study of the postindustrial transformation of America's urban ghettos, sociologist William Julius Wilson argues that the movement of middle-class African Americans from ghetto neighborhoods had traumatic consequences for the low-income residents left behind—not just because middle-class families took much-needed financial resources with them, but also because their absence deprived the poor left behind of mentors, role models, and labor-market connections. There is some evidence that this middle-class exodus affected the job prospects of the ghetto residents whom we came to know. If young people in decades past could look to their local "old heads"—the seniors who held the good jobs in manufacturing and civil service that have since dwindled away—this newer generation seems to lack such a support network.[24]

Among the respondents situated in the middle- or high-wage categories in our 1997 sample, only 28 percent said that their friends, neighbors, and relatives were "good sources" of job information; in contrast, 40 percent of workers in the low-wage category, said this was the case. The vast majority of the highest earners did not live with people who made more money than they did, nor did they socialize with them. Having achieved a level of relative success within their social circles, these young workers had a tough time finding local mentors with the knowledge or contacts to help them continue moving up. Instead, they increasingly found it necessary to tap influences outside of their enclave.

Francisco's case is a good example. When we interviewed him in 1997, he was a low-paid office clerk at a top-tier Manhattan financial conglomerate, making just $6.50 an hour. He was sensitive to the fact that he was working outside the world he knew (Harlem and Queens), in a fast-paced workplace where a million dollars was leftover change. Though he worked on the lower levels of his office building, he would sometimes go out onto the trading floors for inspiration. "We're not so much allowed," he admits. "I just go up to the twenty-ninth floor to use the bathroom, but sometimes I go up to the floors, and I'm like, 'Wow'—looking inside, big, and there's so many people and they're in a business setting. And it's fascinating."

Francisco eventually found a mentor—not at that company, but at another firm also outside Harlem. He took a job at the dot-com start-up Big Apple Delivery just to pick up some cash after school (he was taking college courses at the time), but his manager, Tony, took a liking to him and started teaching him the ins and outs of management. "I just watched him and listened and he taught me," Francisco remembers. "In less than a year, I was a manager." He has left Big Apple, but Francisco still talks to Tony. "I still get advice from him. He's like, 'Come back. I can do a lot for you.' So I'm just like kind of waiting until my pockets are really low and I got to reach out to this guy."

Under Tony's tutelage, Francisco began to envision his path up the job ladder—from worker to assistant manager to manager. He distinguished himself quickly from his co-workers in skills and attitude. The job wasn't hard, he claims, but other workers proved less reliable and were not as adept at following instructions; Francisco, on the other hand, would do anything asked of him, with minimal errors. "I'm basically like a sponge," he says. "I like to soak as much information and resources. Whatever I can learn from you, I want to learn it, because you never know when you can use it." The more Francisco proved himself, the more Tony relied on him.

The more he pushed himself on the job, the more Tony invested in Francisco's informal education. "He would ask me questions like, 'What are you doing with your life? Are you going to school?' He was like, 'If you're willing, I'm willing to teach you. Come aboard and I'll give you as much money as I can.'" A fifty-cent raise here, a fifty-cent raise there: "He was giving it to me and I was producing. . . . I was showing and proving, and he was showing and proving. We kind of became cool."

Francisco rose into the ranks of management, and with his promotion the expectations grew. Tony now watched over him from a distance. "So it was like, I need things to run smoothly there. . . . He be like, 'We need you over there.' And I would take care of it. I basically did whatever he did and the way he did it, because that's how I was taught."

By the time of our last interview, in 2002, Francisco was firmly ensconced in the world of management. His job situation had dimmed somewhat after he left his senior position at Big Apple when the company was floundering, but he was still pulling down a decent wage as a supervisor. Just as his former boss did for him, Francisco was serving as a mentor— but in his case, mostly for family. He was careful, however, in deciding whom to help. He wouldn't recommend just anyone for a job; the person had to have a good "track record." It helped that most of the jobs he was hooking people up with were entry-level positions that "didn't take a degree to do" and do well. "Knowing these people and knowing the jobs they had in the past or their experience or having an education, I would take them," Francisco explained. "Just everyday life with them, I would know off the bat if he could do this job. And if he can't, I'll help him function at his job."

Gaining the respect of someone with seniority provides workers like Francisco with valuable advice about what to do (and not do) and where to look for a better job. It's not just a matter of improving their skills on the job; workers also need to learn how to behave and how to present themselves in ways that signal to the higher-ups that they have potential. The help that workplace mentors provide can extend beyond the office or shop floor, as well. When he decided to start his own business, Adam found the help he needed from his morning supervisor at Air Express. "Even before then, he was really there," Adam told us in 1997, when his T-shirt company was still in its fledgling stage. "I look up to him a lot, and he's there for me. Like I told him, he ever need me, I do for him, because he does for me." The encouragement from his supervisor came in many forms. After

Adam was in a serious car accident and was out on worker's compensation, his supervisor dropped by to see how he was doing. "[He was] the only supervisor to call, come by, and even give me money—his wife even cooked for me," Adam recalled. "And [he] made sure I was taken care of. And that there . . . puts morale into people like me. . . . Even though he's just a supervisor; he's not even the top supervisor there. But he took care of his workers."

At times, low-wage workers find that customers at the workplace can be useful sources of information. When she used to spend her days behind the cash register at Burger Barn, Latoya impressed people so much with her gregarious, obliging personality that she was offered other jobs. A tenant at the co-op where Reynaldo is employed as a hall man advised him on how to pick a preschool for his young daughter. "Look, the best way to do it is to join the Parents League and they'll help you," the tenant, a school dean, told Reynaldo. Reynaldo and his wife joined the Parents League, a network of independent schools in New York, and found their daughter's current preschool in one of the league's brochures. It pays to work at a co-op with wealthy tenants. As Reynaldo points out, "Their kids go to the best pre-Ks."

Young workers cannot always find a mentor to work with them at the office or a customer willing to drop them a helpful lead. (In fact, when we asked them who had been influential in their lives in recent years, only one in ten of our respondents mentioned someone at work.)[25] Nevertheless, they can usually think of at least one person in their personal network—a family member, neighbor, or friend with a good job—who can serve as a positive role model.

Vicente was inspired by an uncle who was a popular and well-respected lieutenant in a New Jersey police department. Karen saw how far her mother, a former drug addict who kicked the habit and got a job with the city transit agency, had come in the past six years, and it made her hopeful that she could turn her own life around. Victoria looked to her ex-fiancé, a former drug dealer who had spent years in prison but nevertheless had managed to land a job—his first job—working downtown at a university: "It made me feel like, if you could do this, I can get me a good job." Randy turned to the example of his wife, who worked at a police car pound in New Jersey and had been tough enough to speak out against corruption in the department. "She's respectable, so it makes me be respectable," he said. "She don't cheat, and neither do I." In more recent years, Randy has also found inspiration in the stories of friends who have managed to overcome their upbringing on the streets and put their histories of drug addiction and crime behind them. "A lot of my friends is doing really well, and that's what keeps me going," he said. What these friends and family members teach is that even people who enter the labor market with serious disadvantages—from growing up poor in the ghetto, or from the bad decisions they made when they were young—can pull themselves up and work their way into the ranks of the respected, and self-respecting.

Personal relationships can also be instructive in the opposite way—revealing what not to do. As a teenager, Reynaldo spent his days selling drugs, hanging out with his friends, and drinking, but today he hardly sees his old mates in Washington Heights. That's for the best, because Reynaldo has cleaned up his life: he works long hours at two well-paying jobs, is married with two young children, and spends what free time he has buying megapacks of Pampers at Costco or playing with his four-year-old daughter on the swings in the park. His old-time associates are cautionary tales of the fate that could have befallen him. "I had one friend, his father was a teacher and he ended up in nothing. A lot of my friends are really f——ed up," he says. These days, Reynaldo steers clear of his old life, keeps to himself at home in the South Bronx ("I just say hi and bye"), and doesn't consider for one moment getting involved in his low-income neighborhood ("F—— the community").

Kyesha gets riled up by the incessant excuses she hears from people around her. The twenty-eight-year-old single mother is hardly a saint herself, but even she is aghast at the behavior of her mom, a longtime welfare recipient who has raked in extra cash for years by scamming the Social Security system. "If it ever get found out, yeah, she's doing federal [time]," Kyesha says. Her nineteen-year-old sister, Irene, is even a worse: a drug user and seller who spends her days smoking pot, lives like a parasite in their mother's house, and thinks only of herself. Because of her success in finding well-paid, stable work, Kyesha finds herself deluged with entreaties from friends and family—her sister included—who want a job hookup or are fishing for a loan. Ordinarily Kyesha wouldn't give someone like Irene the time of day, but she feels a sense of obligation that overrides good sense, so she is trying to help Irene find work, even though in her heart she knows the girl won't work hard and will bring a bad attitude to the job. Fortunately, other people in Kyesha's extended family are better bets, and she has succeeded in helping six of them get jobs.

High flyers like Kyesha have risen to the top of their social network and are now the "go to" people whenever someone needs a job or advice. They may not be able to benefit anymore from the career help that their friends and family can give them, but they are expected to help hook up their loved ones (and not so loved ones) with good jobs like theirs. Adam, like Kyesha, doesn't mind that extra responsibility. He has made a habit of looking out for job leads for the bevy of friends and acquaintances who come to him hoping for a sprinkling of his success. Whenever he drops by Columbia University for a delivery, for instance, he'll stop by the campus employment office and see what positions are available. "I would tell anybody in a heartbeat where to go look for a job," he declares. His largesse also extends to making loans to friends and family. "I'm the banker. Everyone is calling me for all types of loans, and needing help with computers. Like my sister just started her real estate business and she wants me to get her a computer and all of this. It's been great."

That said, Adam has also run into problems trying to help others. Con Edison cut the electricity to his sister's apartment and she was facing eviction; Adam stepped in with money to pay off her bills. "I told her she could make a payment plan to me and I would accept it, just pay me back. To this day I haven't received a penny, and that was back about four years ago." Adam says he takes these disappointments in stride, though he's wiser for them. "Like I tell her, if she ever needs, I'm going to think twice now, because I do work hard for my money."

Yet most low-wage workers who are in a position to help their friends and family aren't as generous as Kyesha and Adam. Research by sociologist Sandra Smith offers some reasons why. Drawing from interviews and surveys of 105 low-income African Americans, she found that 8 out of 10 of her respondents expressed concern that job seekers in their social networks "were too unmotivated to accept assistance, required great expenditures of time and emotional energy, or acted too irresponsibly on the job, thereby jeopardizing contacts' own reputations in the eyes of employers and negatively affecting their already-tenuous labor market prospects." As a result, these individuals tended to keep their stock of job leads to themselves—a decision, Smith says, that could have serious repercussions for job seekers in low-wage labor markets "where employers rely heavily on informal referrals for recruitment and screening." When Smith's respondents did decide to pass on information to their friends and family, they usually had a strong faith in the recipient's ability to deliver on the job, based on that person's track record—work history, known personal habits, and the like. There were some friends and family who were deemed "worthy" of help, and some who were not; there was little tolerance for risks, because a bad recommendation could ruin the respondent's own reputation at the workplace.[26]

Many of the workers in our study followed this selective logic in deciding when, and whom, to help. Faced with requests from friends and family, they err on the side of caution, giving information or resources only to those they deem worthy. Pedro, a twenty-five-year-old forklift driver who makes more than $30,000 a year with benefits at his job at Costco, says that he does his "best" to help out any friend whom he thinks has potential, yet he also acknowledges that he plays favorites: "There are certain things that catch my eye that make me favor that one person. It is favoritism, in a way—you see something you like and you focus on that. And you let them know when you are looking at them, and you keep an eye on them and [tell them to] keep up the good work." Helena, on the other hand, is reluctant to recommend anyone—friend or not—for work at her company. "I just tell them they don't have any openings or go to the Internet and look [it] up yourself," she says. "I mean, [I'll] give them the listing of job postings. But I wouldn't recommend. I wouldn't put my name to it."

Now that she owns her own business, Anita hears from friends and relatives all the time who are looking for a job. She wants to help but notes, "If the demand is not there, I can't do anything." She is blunt about the limits of her generosity. "I'm thinking, this is my business. If I can't control what I spend, why should I spend money on you, when I don't need you to do nothing that I can't do." Of course, "no" is often not enough: before Anita started her own business, her friends would drop by the stores where she worked, looking for favors. She decided she didn't want to work in the Bronx anymore because she was tired of friends importuning her. "I know too many people in the Bronx," she says. "Because people, they always look for favors when they know you work somewhere. . . . [I'd have to] worry about doing my job and worry about people I know coming in."

Ebony reminds us that many friends who want help have no idea what it takes to get ahead. Her younger sister begs her to help her find a job. "Why can't I work where you work? Why can't I have your job?" twenty-one-year-old Renee asks Ebony. Ebony has to patiently explain that she needs more experience. Any office manager at a law firm like hers, Ebony points out, will take one look at Renee's lackluster résumé and throw it into the recycling bin.

Sure, Ebony can put in a good word for Renee. She can help her nail the right look and attitude. She can even "embellish" Renee's work history if need be. "We can make it up, because that is what a lot of these people do," Ebony says. All the same, presentation only goes so far in the white-collar world, Ebony tells her sister. There are skills in this workplace that need to be learned. "They look at what you have on your résumé to decide whether or not you are teachable. It doesn't mean that you are not, but that is the way that they see it." Even those lucky individuals who know how the game is played—even those people willing to put on a happy face and fudge facts to get the job—may not have what it takes to make it in to-day's labor market.

In the early 1990s, a sputtering economy and cutthroat labor market taught young workers some hard lessons. Back then, many were struggling to find work at places like Burger Barn. They were high school dropouts with children, grown men and women who seemed destined to remain stuck in the projects or in mom's Section 8 apartment. Yet, in the span of several years, a surprising number moved up into the white-collar world. The booming economy of the late 1990s helped, but so did the experience that these workers had gained—experience that proved valuable on the way up, even if it was earned with arms elbow-deep in grease or backs sore from lifting laundry. Over the years, they sketched in their minds a field guide to the labor market, a model of how employers behaved, a map of where to head in the working world.

This "education," a mix of common sense, time spent learning the trade, tips gleaned from other workers, and trial and error, has guided them in making decisions about their careers, schooling, and families. It has given them some basic principles for evaluating their options—and for evaluating the would-be workers who come following in their footsteps. With the knowledge they acquired, some have been able to break into the corporate offices and union halls familiar to America's middle class. Their résumés may never bear that ultimate marker of middle-class status, the college degree, but they can proudly point to themselves as homegrown success stories.

Nevertheless, success can be elusive, or short-lived. These workers may know a good deal about the way the labor market works, but they are not always able to act on that information. They may still wind up where they planned, but probably not without some detours or setbacks. The deci-sions they made as young people constrain them. The responsibilities they shoulder—as mothers and fathers, providers and caregivers—siphon off their time and drive. And the social policy choices the rest of us make—to fund or starve child care, to let welfare recipients go to school or force them into bad jobs—set terms that also constrain their options. So they wait to get the GED or to go to college, they put off saving up for the house or the move down South. If they're lucky, they're able to pick up again where they left off—sometimes, a decade later. If not, they may still make it, or they may remain mired in the labor market's muddier patches, stewing over their inability to do better. Either way, they run into the reality of the working world, a reality familiar to many in America's middle class: no matter how successful they are, no matter how busy their schedules become, there is always time for regrets.

7

"This Is the Kind of Life I Want": Work and Welfare in the Boom Years

It has been five years since I last talked to Kyesha. She has gained some weight—maybe twenty pounds, maybe thirty—and she wears it well, her face fuller, her body sturdier. Since 1997 she has acquired four tattoos (her right arm boasts her elaborately etched nickname), and a stud now dots her tongue. Her hair is long now, too, threaded into tiny braids dyed maroon and purple.

On the day we connected, Kyesha was at work in the Malcolm X Housing Project where she grew up and her mother, Dana, still lives. Her workday had just ended, so Kyesha needed to pick up her son, Anthony. Her mother takes care of the rowdy ten-year-old when she's at work and he is done with school for the day. When Kyesha walked into Dana's apartment, her mother was shrieking from the end of the hallway, calling Anthony a "bitch" for some infraction. Dana stopped abruptly when she noticed the company, quickly welcoming the visitor with a good-natured hello. Though Dana heads out to a clinic on Long Island every two weeks for cancer treatment, this "out there" grandmother looks surprisingly strong and healthy and somehow manages to keep her condition a secret from the neighbors.

Kyesha displays a photo of her mother decked out in her crossing guard uniform. She looks like a cop, and kind of proud. This is Dana's new job. Several years ago, New York mayor Rudolph Giuliani started telling welfare recipients that they had to find work if they wanted to keep receiving benefits. "Work is hard," Giuliani said. "Getting up every day, making sure you get a job, getting yourself cleaned and ready to do it—there's a certain discipline that's required for everybody in that. And what we were doing in welfare before was training, training, training."[1] As part of the mayor's Work Experience Program, tens of thousands of men and women donned bright orange vests and blue jackets and started picking up trash and sweeping streets. Dana was not one of them. For years, Dana had supported herself with government assistance—welfare, Social Security payments stemming from the death of her husband, and so on. The city wasn't going to let her do that anymore. But the housing office wanted Dana to clean elevators, and she decided she had had her fill of urine-sprayed floors; she went out looking for a job on her own. She eventually found the crossing guard job.

Kyesha approves. As a city housing employee and Local 545 union member, she complains about how hardworking individuals like herself are getting their "taxes tooken from them," so that other people—people like her mom—can sit at home and watch *Ricki Lake*, *All My Children*, and *One Life to Live* (Dana, incidentally, had cable TV installed in every room of the apartment).[2] "While I'm out there busting my chops," Kyesha says, "they're getting my free tax money. They need to come out there and see what it feels like to work." Some might complain they aren't getting paid enough for the work they're required to do, she says, but so what? If they want more money they should get a job.

Most of the respondents in our study—even those who relied on public assistance to make ends meet—agreed with Kyesha (Table 7.1). Though a substantial number gave the welfare changes mixed reviews, only 9 percent of interviewees in 1997 and 11 percent of interviewees in 2001–2002 had a negative opinion of welfare reform.[3] The five-year lifetime limit on benefits is especially popular among the working poor. Overall our respondents agreed that welfare was intended to provide only temporary assistance. Five years was more than enough time to get back on one's feet financially. Even those individuals who received public assistance said they were disgusted with those (other) people who stayed on welfare for years and scammed the system.

Several months before we caught up with her again in 2002, twenty-six-year-old Deanna had quit a $33,000-a-year job as an administrative assistant at an architectural firm. She was pregnant, her rent was $565 per

Table 7.1 Evaluations of welfare reform by Harlem sample

	Wave 2 (1997)	Wave 3 (2001–2002)
Positive	51.6%	72.2%
Mixed	39.8%	16.7%
Negative	8.6%	11.1%
N	93	18

month, and her husband was making only $7 an hour in computer sales. So, after years of holding menial jobs—everything from Yankees Stadium concession worker to KFC cashier to Department of Transportation switchboard operator—Deanna decided to apply for food stamps and Medicaid. She didn't expect to be on public assistance for long—and certainly not five years.

> At first I didn't want to have to deal with the public assistance or welfare system at all. But I felt like, you know, this is just—for me I felt this was a time of need. Shit, I worked for all of these years, and they taxed me so much, I feel it's money owed to me anyway, so that's why I kind of said OK, I gave into it.
>
> I think it's good as far as the time line because it shouldn't be something that you solely depend on for the rest of your life. It should be for . . . people like me and my husband—for when you're down and out, you know what I mean? We were laid off, so it's assistance that we need right now. I think that's all it should be used for. But because over the years people have taken advantage of it and got comfortable with it, that's why they have to make up these time lines. So I agree with them, totally. If they would have said you have one year, I still would have been like, "That's fine." Because I know I'm going back to work. It's not a problem.

Conservatives argue that what became a welfare "culture" created a sluggish, parasitic class, happy to live off the fat of the bureaucracy. People like that are rare, in my experience. But low-wage workers agree to an extent with the thrust—if not the details—of this perspective.[4] For workers staring up from the bottom of the country's labor market barrel, there is a need to draw distinctions between themselves and those nonworkers with whom many middle-class critics might confuse them. You can hear this defensive concern in the voices of people like Kevin, who earns $9.50 an hour as a child care worker. He was upset by the fact that people on welfare were just sitting on their butts and not doing anything. "If I'm getting a low pay and I can get the government just to pay me to sit at home, why would you argue about that?" he said. For Kevin, his unwillingness to cave in to that enticement was proof that he is a morally superior person.

Tyandra didn't have much to show for years of working low-wage jobs, either. But she, too, was supportive of welfare reform. The twenty-year-old African American could simply point to her cousin, a ne'er-do-well who used to lie in bed until two or three in the afternoon. "Her kids was running around everywhere, but she would sleep and she would hang out at night," Tyandra said. Then the welfare agency told her if she didn't get a job, there would be no more checks in the mail. So Tyandra's cousin started attending a skills-training program and soon found a full-time job at a pharmacy. "It made her more responsible, because now she puts her kids in bed by 10:00 because it's the summer," Tyandra said. "She's home in bed by, like, 10:30, 11:00. She gets up, she goes to work." Tyandra sees a huge difference in her cousin's attitude, too: "She's happy where she's at. She's motivated to work. She's motivated to finish school now. Because before, she was, like, I don't even feel like doing this. I don't feel like staying in school. Now she wants to stay in school, she's working hard, she gets up, she's on time to work. She has fun. She comes home, tells us about her day, how great a day she had. And she likes it. I don't see a problem with that [welfare reform]. Because I think it motivated her to be positive and responsible now."

Is welfare reform fair? Yes, thought most of our respondents—but not all. A minority, about one in ten people we interviewed, thought it was unjust.[5] Workfare, they felt, was about doing degrading manual labor for "chump change." Cassandra, a former drug addict who now holds down a $26,000-a-year job as a customer service representative, told us she felt welfare recipients were being exploited under the new system. "I think the whole program sucks," she said.

I think that's just an excuse for [New York governor George] Pataki to not issue the funds that they've been issued for years. Now, granted, there are people that are on welfare that are sheer laziness, that are capable and should be working. I have a few associates who just kick back. I think it's disgusting. . . . But I don't think that they're really trying to help these people do a damn thing, because if you're going to hire me to clean the streets, at least give me a base salary. You know what I'm saying? Don't have me working for something that I sit on my ass for years to collect. You know, give me a salary, because if you give me a salary, this will make me want to get up every day to go and do this.

Not all welfare recipients were on the rolls because they were lazy and lacked an education, Cassandra pointed out. "It's a lot of things that happen in people's lives, where they have to go there. You know what I'm saying?" she said. "And if you're going to say, 'OK, I'm here to help you,' [then] help me. You know? Help me." It's not that people love being stigmatized. But they do look out on the hurly-burly of the work world with a lack of confidence. They do fear being shunned by employers and want to preserve their dignity in the face of a market that accords dignity mainly to others with more credentials. For those who have already swallowed those lumps, the view from below is, mostly, "tough." I did it. You must. From Cassandra, we hear something more like empathy.

Critics of welfare reform like to pose a simple question: If the government really wants welfare recipients to work, shouldn't it be providing permanent jobs that pay decent wages? Otherwise, its campaign to push people off the rolls is really about creating a cheaper, more submissive labor force. "The regular people that's been working is getting pushed out [of their] jobs by the people on welfare," says Silena, who had been on welfare for two and a half years when we last spoke to her in 1997. "Then the people that's working, they're not getting nothing but their welfare check. I think that's a gyp." For George, a twenty-four-year-old often unemployed black man who was in his fifth low-wage job in four years, there was only one way to describe the work that welfare recipients were being forced to do: "Very, very degrading." "And they pay them pennies for it," he said. "It's almost like the city's using the people to do harder work, to clean up what the people who have these professional positions don't clean. I think it needs to be changed, but the way they're going about it I think is wrong."

It is mortifying, for example, to go around in an orange vest, skewering pieces of trash while passersby gawk. Florida, a twenty-eight-year-old security guard, told us about her sister, who was forced to work in order to collect her benefits. "They had her in her neighborhood picking up paper—it's humiliating personally, because people know when you're doing it." When we last spoke to Florida in 1997, she was earning five dollars an hour and receiving both AFDC payments and food stamps. As part of her work requirement, she had temped at an accounting department for six months. "I picked up . . . how to do the records and the books and stuff like that. But after the six months, they tell you, 'Well, maybe you'll get a position with this company if something open[s]. Nothing opened after that. I still didn't have a job, still was on public assistance—I worked for the money they was giving me."

Even if they believe that benefits should be time limited and welfare recipients should work for their keep, the people affected by these policies have serious objections to the way they have been implemented. For one thing, the government doesn't exactly set up welfare recipients for success. Nolita, a high school dropout and mother of two young children, worked sporadically throughout the years we followed her. She told us in 2002 that she was genuinely trying to find work but that, with the new rules, "everything's harder now." There was no decent child care to be found. There were no buses to take her kids to their after-school program. "They're insisting that I find child care as if it's easy," Nolita scoffs. "As if it's out there somewhere. So basically they're telling me if I don't find child care I get nothing." Nolita had just applied to work in a supermarket and was trying to work out a schedule that would allow her mother to watch her baby daughter while she attended a nurse's aide program. She wanted to work, but she also wanted to be a good mother.[6]

Conservatives—and a good many liberals—argue that nobody insisted Nolita should have children she cannot support.[7] Nothing riles Nolita faster. From her perspective, poor women are entitled to have children just like other women, many of whom don't work. What's more, at the time she had them, she didn't expect to have so much trouble providing for them. There was a man in the picture and he made promises.[8] He just didn't keep them. That is a familiar story for many women who land on the rolls for Temporary Assistance for Needy Families. Enthusiasts of welfare reform were clearly looking to drive home the lesson that there will be a steep price to pay for having kids "beyond your means." Poor women—even those who reject this message—retort that the kids are here, nevertheless, and have to be taken care of.

Arbitrary bureaucracy is the bane of existence for poor people, on or off welfare. They are constantly at the mercy of rules that change, administrators in revolving chairs, the whims of policy fashion. It feels to them as though traps are set deliberately by authorities who delight just as much in confounding innocent mothers trying to get health care for their kids as they do drug addicts trying to put one over on the system.[9]

The system tells you to take care of your kids. The system tells you to get an education. The system tells you not to cheat. But time and time again, people living at the bottom of the labor market see the system actively thwarting their attempts to do the right thing. They observe welfare recipients who cheat the system and stay on the rolls, and others who try to get an education or look for a decent job, and get their benefits slashed.

Back when Lauren, then a twenty-two-year-old single mother, was going to a community college to get her associate's degree—studying full-time and doing fifteen hours per week of work on top of that—the city told her she needed to work more hours to keep receiving public assistance. Lauren was irked that the government bureaucracy couldn't differentiate someone like her from all the people out there who didn't care— the idle poor who weren't trying to improve their lives, the welfare moms who weren't concerned about their children's future. "What about those people who aren't doing nothing?" the Brooklyn resident complained back in 1997. "Why don't you bother them? I'm trying to better my life."

Ebony, too, was trying to get a college education when the welfare office called. "At one point, they were helping you to get into school," she said in her 1997 interview. "[Now] they're like, 'Well, you have to work this job, and I don't care if you go to school or not. You have to schedule your school hours around [your] job.' And that's like backwards to me. I'm trying to get an education so I don't have to be on this, and instead of you helping me so that I don't have to be on it, you're hindering me." At the time, Ebony was living with her grandparents, both of whom have since died. She had worked four different jobs in four years, never earning more than seven dollars an hour. And now that she had finally made it to Bronx Community College, the city wanted her to work for her benefits. "Instead of maybe finishing school in two years, it'll take me four, because I had to go work this program and do this and do that," she told us at the time. When we caught up with her five years later, Ebony had finished up her associate's degree and was working on her BA in political science. She was working as a receptionist at a corporate law firm, making $28,500 with full benefits, and looking forward to the possibility of getting her tuition reimbursed should she go to law school.

By 2002 Ebony had also changed her mind about all those pesky rules.

The culture of dependency was the enemy. "It is the same thing with the environment, people around you," she said. "No one goes to work. No one does anything. They just stand around or whatever, and if you are struggling you can pull out of it, but if you are weak, you can get sucked in—and God knows how many times I was almost sucked in, sucked in and then pulled backed out or whatever." But Ebony had been saved.

The Penetration of Mainstream Values

Adam is the kind of person that Horatio Alger might have had in mind when he penned his late-nineteenth-century novels about impoverished souls who pulled themselves "up by the bootstraps" to fortune. He grew up black and poor in Brooklyn. His mother went on welfare after his father left her. Adam made it to tenth grade and then dropped out of high school. At the age of twenty-seven, he applied for a job at Burger Barn—and was rejected. Today Adam is solidly—enviably—middle class. "You know that saying, 'Keeping up with the Joneses?'" Adams says. "Well, I'm not keeping up with them. I am the Joneses."

His ascent from Burger Barn reject to suburban home owner—better yet, home *builder*—may explain why Adam doesn't have much patience for people who do not work. He endorses welfare reform and votes Republican. And he's adamant that his tax money should not go to pay "for someone else's kid." True, his mother was once on welfare, but she got off after a few years and has "been working ever since"—that's the way the system should work. In Adam's eyes, welfare recipients could all be doing what he and his mother did: start at a low-paying job, put in long hours, work their way up. "Of course there's no work if you want to get up twelve o'clock, one o'clock in the afternoon, and then say, 'I want to look for a job,'" he says. "Put in one or two applications . . . a day . . . and then say there's no jobs. You got to get up early. You got to move."

While Karen would probably agree with these sentiments, "moving" has an altogether different meaning for her. In the past decade, she has shuffled through a succession of underpaid, underappreciated jobs—with little to show for her effort. "You know how some people fantasize about sexual things? I fantasize about money," Karen sighs.

Karen applied for a job at Burger Barn in 1993. Like Adam, she was rejected. And like Adam, she was determined not to let that setback stop her. Karen started attending a local community college and continued to hunt for work, doing brief stints as a day care assistant, a Christmas season salesperson, a college work-study student, and an office worker for a temp agency. But over the next few years, things started to fall apart. Karen dropped out of one college, then another. She cycled through jobs as a teller, cashier, and dispatcher, but never found steady work. She paid for a course at a beauty school, but then dropped out when she was evicted from her apartment.

When we last spoke to her, in 2002, Karen had just spent several months living in a city shelter. She was about to move into a Section 8 apartment in the Bronx. She had a baby boy, and was living off food stamps, TANF, child support for her son, and a $100 "allowance" from her boyfriend.

Adam's fortunes kept getting better and better, while Karen's quality of life declined. Yet ask Karen about public assistance, and she sounds just like Adam. People just "sit on welfare" and "have more kids," Karen complains. Welfare reform was about bringing fairness to the system. As she puts it, "Get the job and we'll see what we can help you with. But don't say, 'Here, take care of me, I'm not going to do anything.'" Karen speaks with shame about her mother, an alcoholic who raised her and her three siblings on government checks. Decades later, she still cringes at the memory of those elementary-school years, watching as mothers arrived to pick up their kids at the end of the day—all of them dressed in suits because they had just come from work. "How come my mother couldn't work? That's all I kept thinking. I want my child to be able to look up to me," she had told us back in 1997, four years before she moved into a shelter.

Whether they grow up in poverty or are raised in middle-class households, Americans tend to despise welfare and respect the employed. *Hands to Work*, LynNell Hancock's gripping account of three women living through the welfare reform of the Clinton years, starts with the story of her own family's brush with poverty: her proud grandfather, laid off from his job at an Illinois railroad company during the Depression, scrambling for piecemeal work as his family slid deeper into poverty. "I should be able to take care of my own," Pat Hancock told his wife, and he persisted in refusing government rations and relief until the family could not say no. Even through the worst economic times this country has ever seen, there were huddled masses yearning to be bound to a wage and chained to a time clock. If much has changed in seven decades, many millions of struggling Americans—including minorities in the inner city—still cling stoically to this attitude of self-reliance, turning resolutely away from government assistance.[10]

The fact that Adam, who has made enough money to build his own

home, and Karen, who has lost her savings and her home, have similar beliefs about work and welfare speaks to the strength of this mainstream
value. And it also reveals a subtler truth: even the experience of downward
mobility doesn't necessarily shake deeply rooted American attitudes about
work and welfare. Nor does the experience of upward mobility necessarily
strengthen them. Instead, opinions tend to remain fixed, regardless of
the fluctuations in a person's economic fortunes.[11] That tells us something about the power of mainstream culture. The thrust of sociological
research on concentrated poverty points away from this perspective, em-
phasizing instead how the inner-city poor are separated from the rest of
American society. It posits the grip of a debilitating oppositional culture
that screens out the normative messages that infuse the social mainstream.

Of course, sociologists were Johnny-come-latelies to this view. Ronald
Reagan got there first, with his stump speeches about welfare queens
waltzing up to grocery store checkouts to buy steak with food stamps,
trundling back to their Cadillacs with overloaded shopping carts that
hard-hat Americans could not afford. He was among the first social critics
to link persistent poverty with a broken culture, to suggest that the causal
pathway moved from bad values to bad practice, supported on the backs of
hard-working, tax-paying citizens. Richard Sennett's seminal book, *The
Hidden Injuries of Class*, noted the consequences: upstanding citizens had
come to feel like chumps who had been taken for a ride by people who had
figured out how to game the system. The anger directed at welfare abusers
colored the whole issue and obscured from view the genuine neediness of
many who had no other choice. And the sociological literature implied
that this was a view that the payers—certainly not the receivers—endorsed.

In this chapter we see, through the lens of work and welfare, how mistaken these views are. We look at how workers and job seekers in Harlem
have changed—or persisted—in their views about the legitimacy of public
assistance, in how they see the halo of the deserving poor and the horns of
those who are dependent though able-bodied.[12] What we see through
their eyes, I argue, is a powerful commitment to values that pull them
closer to a conservative, "red state" perspective than the liberal, "blue
state" view that most sociologists, myself included, subscribe to. That this
is the case in a population with firsthand experience of poverty and the
strictures of the welfare system—people who in many cases owe their own
success to the child care that a welfare mom contributed so that they could
remain on the job—is powerful evidence of their conventional orientation.

Of the hundred individual Burger Barn applicants we followed over four years (1993 to 1997), and the forty we followed over the course of nine years (1993 to 2002), some experienced rapid gains in their wages and education, while others saw their earnings stagnate and their households sink deeper into poverty. How have their personal experiences of mobility (or immobility) shaped their views about the importance of work and the stigma of welfare? What do they think of those people in their neighborhood who do not work—who survive thanks to a twice-monthly check from Uncle Sam? What moral framework guides these judgments?

"How Bad Do You Need It?"

All of the people we followed were in the labor force—working or looking for work—at the time we conducted our first interviews. Back then, few of them had good jobs. Many were unemployed. Nevertheless, in our initial conversations nearly all of them expressed strong mainstream attitudes about the virtues of work and the pitfalls of welfare dependency. Frequently respondents justified their preference for work over welfare on moral grounds, expressing a belief that work brings dignity and dignified people work. But they also reeled off very practical reasons. A job—almost any job—meant "getting on the escalator," finding a toehold amid the tumult of a fiercely competitive labor market and setting oneself up—hopefully, possibly—for a better job to come. Even poorly paid employment was better than relying on government support. This was a widespread sentiment among recipients and abhorrers of welfare alike, and some who straddled both categories.

When we first met Sean, he was working six days a week at Burger Barn and five nights a week at a security job. He and his wife managed to pay rent and care for their eight-year-old daughter without any public assistance. Anyone could "make it" if they worked hard, the twenty-nine-year-old African American declared; welfare recipients just didn't want to get a job. Having already spent half her life manning the counters at Burger Barn, Patty was receiving food stamps left over from her days on welfare and in consideration of her paltry wages. Nonetheless, she insisted to us that public assistance was just another albatross weighing a poor black woman down. "Best thing you do is do something for yourself and get away from it," she said. You may be as poor as you were under welfare, but you've gained a shot (however slim) at upward mobility.

And you still have your self-respect. "It doesn't matter if [it's] a McDonald's job," said Tawana, a former fast-food worker. "At least you have your dignity. You have a job."

William joined the ranks of the employed when he was in his early teens. At the time, his mother was on welfare, and both she and his father encouraged William to get a job. So, while other children were spending their summers lazing on the deck of the public pool or "vegging out" in front of the television, William was working shifts at city parks, picking up bottles and cigarette butts off the public lawns. "And it was right there that I realized I loved to work," says William, who is now twenty-nine.

As William sees it, work fosters responsibility and builds character. "A person who works is a person who's not afraid to go out and do what they gotta do to earn whatever they got to earn," he says. When he speaks in this way, you get the sense that William is talking about more than just a nine-to-five job: he's really talking about morals, about manliness, about the way he lives his life. "[Working] helped me realize that little things are important," he says. "Like getting to work on time, not being late, not being absent. You know, reliability, dependability. Assurances, security. All these things play a part. Things that you take for granted probably every single day, you get paid for that." A few years after his summer stint cleaning city parks, William started working at Burger Barn. His respect for the working life didn't mean William loved his new job. Burger Barn was as low on the employment totem pole as it was possible to stoop, as William's friends were quick to remind him. The customers were rude; the long hours of flipping, frying, and mopping wore him down. He only worked there, he told us during our first interview in 1993, because he had bills to pay and his mother could not afford to help him. After years behind the counters, William still wasn't used to the feeling of shame that would creep in whenever he told someone where he worked. "When people ask, it's like, 'Yeah, I work in [Burger Barn],'" he said, his voice dropping to a mumble. "I still do that."

But a job at Burger Barn is a job—something to be preferred over being unemployed and on welfare, as William knows well. His mother was receiving welfare checks until he was eighteen, but William has few good things to say about AFDC or public assistance in general. "It's a question of character and it's a question of being trapped," William explained in 1993. By 1997 he was working as a janitor at a New York hospital, making twelve dollars an hour and paying for college classes out of his own savings. Welfare reform was now the law of the land, and William had no problem with that. The system had "gotten totally out of control." People were having kids as casually as they might go downstairs and get a soda, he said. What had started out as a helping hand had turned into a handout, and then an "institution." True, William's own mother had been on welfare for many years, but she had been working in one way or another ever since he was thirteen. There's nobody lazy in his family, William insisted.

William's story is a common one. Many low-wage workers live in a starkly moral universe, holding a strong personal belief in the value of work even as they are confronted, day after day, with lifestyles or attitudes that contradict their beliefs—often within their own families. Many of them dislike welfare, even when it is critical to their own household's survival. Their days on welfare or flipping burgers may be long gone, but the old attitudes remain, continuing to influence the way they approach their work, their family, and their future.

During each of the three waves of interviews we conducted for this study (in 1993–94, 1997, and 2001–2002), we asked the following question about the trade-off involved in welfare versus low-wage work: "Some people think that some jobs pay so little that it's not worth it to work at all if that's the only kind of job available. For women at least, some people think it makes more sense to get on welfare, especially if they have kids and can't afford babysitting. Other people say that no matter how low the pay, it's still better to have a job than to be on welfare. What do you think about that?"

Every time the question was asked, a clear majority of our respondents told us they would choose work over welfare. For many, there was nothing to be discussed; having a job was clearly the better option. Others thought a certain "deserving" group of people ought to receive government handouts—the sick, the elderly—but everyone else should be working. Then there were those who had mixed feelings because, as they pointed out, the jobs available to people trying to get off welfare simply didn't pay. Only a very small number of the people we spoke to suggested that welfare was, on the whole, preferable to even a low-paying job (Table 7.2).[13] Among the respondents in our final wave of interviews, not one said public assistance was the better option.

Deanna was one of the few individuals we interviewed who had trouble deciding between (low-wage) work and (low-benefit) welfare. Back in 1993, when she was taking orders and counting change at Burger Barn, Deanna told us that work was the way to go. Nine years later she was hav-

Table 7.2 Value of low-paying job versus welfare

Would you prefer welfare or a low-paying job?	Wave 1 (1993–94)	Wave 2 (1997)	Wave 3 (2001–2002)
Job	81.7%	72.8%	77.8%
Depends	15.1%	22.8%	22.2%
Welfare	3.2%	4.3%	0%
N	93	92	27

ing second thoughts. She was twenty-six and was about to have a baby. Her husband was pulling down a meager seven dollars an hour as a computer sales rep and just couldn't pay the couple's bills. For the first time in her life, Deanna applied for food stamps and Medicaid. She was finally starting to understand why people turned to public assistance. "They give you cash," she said. "They give you food stamps. They pay your rent. They pay for child care. So if you have someone that's paying for all three of these things, you feel like, 'You know, let them do it.' Because once you get a job and you go and you work, they cut it." Sure, she said, maybe you could start working a fast-food job, but then you'd have your benefits slashed—so what was the point? "It's like, why work there and they're cutting everything and I still can't pay my bills, when I can just let them pay it and not work at all?" Deanna said. "That's the logic that people have towards it."

Welfare reform, which went into effect between our first and second waves of interviews, does not appear to have made work more attractive (Table 7.3). In fact, support for the job option diminished slightly as the years went by. Like Deanna, many of the respondents were teenagers when they first sat down for an interview. After these people had lived a little and learned what it meant to support themselves and their children, the views of some had softened.

In general, however, responses were quite stable over time: more than half of the individuals we followed for the entire decade said they preferred work over welfare at both the beginning and end of our study.[14] Francisco is a case in point. Back in 1993, when "workfare" was still a word used only by policy wonks, Francisco insisted that those on public assistance should be working for their benefit checks, at least a couple days every week—if only to show other people that they weren't "taking your

Table 7.3 Stability of work and welfare attitudes over time

Would you prefer welfare or a low-paying job?	Respondents giving same answer at waves 1 and 2	Respondents giving same answer at waves 2 and 3	Respondents giving same answer at waves 1 and 3
Job	65.8%	58.3%	56.5%
Depends	6.8%	0%	0%
Welfare	0%	4.2%	4.3%
Answer changed in direction of job	11.0%	25.0%	21.7%
Answer changed in direction of welfare	16.4%	12.5%	17.4%
N	73	24	23

money, using it, and then just relaxing." Nine years later, he was working as an assistant manager at a high-end candy shop and café, and living with a roommate in a sparsely furnished, two-bedroom public housing apartment listed under his aunt's name. The twenty-seven-year-old Puerto Rican still believed in the virtue of work. "It opens up doors for other things, whether you know it or not," he said. "It just does. It sucks if you have kids and stuff like that, but I don't think you should let it deter you from trying to get a job, whether the job is minimum-wage or not."

For Francisco, working means acquiring skills, learning how to interact with people, and building self-esteem. "Things happen when you have a job, and you're more apt to say, 'I'm doing this job. [The] pay sucks, but I feel maybe I can do something else.' It kind of boosts your spirits to do other things." He speaks from personal experience: when we first interviewed him, Francisco was bouncing from one low-wage job to the next every few months—dishwasher, then security guard, then office clerk—augmenting his income with food stamps and Supplemental Security Income (SSI) payments. His movement from that low station to dot-com management by the time of our second interview reinforced his view that staying in the game is critical; that it is only by doing so that you can hope to see your lot improve.

Francisco is one of the lucky ones. About half of the individuals we followed for the entire span of the study remained trapped at the bottom of the labor market. These low riders cycled through jobs, lacked benefits, and sometimes became homeless. They include people like Randy, a former drug addict and ex-con who was living off unemployment when we last spoke to him in 2002. Though his financial outlook was grim, Randy was strongly supportive of the idea that working a low-wage job was better than being on welfare. "It's better to have a job, because you feel better about your money when you get it," he told us. This was quite a common attitude among the low riders we interviewed. In fact, during the second and third waves of interviews the low riders were slightly more gung ho about work than any of the other individuals we followed.[15]

Of course a substantial number of low riders do not follow through on their general prescriptions. They believe in work, but they aren't working. They denigrate welfare, but they accept it when circumstances dictate the need. There are many reasons for these paradoxes, including a general disconnect between values and action, and a desire to appear socially acceptable to an interviewer. But the most common reason for the disconnect is the difficulty of combining family responsibilities and work when wages do not cover the cost of caring properly for children through paid child care, when neighborhood safety problems expose kids to danger when they are left alone, and when the responsibilities of motherhood conflict with the desire to work.[16]

Working poor Americans have practical reasons for preferring a low-wage job. They may believe neither option provides an adequate income but insist that minimum-wage work pays better than public assistance. After all, welfare recipients receive their checks only every other week. Getting an actual paycheck often means more money, more often. "They wasn't paying my bills," said Patty of the benefits she used to receive. "It wasn't helping me. . . . You could just get a minimum-wage job and do better than you could ever do" on welfare. This observation has become even more true in the wake of welfare reform. The real value of TANF stipends has been falling dramatically, while the combination of even minimum-wage jobs and the Earned Income Tax Credit has increased the take-home pay of those in the labor force. Many of the working poor are still poor, to be sure. But the welfare-reliant poor are far more impoverished than they once were.

More important, low-wage work has the potential to lead to something better, either directly (through promotions) or indirectly (thanks to the skills and experience gained on the job). A job is a gateway to advancement; welfare is a dead end. In fact low-wage workers are often critical of people who expect too much from a first job and don't seem to understand that it is only a stepping-stone—an "escalator" that, with persistence, will reward the worker with something more stable. "If you do well at a job . . . eventually you can go higher," says Falasha. "That's how I feel. I don't understand when people say they're looking for a job, but they won't go into a fast-food restaurant that [pays] only $4.25 [an hour]. . . . Well, you're the one that needs a job—how bad do you need it? You can't be picky. It's like, how can you say that 'I'm not going to take a job because it only pays minimum wage' but yet you're still on public assistance? That means you need a job. You need some kind of income coming in."

Both of Falasha's parents died in the years between our first and second interviews. In 2002, at twenty-five, she was responsible for her younger brother and sister, as well as her four-year-old son. But even for a person saddled with as many family responsibilities as she has, working minimum-wage jobs is preferable to taking money from the government, Falasha insists. "If you have a job, you don't necessarily have to stay where you're at," says this daughter of African immigrants. "But public assistance is just—you're going to get the money, you're living off a check every two weeks, and how much more can there be? Because you're getting that money based on how many kids you have. Then you have to buy food with the food stamps. I mean, I don't know, just to me, I think it's better having a job." When we last spoke to Falasha, she, her siblings, and her son were still living in a public housing apartment, paying $363 per month in rent. Falasha had found a job as a school safety officer—$26,000 per year, with full benefits. She didn't particularly like the job, but it was the most money that she had ever made on her own, and at least she wasn't living "paycheck to paycheck" anymore. "I am proud of myself [for] being able to get up and go to work and do a job that I probably wouldn't have normally taken," she said. "In my eyes, it's like, 'OK. I'm probably not where I want to be.' But [in] other peoples' eyes, it's like, 'That's good.' You know, 'Keep up the good work.'"

Regardless of whether they had parents with steady jobs or were raised in households on the dole, many of the working poor insist they grew up to believe in the value of work—the former by example, the latter in reaction. Tawana told us that her mother, a teacher, always believed that her job was important because she was helping children learn. Her father, a mechanic, just wanted to provide for the family. Having grown up seeing her parents making money, Tawana wanted a paycheck of her own. "I love to make my own money," she told us in 1997 when she was just twenty. "I can't see how anyone would not want to work for their own." For Karen, in contrast, it was a childhood spent watching her alcoholic mother just "sit on welfare" that motivated her to work and make something of herself. She wants to get off public assistance. She wants to get a college degree. "I'm not a welfare baby," she says. "I can't stand it. I have to have money. I have to be independent. . . . I'll take almost anything, except for Burger Barn."[17]

For women with children, finding a job is often about carving out space for themselves within their relationships with men. Kyesha speaks with resentment about a previous boyfriend who treated her like his "house pet." At our last interview, Kyesha explained that her current boyfriend, Ramsey, is in and out of work, and even when he is unemployed, he still tries to tell her what to do. "When you start living with a man, now he's acting, like, 'Where are you going? What time are you going to be back?'. . . I can't even be trusted," she complains. If she and her boyfriend ever get married, she will continue to work, Kyesha says: "I gotta stay independent. Housewives have to have their private stash, always."

Men, too, talk about working their way to independence. It was the reason that Reynaldo got his first job, at the age of fourteen. He was hungry for CDs and fun money and found a way he could afford them on his own dime—bagging groceries at a store on his block for under-the-table wages. When we first met him in 1993, he had graduated to a job behind the counter at Burger Barn. The job was grueling, the customers were "assholes," the wages as minimal as they could lawfully be—but it was good work experience, teaching Reynaldo how to be punctual and responsible and how to deal with people. His immigrant Ecuadorean father drove cabs, cut hair, repaired TVs. His immigrant Colombian mother worked at a bra factory. She would tell her American-born son, "Until you work hard for a little pay, you never gonna know what a job is." And Reynaldo listened.

Well, sort of. Although he put in two days of work on the weekends at Burger Barn, the job was really just a cover for the two illicit jobs that really fattened his billfold: "running" license plates at the Department of Motor Vehicles on 125th Street ($100 per day), and selling marijuana out on Long Island ($600 to $700 per week). As a license-plate runner, he processed the paperwork for license plates while his employer pocketed money from the insurance companies; as an eighteen-year-old entrepreneur in the drug trade, he'd "bag" marijuana in the back of his car and then hand it off on Long Island to his associate, the pusher. The $80 he made every weekend at Burger Barn might as well have been spare change. "The reason why I did that was so that I could show money in the bank," Reynaldo says. "How could I have all that money and not be working?" The Benjamins flowed liberally into his bank account and out again, buying Reynaldo the kinds of toys that a high school senior craved: clothes, sneakers, booze, a car (in his father's name), and a handgun ("for my protection"). He didn't end up saving any of his ill-gotten gains. Nor did he give any to his parents ("selfish") or his brother ("very selfish"). "I put some money in the bank, but I ended up blowing it all," he says. "I think that's why I stopped doing it. It's not worth it. You don't work that hard for the money, so you just blow it."

Flash forward nine years, and Reynaldo is a very different man. The light-skinned Latino no longer punctuates his sentences with a Harlem homeboy's "nigga." He has a five-year-old daughter and a two-month-old son, and these days when his cell phone rings it's usually his wife, asking him to pick up things like disposable liners for the baby's bottle. During the week, Reynaldo and his family live with his in-laws so that his daughter can attend the kindergarten near their home, which is superior in quality to the school near their apartment. He has his eye on his daughter's future. Instead of roaming the seedy parts of Long Island, Reynaldo works as a doorman on the 3:00 to 11:00 PM shift at a luxurious co-op, making $42,000 a year with benefits. And that doesn't count the tens of thousands of dollars he rakes in during his morning hours as a handyman. He still keeps up with the side jobs, but now they're more respectable—walking dogs and remodeling bathrooms and building basement offices (though still paid in cash, of course). He owns the apartment building he lives in, in the Bronx, which brings him $15,000 in rent every year, and is looking into getting a mortgage loan to buy a second.

The self-reliant attitude that Reynaldo observed at an early age in his parents sticks with him today. "I always was, like, independent," he says. "My parents didn't have money, but they always did their own thing. Like my mother use to do *costura*, sewing, and my father use to do repair work, so everybody used to work for themselves. I didn't really like the idea of working for somebody." Reynaldo says he sold drugs and ran license plates in part to be his own boss. Almost a decade later, he's still working hard for his weekly pay. The fast food and fast money have been transformed into a different kind of hustle—the hustle to support two young kids and also find the time to be with them, to stake a claim on property and also pay off tens of thousands of dollars in credit card debt.

The Wages of Low-Paid Work

We tend to think of work as a means to practical ends—and, of course, it is. But as I have argued before, work is also a moral universe in a culture that has always seen it as the proving ground of character.[18] Nelson Aldrich, Jr., shows us how the independently wealthy flunk this test, and William Julius Wilson shows us how those out of the labor force do, too.[19] The moral high ground belongs to those in the vast middle who are in the labor force.

In this, the working poor are not very different from the rest. True, working a job is sometimes just that—clocking hours, getting paid, establishing a bank account. But it also sustains a person's sense of place in the American cultural universe by locating even low-wage workers on the right side of the moral barrier that separates them from those who have absented themselves from the work world. This belief in the moral value of work remains when low-wage workers become high-paid workers, and when working moms can afford to become stay-at-home moms. Like Carmen, many people want to work even when they don't have to, because working is about becoming the kind of person you want to be. Reynaldo may accept the idea that some people need welfare—in two different interviews, Reynaldo told us that the proper choice "depended" on the circumstances—but he insists nonetheless that work is the basis of a person's morality. "You have to think, 'Well, now I have a job, so I can't be outside hanging out so long. I'm gonna go to the job. I'm gonna go home and do my homework and then I'm gonna go to sleep until tomorrow for school.' Like that."

Especially for the young male workers we talked to, legal employment is a worthy path not just because it means staying off the streets and keeping safe.[20] It is also a decision that broadcasts to other people the kind of men they really are. By accepting poorly paid, underappreciated work, they are consciously rejecting the fast-money, high-risk lifestyle of drug dealing that is often the most visible alternative in the neighborhood. And once they have established themselves in better jobs, they see themselves as role models for their communities. "Working, to me, means so much," said Sean, a twenty-nine-year-old married furniture mover who used to be a swing-shift manager at Burger Barn. "'Specially as a black person. It's a black man getting a job. . . . And when I walk through the neighborhood, I don't think I'm better than nobody. I speak to everybody. But they give me respect."

Cassandra got her first job at the age of fourteen and has held a variety of jobs—Burger Barn worker, shoe salesperson, cashier, telephone operator, and finally customer service representative. While none of these jobs was glamorous, they made Cassandra feel like she was part of the mainstream hustle: "I used to like the fact of getting up early in the morning to get ready for work, and being on the train. And I used to love it when I got off. Because I was tired from doing something. And taking a ride home, and just talking about, 'Well, I have to go to work, so I can't talk long.' Or 'I can't hang out.' So, it made me feel good, because I have something that was positive going on in my life. I wasn't depending on somebody to give me anything. I was doing on my own. It wasn't much, but I was doing it. And it was money that I earned. Nobody put it in my hand saying, 'This is yours for nothing.' It was mine for doing something."

At one point in her life, the only thing Cassandra had looked forward to was her next hit. "I was strung out on drugs, and my life was just totally unmanageable," she says. When we meet in 2002, she is making $26,000 a year working at a health insurance company, with full benefits and the protection of a union. She has started writing and performing poetry, and is trying to get a second job to help her pay tuition for her college-bound teenage son. Clean for many years now, the devout thirty-eight-year-old single mother credits Jesus Christ for leading her out of the moral wilderness of her addiction. She has been free of welfare, too, for more than five years.

In our very first interview, Cassandra didn't give us a clear answer when we asked her about whether she preferred low-wage work or welfare. But at our last meeting Cassandra had come to a definite conclusion: taking a job—any job—was worth the risk, she told us. Being on welfare "means that your life is on this corner and that you don't want to cross the street," she said. "You put limitations on yourself like that. I believe [in] just keep going with it, because if you keep rolling and you take one step, Jesus is going to take two right in back of you. I believe in just keep rolling with the punches. It's like riding a bike—you get on, you learn, you fall down, you get back up, and you try it again."[21]

But what if you were working and still not making enough money to feed your family? Wouldn't that be a blow to your pride? "You'll be like, 'Mommy has a job but we're not eating. Something's wrong with Mommy,'" says Belinda, a thirty-four-year-old African American who worked as a nurse's aide before she was injured on the job. "I mean, you have the work ethics but you have no place."

Sociologist Loïc Wacquant has argued that the devotion that these low-wage workers express toward the moral ideal of work is not something to be celebrated or admired, but is merely an indication of their cultural brainwashing by corporate America. "By complying with the holy commandment of work in that deregulated service sector, they bind themselves to capricious employers for famine wages and thereby desecrate the value of independence; by submitting to degrading mistreatment at the hands of managers and customers . . . they daily violate the ideals of autonomy and dignity that are also core American values," Wacquant writes.[22]

What Wacquant forgets, however, is that these individuals exist in a world not entirely of their own making. As I have argued before, the working poor are neither passive victims nor heroic resisters—they are simply men and women trying to make do and faced with often overwhelming odds. Their devotion to work may seem naive and misplaced to some. But it emerges out of a concordance with mainstream American culture that places work at the center of moral existence and also rests compatibly with frustration over exploitation or the arrogance of high-handed managers. More than a few "love working" but don't particularly like this job or that boss. The high-paid chemical workers David Halle studied bond together in their mutual disrespect for management and disdain for the official work rules, but their identities as "working men" remain.[23] Having spent decades describing poor urban minorities as the source of an oppositional subculture, sociologists have become blind to the long reach of middle-class values. These values are communicated daily by the institutions ghetto kids participate in—schools, churches, and workplaces—and are reinforced by the barrage of the media. Even when their personal experience departs from the expected middle-class path, the normative universe is strikingly familiar and far from oppositional.

Low-wage workers aren't stupid. They know when they are oppressed, when employers take advantage of the fact that they're powerless to complain, when the rules are set up to ensure that they fail. And the whole package makes them righteously angry. They recall times when their pay was cut or their children were left waiting on the corner because the boss wouldn't let them off work on time. Carmen boils when she recalls the sacrifices she made, from waking her kids in the middle of the night to enduring the disapproval of her husband, in order to keep her job. Nonetheless, she will risk the stability of her own marriage to stay on the job because she wants to be her own person, and in this society, that means being a worker.

"Like You Are Half a Person"

In 1993, after nearly a decade of receiving welfare checks, Patty decided she had had enough. She was a single mom with seven children. But welfare "just wasn't worth it," says the thirty-seven-year-old African American. "When I got out of it, they [were sending] not even a $100 every two weeks. Am I supposed to jump through hoops for less than $100? I was like, No, I'm not doing this." The welfare bureaucrats were a nightmare, constantly telling her she was worthless, constantly humiliating her. She was in tears every day. "I thought this was something I would never have to do," she says.

The worst thing about welfare, though, was the public stigma: "Wherever you go and you tell me you are on PA [public assistance], automatically you are treated differently. You are not treated like a hundred-percent person. Just like you are half a person—that's how they treat you, anywhere you go."

Patty was determined to get off. Burger Barn was the only employer that would take her. She started as a crew member and quickly rose up the ranks, eventually becoming a general manager. By 2002 she was enrolled in college full-time—not bad for a former C student. Welfare had kept Patty's bills paid during some of her darkest moments, and partly with its help, she was able to rise above poverty. But she never saw it as a legitimate alternative to work. Welfare made you lazy, kept your self-esteem low, and punished you if you tried to get a job. While low-wage workers could eventually become respected figures, welfare recipients were destined to remain objects of unending ridicule, outcasts whose children were teased mercilessly at school. "It's better to have a job for your self-esteem," says Patty. "If you have no pride, if you have no ethic, and if you really don't care about nothing, go get your check. You will work for it."

The way many Americans see it, welfare recipients are, at best, lazy freeloaders, and at worst, miscreants trying to cheat the system.[24] They are, in short, the moral and psychological opposites of the "honest" citizens who pay their share of sweat and stress for every dollar earned. Poor workers are often more scathing in their criticism than anyone else. "These people that get welfare, have fifteen, sixteen kids," says Rochelle. "[They're] scheming the system. I'm serious. Ain't nothing wrong with them." Rochelle is no stranger to uncertainty: as long as we've known her, she has never been able to hold down a steady job. One month she was behind the cash register and working the grill at Burger Barn for minimum wage; the next she had a job as a telecommunication specialist for ten dollars an hour; skip a few months ahead and she was laid off—and so it went. When we last spoke to her, in 1997, the twenty-two-year-old African American was working at a local YMCA as a day camp counselor and living with her boyfriend and his four-year-old son.

Given that they were supporting their household in part on AFDC payments and food stamps, one might expect Rochelle to be more sympathetic toward other people who receive public assistance. But she had few kind words for them. "They don't have no physical disability, so why can't they get up off their behinds like the average American out here trying to make an honest dollar, and go and work?" she said. "You could work in McDonald's, White Castle, get two jobs—it's better than nothing and being on public assistance." Rochelle told us she was a true believer in welfare reform. As she put it: "Put their behinds to work."

Like Rochelle, many of the working poor believe that public assistance is unfair to hard-working taxpayers like themselves. And they insist that long-term dependency harms welfare recipients, particularly by dissuading them from accruing the work experience that will eventually allow them to rise out of their poverty. In other words, welfare will cause these people to get stuck—and not just for the reason that conservatives often give (that is, by blunting their motivation to succeed). The working poor are also keenly aware that their welfare-receiving neighbors and cousins don't exactly have the résumés that appeal to the average employer. Tawana, for instance, points to her friend's mother, who has been on welfare for twenty-two years. "Now she wants to get a job, you know what?" she says. "They ain't nobody hiring her. You know why? She's been on welfare twenty-two years. No work experience. That's sad. That's sad. She has to go to school all over again, and she's middle-aged. She does not want to do that. She doesn't feel she has to do it. But you know what? Welfare reform say, 'Either you work or you're not going to be on welfare.'" As Tawana and many other low-wage workers see it, welfare is a lie that

starts with the premise that everything will be fine if you accept the government's money. "If you have kids, it's OK to be on welfare?" Tawana asks
incredulously. "I don't think so. I mean, any young teenagers that think it's
OK to be on welfare, how long you going to be on welfare waiting for a
high-pay job to come? And then you're on welfare so long you don't have
any experience."

Vanessa has been on welfare all her life—and has hated herself for it.
"That's all I knew," says the twenty-eight-year-old African American. "I
didn't want that cycle to keep repeating itself. I was on PA, and when I had
my children, they were on PA. I don't want my children's children to be on
PA." She worried in particular about what being on welfare was doing to
her young daughter: "It really struck me one time, because they have these
little plastic EBT [electronic benefits transfer] cards and my daughter said,
'Mommy, I want one of those when I grow up.' And I was like, 'No,
sweetie. You want a bank card. You want a credit card. You don't want this.
You want to be better than this.' And that bothered me. That really bothered me. I said, 'I have to do something because this is a poverty cycle that
just keeps repeating itself.'. . . I want my kids to see that you have to work
in order to make things happen. Don't depend on anybody to take care of
you, because if you do, you'll be disappointed every time. And that's one
lesson I want them to have."

Vanessa was fortunate: she landed a work-study job at her community
college and eventually got off public assistance. Because the low-wage
world doesn't provide workers with enough cash to make it, many at the
bottom of the work world are still entwined in welfare through their dependence on kin. They must rely on family members who receive welfare,
because they can't afford to pay for professional child care, or don't trust it.
Bridget, for instance, will sometimes leave her three young children in the
care of her mom, who is a longtime welfare recipient ("she's been on public assistance since I was small"). The twenty-eight-year-old used to be on
public assistance herself but now works at a college bursar's office. Bridget
happens to be more supportive of welfare than most: "If you need to get
on public assistance, by all means, do it," she says. "Don't be prejudiced
against it, because that public assistance helps you. For example, if you
need to go to school and get your high school diploma, you need to concentrate on school. . . . You need food in the house to make sure your children have [something] to eat. They have to be clothed, and you have to do
your education."

Low-wage workers do make distinctions—some quite familiar to middle-class Americans who have never been near a poor neighborhood or a welfare office. For instance, many of these workers believe the government should support "deserving" individuals who are seriously ill or otherwise physically unable to work.[25] Even Lakisha, the daughter of West Indian immigrants, who calls welfare recipients "a bunch of lazy people . . . [who] just don't want to do nothing," agrees that her tax money should go toward helping people with disabilities. "I feel that if they're going to give welfare to people, give it to people that really can't do nothing for theyselves," said the nineteen-year-old administrative assistant, who was also studying at a local college. "[People who are] disabled, you know, [who] can't really do nothing. Blind. Can't work." Single mothers may be deemed "deserving," at least those whose children are very young or who cannot obtain good child care. At the same time, a lot of resentment is expressed about recipients like Kyesha's mother, Dana, who are thought to be having more babies to bump up their benefits.

There's another criterion that distinguishes "deserving" welfare recipients from all the "riffraff": the fact that they take welfare money for only a short period of time. Low-wage workers almost unanimously believe that welfare should be temporary, to provide unfortunate people with just enough assistance to get them back to the point where they can support themselves. "If you're going to use welfare for a backboard, I have no problem with it, because my mother did it," says Adam, the self-described Republican. "She got on welfare after my father left her. I don't even think [she] was on for five years. She got off. The next thing you know, she worked in the hospital." Relying on welfare for long periods of time—because you don't want to work or you hope to get away with fraud—is roundly condemned by the working poor. Their taxes pay for welfare, they say. It isn't fair for them to have to subsidize welfare recipients who just watch television, hang out in the streets, or do drugs. "I don't want my tax money going out there paying for someone else's kid," Adam says. "I'm paying for my own children."

The welfare bureaucracy has internalized these notions about who deserves to be supported at the public's expense. Its intrusive, antagonizing red tape creates exactly the experience that the architects and supporters of conservative welfare policy had in mind: it makes people feel terrible—infantilized, disrespected.[26] It "works" in the sense that the system generates sufficient distaste to incline most people to get out of it. (It also demoralizes those whose life circumstances make an exit unlikely.) "I constantly got tired of people being in my business," says one former welfare recipient, Vanessa. "You have to report to somebody who acts like the money is coming out of their pocket. That bothers me. Then they treat you like crap. That hurts, and they don't realize how they treat people. And then they sit you in this big office and tell you to be there at ten while they have fifty other people that they told to be there at ten. That's not right. . . . And they will sit there and they will talk to you nasty, like you don't mean anything. You're not an individual person. You're a number." Things were so bad that Vanessa, a devout Christian, felt she needed to pray before going into the welfare office.

Eventually Vanessa got a job as an administrative assistant in the admissions office of the community college she was attending. Even though this work-study job paid just $4.25 an hour, it gave her a liberty most of us take for granted: she could keep her personal life private. She no longer had to plead with a superior-acting clerk when her check failed to arrive. When we first spoke to Vanessa, in 1993, she couldn't really tell us whether she thought a low-paying job or welfare was better—it depended on the circumstances, she said. But in our last interview, Vanessa came down definitively on the side of work: "If you have a choice to work or be on welfare, I suggest you work," she said. "It's not worth it. The humiliation is not worth it. And you will feel better about yourself bringing home a piece of paycheck than no paycheck at all."

Patty remembers the humiliation well. The welfare system seemed to be designed to keep people like herself down.

> They control your life too much. They control your life and they don't let you advance. . . . It's no way you can do better for yourself. All you could do is take what they give you. Settle. Or lie. But who wants to lie to live? Who wants to? Not me. I wasn't raised that way . . . uh-uh. It's not worth it. . . . When I got on public assistance, from the time I got on until the time I got off, it was harder and harder to keep you there. And it's a system made up to keep you there, because otherwise they would help you to get out. These are people that was paying thousands of dollars for a hotel for you to stay in every two weeks and they won't pay four hundred dollars for your rent.

When we last spoke to her, in 2002, Patty still felt a great deal of bitterness toward the mistrustful government bureaucrats who treated her and other welfare recipients like enemies. "Anybody that says you don't work to be on PA is a liar," she said. "You have to tell lies [to stay on assistance]. You got to make up lies that you don't even know about." The last straw for her was when someone came to Patty's co-op and knocked on her neighbors' doors. The welfare agency wanted to know with whom Patty was living. "I was pissed, because I felt that was like a total violation," Patty said. "Who are you to walk around and question my neighbors? Who are you to talk my business like that to my neighbors? I just thought that was the biggest violation, and I never went back."

Making Compromises

One morning Latoya and her husband Jason pile the kids into their minivan. The daughters Ellie, fifteen, and Keena, thirteen, are both scheduled for physicals at their family doctor's office. While Jason drives, Ellie pops open a can of Pringles—the family has stashed a whole case of the chips in the back luggage space, a gift from their church's food bank. As the 1995 navy blue Dodge Caravan departs from the family's Bronx housing complex and weaves into the city traffic, Latoya and Jason start reminiscing about the road trips they've taken in recent years, many of them down South, where their late, much beloved church pastor had family. They plan to take an investigatory trip to South Carolina in the coming summer, to help them make up their minds about moving there. Their littlest child, eighteen-month-old Jacob, has severe asthma. He needs to get far away from the Bronx and its sickly industrial air, Latoya reasons.

Today's visit to the doctor is bound to be less stressful than most, thankfully. Latoya's daughters are seeing their family doctor—the same one they've had for years, a round, middle-aged African American woman with a soft, warm face. She holds court in a housing project in Harlem, in an office adorned with clues about the clientele: placards in Spanish and English, notices touting information about Medicaid and a state program for free or low-cost health care for children, photos of smiling black and brown children on the bulletin board above the reception desk. Ellie, not seeing her own picture on the board, rifles through her mother's wallet to find one to post. Meanwhile, young parents wait more or less patiently with their children, chatting, dozing, munching on chips, slurping on sodas.

The checkups turn out fine. God is watching over them. Now, couldn't

He do something about the bills, Latoya wonders? Even on one salary, Latoya and Jason manage to pay them off every month, but the medical expenses—especially for little Jacob—have been growing like a virus. Jacob's asthmatic attacks have brought him and his parents to the hospital emergency room on several occasions, and have cleared out the family's savings. Medicaid helps with the kids' bills, but there's always more to pay. The last time Jacob had to be driven to the hospital, Latoya wound up in a knot of icy panic. Without new jobs in South Carolina, the family cannot afford to move. But they have to find a way, because Jacob can't breathe here. Latoya's own mother died of asthma just seven years before. If they cannot make it to South Carolina . . .

At times like these, Latoya calms herself with prayer. Work, too, has been a salvation. Throughout the years, through all our conversations with her, Latoya has held firm to the principle that work— even low-wage work—is better than welfare. But has all the effort paid off? It's true that she has been lucky: she and her husband have been able to get by without government help. "Well, God makes a way for us," she says. "I don't get public assistance. I don't get food stamps." But then she looks at Jacob and realizes how tenuous her hold is on this comfortable and secure reality. No matter how hard she tries, her family continues to only just get by. Maybe she *should* be on public assistance. The last time she tried to apply for food stamps, Latoya spent all day talking to people at the agency, only to be told at the end of the day that she earned two dollars an hour too much to qualify. In a way, she was relieved—at least she didn't have to bother with that cold and lifeless bureaucracy anymore.

People like Latoya distinguish themselves from the "undeserving"—as one single mother described them, those people who "don't do nothin' but sit around all the time and get this money." Yet those who get up and run off to work every day can still find themselves spinning in place. The choices can remain few, and the compromises many. "I've been on welfare for maybe about a year and a half," Silena told us in 1993. "And I don't like it, you know what I'm sayin'?" Sure, some women had babies so they could get even more money—but Silena wasn't like that. Even when she was taking the government's checks, she was always trying to keep "a little job on the side." Not long after our first interview with her, Silena found something more than a "little job": a position as a receptionist that paid seven dollars an hour. It was the most she had ever earned, and Silena finally had the chance to go off public assistance. Another pregnancy, however, put an end to that opportunity. When we last spoke to her, in 1997, she was twenty-five years old, living in her own apartment with a seven-teen-month-old daughter and a three-year-old, working as a cashier at a local supermarket, and making just five dollars an hour. And she was re-ceiving welfare once again:

> It's rough. The holidays is coming around. Her father's not there to help me now. My parents don't help me. My brother, he has his own child. You understand? So how am I supposed to survive? The wel-fare, all I get is $66 every two weeks, plus the food stamps. The food stamps. I get $200 a month. What am I supposed to get with $66? Mind you, I got to buy Pampers. I need my little personal necessities. Sanitary napkins, soap . . . $66 is nothing. And I'm really not going to be depending on no man too much neither, because every time they do something for you, they throw it up in your face. Depends on, you know, the situation. You get the little knuckleheads that act real crazy. You know.

Low-wage workers want to accept mainstream arguments against welfare, yet the moralism behind those arguments goes only so far. Difficulties with child care, transportation, and health care often force these individuals to move from morality to reality. While virtually all of them may feel that work is better in an absolute sense, when it comes right down to their personal lives, they can't always make the "better" choice. "If you get a job and it's paying low, if it's helping you survive until you can find something better, then I will prefer to do that than get on welfare," says Deanna. "But if you can't do nothing with the job that you're at, and it's not helping you eat, helping you feed your children, then you . . . take the welfare."

For these individuals, the choice between welfare and low-paid work doesn't seem like much of a choice at all. "[There's] always talk of getting people off of public assistance, but there's no work for them to go to," says Latoya. "How do you get people off of public assistance [to] where they can make affordable money to pay for a babysitter and food costs and housing costs and clothing costs? You can't do that. They don't have that yet. So a lot of people still on public assistance and work just so that they can meet their housing, their clothing and babysitting costs."

It's a topic that Kathy Edin and Laura Lein have written about extensively: the barriers that single mothers face in trying to pull themselves out of poverty by their bootstraps—while still respecting themselves as mothers. "Not only must mothers ensure that their children are sheltered, fed, and clothed, they must also see that they are supervised, educated, disciplined, and loved," Edin and Lein write in their 1997 book, *Making Ends Meet.* "Since neither affordable health insurance nor child care was available to most low-wage workers, mothers who chose work over welfare often had to trust their family's medical care to county hospital emergency rooms and their children's upbringing to the streets."[27] Some single mothers want desperately to get off public assistance, but they also know that breaking free of the welfare cocoon places their children at the mercy of other dangers. Women worry about how their children will be treated by child care providers. They mention cases of abuse and insist they couldn't leave their children with "just anybody."

"They want so much money for child care. And you either on a long waiting list, it's too much money, or you got to rely [on] somebody you know," says Karen, who has a three-year-old son, Roy. "Either way, I think it's stressful." When Karen found a job as a teller at a bank, her son's father was taking care of the boy. Then the couple broke up and he refused to care for Roy anymore. Karen found a babysitter, only to discover that she was smoking marijuana and sending Roy downstairs to her mother's place. "My son ended up with ulcers in his mouth. His mouth was bumpy, his hands, his feet. And I paid her a hundred dollars a week. . . . I had to quit that job to take care of my son." Even those parents who are able to find good babysitters or day care are concerned that they won't be able to spend enough time with their children. "If you be at work, who's going to take care of the kids, you know?" says Richard, the father of four children:

Now if you're working and you want to get a babysitter, depending on the way the kids are, sometimes you have to pay extra. Now your money's going down, because now you got to pay a babysitter. And you got to pay your rent, you got to pay this, you got to pay that. So your money goes real low. You have to get two or three jobs. Now you get two or three jobs, now you're spending less time with your kids now. And the kids change. . . . If you don't spend time with your kids, the kids are not going to know you. They're not going to respect you. They're going to—when you tell them to do something, they say, "Why should I listen to you? You never here."

Employers who refuse to give working parents time off when their child is sick also take the shine off of the job. Parents don't have to worry as much when they can count on a relative or close friend to provide child care—but such babysitters are themselves often on welfare. Dana, Kyesha's mother, has been on welfare for about twenty-five years, and for at least fifteen of them she has been responsible for looking after other people's children, including her own grandkids. Without Dana's help, Kyesha would not have been able to work.

Even if reliable child care can somehow be found outside of family and friends, the cost is sometimes too exorbitant for one or even two wage earners to shoulder. If all the money goes to child care, then why even work? "If the job is paying that low and welfare can pay more, then go with the welfare," Florida suggests. "Because if you've got kids, you don't want to hear them saying they're hungry. That's something that would kill a mother."

In a similar way, the costs of commuting present a barrier for aspiring workers from ghetto neighborhoods. Those who can't find a job in their neighborhood, or who prefer not to work there, have to spend both time and money traveling to and from work, which eats into wages, cuts down on family time, and reduces the net advantage of working. The respondents in our study were lucky, in a sense, because New York has the most comprehensive public transportation system in the country—with relatively expensive fares (now two dollars) but a frequency and extensiveness that can't be beat. Nevertheless, the problems of child care and commuting can quickly compound. At one point, Carmen's commute meant that she had to wake her children at 5:00 AM, take them to the Brooklyn Laundromat where she was working (an hour on the subway), and then blow up an inflatable bed there so that the girls could sleep some more. They would often get back home as late as 7:00 PM.

Health care costs, in particular, are the sort of expense that can collapse a fragile budget built around low-wage work. Latoya barely can pay the exorbitant emergency-care bills for Jacob's severe asthma, even with government help through Medicaid; Kyesha, who makes too much to qualify for Medicaid, was thousands of dollars in debt because of medical expenses for her diabetes and her son's asthma. Even as staunch an opponent of welfare as Adam, the conservative businessman, recognizes that people who want to leave welfare often can't afford to lose their Medicaid coverage. "I believe if the government were to have some way where they would put people to work but keep them with the health benefit, more people would go out there to work," he says.[28]

When the desire to work and practical needs pull in opposite directions, the working poor do what everyone else does: they make compromises. They start combining public assistance with other sources of income. They start getting help with child care and health care from family and friends. Sometimes the welfare bureaucracy is tolerant of the paid work. Other times, the low-wage worker has to keep the extra income on the down low.

In the United States, making the choice between work and welfare is not as simple as weighing dollar amounts and checking off benefits. It has become, particularly in this post-AFDC era, a matter of morality first, with compromise the afterthought.

The dilemma with which this chapter begins presents two options that generate equal incomes: low-paid work and low-benefit welfare. Yet this is not really the choice that people like Latoya or Kyesha, Adam or Carmen are talking about making when they speak about work and the opportunities it affords them. In their minds, the only choice is between welfare and a *good* job—one with high wages, reasonable hours, and good benefits. They are not comparing two scenarios frozen in time. They are looking along the arcs of two distinct life trajectories. For them, low-wage work is not a destination; it is the first step along a career path that ultimately will bring about higher earnings and a better quality of life. The answer, they insist, is obvious.

But there are always moments of doubt. Is it worth it to work so much, for so little pay? And when you finally do make it, will you even be able to appreciate it? Late one night, after a long day of making sandwiches, ironing clothes, and fretting about her job, Carmen lies back on her bed and picks up a glossy magazine. On the cover there are two women enjoying a day's work on a farm, milking cows in their clean, long dresses. "This is the kind of life I want," she tells herself. If only working hard could get her there.

8

Dreams, Deferred

Aspirations and Obstacles in Work and Family Life

❦

The men and women who toil in the underbelly of America's urban economy do not have unreasonable hopes for the future. But reality strays from expectation for many Americans, especially those from poor neighborhoods. Without higher education and the right connections, a well-paying job is often elusive. Tuition money and long work weeks discourage workers from returning to school. Soaring real estate prices keep home ownership beyond the reach of many working-class families. And aspirations for a contented family life bump into the prickly realities of the ghetto. Race and class are themes in this story, though few of my respondents would be willing to attribute their difficulties to those impediments. In fact, they look down on those who blame the Man for their troubles. Despite ample sociological evidence that racial discrimination is both real and consequential, the working poor insist that the best way to get ahead is to ignore racism and prove the bigots wrong.

Their focus instead is on the personal: bad decisions made, projects that didn't pan out, hopes that turned sour. Low-wage workers cling to the belief that they can make it by pulling themselves up by their bootstraps, and in this they resemble most Americans. That is no accident, as Chapter 6 argued. The working poor inhabit a familiar, mainstream cultural universe that preaches self-direction, personal responsibility, and the individual's capacity to control her own fate. American culture blinds most of us—

poor and middle class alike—to the structural forces that play a powerful role in determining life options.[1]

The resolute denial that one's birthright determines the future calls to mind the character Jurgis Rudkus, the strong and brash Lithuanian immigrant in Upton Sinclair's 1906 novel *The Jungle*, who watches his family fall into hunger and despair in the meatpacking ghettos of turn-of-the-century Chicago. "I will work harder," Jurgis insists each time that tragedy strikes his loved ones. But what if working hard gets you only so far?

In this chapter we will look at the dreams that the workers we have met cling to, as they scrub Formica counters, change dirty diapers, and spend weary nights studying for exams. Do aspirations change for those who make it out from under the long shadow of ghetto poverty? Do they wither among those who remain stuck—in Harlem, in the Bronx, in an eternal cauldron of family and financial problems? What, if anything, did the experiences of these workers in the boom economy of the 1990s do to alter their attitudes about the opportunities and obstacles before them?

Making Plans and Making Moves

When we first met up with Lanice, the African American teenager was struggling to find a steady job. The last few companies she had worked for had gone out of business or moved. Burger Barn wouldn't hire her. Lanice wasn't picky: she said she'd work at any kind of company, so long as she had an opportunity to advance. In fact, she told us she'd be happy to stay at the same company for ten years—the idea of stability appealed to her. Her views on relationships were much the same. Some girls liked to chase guys and serial date. "That ain't me," she told us in 1993. "I want the settled life, I want the house and the dog and the two-point-five kids, you know— I want that life."

Lanice finished high school but didn't go any further over the next several years—except for taking some adult-education classes at the Learning Annex. "I will only be able to further my education when everything else in my life starts to even out," she told us. Things took time to even out. In one year, she applied for more than twenty jobs, mostly at retail stores like Victoria's Secret and Pier One. When she found work, it never seemed to last long—maybe a few months, maybe a week, at $7.50 to $12.00 an hour. But Lanice's own attitude was changing as well. Whereas before she talked about keeping at the same job for ten years, Lanice now admitted she found it hard to stay put: "I'm just kind of isolated in my little cubicle, it becomes boring for me," she said in 1997, when she was working as a sales representative for a telemarketing firm.

With almost reckless confidence in herself, Lanice eventually made things work out. When we last spoke to her in 2002, she had been an administrative assistant for a company in the entertainment industry for two years. She was making $42,000 a year and loving every minute of it. Her boss, a demanding taskmaster, had cycled through seventeen administrative assistants in the previous year but had taken an immediate liking to Lanice, who was personable, a quick learner, and a tolerant subordinate—someone who didn't take offense at the stream of Post-It notes left on her desk, with things not done written in big letters and underlined. "Everybody can't seem to deal with that type of temperament," her boss lamented.

Experience—and success—have made Lanice more ambitious. At the age of twenty-six, she has finally found a job she is content with, but she is clear that she doesn't want to stay there the rest of her life. Now she has bigger plans. Lanice is starting her own business, a consulting firm that will help individuals, schools, and small companies with fund-raising and networking. She has already hooked up with an accounting firm and a legal service and is now intent on schmoozing her way to the major leagues. In fact, she told us that just the other day she had met a former star football player for the Dallas Cowboys at a business seminar. "There are people already actively doing this, [who] are already at a nice level," she says. "And with their assistance, I feel that I can actually propel [myself] to the same level."

While Lanice has been forging her own successful career path, she has veered off the traditional family track. When she was younger, she told herself that if she didn't find someone and have children by the age of twenty-eight, she "wasn't going to do the child thing." But now she is willing to be more flexible. "Although I was putting those limits on myself, I wasn't actively [dating or] . . . being in places where I could meet people or people of quality," she says. "Because I don't think I'm a bad-looking person, so sure I get approached, but it's not the right quality of person that I want, so what good is that?" She hopes to get married and have children in the next five years, but "if not and it's just me," she says, "I hope that I can say that I'm fulfilled in my life."

Lanice's designs on the future are fairly typical among those voiced by the people we found working in Harlem's Burger Barn restaurants in the mid-1990s. First, they want a job that pays well, is secure, and comes with health insurance and other benefits. They desperately want to leave their days doing retail or slaving at Burger Barn behind them. Then, those who do make it—those who find their way into more exclusive circles of white-collar work—set new objectives for themselves. Like Lanice, many of them hope to be more autonomous, to start businesses of their own, and get out from under the thumb of a bureaucratic boss.

These men and women do not dream about completely unattainable goals. Age alone inclines them toward realism. "My ultimate goal in life? Like, what would be my dream?" Patty—a thirty-seven-year-old mother of seven, a veteran of countless tours of duty at Burger Barn—ponders the question for only a second. "My dream is to pay all my bills with my first week's pay," she says. "That's my dream."

Lanice, too, is not asking for much. "Financially secure does not mean that my house is going to be on MTV *Cribs*," she points out. "It means that I will be working for myself and able to pay my bills and not worry about money. It just means that I'll be able to take care of me, do the things that I want to do and help my mom and just live a real fulfilled life. That's secure to me."

Lanice's trajectory is typical in another sense: her career aspirations evolved over time. More than four out of five of the individuals we followed throughout the eight years of the study changed their views about what a "dream" job would be. Lanice wanted to be a pharmaceutical salesperson, then a public relations manager, then a model. Amy was determined to become a nurse, then an obstetrician, then a social worker. Anita hoped to become a hotel director, then an accountant, then the owner of her own restaurant. This is to be expected. Whether middle class or working class, the dreams one has for the ideal job at eighteen will most likely take a different shape by twenty-eight.

Higher flyers tend to become more ambitious with time, while low riders often see their expectations dwindle away. Consider Nolita. When she was younger, she had a fascination with hair and aspired to be a beautician. Nolita was accepted to a cosmetology school after dropping out of high school, but then she ran way from home and moved into a group home, and her new school near the home didn't offer cosmetology. When we first met her in 1993, the African American teenager had decided she wanted to be a model—she went to a modeling agency with a friend and was accepted. But Nolita soon gave up on that option: she had a child, got married, and then had another child. In 1997, she told us she intended to become a home health aide—she was mulling over possible programs—but it was difficult finding child care, and she never followed through on her plans. When we last met up with her in 2002, Nolita was still talking about finishing her home health aide certification, but told us she would be happy if she could just return to her old job at a movie theater. "It was interesting, [you] got a chance to move around. You're not confined to one space. [It's] not so boring," she said. By then, Nolita was separated from her husband, living in Section 8 housing, and supporting herself and her children solely on public assistance.

Patty, in contrast, rose methodically up the management ladder at Burger Barn, and her expectations for the future grew with each step. She had started off as a crew member making the minimum wage. By the time we met her in 1993, Patty had been promoted to crew chief, and she told us she had her eyes on a bigger prize. She was confident she had the experience and people skills to run the show at the restaurant. Plus, she had five kids to feed; she needed more money. "My goal is to be a manager. And until I make management at Burger Barn I will not even consider another job," she said. Patty did eventually become a general manager at Burger Barn, pulling in $545 every week. But she left the fast-food chain in 1998 and headed back to school full-time to get an associate's degree. Fast food wasn't good enough for her anymore: "Now I need to get what I deserve, and I won't settle for Burger Barn," she said in 2002. "I won't settle for what [they] think [they're] going to give me. I'm never going to get on a floor again. Certain things I'm never going to do again. I'm not going to run [a] register all day, no more."

Other workers cling to the same career goals no matter what happens—and there's no clear trend line for them, upward or downward, in terms of their future prospects. Jesús, for instance, is one of the low riders in the study, a high school dropout whose wages remained stuck below the fifteen-dollars-per-hour mark. Ever since he was a boy, Jesús has wanted to become a veterinarian. "With the attitude and the people that I got behind me, I should be somewhere in the veterinarian field—out there studying in Africa or something," the twenty-four-year-old Puerto Rican told us in 1997. "That's what I really want." But he left high school in the tenth grade and got in trouble with the law. Veterinarian school seemed completely out of the question. He was living at home with his mother in Harlem. But Jesús persisted. He got his high school equivalency degree. He landed a job in a veterinarian's office as a technical assistant—the pay was $11.50 an hour, with full benefits. He wasn't a doctor yet, but at least he was one step closer to his dream.

One might argue that low-wage workers like Jesús need a reality check: How is he ever going to become a veterinarian if he can't even finish college? But if their career aspirations end up being unrealistic—thanks to limited opportunities, abilities, or willpower, take your pick—at least these determined workers move *part way* toward their goals. Deanna, for instance, may not lay claim to the keys to the executive washroom within five years, but it's clear that she is headed in the general direction of success. Her last two office jobs have paid her more than $35,000 a year, and at the telecommunications and cable company where she used to work, she had plowed her way from sales-rep peonage to low-level management in two years.

Of the individuals we followed throughout the study, perhaps half had career aspirations that could be called realistic, given their past performance and achievement; you could reasonably see them completing the requirements for their dream job in five to ten years. But almost as many low-wage workers weren't anywhere near their desired profession. Take Victoria, a forty-four-year-old African American who can't seem to hold down a job but still talks wistfully about her dream of running a hair salon. Or consider Belinda, a thirty-four-year-old African American who wants to be a lawyer but is struggling to finish her bachelor's degree; her last paid employment as a nurse's aide ended when she severely injured her back. Of course, dreaming the improbable dream is not behavior unique to the working poor: many of today's college students believe they will someday be millionaires.[2]

Workers who acquire additional years of education tend to become more ambitious about their career plans. Natalie, for instance, told us back in 1993 that she wanted to be a registered nurse. Getting an education is important, she told us then, because you can't get anywhere without it. In 1995, she studied for three months at a state college, then dropped out because she couldn't afford the tuition. But even that brief time in school had helped her to reevaluate her career options. When we caught up with her two years later, she told us she wanted to be a doctor. She had started to major in biology at her old state college, and was planning to head to another school upstate to continue her studies. Natalie confessed to us in

2002 that she had an intensely personal reason for her career choice: as someone who suffered from sickle-cell anemia, she wanted to be able to help other people in her situation.[3]

Of course, it isn't always clear which way the causal arrow points. Did tacking on more years of education propel Patty from her initial dreams of managing a Burger Barn to later dreams of managing a human resources division, or did she go to college because she was a driven person to begin with, with bigger dreams in her future? Did getting her bachelor's degree transform Tamara's sense of possibility, or was her early desire to become a beautician just a hesitant half-step for an ambitious woman who would later realize she *really* wanted to own her own restaurant (although she actually became a social worker)? Whatever the reason, more than seven out of ten of those workers in our study who were moving up the higher-education track expressed more ambitious career goals as time went by—moving from salesperson to paralegal, from physical therapist to lawyer, from "whatever makes money" to a job in the computer industry.

Then there are people like Francisco, whose career goals simply drift. A twenty-seven-year-old Puerto Rican, Francisco told us back in 1993 that he wanted to go to law school and ultimately become a judge. Then Francisco took an introductory psychology course in college. He was fascinated by the teacher and the way she taught; soon afterward, he was talking about his plans to work in a hospital or even to start a therapeutic practice of his own. "What happened is I went to college and I found out that there's so many other things out there," he said in 1997. "You know, how college really . . . [had] a big impact in my life. It's changed everything. I was exposed to so many different things. That's why I tell everyone, if you can really go away to college—even if you do it for [a] year—do it, because the experience is like—there's nothing like it." Francisco didn't end up finishing college, and he has not taken any significant steps toward achieving his career dreams in law or psychology. He believes that not getting his degree has held him back from trying out new lines of work: "I don't have anything to fall back on. . . . I wish I had this degree to say, 'I have a degree in this. I'm pretty sure this allows me to do this or get into that. You can see that I have an education.' Without it, some jobs that I would like to apply for, they're like, 'As long as you have a B.A., it doesn't matter.' Then they're like, 'Come on. Come aboard.' But not having it, it's just, like, 'Do I apply?'"

For many of the former Burger Barn workers, higher education is a means to a higher income and a job pushing paper instead of a mop. For others, however, getting that diploma is also a matter of getting respect— self-respect, and respect from others. Vanessa, for instance, wants to finish college so she can be a good role model for her two kids. "I don't want my kids to come to me with an excuse," she says. "Like, 'I don't want to go to school. You didn't go.' I want them to see, 'Here's my high school diploma, here's my associate's, here's my bachelor's. I don't want an excuse from you.' That's how I feel. I've never really had anybody to really look up to, and I want my kids to have somebody to look up to."

Running into Roadblocks

Many Americans fall short of the goals that they set for themselves, even if they come from a privileged background. Still, disappointed ambitions are, not surprisingly, more common for people who venture out from poor neighborhoods. About a third of the respondents we followed through the decade of the study expressed a desire to become a doctor, a lawyer, or an accountant. By 2002, none of them could lay claim to these professions. The person who came closest was Helena, a twenty-six-year-old Dominican American who, instead of becoming an accountant, had landed a management job at an insurance company. The last time we spoke with her, she was making $62,000 a year with full benefits and managing an office of thirteen people.

What holds these individuals back? Many have no real idea what it takes to get there: the long years of schooling, the high level of academic performance. They lack the connections, time, and resources to find the kinds of internships that their more advantaged competitors can boast of on their law school applications. They may not know such things are even required, in part because they are unlikely to know anyone personally who has realized such a lofty ambition. And the schooling costs, big time. Every year of added tuition and forgone earnings is another barrier that makes it harder for someone "graduating" from Burger Barn to find their way to med school.

The disparity between dreams and opportunities does not go unnoticed. Vanessa, for instance, laments that even when she gets her college degree, she still won't be able to find a job she truly loves. "A high school diploma doesn't mean anything, a college diploma doesn't really mean anything," she told us in 1997. "And it's sad because people used to say to me, 'Oh, it's not what you know, it's who you know.' And I used to look at them and be like, 'Yeah, right, I don't believe that.' But now I do. I really do."

For many who aspire in vain to join the professional class, it comes down to a lack of money. Falasha has long dreamed of becoming a lawyer—corporate copyright at first, then entertainment—but the twenty-five-year-old daughter of African immigrants has had trouble paying for college. After a short stint at a local college, she had to drop out because the tuition was too expensive. She's back in school at another college now, but she is struggling to study hard, work full-time as a school safety officer, and take care of her five-year-old son. Falasha has dropped her sights from law school; she now hopes that one day she will get a master's degree, go into journalism, and start her own magazine. But given how far she still has to go to complete her education, this may just be more wishful thinking. "I don't feel like I'm where I need to be in life," Falasha says. "I wouldn't even be proud to tell [people] that I'm still in school because . . . it's been an ongoing battle for me and school for a long time."

The communities in which they are brought up don't always support these workers and their big dreams. Lanice complains that she can't get any encouragement from her family. They don't expect to see her do well and tend to throw cold water on her ambitions, she says.

> No matter how enthusiastic I become, no matter how many facts I bring to them, it's like, "No." It's not that they say bad things about me personally, but they don't try to even share for a second to get out of their own negativity . . . and it becomes very draining, because every time, then, that I see them, especially once I mention that I'm doing something, it's like, "Well, what happened? Where's all this money? Or where's all this fame or where is all this?" So it's like a constant reminder that these particular people, no matter what you do, are always going to have something negative to say about it, especially if you can't show them the money, as Jerry Maguire said.

Of course no discussion of blocked opportunity would be complete without mention of race. More than two-thirds of the men and women we interviewed throughout the ten years of this study believed that employers practiced racial discrimination (Table 8.1).[4] (Answers to this question were not terribly stable: about half of respondents changed their answers—in either direction—the next time they were interviewed.)[5] African Ameri-

Table 8.1 Beliefs about racial discrimination by employers

Do employers discriminate?	Wave 1 (1993–94)	Wave 2 (1997)	Wave 3 (2001–2002)
Yes	77.9%	69.2%	70.8%
No	22.1%	30.8%	29.2%
N	86	91	24

cans in particular were seen to be the targets of workplace discrimination. Many black respondents volunteered that immigrants, "Mexicans," and whites were favored at their expense, though some thought Hispanics were also treated unfairly.

More broadly, many low-wage workers believe that people judge them not on their individual merits but by their status as a member of a group—whether racial, geographic, or some other kind of identity. To gauge the prevalence of this perspective, we asked our respondents this question three times over the course of our study: "Some people believe that they will always be treated as individuals, that whatever they're like as individuals is all that matters. Other people say, 'No, your individuality doesn't matter. People will judge you by your skin color or the neighborhood you come from.' What do you think?"

In each wave of interviews, large majorities said that people were judged by their skin color, the neighborhood they came from, or another kind of discernible identity (Table 8.2).[6] The proportion of respondents professing this belief grew over time.[7]

When the workers we interviewed mentioned employers who discriminated, they usually referred to cases in which bosses had shown an aversion to hiring or working with African Americans, or people of color more broadly. Belinda, for instance, describes one time when she spoke to a hiring manager about a job over the phone. The woman must have assumed Belinda was some race other than black, she says, because when she arrived for her interview and said she had an appointment, she was told to wait—and had to cool her heels for three hours. Eventually Belinda overheard the woman on the phone saying, "She's not special," and she decided to leave. Then there was the time that Belinda was working as a nurse's aide and her assistant supervisor was Puerto Rican. The woman went to great lengths to intimidate the black female workers, Belinda says, but she left the Hispanic workers alone—even though they didn't work as hard.

Table 8.2 Beliefs about discrimination generally

Do people judge others by skin color, neighborhood, or other group identity?	Wave 1 (1993–94)	Wave 2 (1997)	Wave 3 (2001–2002)
Yes	64.2%	82.4%	88.9%
No	35.8%	17.6%	11.1%
N	67	74	27

Larry, a twenty-nine-year-old Puerto Rican, remembers the discrimination he routinely saw at his old job at Burger Barn. Employers discouraged Caribbean immigrants from working at the restaurant, he alleges. "You know, they was like, 'Well, your body odor,' or 'You can't speak English.' Little things like that. But they dressed it up with, 'You don't have the qualifications that we're looking for at this particular time.' You know." The manager at that Burger Barn was African American. When we last met with him, Larry was working as a computer technician at a municipal office, and he said he still encounters discrimination—this time, from his supervisor's boss, who happens to be Puerto Rican. "He will do everything in his power not to be Puerto Rican, and he will hire only people who are nonethnic," Larry says. "If you're not from England or from the Midwest, he won't really hire you. . . . If you're ethnic of a tan complexion, he will have a hard time hiring you. He'll deny it, but it shows otherwise."

Some workers are convinced that they have two strikes against them— race and neighborhood. "For a job, they'll look at your address or see you come from Harlem or Brooklyn or whatever, and they'll think, 'Well, we'll hire him, but we got to watch him,'" says Randy, a forty-three-year-old African American who has spent much of his life shuttling between low-paid jobs. The problem is most acute, he thinks, among black bosses, who are more inclined to think themselves superior to the man at the bottom. "I'd rather work for a white man," Randy notes. "They'd treat you a lot better. A black man is going to make you, you know, lose your head, and you don't know what you might do. The way they talk to you, it's a shame." The lack of respect that black people have for one another is visible not just in the workplace but everywhere, Randy says. "The white people don't come in our neighborhoods and rob us. . . . So I don't believe in all that brother stuff. If you didn't come out of my mother, you ain't my brother."

Ironically, the conviction that discrimination matters grows more powerful for those who do well in the labor market. When we first met Adam in 1993, he told us flat out that he didn't think race had ever played a role in his being turned down for a job. Of course, whites tended to get more of the jobs, he said, but that was because they had more education. Nine years later, Adam had risen up the ranks at a unionized courier company; he was making $70,000 a year with full benefits, and people in the company were encouraging him to become a supervisor. By then, he had a more nuanced—and less optimistic—picture of the employment scene. On the bottom rungs of the corporate ladder, he said, "they don't judge by skin color or anything like that." But once you move up into the rarefied ranks of management, things change:

> The supervisor—what they call a street supervisor, one who is on the lower level—I've never seen a minority that got hired [above] that. That was bad. Even though we've seen some great supervisors, even one that graduated from here, who happened to be Hispanic, and he had a Columbia University master's degree and all, he was a street-level supervisor. They would never hire him up to be a manager. . . . That's where I see them judging by the color of your skin. But as far as working in the lower level, it all depends on the type of person you are. . . . I can't say why [this is], I don't know why. I mean, I couldn't really speak up on it, because I was the lower level. I tried to get some of the supervisors to speak up on it, but a lot of them would—after a while they get frustrated, [and] they would usually just quit, because they know it's like a dead end. "I'm a supervisor, but here you get another supervisor who is Caucasian who could come in. I've been here six years, and three months after he's here, he's a manager, while I'm still a supervisor." I was like [laughter], "I don't understand it."

Jennifer Hochschild's book *Facing Up to the American Dream* provides some context for Adam's observation: surveys show that middle-class African Americans are far more likely to express frustration about racism and anxiety about their future progress than poor African Americans.[8] If Adam is to be believed, the brunt of employment discrimination may be occurring at the higher job levels, and this would help explain why less successful African Americans—relatively speaking—aren't so conscious of it or concerned about it. Take Kevin, for example, a twenty-five-year-old African American who makes $9.50 an hour in his position as a child care worker for the city's Department of Juvenile Justice—the equivalent, he quips, of an underpaid corrections officer. At his office "everyone is my color," Kevin points out, and he says he hasn't experienced any problems there. "Sometimes race is an issue, but if you have the skills and the smarts and intelligence or whatever, it sometimes doesn't matter," he says. People like Kevin may be too far down the ladder to see active discrimination. Those who climb into management have a different vantage point.

That said, many of the least successful of the respondents were convinced that discrimination is an active force in the labor market.[9] They include people like Victoria, an unemployed forty-four-year-old African American who believed she had run into racist employers while looking for work. "I don't care how bad I need the job. I'm not going to take no shit like that," she says. There are also high flyers who insist that racism is not a factor in their own job prospects. "I haven't experienced . . . being judged by my skin color," says Bridget, the African American woman who works in the college bursar's office. What Bridget sees out there is not racial discrimination but class-based reactions on the part of employers who don't want to hear African American vernacular at work or to hire people who wear hip-hop styles. So long as black job seekers don't display hallmarks of the ghetto, discrimination shouldn't be a problem, Bridget says— and that seems fair enough to her. A willingness to compromise is part of what makes someone worth choosing among the many job applicants out there.

"That Man Lost Me"

When Belinda was a girl, she told her mother that she wanted to be a lawyer. "No, you're not," her mom replied. "You're going to be a nurse."

"I'm going to be an attorney," Belinda insisted.

"Let me tell you something. Black girls are not attorneys."

"Yes, they are. You just don't know any."

Mother and daughter kept going back and forth—for years. "Every time I would try to get to law, she'd turn me around and try to get me into medicine," Belinda recalls. Her mother had grown up in Jim Crow Arkansas; she thought her daughter was pursuing an impossible dream. A black girl doesn't sit behind a desk, she maintained.

Belinda's confidence eroded, and she eventually gave up on her plans to become a lawyer. When we first met her in 1993, Belinda told us she was going to college and planned to study medicine. Several years later, she had found a job as a nurse's aide at a New York hospital, making $14.29 per hour.

But her desire to become a lawyer did not go away. In 2002, when we spoke to her last, she was bitter about the "raw deal" she had gotten from her parents. From the time she was young, she had been put in a "box," she said, and the possibilities of her future life had been circumscribed. It was not that Belinda believed her mother's assessments of a black woman's chances in the legal field were utterly mistaken. Belinda was mad because, in her view, the best response to the knowledge that racism is out there is to commit yourself to the proposition that people can succeed if they try hard enough—even if it's contrary to personal experience. "You [should] tell me, if I be good and if I respect people, I can be anything I want to be," Belinda said. In fact, the vast majority of the men and women we followed over the course of our study expressed this point of view. At each of our three waves of interviews, we asked this question: "Some people say that anyone who wants to make it in this city or in America can do it. All they have to do is try or work hard. Other people take the opposite point of view and say that they have many obstacles against them from the beginning. This is a very general question, but what do you think? Can anyone make it? Why or why not?"

At each point, an overwhelming majority of respondents—from 72 to 88 percent—told us that they believe in that quintessentially American dream that anyone, by dint of hard work and persistence, can succeed. In fact, most of those who said that people were judged by their race or other group identity also said anyone can make it (Table 8.3). These individuals acknowledged that racism exists and that they might not always be judged on their own merits, but they still insisted that everyone—even racial minorities—can make it if they try: they simply have to fight past the racism.

Many low-wage workers of color who aspire to a brighter and better-compensated future in the American labor market believe that they need to downplay potential barriers, like race, that stand in the way. They say that focusing on racism—as Belinda's mother did—simply erects road-blocks in the mind that keep people from ever making the effort to realize their ambitions. As Adam sees it, the best way to respond to discrimination is with determination to turn a blind eye. An employer may be racist, he says, but you have to steel yourself to the abuse. You can't let it eat away at your own morale. "'He prefer[s] a white person over me.' Don't look at it

Table 8.3 Beliefs about socioeconomic mobility

Can anyone make it?	Wave 1 (1993–94)	Wave 2 (1997)	Wave 3 (2001–2002)
Yes	83.7%	71.9%	87.5%
No	16.3%	28.1%	12.5%
N	86	96	32

like that. [Instead think,] 'That man lost me. I didn't lose him. I could have made his job or his business better.'" In other words, racism might be a barrier, but if you dwell on that fact it simply shows you are spiritually weak and defeatist. "Get over it" rather than dwell on it—that is Adam's credo. Life is full of barriers, he says. The success stories are the people who bracket their fury and push past it hard enough to prove the racists wrong. People who don't follow this rule, who insist on dwelling on the Man, are to be either pitied or criticized, Adam believes—not necessarily because they are wrong, but because they have run full tilt down a blind alley.

Faced with obstacles, Americans of all backgrounds, the working poor included, tend to emphasize the individual and personal rather than the structural and systematic. Jennifer Hochschild wrote that "workers generally accept, even if they have some doubts about, the American ethos of rugged individualism and the American dream of upward mobility. They fear equality; they have little or no class consciousness; they believe the world is just and people get what they deserve; the poor limit their aspirations and dreams to reduce dissonance between desires and possibilities."[10] As I pointed out in *No Shame in My Game*, low-wage workers share this dominant view—in fact, they often revel in it. In their drive to become the Joneses, they start thinking like the Joneses. Adopting this attitude may be a form of protective denial, for with so many obstacles in your path, the sanest thing to do is not to dwell on them but to just barrel straight ahead. But low-wage workers also take on this attitude because they *are* mainstream America, not some deviant subculture.[11]

Even individuals in our study who suffered from chronic unemployment, treacherous finances, or spells of incarceration during the 1990s expressed this distinctively individualistic outlook. Across the three waves of interviews, between 75 and 92 percent of low riders maintained that anyone can make it—in fact, they were more likely to believe this than the more successful respondents in the sample.[12] Years of stagnant wages did little or nothing to shake this belief. Take Randy, for instance, who was unemployed in 2002 and has a sporadic work history and a prison record to boot. When pressed, he says that his race, his neighborhood, and his criminal record have harmed his chances of getting and keeping a good job. Nevertheless, he says he doesn't blame the employers who constantly turn him down. "Those people are not the ones who made me go out there and get on drugs and go get arrested," he says. "And this is their company. They have that right." Facing a labor market hostile to people like him, Randy invokes the spirit of Jurgis Rudkus. "What do I do? I just work harder. Doors get closed in my face. I keep going." In fact, Randy is more willing to point fingers at other African Americans than at white people. The fact that poor Hispanic immigrants can make it in America shows that black people just need to get their act together, he says. "These people are out there working. They're working hard. If there ain't no jobs, they create their own. They'll go buy batteries. They'll sell them. The blacks will sit back and laugh at them selling batteries on the train, but you not working. See? . . . Most blacks are lazy, they don't want to work. They'll hang out all day and then, you know, want to rob somebody else's hard work. And not all of them, now. But a lot of the young ones these days, man— our race is going down is because the parents are not teaching them right."

Randy blames a culture of permissive parenting for the problems that beset the inner city. Kids wear their pants on their hips? That would never happen when he was growing up. His mom made sure Randy "got the belt" whenever he acted up. It's true that kids today can't be disciplined in the old-fashioned way because the authorities will step in. But parents are also guilty of turning a blind eye to serious misbehavior on the part of their children, Randy says. "You know your child is not working, but you know he's coming in with two- or three-hundred-dollar sneakers and all this money? You know what's going on." Spoiled all their lives, he says, kids don't understand that working hard is the only way to get ahead. "You have to be out there," Randy says. "It's not going to come to you." He should know.

It's not that these individuals are just mouthing the politically correct line. They truly believe in the American gospel of work and ambition. Then, when they are faced with the reality that hard work does not necessarily pay off, they are left scratching their heads in genuine disbelief.

When we spoke to him in 1997, Francisco complained that, for all his hard work and sacrifices in the military, in college, and in the working world, he was still doing worse than his older brothers. For years his brothers had shuttled between courts and jails on account of their sundry criminal activities, but now they had their GEDs, were working for the city, and every payday took home fat paychecks. Francisco wondered what he had done wrong to become the underdog. "I joke about it. I'm like, 'Should I start troubles with the law and then go, you know, go seek a . . . probation officer? Should I go to [a] probation officer and have him hook me up with a good job like that?'"

Five years later, there wasn't much reason to envy his eldest sibling anymore: big brother had wound his way back to the jailhouse. "He's not doing well at all," laments Francisco in 2002. His other elder brother was still working for one of the city's social service agencies, making good money; his younger brother was just "hopping around," never content with any line of work—and never advancing. As for Francisco himself, he had managed to climb a few feet up the golden stairway during the Internet's boom years, when he was working for a start-up "deliver anything" service in Manhattan, helping to build up an exciting new company and relishing a dot-com yuppie's freedom and fat bonuses. But since that venture had crashed, Francisco had gone back down to working for eleven dollars an hour and no benefits and was caught in promotion stasis as the manager of a small, upscale café owned by a celebrity's daughter. "I thought there'd be much more people involved in different areas doing different [things], but there's only, like, one guy," Francisco says. "Right now, I'm thinking it's going to be hard for me to move up." Having more education and more drive than his brothers has paid off in some ways for Francisco, but then again, has it really? None of them has made it big. "Everybody seems to be OK. We're not at jobs which we'd love to be our ideal job—you know, that fantasy job that you have in your head, making a million bucks and sitting in a plush office. But everyone's working." Except big brother in jail.

A Piece of Heart, a Piece of Heaven

Work is only part of life's equation. Family is the other half and often the more vexing element. Finding a partner, for emotional support and satisfaction, for the help he or she provides in maintaining a household and taking care of kids, for the comfort of growing old with someone by your side, these are simple desires, but they're as complicated to satisfy as they are universal in their appeal.[13] As the complexities of searching for a mate—and keeping one—have grown, women in all walks of life, from those struggling with poverty to Hollywood stars, have opted to have children without having a steady man in the picture.[14]

For many women, the almost audible tick-tock of their biological clock spurs the impulse to have kids. Among the working poor, though, marriage and children often appear as two distinct propositions that do not necessarily follow one from the other. First comes love, then comes a baby in a baby carriage—and only then, if things are going swimmingly, does marriage come into the picture. David Ellwood and Christopher Jencks point out that this trend of having children first and getting married later (a reversal on the norm for women born in the 1940s) is particularly prevalent among women with less education—and among high school dropouts above all. College graduates who are now in their forties tend to have postponed both marriage *and* childbearing in comparison with women born a generation earlier. Meanwhile, high school graduates and high school dropouts tend to have postponed marriage but not childbearing. "The result has been a rapid rise in the fraction of less-educated women who have had children but have not married," Ellwood and Jencks write.[15]

In their book *Promises I Can Keep*, sociologists Kathryn Edin and Maria Kefalas help us understand why. Their study of single mothers in Philadelphia and Camden, New Jersey, reveals that poor women, lacking the same opportunities as middle-class women to find rewarding careers and meet marriageable men, often get a sense of purpose and identity by having children without marrying. And because they have such dismal prospects in the labor market to begin with, Edin and Kefalas say, having children rarely hurts the earnings of these mothers over the long term. Poor women are not trying to have kids out of wedlock, exactly, but neither are they making determined efforts to prevent a pregnancy. "Someday I'm going to *plan* my pregnancies," says a twenty-two-year-old African American single mom in their book, "like . . . *white* [middle-class] women do. You know, like Murphy Brown! You have your fancy car, . . . your fancy house, your career all set, and *then* maybe you'll have a baby!"[16]

The women we came to know did not think—at the outset—that having children would impede their progress in the labor market. Seven out of ten women in the study group gave birth to one or more children during the years of our research (slightly more than two-thirds of all the respondents, male and female, were parents). When we compare the more successful workers with the less successful in the sample, we find about the same percentage of parents in the two groups. By 2002, however, many of the women were at a stage in their life where their careers were picking up—or their friends' careers were picking up and they were being left behind. The consequences of childbearing were clearer to them at this point than they had been in their youth, and some doubts began to emerge. The last time we spoke with Lauren, in 2002, the twenty-six-year-old African American (the mother of a seven-year-old daughter) was working in the accounting department of a New York nonprofit foundation, making $27,500 a year plus benefits. She said she could have done better. "If I waited to have my daughter, I could have gotten scholarships to get into a better college. If I took advantage of those benefits, I would have gotten further in life."

For the most part, however, mothers emphasized that having children had changed their lives for the better. Having her daughter may have slowed her down "a little bit," Lauren acknowledged, "but I still . . . got back on the train and just keep going, going, going." She insisted that she did not regret having her child. "I think parenting is a beautiful thing. Her growing up is the best thing that's happened so far in my life, out of everything." Bridget, one of our midlevel wage earners, said that having her son motivated her to pull her life together. "That gives me the motivation to want to do things more and work a little harder at the things, even though it's difficult and I know that," she told us in 1997. "It makes me want to strive a little harder for what I want."[17]

Mothers who haven't had much financial stability in their lives tend to cling all the more tightly to their children as a source of inspiration and hope. Vanessa, a low rider and single mother, insists that her lack of success to date had nothing to do with her children. "I wouldn't say having my kids is a bad thing, because it's not," she says. "Actually, it makes me do more. It makes me push myself to do better things. I mean, I got what I wanted. I got two girls. I just want what's best for them." When we last met up with Sabrina, in 2002, the thirty-five-year-old African American mother of three had come through some hard times: a recovering crack addict, she had lost her job as a kitchen worker (which paid nine dollars an hour) after her office building was devastated in the September 11 attack on the World Trade Center, and she was living off a combination of disaster relief payments and a tax refund. Two of her daughters were living with her great-grandmother; she and her partner (also recently laid off) could barely support their three-year-old daughter, who was living with them. Nevertheless, Sabrina considered her baby girl a godsend. "She inspired me to achieve what I wanted," Sabrina told us. Pregnancy had pushed her to get her life together. If it wasn't for her daughter, "I'd probably still been out there doing the same thing or maybe not even being alive," she insisted.

The mothers we talked to want to see their children attain the success that may have eluded them in their own lives. But because they lack the resources of their middle-class counterparts, many of these low-income moms eventually take a hardened view of their children's chances. Patty, for instance, talks bluntly about how kids are either "college-bound" or "penitentiary-bound." "If you're penitentiary-bound, get out; if you're college-bound, you can stay," she says. One of her daughters is doing badly in school, Patty says, and she's been forced to consider drastic action: sending her away from home, maybe to California, or Long Island, so that she can get away from the negative influences of her peer group. "She got in with a crowd," Patty told us in 1997. "Instead of staying with her A-student crowd, she got with this crowd. So now I got to get her away, because she's an A student—always [has] been from the time of school. So I'm going to ship her out so I don't lose her."[18]

Middle-class households have a sense of security—of being protected against crime, lack of money, absence of health care—that the poor can rarely count on. Acknowledging this difference, some social scientists have argued that teenage motherhood may reflect an adaptation to the dangers of a life in poverty. As Arline Geronimus points out, the life expectancy of minority women—particularly African Americans—is significantly shorter than that of majority women. A young girl who plans to depend on her own mother as a source of support will have to "hurry up" if she wants to be sure that support system will still be in place when she needs it.[19] Also, Geronimus points out, teen moms may be hoping to bring the father's female kin into the picture, thus harvesting much-needed resources from the joined families. If teenage motherhood is truly a "social response to disadvantage," this may explain why poor families see such behavior as acceptable (and even expected) at ages that middle-class Americans might find appallingly young. It may also explain why, in poor neighborhoods, a girl becomes a woman at an earlier age. She has to. "For those [teenagers] with less apparent chance of achieving upward mobility, early fertility may be one effective way to pursue personal and cultural survival and development," Geronimus writes.[20]

I would add to Geronimus's argument the point that boys, too, are expected to "become" men more quickly in families of lesser means. Middle-class children, in general, enjoy the luxury of an elongated adolescence, those additional years of leisure that have been tacked on over decades of national affluence—first after high school, now after college—when kids are still kids, and parents are still willing to house them, pay their bills, bail them out of scrapes. Poor children, in contrast, are deemed responsible for their own fate when they are in their teens.[21] For this reason, a single mother like Cassandra can talk frankly about kicking her son—at seventeen—out of the house if he doesn't get his life together: "So that's pretty much his choice, you know. Either you go to college or you pack your bags and you decide what you want to do after that, because I don't tolerate, like, laziness, and well, I can't. I don't even allow that word in my house. And I just believe in striving, because I came from the street. Literally. And if I can do it, you can do it. You know. I just carry Jesus everywhere I go, and He's always like, Yeah, you can do it, Cassandra. Let me just give you this nudge. And you can take the push."

What sounds like fatalism or resignation is, in the case of these parents, an acknowledgment that the course of life in poor communities unfolds at a faster, more furious pace. At the age of seventeen, Cassandra's son is—in her eyes—a man; and yet he is a man in a culture that does not give someone his age the wherewithal to act like one.

If middle-class parents' standards for judging their children's success are unrealistic for poor parents, so too are middle-class standards about marriage. Only one-fifth of the women we talked with in our last wave of interviews in 2001 and 2002 were married.[22] Like the women in Edin and Kefalas's book, many of our respondents expressed frustration that the men in their lives were not marriage material: they were not willing to be serious partners, to support the women financially and emotionally, to offer themselves as loving fathers to their children. "I understand that you have to work on it, it's not just out there, but why can't you have a man that's not on alcohol, that's willing to be your strength and you're willing to be his strength?" asks Belinda. "Why can't you two guys be a team? Why can't you have the child and both of you two work together at bringing this child up into this world? And that, to me, is the perfect family." Problems with drug abuse, criminal behavior, and domestic abuse loom large in the relationships that poor women have with poor men, and they frequently tear mothers away from their children's fathers.

Some men, of course, beg to differ. Contrary to popular image, they too think about family and value children, though they may come to this realization later in their life cycle than women do—in all classes.[23] Kevin told us in 1993 that he just wanted to make money and didn't care for having a family; nine years later, at the age of twenty-five, he was talking about his hope to settle down and "maybe" have a child. Jamal settled down with Selina because he wanted a family and a home. Carmen's husband, Sal, has been a family man for years. True, young fathers, like Adam once was, engage in their urban-ghetto versions of "youthful indiscretions"— infidelities and transgressions that, at best, keep them distant from their partners and children, and at worst break their families apart. But give them a few years, and they'll learn to be decent dads, they say. In 1997 Adam already had two young children but was convinced he was not marriage material. He was seeing several women at a time; his mother was on his case for not being able to settle down in a committed relationship. Fast-forward four years, and Adam is happily married (his third try). His two children are both living with him, and he's building a house for his family in North Carolina, where the schools are supposedly better. This model dad is now trying to help his wife's daughter land a steady job— even as he complains that people like his stepdaughter, a welfare recipient with children, need to stop living off of charity.

Given Adam's particular trajectory as a deadbeat-dad-turned-Father-Knows-Best, it may be that the bleak picture of male partners that Edin and Kefalas paint is a function of time and their age—men who are still searching for their identity in their twenties ultimately settle on the traditional role and responsibilities of fatherhood in their thirties (Adam is thirty-six). Adam's decision to marry a woman who already had a child also calls into question the idea that women with children will always be undesirable in the eyes of potential suitors—eventually some of these men "grow up" and learn to look past such distinctions. This is small comfort to the mothers of Adam's older children, however, who were deprived of the kind of contribution to their well-being that he now offers routinely to his wife and younger children. Nonetheless, his is not an undifferentiated pathway. Instead, he has matured into the kind of fatherhood role society expected him to play all along.

Jamal, too, has grown up—though his added maturity has come only after many years, and at some price. By the time I caught up with Jamal again in 2002, he had abandoned his life in New York, and with it, his common-law wife and young daughter. The ties were broken, the photos burned, and Jamal was now living across the country with his (legal) wife, Selina, and their three children. At thirty, he had put an end to his drug use and was working hard to calm his temper. His relationship with Selina has its ups and downs, but they have preserved their marriage and they plan to stay married.

In short, men may get better with age, but a good man is still hard to find. As their search for a responsible partner continued to net nothing, the women in our study confided that they were drifting increasingly toward despair. "I have this vision that I'm going to be with this guy," Belinda said in 2002, at the age of thirty-four, after years of being unable to find a man, "that's not on alcohol, that's willing to be your strength." Her loneliness had metastasized into fantasies. "We're going to have, like, one child. I don't know this guy. He doesn't know me. And that's what I'm seeing. I just have this vision. I see this guy every night. I don't know who he is. He doesn't know who I am, but I'm going to marry him. And I'm going to tell the man. And the funniest thing is, he's going to pay for my— our—honeymoon in Paris. It's between Paris and Italy."

Just because poor women don't marry right away doesn't mean that they are against the idea. Edin and Kefalas argue that the institution of marriage is so sacred that their research subjects claimed they would not marry until they were sure it would last. Though this is undoubtedly true for many, it does not quite square with what we heard over the years we followed the work and personal lives of our Burger Barn workers. Sadly, many women find that the men they set their sights on are not interested in marriage. African American men, in particular, know they are in a sweet position in the marriage market, and some take advantage of it by having serial girlfriends without committing to any one of them until late in life.[24] Latoya married a man who ended up in prison only a few years later. Kyesha would marry her boyfriend, Ramsey, if he were willing, even though she knows he is a bad bet. The desire to marry, particularly for women, often overwhelms common sense. It is easier for them to say the men are no good, and thus not worthy of marrying, than to admit that a wedding ring cannot be coaxed from their lover.

Kyesha admits as much when she is being totally honest with herself. But out of either embarrassment or the simple need to adapt to the paucity of options for marriage partners, she maintains that she, too, wants to have her fun. "I think I've worked so hard so far that I really haven't had time to enjoy life," Kyesha said in our last interview with her, in 2002. "Everything is just tooken so seriously when it comes to me getting my money, when I finally unwind it's like for a second, and that's when I explode and do just crazy shit for, like, two days and then it's, like, I'm back to, OK, it's dah-dah-dah, and I need to do a little more unwinding. I had no childhood. Like, I didn't have no twenty-one, twenty-three, twenty-four phase, because I was a mother so I didn't have time for it, and now I'm kicking into that zone when I should be doing more serious shit. Now I'm trying to live my twenty-three, twenty-four."

For Kyesha, living her "twenty-three, twenty-four" sometimes seems to come at the expense of her young son. A friend of hers points out that Kyesha often shows up at kids' events—children's birthday parties, for instance—without Anthony in tow. (Anthony had lied to Kyesha about homework he was supposed to do, the explanation goes.) Yet the same Kyesha devoted nearly two years to dreaming about the day she would walk down the aisle with her old boyfriend Kevin, followed by a married man she set her cap for, and so on. Had any of them been willing, she would have been there with the wedding dress, like a shot.

That said, there are also single mothers like Natasha, who prefer to spend their nights reading to their children, helping them with their lessons, showering them with positive attention. Natasha is good friends with Kyesha, but they couldn't be more different in their views on relationships. It's not like Natasha doesn't get her share of attention from the menfolk: the last time we talked to her, she was dodging calls from a friend who has been doggedly pursuing her—for the past five years, in fact. Natasha is just not ready to commit.

Get Me Out of Here

Adam and his family are heading down South. They're building a new house in North Carolina—a custom-built estate squatting atop a full six acres of land—and have already poured thousands of dollars into the project. It was such an expensive undertaking that the local banks started giving him static. "Not only did I have the biggest house, I had the most expensive house in the city," Adam says. "So they were like, 'Hold on! What's going on here?' So I've got to keep coming up with a couple of thousand—'Here, here are $10,000 to satisfy you, all right?'" For Adam, though, the expense is well worth it. He wants to live near the extended family again. He wants a house of his own—one he couldn't dream of affording in New York. And he wants to provide a better quality of life for his children.

For the most part, the people who express a desire to get out of New York are the ones with the most financial wherewithal—the high flyers. They are people like Edward, a twenty-five-year-old Dominican American who sees himself "sitting in Miami Beach in my own house." Working as a security guard at a federal building for fifteen dollars per hour, Edward is looking for a better quality of life (and a lower cost of living) for himself and his young daughter. Deanna, a former administrative assistant who was making $33,000 before she left her job to have her baby, is not thrilled about raising her son in the city either. "We went out [to Florida] for vacation to Disney World, and we were only there for a week but it was just, I don't know. It was so calm and peaceful," she says. "It's a different vibe than New York. It just seems like someplace better to raise your children than here."

For immigrants, the allure of home often grows stronger as they establish a financial foothold and are able to entertain the prospect of returning to their country of origin for good. Take Maria, a twenty-eight-year-old Dominican American who has lived in the United States for thirteen years. After years of struggling at Burger Barn and elsewhere, she and her husband, Tomás, now have decent office jobs and finally feel in the position to make "very big" plans to move themselves and their six-year-old son to the Dominican Republic—the island nation that, as she emphasizes, is her true home. "We plan to buy a house in our country, God willing," she says. "In the next five years I might see myself in my country. My husband's plans are to open a business over there, computer systems and all of that stuff. My project for the next five years is in Santo Domingo, my country."[25]

Internal migrants—those individuals, for example, with family ties that draw them to the South—speak in remarkably similar ways about their dream of returning to that other "old country," below the Mason-Dixon line. Patty is one of these "transregional villagers": though she grew up in the Bronx, she talks with an immigrant's longing about moving to Georgia, where her late grandmother was born and her uncle still lives. The idea of country life—wide-open spaces, close-knit families, a big house—

appeals to her. "I want to raise a chicken and a cow and a pig," she says. "I want to know how to make bread from scratch. I think that these recipes need to be somewhere in a book in the family, because God forbid the supermarket's not there no more. . . . I don't want my kids not to know how to take care of themselves from scratch." They are people like Mike, a twenty-three-year-old sales associate of West Indian and Dominican descent, who has had his fill of fast-paced city life and frigid city winters. Mike wants to move to a quiet part of Virginia—the place where his mother is from, the community that his relatives call home, an exotic land where trees don't have to ask permission from the sidewalk to grow.

Cassandra is another sojourner in the North. She speaks with obvious longing of a recent family trip to North Carolina, where she had lived for a few years as a child. "It's so serene. And I woke up in the morning to the smell of pine trees, and no niggers, no cars, no . . . it was like heaven." Her son loved it. All the kids wanted to stay. "I mean, none of us wanted to come back. None of us. You know, because it was like a whole new world. It was clean, it was peaceful . . . you could breathe. It was stress-free. No drug dealers on the corner that my son and my nieces and my nephews had to pass. You know, oh God."

Anthropologist Carol Stack has chronicled the geographic and emotional journeys of internal migrants in her book *Call to Home*. Reversing in trickles the Great Migration, over the last two decades African Americans have been leaving northern cities (and their northern lifestyles) in search of more tangible roots to family and community in the South.[26] Yet for many, relocating is more easily said than done. In 1993 Cassandra told us that she hoped to move to Atlanta with her young son, because New York was no place to raise a baby; four years later, she said she and her boyfriend, a tractor-trailer driver, had plans to relocate to New Jersey for his job. But in 2002 Cassandra was still living in the same apartment in the Bronx, still talking about moving: this time, to Orangeburg, South Carolina. "I'm stressed and frustrated, and my son is stressed and frustrated," she said. "We need to be where there is tranquility. We're just not finding that here."

Of course, it's not just nostalgia that entices people like Maria and Patty and Mike to want to plant roots outside of New York. There is also the fact that, even for families with decent-paying jobs, buying a house in the New York metropolitan area is an unlikely—almost laughable—prospect. "You just don't own land in New York. And I don't see me building a house on land I don't own," says Patty. Leaving the world's greatest city is, ironically, all about upward mobility. A dog in the backyard, a picket fence—these are things that a college-educated former Burger Barn manager like Patty must have, she insists, before she dies. "Yes, I do want the American dream," she tells us.

Low riders, on the other hand, seem to prefer staying in New York. For most, the reasons have to do with the family ties that are both emotionally valuable and pragmatically indispensable. Natasha might dream about relocating to the Boston area, but she really cannot do without her mother, Lizzie, to help with her kids. The webs of kin that make life possible cannot be relocated easily.

For some, health problems—which compromise their economic fortunes as well—keep them rooted in the city. "I really don't want to leave New York because . . . all my doctors are here," points out Natalie, a twenty-five-year-old unemployed African American who suffers from sickle-cell anemia. Victoria, too, insisted she couldn't leave the city. When we last met up with her in 2002, Victoria was not working and was living off of Social Security income from her deceased husband. Her résumé amounted to just a bunch of short-term retail job at Macy's and Sears and the like, and she had never obtained any education past high school. But the main thing that kept her in New York, she said, was her elderly and sick mother. "I can't leave her," she told us in 1997. "That's one thing that keeps me here. She doesn't like the country. She doesn't like things like that. She's a city person. . . . I will feed bad because I know she took care of me all my life. So I think it's my turn." Other people don't have obligations that keep them in New York but simply can't imagine leaving. "I'm so used to the city," says Vanessa. "Born and raised here. I have family down South and I've been down South, but that's more like when you're looking to retire. It's a slow pace, and right now it's not an option."

Finding Dignity

Randy can offer some perspective on the dreams that arise from American poverty. He has seen his share of them fall short. Back in the seventies, when he was just a kid hanging out on Harlem's street corners, rap music was the sound of the underground—and Randy was one of the elite few who knew how to get a crowd jumping. "This was when there was no rap records out. All these groups wasn't even out then. We used to bring our music in the park." The thin, dark-complexioned teenager would hang with the likes of Grandmaster Flash and Kurtis Blow—the pioneers of a new music not yet sullied by "bling bling" and gangsta wannabes. Those artists went on to record smash-hit albums; Randy sank his money into crack cocaine. His friends signed record deals; Randy robbed his neighbors to feed his habit. He would lurk on the corner of 115th and Third Avenue, buying whenever he could, taking whenever he couldn't. "I would go over there and I would rob them at gunpoint, and go back upstairs—right in the neighborhood." In his own words, Randy was "treacherous": "If you had something I wanted, I would take it."

Randy broke his mother's heart. She had raised him to be respectable—to dress nicely, to say his "yes, ma'ams" and "no, sirs," to work hard and be independent. But as a man in his twenties, he was just another crack fiend. "I was greasy as a bodega pork chop," Randy says. He would eat out of garbage cans. His hair was nappy. His own mother could not bear the sight of him. "I should have never borned you in the world," she once told him. "You ain't nothing."

Randy didn't care. All he could think about was his next hit.

The law finally caught up with Randy. As he was being hauled off to jail for robbery, he learned that his mother was seriously ill. The news stunned Randy. There he was, staring down a three-year sentence, while his mother was dying of diabetes. "When I got locked up, the first thing I thought about was, 'Wow, I'm not going to see my mother a lot again.'"

In jail, Randy found Islam. He sat alone in his cell and prayed to God—begged Him to change his life. "I . . . asked God to let me see my mother alive," he says, "so I could make her happy and be proud of me, because she worked real hard." In his jail cell, there was no one to talk to. No one to watch him pray. No one to stand between him and God. "And He answered my prayers," Randy says. When he came home three years later, his mother was still alive. They had cut off one leg; they had cut off the other. She was going blind. But when he went to her in the hospital, she recognized her son. "She had her right mind," Randy says. "She knew who I was."

Randy vowed to turn his life around. He began working. He had to take a train and a bus to work, and had to borrow money to pay the fares, but he kept at it for his mother's sake. "She meant everything to me," he says. His mother died in 1996.

Now in his forties, Randy is a changed man. When we met him last, in

2002, he looked great—dressed nicely, but not expensively, with stylish sunglasses perched on his nose. He doesn't do drugs anymore. He doesn't hang out. He is married, and Randy and his wife, a former police department employee, take care of their two granddaughters. "Before, I didn't want anything but just the drugs—and lots of it," he says. "The most important thing to me now is my wife and my grandkids. If something happened to me, I want it where she don't have to ask nobody for nothing, and my grandkids won't have to ask nobody for nothing. So that's the only thing. Material stuff is really nothing to me."

Randy is a low rider: he has never been able to hold down a job for too long, and he didn't have one at the time of the last interview. Nevertheless, Randy and his wife somehow manage to make ends meet. He insists that he is grateful, too, for what he has and for how far he has come. Randy's best gig so far has been as an ambulette driver. Sometimes he would wander through the hospital after dropping off a patient. "I'd see people with tubes in every hole in their body," he says. "The only thing that they would wish for is that that day would be the day that they pass away." When things are rough for him now, when he feels sorry for himself, Randy remembers those people in the hospital, he says, and tries to "live right and treat people right."

The working poor—and their more successful counterparts—do not seek more than what most middle-class Americans want: jobs with decent pay and possibilities for advancement, families that are loving and supportive, marriages that are good matches, homes that are situated in pleasant, safe neighborhoods. Even the most desperate among them—individuals who find themselves unemployed or underemployed for long stretches of time, who struggle to survive on a dwindling income—cling to the values of mainstream America. Whether flying high or perched precariously, in the boom economy of the nineties these men and women believed that they could succeed with hard work, in spite of racism or a lack of opportunity. They put one foot in front of the other and edged just a bit closer to their goals.

9

Opening the Gates

❧

Tight labor markets and high levels of economic growth are boons to the working poor, particularly if they last long enough to sop up the surplus labor that is left idle or underutilized in low-growth periods. Such happy conditions prevailed in the late 1990s and the first year of this decade, and while they did, labor shortages inclined employers to take chances on people they might have bypassed before. Young black men— traditionally the group most disadvantaged by employer preferences— found work in record numbers. Earnings rose as the hours worked increased.[1] Inequality began to stabilize, and poverty started to shrink for the first time since the mid-1970s.[2]

Did these favorable conditions improve the prospects for upward mobility among those who were already in the labor market? Here the evidence is mixed. We certainly see some remarkable success stories in the lives of the people chronicled in this book, and the dispersion of wages suggests that movement to better-paying jobs was far more likely than the pessimists would have predicted on the basis of the literature reviewed in Chapter 2. Among the workers we followed, who started out in the early 1990s in minimum-wage jobs, 22 percent saw their income increase by more than five dollars per hour in real wages. But would we have seen the same pattern during a slow growth period? Several of the studies reviewed in Chapter 5 corroborate the findings in *Chutes and Ladders:* favorable conditions that enhanced the fortunes of new entrants to the labor market also created opportunities for mobility among those who were already on the job. Yet the Survey of Income and Program Participation (SIPP) analysis described in Chapter 5 tells us that the effects of a good economy are modest. Moving up happens in both slack labor markets and tight ones, even if it is slightly easier in the latter compared with the former.

Everyone is in favor of growth, but today we seem to have difficulty re-creating the conditions that made such extraordinary economic prosperity possible. Certainly the economic problems besetting the United States now, with skyrocketing deficits, a huge trade imbalance despite a weak dollar, and anemic job growth, do not point in the right direction if we are to keep the up escalator running for the working poor, or for anyone else. Nonetheless, because upward movement happens under many circumstances, it is worthwhile asking which policies will create more high flyers like Kyesha, rather than low riders like Natasha.

The answer varies according to the interests of those doing the talking. The business community generally favors higher productivity and looks for ways to create a workforce with more human capital to offer, which permits employers to recapture the cost of paying out more money on the salary line, often to fewer workers. This approach favors the well edu-cated, to whom the lion's share of wage increases have gone in the past thirty years. Even so, there is evidence that corporate profits have gone up much faster than wages, even of those at the top of the earnings distri-bution.

Strategies to enhance earnings through human capital will help the working poor only if opportunities to increase their skills and experience are readily available to them. But to put this type of approach in play on a large scale would require the commitment of public resources that the nation has not been willing to underwrite: heavy investments in early childhood education, higher education, and workforce training. Instead, we see cuts in education budgets and little enthusiasm for the kind of training initiatives that were popular in the Clinton administration. Re-cently we have heard more about high-stakes testing and, to a lesser de-gree, school vouchers as ways of boosting the quality of education. The track records thus far for these initiatives do not seem to indicate that they will pay off for the working poor or their children.

Labor enthusiasts point to union organizing and international fair labor standards as methods for preventing wages from eroding and keeping well-paid jobs from disappearing in the United States.[3] It would be a blessing for many of the people whose lives are chronicled in this book if unions were to grow in strength; instead, we see union membership shrink every year and organizing efforts falter, especially when faced with corporate threats to pull out of a region if a union gets its foot in the door.[4] The patterns of occupational growth in the United States do not seem to favor strong unions, which were built on the backs of steel mills and auto plants rather than Burger Barns and Wal-Marts.[5] This is not to say that a strong union movement is either impossible or undesirable, but as a way to secure upward mobility for poor workers, it is only a distant possibility, albeit one that more progressive unions are fighting for.[6]

What, then, are the politically practical approaches that would assist more people to follow in the footsteps of people like Helena, who started out working at Burger Barn and at the end of our study was earning $60,000 as a call center manager? A number of think tanks have contributed some answers to this question, and I rely heavily on them here. The Center on Budget and Policy Priorities, the Brookings Institution, the Economic Policy Institute, the Rockefeller Foundation Program on the Future of Work and its collaborative partner, the Russell Sage Foundation, the Annie E. Casey Foundation, Jobs for the Future, and the Urban Institute—to name only a few—have focused a great deal of attention on federal and state policies that would enhance the chances for the working poor to cross over the poverty line. These institutions deserve all the credit for the ideas reviewed here, but since they are generally familiar only to wonks who haunt public policy Web sites, they bear further discussion.

Holding the Door Open

The Adams of this world—who earn $70,000 a year even though they haven't finished high school—are unusual. On average, high earnings go to those who complete college, and poverty awaits the high school dropouts. That message has clearly gotten through to most people in the United States, and that is why we have seen the rates of high school graduation climb higher and higher, even among poor minorities.[7] Although serious problems remain for Hispanics at the high school level, the real action now lies in access to college. Higher education, from vocational training in practical fields like nursing or accounting to the more traditional liberal arts education, is now critical for most people who hope to become middle class. Even without the degree, every semester spent in college improves workers' prospects in the labor market, especially for those in our Up but Not Out Club (see Chapter 3) who are seeking better versions of clerical and administrative jobs.[8]

Financial barriers prevent many qualified students from moving into higher education, and those barriers multiply for single parents, and for adult learners more generally.[9] This can be a problem even for our high flyers, like Kyesha and Lauren, who earn enough to manage the expense of raising their children but may not have enough left over to pay for college tuition for themselves. The financial aid system for higher education is problematic for these working parents, since it is oriented toward traditional students who go to school full-time.[10] The Higher Education Act was authorized by Congress in order to increase access to college, but it did not focus much attention or provide much money for working adults with dependent children, even though "*non-traditional* students—that is, students older than twenty-four years or enrolled on a part-time basis— are the majority of all students (an estimated 53 percent in 1999)," according to the Almanac of Policy Issues.[11]

More than $9 billion a year flows from the federal Pell Grant program to students to pay for tuition and education-related expenses. Although adults who have jobs and families are technically eligible for these funds, they often cannot qualify because the model this program is based on is that of a full-time student who can make substantial progress toward the completion of a degree year by year. Pell Grant regulations make it clear that the program is for "regular students" who are making "satisfactory progress." The Annie E. Casey Foundation advocates expanding the program overall and extending its largesse to students who are enrolled in short-term, nondegree programs to build their skills, rather than limiting it to the current types of recipients, who must be enrolled in formal degree or certificate programs. If students who are making satisfactory progress included adults enrolled part-time who must take long breaks between courses, as well as young students who are in the classroom full-time, we would see more adult students improving their skills.

The Lifetime Learning Tax Credit was supposed to address the needs of adult learners. Authorized in 1997, this credit was a brainchild of the Clinton administration, especially of Secretary of Labor Robert Reich. Reich recognized that increased turmoil in the labor market was disrupting the long-term affiliation of workers (both white collar and blue collar) with a single employer, and that periodic unemployment and job shifting were likely to hit millions of Americans. The Clinton administration wanted to make it easier for adult workers to retrain, and this tax credit was an important policy instrument for achieving that end. Yet low-wage workers, who owe little in income taxes to begin with, have not been able to benefit from this legislation. Beneficiaries receive the tax credits after they have paid their tuition, and many lack the resources to pay that bill in the first place. If the Lifetime Learning credit were refundable, so that those who had already satisfied their tax obligations would receive a cash payment, it would reach more nontraditional students.[12]

These initiatives would be of greatest benefit to the kinds of workers who are in the labor force, including the vast majority of the people we followed over the course of the research in *Chutes and Ladders*. A minority of the subjects moved in and out of the work world and continued to receive TANF payments, at least until their time limits expired. They should not be forgotten where higher education is concerned. Indeed, as Lauren's experience shows, mothers on welfare who are permitted to go to school, even for a year, can make a break from public assistance and land a good job. The Maine Parents as Scholars Program makes it possible for welfare recipients in that state to complete two- or four-year degrees. "Graduates increased their hourly median wages from $8.00 before college to $11.71 immediately after college—a 46 percent increase."[13] CalWORKs (California Work Opportunity and Responsibility to Kids), the welfare program in the State of California, found even larger upticks in earnings for its recipients who attended college, even for those who did not have a high school diploma or a GED beforehand. "Those who obtained an associate degree dramatically increased their earnings (from about $4,000 annually before college to nearly $20,000 two years after graduating) and those in vocational fields saw even larger increases."[14]

The Center on Budget and Policy Priorities has given some thought to how community college programs supported by the states could be tailored to benefit low riders, those who are in and out of work and episodically on public assistance. It points to some key design features that need to be taken into account if the payoff is going to be significant:

- "The longer the program, the greater the economic payoff. . . . Vocational certificate programs needed to be at least . . . ten courses in

length to yield earnings that topped $15,000 by the second year out
of school. . . . Better paying health professions required longer support."

- "New services, such as child care, work study, service coordination,
  and job development and placement programs . . . [are] often a key
  factor" in making community college programs work for welfare recipients. Work study positions are particularly important, not only
  for the income they generate, but for the experience they provide,
  "especially when located off campus with private employers."
- "Anticipate realistic time frames for completion of credits." Community college students, who often work while going to school (even if
  they are not parents), generally need more than three years to complete an associate's degree. Low-income parents, particularly those
  who need remedial education, may need longer.[15]

California permits welfare recipients to satisfy their work requirement
for up to twenty-four months by enrolling in community college. As of
2002, 28 percent of the adults on the TANF rolls in the Golden State were
taking at least one course, and most of them also worked while going to
school. Twenty-two other states allow their public-assistance clients to enroll in school and count their efforts toward the "work participation rate"
that the federal government requires states to show. These policies pay off
in higher earnings over the life course and should be expanded as much as
possible.

Taxes, Taxes, Taxes

Working-poor families have benefited immensely from the introduction
in 1975 of the Earned Income Tax Credit. Many of the workers profiled in
this book now earn too much money to qualify for the EITC, but more
than half are still earning wages that entitle them to it. The federal EITC
is a refundable credit that goes to families who work but earn less than 200
percent of the poverty level. According to the Brookings Institution, the
EITC delivered more than $30 billion to 18.4 million low-income families
across the United States in 2001.[16] This makes the EITC the largest federal aid program targeted to the working poor and the most valuable, because it puts real dollars in the pockets of workers. When the taxpayers
reach the zero point in their tax liability, the difference is refunded in cash:

87 percent of all EITC dollars are refunded.[17] That money works wonders for the poor. In 1999, it lifted 4.7 million people above the poverty line, including 2.5 million children.

Welfare reform advocates saw the EITC as a way of rewarding work, where other measures merely punished those out of the labor force through drastic reductions in the amount (and duration) of their public assistance. As the Brookings research shows, in 1984 73 percent of single mothers worked. By 1996, before time limits were enforced, 81 percent were on the job. Big-city mayors are certainly aware of the benefits of the EITC, because the credit puts money—lots of money—in the hands of low-income consumers. "Low income working families . . . are most concentrated in the central cities," Brookings scholars Alan Berube and Benjamin Forman note, but surprisingly even more of these dollars—60 percent of the total—wend their way to America's suburbs.[18]

Only seventeen states have followed the federal lead in establishing Earned Income Tax Credits of their own, and among them, thirteen declare it refundable. The other four reduce the recipient's tax burden to zero so they don't owe state income tax. It would be a boon to the working poor if the other thirty-three states would follow suit and at least relieve low-income citizens of their state tax burden. Rewarding them through state tax refunds would be even better, for that would mean money in their pocket.

Perhaps we should count our blessings, though, because "nearly half of the states impose income taxes on families with incomes below the poverty line."[19] Southern states are particularly aggressive about taxing their poorest residents, and the politics of doing otherwise are fraught with controversy. In 2003 the Republican governor of Alabama, Bob Riley, asked his constituents to vote for a modest tax increase on higher-income residents in order to increase support for the state's poorly funded public education system and eliminate the income tax for those below the poverty line.[20] His bold proposal was resoundingly defeated. Hence, an Alabama family of four with annual earnings of $4,600 still owes income tax, which makes them even poorer than their income suggests. This absurd and damaging policy helps to trap millions of families in poverty both by taxing much-needed income and by stripping the state's budget of the resources needed to improve the public schools.

Income taxes are not the only revenue-collecting instruments that are hard on low-income families. State sales taxes—particularly on items like cigarettes and gasoline—make up one-third of most states' revenues. As researchers at the Center on Budget and Policy Priorities (CBPP) point out, these taxes are particularly regressive: "These consumption taxes impose a disproportionately high burden on lower-income families, who must spend a larger share of their income on items subject to tax in order to meet basic needs. In 2002, sales and excise taxes alone took up 7.8 percent of the income of the bottom 20 percent of taxpayers."[21] What could be done to relieve these burdens on low-income taxpayers? Some states have established "no tax floors," meaning that families who earn below a set amount of money do not owe tax at all. After all other taxes are factored in, families below the floor can write "zero" on the tax-due line on their state income tax form; those just above the floor gradually lose the break. CBPP recommends additional measures that would make a difference, including creating sales-tax rebates for families below the poverty line, adjusting tax credits so that they are conditioned on family size, and annually adjusting the income level that qualifies families for credits so that inflation does not push them above the eligibility line. All of these proposals would have the effect of relieving low-income families of tax burdens and therefore permitting them to keep more of their earnings. In states that permit cash rebates in excess of tax liabilities, the consequences would be even more progressive, for the measures would transfer funds to the working poor who do not owe taxes at all.

The property tax system is another venue for addressing the needs of families, including those we might regard as lower middle class, like Carmen and Salvador. Property owners in their state (New York)—and many others—are allowed to deduct their real estate taxes and thus lower their overall tax liability that way. In theory, landlords should pass some of those savings on to their tenants, because it costs them that much less to hold their buildings. Landlords are not compelled to do so, of course, and so to ensure that renters receive some of the benefits of property tax relief, "twenty-six states and the District of Columbia have property tax relief programs that provide relief to renters and homeowners alike."[22] The other twenty-four states permit deductions to home owners only. Extending renter rebates to those states would help both low- and middle-income renters by providing them with a benefit equal to that received by the real estate owners in their communities.

Many property tax relief measures are directed at sheltering the fixed-income elderly rather than families whose members are still in the labor

force. As the CBPP points out, twenty-four of the thirty-six states that offer so-called circuit breakers, tax floors for those with low incomes, make
them available only to the elderly and disabled. Low-income working families are in need of this relief as well, and if these programs were means
tested rather than status defined, they would help the kinds of people described in this book to support their families and to build assets, like
homes. In addition, when means testing rules are set, it makes a huge difference if the cutoff is a function (or multiple) of the poverty line rather
than a fixed dollar amount, because the former approach permits eligibility
levels to rise as inflation increases earnings, and it takes family size into account as well. Child care expenses can be treated in exactly the same way,
which could be another huge shot in the arm for working families.

These are not pie-in-the-sky ideas. They are in place in many parts of
the United States, as the CBPP points out: "At least eight states . . . use a
no-tax floor in their income taxes. More than half the states . . . provide income tax credits or deductions for child care expenses." And five states
provide either credits or rebates to offset some of the sales taxes on food.[23]
Extending these policies to the states that do not currently make use of
them would be a boon to the Latoyas, Jamals, and Carmens in this country. If these programs were coupled with steady increases in the minimum
wage—a measure that the Republican-controlled Congress has rejected
even as it has authorized massive tax breaks for the wealthiest Americans—
we would see more families pull themselves above the poverty line and
fewer children growing up with material hardship.

Doctor, Doctor

This country has been awash in the politics of health care reform for many
years now, spurred on by the skyrocketing cost of medical care, out-of-
control insurance rates (for consumers and physicians), and the ever-grow-
ing population of uninsured Americans, many of them workers and their
children. This is one policy front where a lot has been accomplished already, particularly in extending insurance coverage to children in poor and
near-poor households. Latoya's children receive their health care through
the State Child Health Insurance Program (SCHIP), which provides state
and federally funded health coverage to otherwise uninsured children.
Having a young son with chronic asthma, the family finds it a huge relief
to have his medical needs addressed.

Yet our concern for uninsured children has not been matched by attention to the health care needs of their parents. Delivering health insurance
through employers often leaves in limbo those workers whose jobs pay
only a modest salary. Their firms may not offer health insurance or, like
Natasha's employer, may provide it at an exorbitant cost to employees.
Only sixteen states offer Medicaid coverage for parents with incomes up to
the poverty line. In one state, "parents with incomes of more than 20 percent of the poverty line—about $3,100 annually for a family of three—are
ineligible for Medicaid," even though their children are covered. "In a
typical state," CBPP tells us, "a working parent earning about 71 percent
of the federal poverty line (about $11,000 for a family of three) is ineligible
for public coverage."[24] Anyone earning more than that is automatically
disqualified, which is absurd given how low the poverty line is and how far
short it falls from covering the real cost of living in a city like Los Angeles
or New York. Until we secure a better system altogether—which would
entail a debate beyond the scope of this chapter—we need to think about
incremental changes that will help workers, particularly low-wage workers, address the problem of health care access. Even if we didn't care about
their physical well-being—which we should—just keeping adult workers
on the job requires that we face the issue of the uninsured. Holding down
the expense of emergency treatment, which is where workers end up if
they don't have preventative care, is another worthy goal. What, then, can
be done?

The Center on Budget and Policy Priorities advocates extending state
child health insurance programs or Medicaid eligibility to parents above
the current income limits. Would this bankrupt states that are already
reeling under budget cuts and wrangling with the federal government over
who should pay for what? It wouldn't be cheap, that's for sure. And demands to increase the generosity of Medicaid will generate howls from the
feds, who are driving in the opposite direction: cutting reimbursements,
starving states, which then turn around and cut the poor from the rolls,
and shaving physician fees to the point where doctors refuse to serve uninsured patients.

The political conflict is reaching a boiling point, and in many states it
is being resolved by denying low-income working parents access to health
care, hardly a solution to the dilemma and not one that is foreordained.
Twenty-one states have eliminated the Medicaid assets test, so that families do not have to lose their cars, houses, or modest savings accounts

before they can get health care. Seven states—California, Connecticut, Maine, Ohio, Rhode Island, Arizona, and Illinois—and the District of Columbia have extended Medicaid to poor parents. They range from staunchly Republican states to hard-core Democratic ones, suggesting that it is possible to do more in many political climes.

Even with the best of health care, kids get sick. Who is going to take care of them when that happens? The Family and Medical Leave Act was a first step in making it possible for parents to attend to their children and elders who need help. Hard as it was to pass this federal legislation, all that it accomplished was to protect the jobs of those who make use of it. It exempted millions of small businesses, and it provided no income replacement for anyone. Most families cannot go without the income that the working members of their households earn. California was the first state to address this problem in a fashion that genuinely lightens the burdens illness imposes. In 2002, Governor Gray Davis signed a bill that provides for up to six weeks of partial pay "for eligible employees who need time off from work to bond with a new child or care for a seriously ill family member." The program, funded entirely by a payroll tax on employees, builds on California's existing State Disability Insurance system; virtually all private-sector employees are included.[25]

Although it has proven difficult to spread the news of this dramatic change to California's low-income workers, in time it will make an enormous difference, particularly for working families whose members suffer from chronic conditions. If workers like Latoya could recoup some of the wages they lose when they have to take time off to care for an asthmatic child, for example, their families would not be so stretched.

What about the Kids?

Middle-class mothers have a hard time finding comprehensive, affordable child care. Working-poor families, and those who have pulled themselves out of poverty but fall short of affluence face even more difficulty, particularly if they cannot turn to relatives for help, as so many of the families in this book have done. In California, where the state's budget was hammered by the energy crisis that brought Governor Arnold Schwarzenegger into office, nearly 280,000 children are on waiting lists for day care.[26] In New York City, about 11,000 low-income families are lining up for nonexistent spaces, a consequence of "relatively slow growth in the number of available . . . slots, combined with a huge increase in demand as nearly a million women left welfare rolls in the city since 1996."[27] Budget proposals on the desk of New York governor Pataki in 2005 were expected to cut even more deeply into support for child care. Like many other states, New York faces a shortfall ($6 billion in 2005), and the governor looks on the social service budget as the place to hold the line. Twenty-two thousand families would lose the slots they currently hold, and those on the waiting list would have to wait some more.[28]

Nationwide in 2001, only 14 percent of the children who were technically eligible for federal assistance with child care costs actually received it.[29] The population served is declining in size, as the states have lowered the income eligibility limits, frozen waiting lists, cut provider payments, and increased the amount families are expected to pay above the level of their grants. Yet the availability of reasonably priced child care is essential to keeping parents in the labor force, whether we are speaking of welfare recipients or families, like Carmen's, who earn an amount significantly above the poverty line but still don't make enough to afford child care without a subsidy.[30] If for no other reason than to make it possible for parents to remain on the job, we need to increase the number of kids who have subsidized child care by increasing the supply of places, lowering the threshold of eligibility, increasing the funds directed at providers (so they can afford to accept more children and provide them with quality care), and reduce the copayments for families.

The most enlightened child care policies are those that transition young children into enriched early childhood development programs that will improve cognitive skills and increase school readiness. In his 2004 book *Exceptional Returns*, economist Robert Lynch points to the smart investment that high-quality early childhood programs represent in terms of improved academic performance, increased lifetime earnings, and decreased rates of criminal conduct for poor children who participate in these programs. We now have several decades' worth of experience with Head Start, the ambitious federal initiative to boost the cultural capital of poor children, and it largely bears these findings out. Indeed, Lynch forecasts that benefits would outweigh costs by $31 billion by the year 2030 if we were to implement a universal program of early childhood development today.[31]

The need is all the more pressing in some of our most populous states, where immigrants form a large part of the poor and near-poor population.

That description fits many more states than it once did, since the traditional gateway cities of Los Angeles, Miami, New York, and San Francisco have been superseded by the Southeast and the Midwest in the rate of growth of the immigrant population. As the Foundation for Child Development points out, "Immigrants comprise 12 percent of the total U.S. population, [but] children of immigrants make up 22 percent of the 23.4 million children under age six. By 2020, almost 30 percent of all children will have one or more foreign-born parents."[32] These children will grow up to be productive citizens if the educational resources directed at them prepare them for the labor force. If not, they will not be the only ones to suffer. The rest of us—who will depend on them to keep the country productive when they reach working age—will pay a huge price if the system fails them.[33]

Fortunately, some states have moved ahead with ambitious plans for early childhood education. Georgia, Oklahoma, and New Jersey provide prekindergarten (pre-K) classes as part of the public school system for most, if not all, four-year-olds. In December 2004 the Florida legislature voted to provide universal pre-K instruction to all four-year-olds in that state. (Even more impressive, the lawmakers set goals for increasing teacher credentials and lowering the ratio of teachers to children until it reaches one to ten.)[34] Several months later, New Mexico's legislators approved a pre-K pilot program for four-year-olds in high-poverty areas.[35]

These are important steps toward addressing the long-term educational needs of the country's youngest citizens, to put them on a footing that will help them avoid poverty in the first place. At the same time, these policies address a critical child care need for parents. We could do even more if the 45 percent of American kindergarteners who are currently in half-day programs were provided full-day instruction. Finally, as early childhood education becomes a norm, there are equity issues to worry about. In 1965, only 5 percent of three-year-olds and 16 percent of four-year-olds were enrolled in preschool of any kind. By 2002, those numbers had exploded exponentially: 42 percent of three-year-olds and 67 percent of four-year-olds were attending school.[36] "According to the National Center for Education Statistics, children whose mothers have a college degree are twice as likely to be in some type of center-based school setting as those whose mothers didn't graduate from high school."[37] This is class reproduction at work. Children who have been to preschool are ahead of their nonattending classmates because they have already mastered much of the curriculum before they greet their teacher on the first day of kindergarten. It is important to provide all children with the tools they need to do well in the early years of school; we are seeing a divide open up, even at the tender age of four.

One-Stop Shopping

SeedCo, a nonprofit organization in New York City, has some innovative ideas about how to make it easier for low-income families to claim benefits they are legally entitled to, whether in the form of the EITC, housing vouchers, or child care subsidies. It has developed a Web-based tool that will permit case managers to process client data so that, in one fell swoop, they can determine a family's eligibility for virtually all benefits *and* complete their enrollment. Ending the cumbersome and time-consuming tradition of traipsing from one agency to another, only to be told that a document is missing, or to come back again in three weeks, would be a blessing for millions of poor families.

A system of the kind SeedCo has developed would help to address what remains a vexing problem: millions of families that are entitled to benefits just don't receive them. For example, only half of the working families who should be getting food stamps actually claim them. Only a quarter of the workers who are entitled to the EITC receive it.[38] According to the Kaiser Commission on Medicaid and the Uninsured, 40 percent of families whose children were eligible for Medicaid but not enrolled did not know that children of working parents were qualified.[39] Minorities, especially low-income Hispanics, are less likely than virtually any other eligible group to know about the EITC.[40] Poor education, lack of access to information, language barriers, and the sheer complexity of navigating the bureaucracies involved in dispensing benefits helps to explain why so many people who should be assisted by these programs are not benefiting from them. Compare this with the mortgage tax deduction or any of the myriad government benefits that middle-class Americans are entitled to, and the difference becomes clear.

Some scholars have argued that this is not an accident, that we design our benefits so that they will be hard to claim, both to discourage them from becoming expensive to support and to keep as many people independent of government support—and on their own—as possible.[41] Anyone who has read *Angela's Ashes*, Frank McCourt's moving account of his childhood poverty in Limerick, Ireland, will recall the heartbreaking description of the humiliation his mother endured as she sought help from Catholic charities so that she could put shoes on her son's feet. The theory seems to be the same in the United States today: Don't make it easy to access the safety net.

We have enacted benefits for good reasons. Erecting labyrinthine paperwork barriers in order to deny the poor—particularly the working poor—what they are legally entitled to claim serves no real purpose. It is simply an attempt to balance the budget on the backs of those least able to bear its weight.

What are the chances the reforms discussed here will come to pass? Some already have, particularly those in the area of prekindergarten education. Others are likely to flounder in our government's sea of red ink. The tax cuts enacted during President Bush's first term, coupled with the cost of war in Iraq and Afghanistan, have bequeathed this country deficits as far as the eye can see. Liberals are wondering what happened to the economic discipline that was characteristic of the Clinton presidency. Fiscal conservatives are stunned by the increases in government spending.

The question is, where will the savings come from to beat back this fiscal monster? The military budget is not on the cut list. Instead, social programs of precisely the kind discussed here are being slashed right and left. Job training, housing, higher education, and social services have taken a beating. A six-month investigative report by the *Detroit News* concluded that "the working poor and destitute Americans are increasingly likely to be placed on waiting lists, receive reduced services, or be denied service entirely."[42] In 2003 Massachusetts governor Mitt Romney imposed a fee of nineteen dollars a month on Medicaid recipients earning less than $13,300 for a family of three. Poor families who can barely make ends meet are required for the first time to make copayments when they visit the doctor.[43] Fortunately, the legislature passed a more progressive policy in April of 2006 that mandates the purchase of insurance by small business owners for their employees and eases the way for young adults, the group most likely to be uninsured, to get their hands on coverage. Hence, even in a state that seemed to be headed in a punitive direction in 2003, we see signs of progressive reform several years later. All eyes are on Massachusetts now, since it is the first state to attempt a form of universal coverage.

The Bush tax breaks gave the richest 10 percent of Americans a gift of $148 billion. That is twice as much as the government will spend on job training, Pell Grants for college students, public housing, low-income rental subsidies, child care, health insurance for low-income kids, low-income energy assistance, meals for shut-ins, and federal contributions to welfare. One does not have to be an expert in public policy to recognize that if we strip our must vulnerable citizens of the supports they need to educate their children, train for decent jobs, attend college, and stay in the labor force, we will drag ourselves back to the bad old days when those born poor stayed that way.

Chutes and Ladders chronicles the efforts of inner-city workers to move ahead in the American labor market. The single mother whose own mother was a long-term welfare recipient, the son of a heroin addict who never held more than a part-time minimum-wage job, the Burger Barn worker who was forced onto Medicaid so that she could see a doctor while in the midst of a dangerous pregnancy—Kyesha, Jamal, and Carmen are, at the end of this study, no longer stuck in the ranks of the working poor. They are budding members of the minority middle class, and the chances are good that their children will not repeat the pattern of their parents' lives. Government benefits played a role in making that possible. Even more important, these individuals were ready to go when jobs opened up that could ensure them a better standard of living. No one had to tell them they could do better for themselves; no one had to recast their culture or their values to persuade them to grasp that brass ring. They jumped at the opportunities they could find, and they made it—sometimes with the help of family, sometimes with the support of friends, and occasionally with the subsidy of public housing or health care. Theirs is not the majority's story. Many of their co-workers from their Burger Barn days are still treading water, earning enough to get by but not enough to rest easy. But the experience of these high flyers tells us what is possible.

APPENDIX A

Study Design

❦

We began this study in 1993–94 with close to three hundred workers from Harlem's fast-food labor force. During the first wave of the research, more than two hundred in this group were employed at one of the four Burger Barn outlets in Harlem. The rest had applied for a job at one of the restaurants but had not been hired. In 1997–98 the second wave of research reconnected with more than one hundred members of the original sample. In the second wave, the group was more evenly divided between people who had been Burger Barn employees and unsuccessful applicants. The third and final wave of research, conducted in 2001–2002, involved forty people (Table A.1).

Table A.1 Burger Barn employees and applicants in the sample groups

	Wave 1 (1993–94)	Wave 2 (1997)	Wave 3 (2002)
Employee in '93–94	201 (68%)	56 (54%)	18 (45%)
Unsuccessful applicants in '93–94	93 (32%)	47 (46%)	22 (55%)
Total	294	103	40

Who Is in Wave 3?

The wave 3 cohort is made up of three different age groups. Those in the first group (ages twenty-three to twenty-six) were the youngest workers when the study began—the teens who landed fast-food jobs; those in the second group (ages twenty-seven to twenty-nine) were the young adults of 1993; and those in the third group (thirty and over) were the oldest ones working in fast food in 1993, even though their age at the time might have made them candidates for better paying jobs (Table A.2).

In wave 3, two-thirds of the sample group is female, one-third male. This is similar to the gender breakdown in wave 2; in wave 1 the sample was more evenly divided (Table A.3).

The racial and ethnic composition of the wave 3 group is 60 percent black, or African American, 15 percent Dominican, 10 percent Puerto Rican, and 10 percent other. This is similar to the composition of waves 1 and 2 (Table A.4).

A third of the wave 3 group is married. This is hardly surprising for a group age twenty-three and older. As we would expect, the relationship status of the individuals shifted over time. More members of this group (fourteen) are

Table A.2 Age

Age (years)	Wave 1 (1993)	Wave 2 (1997)	Wave 3 (2002)
15–19	102 (35%)	3 (3%)	—
20–22	64 (22%)	39 (38%)	—
23–26	42 (14%)	27 (26%)	15 (38%)
27–29	31 (11%)	11 (11%)	11 (27%)
30–35	55 (18%)	23 (22%)	14 (35%)
Total	294	103	40

Table A.3 Gender

	Wave 1 (1993)	Wave 2 (1997)	Wave 3 (2002)
Female	155 (53%)	64 (62%)	26 (65%)
Male	139 (47%)	39 (38%)	14 (35%)
Total	294	103	40

Table A.4 Race/ethnicity

	Wave 1 (1993)	Wave 2 (1997)	Wave 3 (2002)
African American	190 (65%)	62 (62%)	27 (60%)
Dominican	49 (17%)	22 (22%)	6 (15%)
Puerto Rican	10 (3%)	8 (8%)	4 (10%)
Other	45 (15%)	8 (8%)	3 (10%)
Total	294	100	40

Table A.5 Marital status of wave 3 respondents

	At wave 2 (1997)	At wave 3 (2002)
Married, living with spouse	9	14
Separated	0	2
Divorced	4	2
Widowed	1	1
Never been married	20	16
Living w/unmarried partner	6	5
Total	40	40

Table A.6 Wave 3 respondents with children

	At wave 1 (1993)	At wave 2 (1997)	At wave 3 (2002)
Had children	15	24	30
No children	25	16	10
Total	40	40	40

married than at any time in the past, and five people are living with an un-married partner. Notably, another third of the group has never been married (Table A.5).

Three-fourths of those in the wave 3 cohort have a child (Table A.6). More than half also had a child at wave 2. Since wave 2, nineteen of the final cohort had a new child (six had their first child, and thirteen had their second child).

Wage Mobility

An important question to ask is, What opportunities did wave 3 respondents have to increase their wages? There are twelve people who were employed at wave 1 (1993), wave 2 (1997), and wave 3 (2002).[1] The average hourly wage for this group in 1993 was $6.09 in 2002 dollars ($4.94 in 1993 dollars) and the average wage in 2002 was $16.90 (Figure A.1).

If we calculate their average hourly wage growth per year, we find that six people out of the twelve (50 percent) saw their hourly wage grow by more than $1.25 per year.[2]

To increase the number of the sample, we can look at the change from wave 1 to wave 3—that is, the seventeen people who were employed at wave 1 and wave 3, but not at wave 2. The average wage for this group in 1993 was $5.84 ($4.74 in 1993–94 dollars), and the average wage in 2002 was $15.98 (Figure A.2). When we calculate the average hourly wage growth per year, we see that six people out of the seventeen (35 percent) saw their hourly wage grow by more than $1.25 per year.[3]

Given the small numbers here, it is not surprising that we see such a high percentage of high flyers. While it is hard to say just how significant is the relationship between the likelihood of being employed at the time of the interview and wage growth, it seems clear that there is some relationship. When we limit the pool to those employed at the time of the interview, we lose people with lower levels of wage growth. The wage growth charts for the hires only,

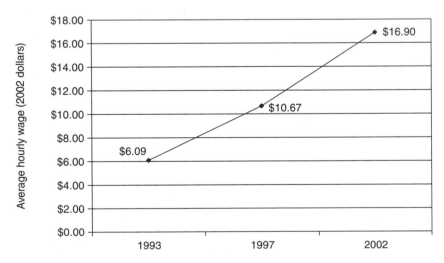

Figure A.1   Change in average hourly wages ($n = 12$).

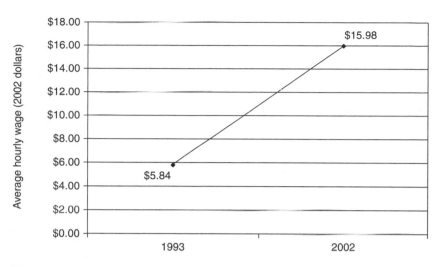

Figure A.2 Average hourly wages ($n = 17$).

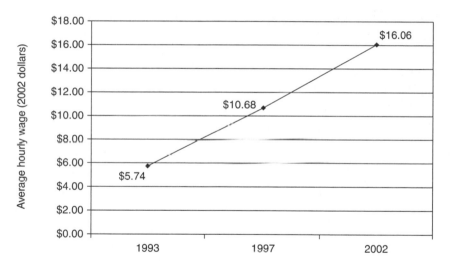

Figure A.3 Average hourly wages, hires ($n = 10$).

looking at all three waves and at just wave 1 and wave 3, are presented in Figures A.3 and A.4.

There are ten hires who were employed at wave 1, wave 2, and wave 3. The average hourly wage for this group in 1993 was $5.74 in 2002 dollars ($4.63 in 1993 dollars), and the average wage in 2002 was $16.06. When we calculate the average growth per year in the hourly wage, we find that four people out

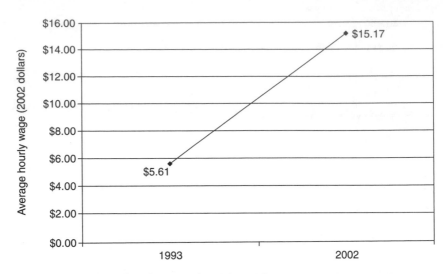

Figure A.4 Average hourly wages, hires (*n* = 14).

the ten (40 percent) had an hourly wage growth of more than $1.25 per year (Figure A.3).[4]

If we look at the change from wave 1 to wave 3 for the hires (*n* = 14), the average wage in 1993 was $5.61 ($4.52 in 1993 dollars), and the average wage in 2002 was $15.17. When we calculate the average wage growth per year, we find that four people out the fourteen (29 percent) had hourly wage growth of more than $1.25 per year (Figure A.4).[5]

APPENDIX B

Sample Definitions

🍇

For the comparative analysis described in Chapter 5, based on data from the Survey of Income and Program Participation, an individual job holder qualified for inclusion if (in addition to the restrictions set down by the particular sample) at some point during the job the following three criteria were met:

> The individual who held the job was between eighteen and forty years of age, *and*
> The individual's family was at or below 1.5 times the poverty level for that family, *and*
> The job paid an hourly wage.

The samples analyzed are displayed in Table B.1.

Table B.1 Sample groups

	Sample 1: Base	Sample 2: All non-managerial jobs	Sample 3: All races	Sample 4: All geographic areas
Geographic area	metro[a]	metro[a]	metro[a]	all areas
Race	black/Hispanic	black/Hispanic	all	all
Job	food service[b]	all nonmanagerial jobs[c]	all nonmanagerial jobs[c]	all nonmanagerial jobs[c]

Note: Each sample builds on the previous sample. For example, sample 2 includes all individuals in sample 1 *plus* black or Hispanic individuals in metropolitan areas who hold nonmanagerial jobs outside food service.

a. See Table B.2 for a complete listing of metropolitan areas.

b. Food service jobs are defined by SIC code 641 and SOC codes 436–469.

c. See Table B.3 for a complete listing of SOC codes excluded from nonmanagerial jobs.

Metropolitan Areas

Table B.2 lists the geographic areas classified as metropolitan areas in the SIPP data, used for comparison with the Harlem study.

Food Service Jobs

Food service jobs are defined for the SIPP by the industrial and occupational classifications used by the U.S. Census Bureau. To qualify as food service, a job must fall under the 1987 Standard Industrial Classification (SIC) system industry group 641 ("Eating and Drinking Places") and the worker must be listed in one of four food service occupations, as defined by the 1980 Standard Occupational Classification (SOC). Details of the industry and occupation codes are listed below.

Industry Group

Industry group 641, "Eating and Drinking Places," is divided into two subcategories: "Eating Places" and "Drinking Places." (While the two types of establishments are identified using four-digit SIC codes, the SIPP provides only the three-digit industry group code. Many of the jobs listed under "Drinking Places" were eliminated from our analysis once the occupations were taken into consideration.)

EATING PLACES

Establishments primarily engaged in the retail sale of prepared food and drinks for on-site or immediate consumption. Caterers and industrial and institutional food service establishments are also included in this category.

- Automats (eating places)
- Beaneries
- Box lunch stands
- Buffets (eating places)
- Cafés
- Cafeterias
- Carry-out restaurants
- Caterers
- Coffee shops
- Commissary restaurants

Table B.2 Metropolitan areas

CMSA/ MSA	Geographic area	CMSA/ MSA[a]	Geographic area
7	Boston-Lawrence-Salem, MA-NH	3240	Harrisburg-Lebanon-Carlisle, PA
10	Buffalo–Niagara Falls, NY	3320	Honolulu, HI
14	Chicago–Gary Lake County, IL-IN	3480	Indianapolis, IN
21	Cincinnati-Hamilton, OH-KY	3600	Jacksonville, FL
28	Cleveland-Akron-Lorraine, OH	3840	Knoxville, TN
31	Dallas–Ft. Worth, TX	3980	Lakeland-Winterhaven, FL
34	Denver-Boulder, CO	4040	Lansing–East Lansing, MI
35	Detroit–Ann Arbor, MI	4720	Madison, WI
41	Hartford–New Britain–Middletown, CT	4880	McCallen-Edinburg-Mission, TX
42	Houston, TX	4900	Melbourne-Titusville–Palm Bay, FL
49	Los Angeles–Anaheim-Riverside, CA	4920	Memphis, TN
56	Miami–Ft. Lauderdale, FL	5120	Minneapolis–St. Paul, MN
63	Milwaukee-Racine, WI	5160	Mobile, AL
70	New York–New Jersey–Long Island, NY-NJ-CT	5360	Nashville, TN
77	Philadelphia-Wilmington-Trenton, PA-DE-NJ	5480	New Haven–Meriden, CT
78	Pittsburgh–Beaver Valley, PA	5560	New Orleans, LA
79	Portland-Vancouver, OR-WA	5720	Norfolk–Virginia Beach–Newport News, VA
82	St. Louis–St. Charles–Farmington, IL-MO	5880	Oklahoma City, OK
84	San Francisco–Oakland–San Jose, CA	5960	Orlando, FL
91	Seattle-Tacoma, WA	6080	Pensacola, FL
160	Albany-Schenectady-Troy, NY	6200	Phoenix, AZ
200	Albequerque, NM	6640	Raleigh-Durham, NC
520	Atlanta, GA	6840	Rochester, NY
640	Austin, TX	6880	Rockford, IL
680	Bakersfield, CA	6920	Sacramento, CA
760	Baton Rouge, LA	7120	Salinas-Seaside-Monterey, CA
840	Beaumont–Port Arthur, TX	7160	Salt Lake City-Ogden, UT
1000	Birmingham, AL	7240	San Antonio, TX
1520	Charlotte-Gastonia–Rock Hill, NC	7320	San Diego, CA
1720	Colorado Springs, CO	7560	Scranton–Wilkes-Barre, PA
1840	Columbus, OH	8000	Springfield, MA

Table B.2 Metropolitan areas (continued)

CMSA/ MSA	Geographic area	CMSA/ MSA[a]	Geographic area
1880	Corpus Christi, TX	8120	Stockton, CA
2000	Dayton-Springfield, OH	8160	Syracuse, NY
2320	El Paso, TX	8280	Tampa–St. Petersburg–Clearwater, FL
2400	Eugene-Springfield, OR	8400	Toledo, OH
2560	Fayetteville, NC	8520	Tucson, AZ
2700	Ft. Myers, FL	8560	Tulsa, OK
2760	Ft. Wayne, IN	8680	Utica-Rome, NY
2840	Fresno, CA	8840	Washington, DC-MD-VA
3120	Greensboro–Winston-Salem–High Point, NC	8960	West Palm Beach–Boca Raton–Delray Beach, FL
3160	Greensville-Spartanburg, SC	9240	Worcester, MA

Source: U.S. Census Bureau, Population Division, 1999 Definitions.
a. CMSA/MSA = consolidated metropolitan statistical area/metropolitan statistical area.

· Concession stands, prepared food (e.g., in airports and sports arenas)
· Contract feeding
· Dairy bars
· Diners (eating places)
· Dining rooms
· Dinner theaters
· Drive-in restaurants
· Fast-food restaurants
· Food bars
· Food service, institutional
· Frozen custard stands
· Grills (eating places)
· Hamburger stands
· Hot dog (frankfurter) stands
· Ice cream stands
· Industrial feeding
· Lunch bars
· Lunch counters
· Luncheonettes
· Lunchrooms
· Oyster bars
· Pizza parlors
· Pizzerias

- Refreshment stands
- Restaurants
- Restaurants, carry-out
- Restaurants, fast-food
- Sandwich bars or shops
- Snack shops
- Soda fountains
- Soft drink stands
- Submarine sandwich shops
- Tea rooms
- Theaters, dinner

DRINKING PLACES (ALCOHOLIC BEVERAGES)

Establishments primarily engaged in the retail sale of alcoholic drinks, such as beer, ale, wine, and liquor, for consumption on the premises. The sale of food frequently accounts for a substantial portion of the receipts of these establishments.

- Bars (alcoholic beverage drinking places)
- Beer gardens (drinking places)
- Beer parlors (tap rooms)
- Beer taverns
- Beer, wine, and liquors: sale for on-site consumption
- Bottle clubs (drinking places)
- Cabarets
- Cocktail lounges
- Discotheques, alcoholic beverage
- Drinking places, alcoholic beverage
- Night clubs
- Saloons (drinking places)
- Tap rooms (drinking places)
- Taverns (drinking places)
- Wine bars

Occupational Classification

The four occupational classifications considered to be food service jobs are drawn from the Standard Occupational Classification (SOC) of the 1980 census:

SOC code 436: Cooks, except short-order
SOC code 437: Short-order cooks
SOC code 438: Food counter, fountain, and related occupations
SOC code 439: Kitchen workers, food preparation.

For all panels, beginning in 1991, the SIPP uses the 1990 census codes. For these panels, SOC codes 436 and 437 are combined under the heading "Cooks."

Excluded Managerial and Professional Occupations

When expanding the sample from food service–related occupations to all nonmanagerial jobs, all occupations were allowed as "qualifying" jobs except those defined as managerial or professional occupations. The excluded occupations are shown in Table B.3.

Table B.3 Managerial and professional occupations excluded from sample

SOC code[a]		
1980 census	1990 census	Job description
3	3	legislators
4	4	chief executives and general administrators, public
5	5	administrators and officials, public administration
6	6	administrators, protective service
7	7	financial managers
8	8	personnel and labor relations managers
9	9	purchasing managers
13	13	managers, marketing, advertising, and public relations
14	14	administrators, education and related fields
15	15	managers, medicine and health
16	18	managers, properties and real estate
17	16	postmasters and mail superintendents
—	17	managers, food-serving and lodging establishments
18	19	funeral directors
19	—	managers and administrators, n.e.c.[b]
—	21	managers, service organizations, n.e.c.[b]
—	22	managers and administrators, n.e.c.[b]
23	23	accountants and auditors
24	24	underwriters
25	25	other financial officers
26	26	management analysts
27	27	personnel, training, and labor relations specialists
28	28	purchasing agents and buyers, farm products

Table B.3 Managerial and professional occupations excluded from sample
(continued)

1980 census	1990 census	Job description
29	29	buyers, wholesale and retail trade except farm products
33	33	purchasing agents and buyers
34	34	business and promotion agents
35	35	construction inspectors
36	36	inspectors and compliance officers, except construction
37	37	management-related occupations, n.e.c.[b]
43	43	architects
44	44	aerospace engineers
45	45	metallurgical and materials engineers
46	46	mining engineers
47	47	petroleum engineers
48	48	chemical engineers
49	49	nuclear engineers
53	53	civil engineers
54	54	agricultural engineers
55	55	electrical and electronic engineers
56	56	industrial engineers
57	57	mechanical engineers
58	58	marine and naval architects
59	59	engineers, n.e.c.[b]
63	63	surveyors and mapping scientists
64	64	computer systems analysts and scientists
65	65	operations and systems researchers and analysts
66	66	actuaries
67	67	statisticians
68	68	mathematical scientists, n.e.c.[b]
69	69	physicists and astronomers
73	73	chemists, except biochemists
74	74	atmospheric and space scientists
75	75	geologists and geodesists
76	76	physical scientists, n.e.c.[b]
77	77	agricultural and food scientists
78	78	biological and life scientists
79	79	forestry and conservation scientists
83	83	medical scientists
84	84	physicians
85	85	dentists
86	86	veterinarians
87	87	optometrists
88	88	podiatrists

SOC code[a]

Table B.3 Managerial and professional occupations excluded from sample
(continued)

SOC code[a]		
1980 census	1990 census	Job description
89	89	health diagnosing practitioners, n.e.c.[b]
95	95	registered nurses
96	96	pharmacists
97	97	dietitians
98	—	inhalation therapists
—	98	respiratory therapists
99	99	occupational therapists
103	103	physical therapists
104	104	speech therapists
105	105	therapists, n.e.c.[b]
106	106	physicians' assistants
113	113	earth, environmental, and marine science teachers
114	114	biological science teachers
115	115	chemistry teachers
116	116	physics teachers
117	117	natural science teachers, n.e.c.[b]
118	118	psychology teachers
119	119	economics teachers
123	123	history teachers
124	124	political science teachers
125	125	sociology teachers
126	126	social science teachers, n.e.c.[b]
127	127	engineering teachers
128	128	mathematical science teachers
129	129	computer science teachers
133	133	medical science teachers
134	134	health specialties teachers
135	135	business, commerce, and marketing teachers
136	136	agriculture and forestry teachers
137	137	art, drama, and music teachers
138	138	physical education teachers
139	139	education teachers
143	143	English teachers
144	144	foreign language teachers
145	145	law teachers
146	146	social work teachers
147	147	theology teachers
148	148	trade and industrial teachers
149	149	home economics teachers
153	153	teachers, postsecondary, n.e.c.[b]
154	154	postsecondary teachers, subject not specified
155	155	teachers, prekindergarten and kindergarten

Table B.3 Managerial and professional occupations excluded from sample
(continued)

SOC code[a]		
1980 census	1990 census	Job description
156	156	teachers, elementary school
157	157	teachers, secondary school
158	158	teachers, special education
159	159	teachers, n.e.c.[b]
163	163	counselors, educational and vocational
164	164	librarians
165	165	archivists and curators
166	166	economists
167	167	psychologists
168	168	sociologists
169	169	social scientists, n.e.c.[b]
173	173	urban planners
174	174	social workers
175	175	recreation workers
176	176	clergy
177	177	religious workers, n.e.c.[b]
178	178	lawyers
179	179	judges
183	183	authors
184	184	technical writers
185	185	designers
186	186	musicians and composers
187	187	actors and directors
188	188	painters, sculptors, craft-artists, and artist printmakers
189	189	photographers
193	193	dancers
194	194	artists, performers, and related workers, n.e.c.[b]
195	195	editors and reporters
197	197	public relations specialists
198	198	announcers
199	199	athletes
243	243	supervisors and proprietors, sales occupations
303	303	supervisors, general office
304	304	supervisors, computer equipment operators
305	305	supervisors, financial records processing
306	306	chief communications operators
307	307	supervisors, distribution, scheduling, and adjusting clerks
413	413	supervisors, firefighting and fire prevention occupations
414	414	supervisors, police and detectives

Table B.3 Managerial and professional occupations excluded from sample
(continued)

SOC code[a]		
1980 census	1990 census	Job description
415	415	supervisors, guards
433	433	supervisors, food preparation and service occupations
448	448	supervisors, cleaning and building service workers
456	456	supervisors, personal service occupations
473	473	farmers, except horticultural
474	474	horticultural specialty farmers
475	475	managers, farms, except horticultural
476	476	managers, horticultural specialty farms
477	477	supervisors, farm workers
485	485	supervisors, related agricultural occupations
494	494	supervisors, forestry and logging workers
497	497	captains and other officers, fishing vessels
503	503	supervisors, mechanics and repairers
553	553	supervisors, brickmasons, stonemasons, and tile setters
554	554	supervisors, carpenters and related work
555	555	supervisors, electricians and power transmission installers
556	556	supervisors, painters, paperhangers, and plasterers
557	557	supervisors, plumbers, pipefitters, and steamfitters
558	—	supervisors, n.e.c.[b]
—	558	supervisors, constructing, n.e.c.[b]
613	613	supervisors, extractive occupations
633	628	supervisors, production occupations
803	803	supervisors, motor vehicle operators
823	823	railroad conductors and yardmasters
828	828	ship captains and mates, except fishing boats
843	843	supervisors, material moving equipment operators
863	864	supervisors, handlers, equipment cleaners, and laborers, n.e.c.[b]

Source: Standard Occupational Classifications, U.S. Bureau of Labor Statistics, Division of Employment Statistics.

a. SOC = Standard Occupational Classification.

b. n.e.c. = not elsewhere classified.

Occupational Prestige Scores and the Socioeconomic Index

The occupational prestige scores we use today date from the North-Hatt study of 1947, which rated ninety occupational titles.[1] Duncan used the North-Hatt information in conjunction with the detailed occupational categories available in the 1950 census of the U.S. population to create a socioeconomic index (SEI).[2] He regressed prestige scores for forty-five occupational titles on education and income characteristics of men. He then assigned prestige scores to all occupational categories in the census. The SEI scores have been routinely updated according to revised classification systems used in later censuses. The SEI has somewhat different properties than the occupational prestige score because of its use of education and income measures, and it enables researchers to cover a wider range of occupational titles.

To expand the prestige score to more occupational titles without relying on the SEI, additional prestige measures were designed. Siegel created a prestige score with pooled data from five separate studies, using occupational titles from the 1960 census.[3] These titles covered a larger range of occupations than the North-Hatt score, which was dominated by high-status professional and low-status service occupations. Updating the SEI between the 1960 and 1970 classifications was straightforward, because there were minimal changes in the occupational titles.

Siegel's prestige score allowed Stevens and Featherman to calculate a revised SEI based on the occupational titles in the 1970 census.[4] The 1970 SEI scores were, in turn, linked to the 1980 census by Stevens and Cho, even though the classification system was significantly altered between the 1970 and 1980 censuses.[5] Stevens and Hoisington recalibrated prestige scores by weighting them according to the size of the labor force in each category.[6] Other methods have also been tried.

Current use of the reworked scores presents some problems: the selection of occupational titles is not representative; old scores have been reworked to fit new occupational categories; public opinion on occupational prestige has shifted; and occupational categories have changed.

Research has shown that shifts in public opinion have altered prestige scores but changes in the classification system have not. The averaging of occupational title scores (over wider classifications) is reflected in some differences between score sets, but different scales tend to produce similar results. The current argument is that new scales, based on new prestige ratings, are better suited to contemporary occupational data.

New Prestige Rankings

In 1989 a new survey was administered to evaluate the prestige of occupational titles. This survey ranked 740 occupational titles (as opposed to the 204 in the original 1964 study). Following the same procedures that were used to construct the original prestige scale, new rankings were linked to occupational titles in both the 1980 and the 1990 census, which were very similar. Additionally, socioeconomic scores were developed using the 1980 census information.[7]

Our SIPP data are classified under the Standard Occupational Classification (SOC) system used in both the 1980 and the 1990 census. We rely on the Nakao and Treas prestige scores, using the new survey and the 1980 census definitions to create an SEI score with the 1990 census classifications.[8] In some cases, where the 1980 categories exist and are a subset of the 1990 classification, the SEI scores of the occupations belonging to the 1990 census category are averaged. Where the 1980 categories were expanded, the 1980 SEI score was assigned to each of the expanded categories in the 1990 classification system. Table C.1 contains a list of SEI scores and occupations for all SOC codes.

Table C.1 Socioeconomic index scores and occupations for all Standard
Occupational Classification codes

SEI score	Job description
14.53	textile sewing machine operators
14.74	pressing machine operators
14.83	private household cleaners and servants
14.85	knitting, looping, taping, and weaving machine operators
14.97	shoe machine operators
15.26	miscellaneous textile machine operators
15.33	cooks, private household
15.38	housekeepers and butlers
15.62	launderers and ironers
15.71	maids and housemen
15.93	nailing and tacking machine operators
15.95	solderers and brazers
16.11	hand packers and packagers
16.22	graders and sorters, except agricultural
16.62	sawing machine operators
16.72	bridge, lock, and lighthouse tenders
16.72	crossing guards
16.77	graders and sorters, agricultural products
16.78	elevator operators
16.87	laundering and dry cleaning machine operators
16.88	nursery workers
17.09	farmworkers
17.24	garbage collectors
17.24	vehicle washers and equipment cleaners
17.54	cooks
17.58	packaging and filling machine operators
17.63	punching and stamping press machine operators
17.70	adjusters and calibrators
17.71	electrical and electronic equipment assemblers
17.75	kitchen workers, food preparation
17.87	precision assemblers, metal
17.88	assemblers
17.95	slicing and cutting machine operators
17.98	child care workers, private household
17.99	textile cutting machine operators
18.03	machine feeders and offbearers
18.03	timber cutting and logging occupations
18.09	upholsterers
18.12	janitors and cleaners
18.20	shoe repairers
18.29	industrial truck and tractor equipment operators
18.33	miscellaneous food preparation occupations
18.41	painting and paint spraying machine operators
18.42	dressmakers

Table C.1 Socioeconomic index scores and occupations for all Standard
             Occupational Classification codes (continued)

SEI score	Job description
18.46	construction laborers
18.51	helpers, mechanics, and repairers
18.62	compressing and compacting machine operators
18.70	miscellaneous machine operators, n.e.c.[a]
18.75	molding and casting machine operators
18.76	washing, cleaning, and pickling machine operators
18.77	hand cutting and trimming occupations
18.79	miscellaneous metal and plastic processing machine operators
18.81	laborers, except construction
18.83	cementing and gluing machine operators
18.85	production samplers and weighers
18.86	extruding and forming machine operators
18.86	food batchmakers
18.88	crushing and grinding machine operators
18.88	folding machine operators
18.88	waiters and waitresses
18.95	mixing and blending machine operators
18.95	shaping and joining machine operators
19.04	hand engraving and printing occupations
19.10	hairdressers and cosmetologists
19.10	tailors
19.16	miscellaneous woodworking machine operators
19.16	roasting and baking machine operators, food
19.23	groundskeepers and gardeners, except farm
19.23	miscellaneous handworking occupations
19.24	hand molding, casting, and forming occupations
19.25	bakers
19.30	numerical control machine operators
19.30	pest control occupations
19.32	supervisors, handlers, equipment cleaners, and laborers, n.e.c.[a]
19.33	waiters'/waitresses' assistants
19.35	drilling and boring machine operators
19.37	machine operators, not specified
19.49	grinding, abrading, buffing, and polishing machine operators
19.52	miscellaneous material moving equipment operators
19.56	freight, stock, and material handlers, n.e.c.[a]
19.73	garage and service station–related occupations
19.74	separating, filtering, and clarifying machine operators
19.75	furniture and wood finishers
19.76	roofers
19.80	hand molders and shapers, except jewelers
19.81	news vendors
19.85	metal plating machine operators

Table C.1 Socioeconomic index scores and occupations for all Standard
Occupational Classification codes (continued)

SEI score	Job description
19.86	bookbinders
19.88	marine life cultivation workers
19.94	machinery maintenance occupations
19.96	explosives workers
19.97	stock handlers and baggers
20.24	mining machine operators
20.24	mining occupations, n.e.c.[a]
20.26	precision grinders, filers, and tool sharpeners
20.29	farm equipment mechanics
20.43	barbers
20.50	grader, dozer, and scraper operators
20.56	construction trades, n.e.c.[a]
20.60	miscellaneous precision apparel and fabric workers
20.61	supervisors, food preparation and service occupations
20.62	furnace, kiln, and oven operators, except food
20.65	hunters and trappers
20.66	welders and cutters
20.74	drillers, oil well
20.77	miscellaneous metal-, plastic-, stone-, and glass-working machine operators
20.79	helpers, surveyor
20.79	painters, construction and maintenance
20.79	supervisors, cleaning and building service workers
20.80	food counter, fountain, and related occupations
20.86	supervisors, painters, paperhangers, and plasterers
20.91	cabinetmakers and bench carpenters
20.95	automobile mechanic apprentices
20.95	automobile mechanics
21.04	forging machine operators
21.10	motor transportation occupations, n.e.c.[a]
21.10	truck drivers
21.11	hoist and winch operators
21.17	butchers and meat cutters
21.22	wood lathe, routing, and planing machine operators
21.30	concrete and terrazzo finishers
21.31	carpenter apprentices
21.32	inspectors, agricultural products
21.40	cashiers
21.42	drillers, earth
21.47	bus drivers
21.50	production testers
21.55	plasterers
21.57	miscellaneous plant and system operators

Table C.1 Socioeconomic index scores and occupations for all Standard
Occupational Classification codes (continued)

SEI score	Job description
21.62	excavating and loading machine operators
21.62	paving, surfacing, and tamping equipment operators
21.71	sailors and deckhands
21.72	operating engineers
21.73	automobile body and related repairers
21.83	bus, truck, and stationary engine mechanics
21.86	milling and planing machine operators
21.86	miscellaneous precision workers, n.e.c.[a]
21.89	telephone operators
21.98	crane and tower operators
22.03	production inspectors, checkers, and examiners
22.09	lathe and turning machine operators
22.40	fishers
22.41	heat treating equipment operators
22.46	taxicab drivers and chauffeurs
22.49	industrial machinery repairers
22.52	heavy equipment mechanics
22.58	carpenters
22.62	brickmason and stonemason apprentices
22.62	brickmasons and stonemasons
22.62	longshore equipment operators
22.62	stevedores
22.63	supervisors, brickmasons, stonemasons, and tile setters
22.69	tile setters, hard and soft
22.71	lathe and turning machine set-up operators
22.86	supervisors, carpenters and related workers
23.00	animal caretakers, except farm
23.06	carpet installers
23.07	traffic, shipping, and receiving clerks
23.11	parking lot attendants
23.20	driver-sales workers
23.20	rolling machine operators
23.22	family child care providers
23.27	horticultural specialty farmers
23.33	data-entry keyers
23.40	paperhangers
23.52	specified mechanics and repairers, n.e.c.[a]
23.55	child care workers, n.e.c.[a]
23.58	nursing aides, orderlies, and attendants
23.60	peripheral equipment operators
23.61	correctional institution officers
23.64	elevator installers and repairers
23.68	drywall installers

Table C.1 Socioeconomic index scores and occupations for all Standard Occupational Classification codes (continued)

SEI score	Job description
23.73	billing, posting, and calculating machine operators
23.73	mail-preparing and paper-handling machine operators
23.76	miscellaneous precision woodworkers
23.81	farmers, except horticultural
23.82	inspectors, testers, and graders
23.88	meter readers
23.89	marine engineers
23.96	bartenders
23.97	office machine operators, n.e.c.[a]
24.01	weighers, measurers, checkers, and samplers
24.02	layout workers
24.13	hand painting, coating, and decorating occupations
24.17	guards and police, except public service
24.23	mechanical controls and valve repairers
24.26	household appliance and power tool repairers
24.40	messengers
24.44	machinists
24.49	machinist apprentices
24.55	glaziers
24.59	baggage porters and bellhops
24.72	billing clerks
24.83	locksmiths and safe repairers
24.83	small engine repairers
24.98	file clerks
25.09	rail vehicle operators, n.e.c.[a]
25.19	communications equipment operators, n.e.c.[a]
25.21	licensed practical nurses
25.22	typists
25.23	stock and inventory clerks
25.37	sales support occupations, n.e.c.[a]
25.37	sales workers, apparel
25.37	sales workers, shoes
25.38	classified-ad clerks
25.38	hotel clerks
25.50	not specified mechanics and repairers
25.50	precious stones and metals workers (jewelers)
25.51	boilermakers
25.53	chief communications operators
25.54	millwrights
25.66	supervisors, farmworkers
25.69	demonstrators, promoters and models, sales
25.83	sales counter clerks
25.96	health aides, except nursing

Table C.1 Socioeconomic index scores and occupations for all Standard
            Occupational Classification codes (continued)

SEI score	Job description
26.12	sheet metal worker apprentices
26.12	sheet metal duct installers
26.15	railroad brake, signal, and switch operators
26.16	mail clerks, except postal service
26.25	supervisors, related agricultural occupations
26.26	duplicating machine operators
26.26	sheet metal workers
26.33	public transportation attendants
26.35	miscellaneous printing machine operators
26.38	heating, air conditioning, and refrigeration mechanics
26.48	printing press operators
26.49	sales workers, other commodities
26.75	miscellaneous electrical and electronic equipment repairers
26.81	water and sewage treatment plant operators
27.07	early childhood teacher's assistants
27.09	engravers, metal
27.10	helpers, construction trades
27.15	dental assistants
27.23	plumbers, pipe fitters, and steam fitters
27.24	plumber, pipe fitter, and steam fitter apprentices
27.38	payroll and timekeeping clerks
27.41	camera, watch, and musical instrument repairers
27.42	supervisors, plumbers, pipe fitters, and steam fitters
27.84	mail carriers, postal service
27.86	telephone line installers and repairers
27.91	structural metalworkers
28.01	insulation workers
28.10	typesetters and compositors
28.16	electrical power installers and repairers
28.26	stationary engineers
28.38	personal service occupations, n.e.c.[a]
28.43	supervisors, personal service occupations
28.60	street and door-to-door sales workers
28.76	protective service occupations, n.e.c.[a]
28.91	attendants, amusement and recreation facilities
28.92	general office clerks
28.92	order clerks
28.95	electronic repairers, communications and industrial equipment
29.00	receptionists
29.02	optical goods workers
29.03	sales workers, hardware and building supplies
29.19	photographic process machine operators

Table C.1 Socioeconomic index scores and occupations for all Standard
Occupational Classification codes (continued)

SEI score	Job description
29.33	bank tellers
29.82	dancers
29.94	stenographers
30.18	supervisors, distribution, scheduling, and adjusting clerks
30.25	postal clerks, except mail carriers
30.29	supervisors, guards
30.43	bookkeepers, accounting, and auditing clerks
30.62	pattern makers and model makers, wood
30.70	dispatchers
30.78	aircraft mechanics, except engine
30.85	aircraft engine mechanics
30.91	supervisors, electricians and power transmission installers
31.04	electrician apprentices
31.05	electricians
31.23	locomotive operating occupations
31.23	pattern makers and model makers, metal
31.26	statistical clerks
31.44	photoengravers and lithographers
31.75	personnel clerks, except payroll and timekeeping
31.90	records clerks
31.95	tool and die makers
31.98	sales workers, furniture and home furnishings
32.03	captains and other officers, fishing vessels
32.41	administrative support occupations, n.e.c.[a]
32.44	cost and rate clerks
32.58	dental laboratory and medical appliance technicians
32.59	telephone installers and repairers
32.61	miscellaneous precision metalworkers
32.61	tool and die maker apprentices
32.68	sales workers, radio, tv, hi-fi, and appliances
32.72	information clerks, n.e.c.[a]
32.72	supervisors, firefighting and fire prevention occupations
32.75	motion picture projectionists
32.76	office machine repairers
32.83	firefighting occupations
32.87	power plant operators
32.93	correspondence clerks
32.93	material recording, scheduling, and distributing clerks, n.e.c.[a]
33.18	supervisors, material moving equipment operators
33.25	ship captains and mates, except fishing boats
33.33	supervisors, forestry and logging workers
34.40	auctioneers
34.48	production coordinators

Table C.1 Socioeconomic index scores and occupations for all Standard
Occupational Classification codes (continued)

SEI score	Job description
34.54	sales workers, motor vehicles and boats
34.62	purchasing agents and buyers, farm products
34.71	broadcast equipment operators
34.73	secretaries
34.75	eligibility clerks, social welfare
34.76	managers, farms, except horticultural
35.23	administrators, protective services
35.25	proofreaders
35.40	supervisors, motor vehicle operators
35.41	bill and account collectors
35.97	expediters
36.20	forestry workers, except logging
36.20	interviewers
36.38	construction inspectors
36.47	railroad conductors and yardmasters
36.84	computer operators
36.87	supervisors, financial records processing
37.07	supervisors, general office
37.78	supervisors, police and detectives
37.96	pattern makers, layout workers, and cutters
38.01	police and detectives, public service
38.59	supervisors, extractive occupations
39.08	transportation ticket and reservation agents
39.10	biological technicians
39.12	sales workers, parts
39.20	radiologic technicians
39.43	surveying and mapping technicians
39.43	surveyors and mapping scientists
39.51	supervisors, computer equipment operators
39.84	managers, food serving and lodging establishments
41.07	fire inspection and fire prevention occupations
41.73	supervisors, construction, n.e.c.[a]
41.79	legal assistants
42.86	photographers
43.38	dietitians
43.68	inspectors and compliance officers, except construction
44.63	health technologists and technicians, n.e.c.[a]
44.80	library clerks
45.21	industrial engineering technicians
45.33	engineering technicians, n.e.c.[a]
45.65	electrical and electronic technicians
45.69	musicians and composers
45.70	welfare service aides

Table C.1 Socioeconomic index scores and occupations for all Standard
Occupational Classification codes (continued)

SEI score	Job description
45.80	buyers, wholesale and retail trade except farm products
46.14	science technicians, n.e.c.[a]
46.25	sales occupations, other business services
46.27	investigators and adjusters, except insurance
46.40	registered nurses
47.26	funeral directors
48.48	drafting occupations
48.48	managers, horticultural specialty farms
48.80	designers
48.82	data processing equipment repairers
48.90	athletes
48.97	purchasing managers
49.33	mechanical engineering technicians
49.57	forestry and conservation scientists
50.01	sales representatives, mining, manufacturing, and wholesale
50.04	chemical technicians
50.11	air traffic controllers
50.48	business and promotion agents
50.75	health record technologists and technicians
51.22	technicians, n.e.c.[a]
51.64	teachers, special education
51.80	actors and directors
51.96	management-related occupations, n.e.c.[a]
52.01	real estate sales occupations
52.99	teachers, n.e.c.[a]
53.43	insurance sales occupations
54.09	underwriters
54.12	recreation workers
54.35	administrators and officials, public administration
54.42	painters, sculptors, craft-artists, and artist printmakers
54.48	purchasing agents and buyers, n.e.c.[a]
54.96	clinical laboratory technologists and technicians
55.39	announcers
55.67	artists, performers, and related workers, n.e.c.[a]
55.78	insurance adjusters, examiners, and investigators
57.08	religious workers, n.e.c.[a]
57.09	chief executives and general administrators, public administration
57.09	legislators
57.93	managers, marketing, advertising, and public relations
58.51	teachers, prekindergarten and kindergarten
58.55	financial managers
58.60	tool programmers, numerical control

Table C.1 Socioeconomic index scores and occupations for all Standard
Occupational Classification codes (continued)

SEI score	Job description
58.71	advertising and related sales occupations
58.82	physicians' assistants
59.58	technical writers
59.64	personnel and labor relations managers
59.80	personnel, training, and labor relations specialists
59.94	occupational therapists
59.94	physical therapists
59.94	respiratory therapists
59.94	speech therapists
59.94	therapists, n.e.c.[a]
60.47	managers, properties and real estate
61.22	archivists and curators
61.54	managers, medicine and health
61.62	other financial officers
64.76	accountants and auditors
64.94	operations and systems researchers and analysts
65.12	statisticians
65.46	librarians
65.71	social workers
66.03	clergy
66.05	computer programmers
67.25	dental hygienists
67.26	public relations specialists
67.27	editors and reporters
67.55	airplane pilots and navigators
68.44	agricultural and food scientists
68.84	trade and industrial teachers
70.00	management analysts
70.64	industrial engineers
70.88	teachers, elementary school
71.38	securities and financial services sales occupations
73.06	computer systems analysts and scientists
73.13	home economics teachers
73.88	social scientists, n.e.c.[a]
74.58	atmospheric and space scientists
75.14	teachers, secondary school
75.49	mining engineers
76.41	engineers, n.e.c.[a]
76.60	judges
76.71	mechanical engineers
76.73	medical scientists
76.87	civil engineers
77.13	postsecondary teachers, subject not specified

Table C.1 Socioeconomic index scores and occupations for all Standard
Occupational Classification codes (continued)

SEI score	Job description
77.32	biological and life scientists
77.57	marine and naval architects
77.76	chemists, except biochemists
78.16	sales engineers
78.27	economists
78.33	sociologists
78.97	electrical and electronic engineers
78.97	foreign language teachers
78.99	agricultural engineers
79.23	metallurgical and materials engineers
79.63	urban planners
79.72	architects
79.91	art, drama, and music teachers
80.05	physical scientists, n.e.c.[a]
80.37	actuaries
80.81	English teachers
80.90	health specialties teachers
81.10	pharmacists
81.10	theology teachers
81.43	physical education teachers
81.61	medical science teachers
81.93	natural science teachers, n.e.c.[a]
81.93	teachers, postsecondary, n.e.c.[a]
82.28	sociology teachers
82.32	petroleum engineers
82.44	administrators, education and related fields
82.46	computer science teachers
82.46	mathematical science teachers
82.48	psychologists
82.89	podiatrists
82.91	business, commerce, and marketing teachers
83.02	nuclear engineers
83.53	aerospace engineers
83.61	history teachers
83.80	biological science teachers
84.22	physics teachers
84.39	mathematical scientists, n.e.c.[a]
84.80	political science teachers
84.86	engineering teachers
85.03	chemistry teachers
85.04	earth, environmental, and marine science teachers
85.04	social science teachers, n.e.c.[a]
85.04	social work teachers

Table C.1 Socioeconomic index scores and occupations for all Standard
Occupational Classification codes (continued)

SEI score	Job description
85.53	psychology teachers
85.71	agriculture and forestry teachers
85.73	optometrists
86.20	education teachers
86.60	veterinarians
86.65	geologists and geodesists
87.00	physicists and astronomers
87.11	economics teachers
87.14	chemical engineers
88.28	physicians
88.42	lawyers
89.57	dentists
90.45	law teachers

a. n.e.c. = not elsewhere classified.

SIPP Analysis of Wage and Status Change

Table D.1 Summary statistics by gender and sample

	Basc (1)	All nonmanagerial jobs (2)	All races (3)	All geographic areas (4)
Males				
Age (years)	24.8	26.9	26.8	26.9
	(0.53)	(0.15)	(0.09)	(0.08)
Married	0.18	0.30	0.29	0.31
	(0.033)	(0.010)	(0.006)	(0.006)
AFDC/TANF recipient	0.01	0.02	0.02	0.01
	(0.009)	(0.003)	(0.002)	(0.001)
Education				
9th grade or less	44 (32%)	423 (21%)	575 (11%)	685 (10%)
10th grade	10 (7%)	127 (6%)	287 (5%)	358 (5%)
11th grade	27 (19%)	196 (10%)	416 (8%)	546 (8%)
High school grad	46 (33%)	793 (40%)	2,260 (43%)	2,969 (45%)
>High school	13 (9%)	466 (23%)	1,730 (33%)	2,058 (31%)
N	140	2,006	5,269	6,617

Table D.1 Summary statistics by gender and sample (continued)

	Base (1)	All nonmanagerial jobs (2)	All races (3)	All geographic areas (4)
Females				
Age (years)	25.0	27.2	26.7	26.8
	(0.57)	(0.15)	(0.09)	(0.08)
Married	0.17	0.25	0.27	0.29
	(0.031)	(0.009)	(0.006)	(0.005)
AFDC/TANF recipient	0.18	0.12	0.08	0.08
	(0.032)	(0.007)	(0.004)	(0.003)
Education				
9th grade or less	21 (15%)	269 (12%)	396 (7%)	473 (6%)
10th grade	14 (10%)	142 (6%)	315 (5%)	374 (5%)
11th grade	29 (20%)	204 (9%)	436 (7%)	534 (7%)
High school grad	54 (38%)	934 (41%)	2,421 (41%)	3,081 (42%)
>High school	26 (18%)	710 (31%)	2,351 (40%)	2,823 (39%)
N	145	2,260	5,919	7,285

Table D.2 Distribution of initial wages (in dollars), base sample

	Males	Females
No. observations	139	145
Mean −2.5%	6.29	5.57
Mean	6.65	5.75
Mean +2.5%	7.02	5.92
10th percentile	5.02	4.90
15th percentile	5.23	5.03
20th percentile	5.30	5.12
25th percentile	5.39	5.32
30th percentile	5.44	5.36
35th percentile	5.49	5.39
40th percentile	5.62	5.42
45th percentile	5.76	5.46
50th percentile	5.98	5.52
55th percentile	6.13	5.59
60th percentile	6.28	5.75
65th percentile	6.51	5.85
70th percentile	6.55	5.91
75th percentile	7.06	6.07

Table D.2 Distribution of initial wages (in dollars), base sample (continued)

	Males	Females
80th percentile	7.66	6.24
85th percentile	8.50	6.43
90th percentile	9.04	6.87

Table D.3 Distribution of 12-month wage growth, base sample

	Males		Females	
	$ (1)	% (2)	$ (3)	% (4)
No. observations	80		72	
Mean −2.5%	−0.29	−2.4	−0.09	−4.4
Mean	0.27	3.8	0.25	2.9
Mean +2.5%	0.82	9.9	0.58	10.2
10th percentile	−1.65	−17.0	−0.71	−11.0
15th percentile	−0.65	−11.3	−0.19	−3.3
20th percentile	−0.38	−5.6	−0.15	−2.6
25th percentile	−0.19	−3.0	−0.12	−2.0
30th percentile	−0.11	−1.7	−0.07	−1.2
35th percentile	0.05	0.7	0.06	0.9
40th percentile	0.17	2.8	0.11	1.9
45th percentile	0.34	5.0	0.21	3.8
50th percentile	0.38	6.0	0.36	6.8
55th percentile	0.46	8.8	0.41	7.4
60th percentile	0.51	9.1	0.46	8.3
65th percentile	0.68	12.4	0.54	9.4
70th percentile	0.89	13.0	0.70	12.0
75th percentile	0.95	16.6	0.80	13.3
80th percentile	1.18	18.2	0.92	16.2
85th percentile	1.24	23.2	1.11	19.1
90th percentile	1.73	28.3	1.42	23.9

Table D.4 Distribution of average annualized wage growth, base sample

| | All individuals | | | | In sample > 18 months | | | |
| | Males | | Females | | Males | | Females | |
	$ (1)	% (2)	$ (3)	% (4)	$ (5)	% (6)	$ (7)	% (8)
No. observations	140		145		83		86	
Mean −2.5%	0.17	2.3	−0.02	0.5	−0.14	−0.3	−0.57	−5.3
Mean	0.58	6.0	0.29	4.0	0.44	5.6	0.10	0.9
Mean +2.5%	1.00	9.6	0.60	7.5	1.01	11.5	0.77	7.2
10th percentile	−0.46	−7.2	−0.80	−13.3	−1.20	−18.8	−0.87	−13.2
15th percentile	−0.32	−4.1	−0.39	−6.5	−0.74	−12.1	−0.46	−8.1
20th percentile	−0.25	−3.6	−0.23	−4.1	−0.49	−7.2	−0.25	−4.0
25th percentile	−0.20	−2.8	−0.19	−3.1	−0.35	−5.1	−0.21	−3.2
30th percentile	−0.16	−2.3	−0.15	−2.7	−0.23	−3.3	−0.17	−2.6
35th percentile	−0.11	−1.9	−0.12	−2.2	−0.20	−3.2	−0.16	−2.5
40th percentile	−0.08	−1.4	−0.07	−1.0	−0.16	−1.9	−0.12	−2.3
45th percentile	−0.04	−0.4	0.00	0.0	−0.10	−1.6	−0.11	−1.9
50th percentile	0.04	0.5	0.08	1.6	−0.05	−0.5	−0.03	−0.8
55th percentile	0.14	1.8	0.18	3.2	0.02	0.9	0.01	0.0
60th percentile	0.27	4.7	0.28	5.0	0.20	2.4	0.09	1.7
65th percentile	0.36	6.1	0.36	6.3	0.30	4.6	0.29	4.1
70th percentile	0.50	7.4	0.58	9.0	0.55	7.8	0.40	6.0
75th percentile	0.66	9.5	0.78	11.2	0.75	9.5	0.66	9.8
80th percentile	0.78	11.9	0.90	14.1	0.97	12.8	0.91	13.6
85th percentile	1.00	14.6	1.09	18.0	2.03	23.7	1.23	19.6
90th percentile	1.52	18.4	1.82	29.5	2.81	40.9	1.93	28.2

Table D.5 Categories of wage growth, base sample

	Males	Females
> $5	16 (11%)	19 (13%)
$1–$5	41 (29%)	42 (29%)
< $1	16 (11%)	17 (12%)
Loss	67 (48%)	65 (45%)
Total	140	143

Table D.6 Distribution of initial wages (by gender and sample)

	Males				Females			
	Base (1)	All nonmanagerial jobs (2)	All races (3)	All geographic areas (4)	Base (5)	All nonmanagerial jobs (6)	All races (7)	All geographic areas (8)
No. observations	139	1,985	5,233	6,578	145	2,244	5,881	7,239
Mean −2.5%	6.29	7.83	8.53	8.51	5.57	6.98	7.09	7.03
Mean	6.65	7.99	8.65	8.61	5.75	7.10	7.17	7.10
Mean +2.5%	7.02	8.15	8.76	8.71	5.92	7.22	7.25	7.17
10th percentile	5.02	5.10	5.29	5.26	4.90	5.02	4.89	4.79
15th percentile	5.23	5.37	5.45	5.43	5.03	5.26	5.22	5.14
20th percentile	5.30	5.46	5.70	5.62	5.12	5.38	5.38	5.34
25th percentile	5.39	5.70	5.94	5.89	5.32	5.45	5.46	5.43
30th percentile	5.44	5.92	6.24	6.18	5.36	5.54	5.59	5.52
35th percentile	5.49	6.13	6.46	6.45	5.39	5.73	5.82	5.75
40th percentile	5.62	6.35	6.72	6.69	5.42	5.95	6.01	5.97
45th percentile	5.76	6.54	7.08	7.06	5.46	6.08	6.23	6.17
50th percentile	5.98	6.83	7.41	7.41	5.52	6.29	6.44	6.36
55th percentile	6.13	7.23	7.68	7.68	5.59	6.54	6.61	6.56
60th percentile	6.28	7.60	8.19	8.19	5.75	6.79	6.99	6.89
65th percentile	6.51	7.95	8.69	8.69	5.85	7.10	7.33	7.27
70th percentile	6.55	8.57	9.30	9.28	5.91	7.52	7.64	7.63
75th percentile	7.06	9.05	10.00	9.98	6.07	7.97	8.14	8.07
80th percentile	7.66	9.83	10.90	10.86	6.24	8.50	8.68	8.61
85th percentile	8.50	10.90	11.99	11.99	6.43	9.25	9.36	9.30
90th percentile	9.04	12.53	13.75	13.65	6.87	10.15	10.39	10.33

Table D.7 Distribution of wage growth (by gender and sample)

	Males								Females							
	Base		All nonmanagerial jobs		All races		All geographic areas		Base		All nonmanagerial jobs		All races		All geographic areas	
	$ (1)	% (2)	$ (3)	% (4)	$ (5)	% (6)	$ (7)	% (8)	$ (9)	% (10)	$ (11)	% (12)	$ (13)	% (14)	$ (15)	% (16)
No. observations	140		2,006		5,269		6,617		145		2,260		5,919		7,285	
Mean − 2.5%	0.17	2.3	0.18	2.3	0.39	4.1	0.37	3.6	−0.02	0.5	0.35	4.0	0.52	5.5	0.45	4.9
Mean	0.58	6.0	0.36	3.5	0.49	4.9	0.45	4.3	0.29	4.0	0.54	5.1	0.64	6.2	0.56	5.6
Mean + 2.5%	1.00	9.6	0.54	4.7	0.59	5.7	0.54	5.0	0.60	7.5	0.74	6.2	0.75	6.9	0.67	6.2
10th percentile	−0.46	−7.2	−1.17	−15.3	−1.17	−13.9	−1.21	−15.2	−0.80	−13.3	−0.86	−12.3	−0.90	−12.3	−0.88	−12.5
15th percentile	−0.32	−4.1	−0.65	−8.6	−0.65	−7.0	−0.67	−7.3	−0.39	−6.5	−0.44	−5.8	−0.43	−5.7	−0.44	−5.9
20th percentile	−0.25	−3.6	−0.40	−4.3	−0.40	−4.1	−0.40	−4.1	−0.23	−4.1	−0.28	−3.9	−0.27	−3.7	−0.28	−3.7
25th percentile	−0.20	−2.8	−0.28	−3.7	−0.27	−3.4	−0.28	−3.4	−0.19	−3.1	−0.22	−3.1	−0.21	−3.0	−0.21	−3.0
30th percentile	−0.16	−2.3	−0.22	−3.0	−0.21	−2.8	−0.21	−2.8	−0.15	−2.7	−0.18	−2.8	−0.17	−2.7	−0.17	−2.7
35th percentile	−0.11	−1.9	−0.18	−2.6	−0.17	−2.3	−0.17	−2.3	−0.12	−2.2	−0.15	−2.3	−0.14	−2.2	−0.14	−2.2
40th percentile	−0.08	−1.4	−0.14	−2.1	−0.13	−1.8	−0.13	−1.8	−0.07	−1.0	−0.11	−1.7	−0.10	−1.6	−0.10	−1.6
45th percentile	−0.04	−0.4	−0.10	−1.6	−0.08	−1.1	−0.08	−1.1	0.00	0.0	−0.06	−1.0	−0.05	−0.7	−0.05	−0.8
50th percentile	0.04	0.5	−0.04	−0.4	0.00	0.2	0.00	0.2	0.08	1.6	0.03	0.5	0.04	0.7	0.04	0.7
55th percentile	0.14	1.8	0.08	1.2	0.15	1.9	0.14	1.9	0.18	3.2	0.12	1.8	0.16	2.2	0.15	2.1
60th percentile	0.27	4.7	0.22	3.0	0.30	3.6	0.29	3.5	0.28	5.0	0.22	3.5	0.27	3.9	0.25	3.7
65th percentile	0.36	6.1	0.36	4.8	0.45	5.5	0.44	5.3	0.36	6.3	0.34	5.0	0.41	5.8	0.38	5.4
70th percentile	0.50	7.4	0.53	6.7	0.65	7.6	0.63	7.4	0.58	9.0	0.49	6.9	0.56	7.8	0.53	7.4
75th percentile	0.66	9.5	0.72	9.2	0.89	10.1	0.87	9.9	0.78	11.2	0.67	9.1	0.76	10.0	0.71	9.5
80th percentile	0.78	11.9	0.99	11.5	1.21	13.4	1.17	13.1	0.90	14.1	0.92	11.8	1.00	13.3	0.95	12.7
85th percentile	1.00	14.6	1.34	15.3	1.72	18.7	1.64	18.3	1.09	18.0	1.25	16.5	1.38	18.4	1.30	17.6
90th percentile	1.52	18.4	1.98	23.8	2.54	26.9	2.44	26.2	1.82	29.5	1.76	24.4	2.06	27.3	1.98	25.9

Table D.8 Categories of wage change (by gender and sample)

	Base (1)	All nonmanagerial jobs (2)	All races (3)	All geographic areas (4)
Males				
> $5	16 (11%)	318 (16%)	1,013 (19%)	1,240 (19%)
$1–$5	41 (29%)	462 (23%)	1,163 (22%)	1,465 (22%)
< $1	16 (11%)	183 (9%)	451 (9%)	590 (9%)
Loss	67 (48%)	1,029 (52%)	2,590 (50%)	3,263 (50%)
Total	140	1,992	5,217	6,558
Females				
> $5	19 (13%)	338 (15%)	973 (17%)	1,140 (16%)
$1–$5	42 (29%)	528 (23%)	1,418 (24%)	1,735 (24%)
< $1	17 (12%)	289 (13%)	662 (11%)	875 (12%)
Loss	65 (45%)	1,094 (49%)	2,815 (48%)	3,473 (48%)
Total	143	2,249	5,868	7,223

Table D.9 Distribution of wage growth, 1986–1992 panels compared with 1996 panel, by gender and sample

	Males								Females							
	Oct. 1985–Apr. 1995 (1986–1992 panels)				Dec. 1995–Feb. 2000 (1996 panel)				Oct. 1985–Apr. 1995 (1986–1992 panels)				Dec. 1995–Feb. 2000 (1996 panel)			
	Base		All geographic areas		Base		All geographic areas		Base		All geographic areas		Base		All geographic areas	
	$ (1)	% (2)	$ (3)	% (4)	$ (5)	% (6)	$ (7)	% (8)	$ (9)	% (10)	$ (11)	% (12)	$ (13)	% (14)	$ (15)	% (16)
No. observations	273		18,520		140		6,617		191		18,951		145		7,285	
Mean −2.5%	0.21	1.8	0.29	2.8	0.17	2.3	0.37	3.6	−0.02	0.5	0.26	3.1	−0.02	0.5	0.45	4.9
Mean	0.39	4.5	0.34	3.2	0.58	6.0	0.45	4.3	0.29	4.0	0.30	3.4	0.29	4.0	0.56	5.6
Mean +2.5%	0.57	7.2	0.39	3.5	1.00	9.6	0.54	5.0	0.60	7.5	0.35	3.8	0.60	7.5	0.67	6.2
10th percentile	−0.75	−11.0	−1.28	−13.1	−0.46	−7.2	−1.21	−15.2	−0.76	−13.8	−0.88	−11.1	−0.80	−13.3	−0.88	−12.5
15th percentile	−0.45	−7.5	−0.74	−6.8	−0.32	−4.1	−0.67	−7.3	−0.32	−5.1	−0.48	−5.9	−0.39	−6.5	−0.44	−5.9
20th percentile	−0.32	−4.5	−0.50	−4.7	−0.25	−3.6	−0.40	−4.1	−0.25	−4.4	−0.34	−4.4	−0.23	−4.1	−0.28	−3.7
25th percentile	−0.26	−3.6	−0.37	−3.7	−0.20	−2.8	−0.28	−3.4	−0.21	−3.5	−0.26	−3.5	−0.19	−3.1	−0.21	−3.0
30th percentile	−0.21	−2.9	−0.29	−3.0	−0.16	−2.3	−0.21	−2.8	−0.17	−3.0	−0.21	−2.9	−0.15	−2.7	−0.17	−2.7
35th percentile	−0.17	−2.7	−0.22	−2.7	−0.11	−1.9	−0.17	−2.3	−0.16	−2.8	−0.17	−2.7	−0.12	−2.2	−0.14	−2.2
40th percentile	−0.15	−2.6	−0.17	−2.2	−0.08	−1.4	−0.13	−1.8	−0.14	−2.4	−0.14	−2.2	−0.07	−1.0	−0.10	−1.6
45th percentile	−0.13	−2.1	−0.12	−1.3	−0.04	−0.4	−0.08	−1.1	−0.09	−1.5	−0.09	−1.2	0.00	0.0	−0.05	−0.8
50th percentile	−0.03	−0.3	−0.01	−0.1	0.04	0.5	0.00	0.2	−0.03	−0.4	−0.01	−0.1	0.08	1.6	0.04	0.7
55th percentile	0.04	0.7	0.10	1.0	0.14	1.8	0.14	1.9	0.00	0.0	0.08	1.0	0.18	3.2	0.15	2.1
60th percentile	0.15	2.4	0.22	2.3	0.27	4.7	0.29	3.5	0.06	1.0	0.17	2.2	0.28	5.0	0.25	3.7
65th percentile	0.34	4.9	0.37	3.9	0.36	6.1	0.44	5.3	0.19	3.0	0.28	3.5	0.36	6.3	0.38	5.4
70th percentile	0.45	7.1	0.54	5.8	0.50	7.4	0.63	7.4	0.32	5.6	0.40	5.2	0.58	9.0	0.53	7.4
75th percentile	0.78	10.6	0.78	8.4	0.66	9.5	0.87	9.9	0.39	6.7	0.57	7.3	0.78	11.2	0.71	9.5
80th percentile	1.29	16.5	1.11	11.9	0.78	11.9	1.17	13.1	0.51	9.7	0.80	10.3	0.90	14.1	0.95	12.7
85th percentile	1.56	23.2	1.59	17.7	1.00	14.6	1.64	18.3	0.83	13.9	1.16	14.9	1.09	18.0	1.30	17.6
90th percentile	2.79	30.7	2.44	26.7	1.52	18.4	2.44	26.2	1.52	23.3	1.80	22.3	1.82	29.5	1.98	25.9

Table D.10 Categories of wage change, 1986–1992 panels compared with 1996 panel, by gender and sample

	Oct. 1985–Apr. 1995 (1986–1992 panels)		Dec. 1995–Feb. 2000 (1996 panel)	
	Base	Full sample	Base	Full sample
Males				
> $5	54 (20%)	3,344 (18%)	16 (11%)	1,240 (19%)
$1–$5	44 (16%)	3,750 (21%)	41 (29%)	1,465 (22%)
< $1	32 (12%)	1,883 (10%)	16 (11%)	590 (9%)
Loss	138 (51%)	9,207 (51%)	67 (48%)	3,263 (50%)
Total	268	18,184	140	6,558
Females				
> $5	22 (12%)	2,598 (14%)	19 (13%)	1,140 (16%)
$1–$5	37 (20%)	4,134 (22%)	42 (29%)	1,735 (24%)
< $1	23 (13%)	2,443 (13%)	17 (12%)	875 (12%)
Loss	100 (55%)	9,384 (51%)	65 (45%)	3,473 (48%)
Total	182	18,559	143	7,223

Table D.11 Annual deflated wage rates (regression coefficients, by gender)

| | Males | | | | Females | | | |
| | Change in dollars | | Change in percent | | Change in dollars | | Change in percent | |
	(1)	(2)	(3)	(4)	(5)	(6)	(7)	(8)
Additional nonmanagerial jobs	-0.125	-0.378	-0.018	-0.079	-0.126	0.162	-0.014	-0.111
	(0.087)	(0.509)	(0.011)	(0.061)	(0.238)	(0.451)	(0.019)	(0.129)
Other races (not black or Hispanic)	0.055	-0.454	-0.004	-0.085	-0.031	0.046	-0.003	-0.128
	(0.081)	(0.504)	(0.011)	(0.062)	(0.236)	(0.455)	(0.019)	(0.129)
Nonmetropolitan areas	-0.159*	-1.162	-0.019*	-0.106	-0.217	-1.308	-0.014	-0.218
	(0.083)	(2.570)	(0.011)	(0.224)	(0.238)	(1.359)	(0.019)	(0.165)
Age	—	-0.244	—	-0.019	—	-0.320	—	-0.031
		(0.166)		(0.017)		(0.195)		(0.021)
Age squared	—	0.004	—	0.000	—	0.006	—	0.001
		(0.003)		(0.000)		(0.004)		(0.000)
Married w/spouse present	—	-0.141	—	-0.014	—	-0.557	—	0.019
		(0.315)		(0.034)		(0.459)		(0.028)
Unemployment rate	—	0.022	—	0.001	—	-0.013	—	-0.002
		(0.054)		(0.004)		(0.042)		(0.004)
Education	—	0.182	—	-0.008	—	-0.204	—	0.017
Completed 10th grade		(0.464)		(0.058)		(0.442)		(0.069)
	—	-0.252	—	-0.027	—	0.032	—	0.052
Completed 11th grade		(0.415)		(0.050)		(0.467)		(0.071)
	—	-0.017	—	-0.030	—	-0.398	—	0.015
Completed 12th grade		(0.399)		(0.039)		(0.422)		(0.052)
	—	0.046	—	0.003	—	0.335	—	0.054
More than high school		(0.373)		(0.035)		(0.444)		(0.052)
No. observations	759,584	10,768			730,024	11,775		
No. individuals	39,634	836			38,680	917		

* Significant at 10%.
Note: Standard errors in parentheses.

Table D.12 Probability of being a high flyer (probit coefficients, by gender)

	Males		Females	
	(1)	(2)	(3)	(4)
Additional nonmanagerial jobs	0.100	0.037	0.054	0.238
	(0.102)	(0.462)	(0.126)	(0.554)
Other races (not black or Hispanic)	(0.232**	0.146	0.206*	0.311
	0.100)	(0.457)	(0.125)	(0.549)
Nonmetropolitan areas	0.091	—	−0.001	1.005
	(0.101)	—	(0.126)	(0.945)
Age	—	−0.067	—	−0.002
	—	(0.104)	—	(0.093)
Age squared	—	0.001	—	0.000
	—	(0.002)	—	(0.002)
Married w/spouse present	—	−0.090	—	−0.198()
	—	(0.162)	—	(0.141)
Unemployment rate	—	−0.027	—	−0.047
	—	(0.031)	—	(0.029)
Completed 10th grade	—	0.221	—	0.146
	—	(0.321)	—	(0.335)
Completed 11th grade	—	−0.110	—	0.037
	—	(0.289)	—	(0.307)
Completed 12th grade	—	0.179	—	0.163
	—	(0.233)	—	(0.243)
More than high school	—	0.418*	—	0.452*
	—	(0.243)	—	(0.254)
No. individuals	39,634	806	38,680	883

* Significant at 10%.
** Significant at 5%.
Note: Standard errors in parentheses.

Table D.13 Summary statistics for SIPP sample by high flyer status, at first month and 18 months

| | Males | | | | | | Females | | | | | |
| | High flyers | | | Others | | | High flyers | | | Others | | |
	Period 1	Period 2	Difference	Period 1	Period 2	Difference	Period 1	Period 2	Difference	Period 1	Period 2	Difference
Demographic characteristics												
High school graduate	0%	0%	0%	37%	44%	7%	60%	60%	0%	44%	45%	1%
> high school	50%	50%	0%	11%	12%	1%	0%	0%	0%	13%	16%	3%
Age (years)	22.3	24.0	1.8	25.4	26.8	1.4	24.8	26.4	1.6	25.2	26.6	1.4
Married with spouse present	0%	25%	25%	32%	34%	3%	20%	20%	0%	16%	21%	5%
Nonwhite	25%	25%	—	33%	33%	—	80%	80%	—	72%	72%	—
Employment status												
Deflated wage rate	$5.64	$7.06	$1.42	$6.80	$7.25	$0.45	$5.22	$7.79	$2.57	$5.66	$6.34	$0.68
Employed	100%	100%	0%	100%	89%	−11%	100%	100%	0%	100%	76%	−24%
New job	—	50%	—	—	58%	—	60%	60%	—	—	60%	—
Hours per week	35.0	31.3	−3.8	33.7	36.0	2.2	27.0	39.0	12.0	28.0	30.5	2.5
Weeks	1.3	4.8	3.5	2.7	3.3	0.6	2.6	4.2	1.6	2.3	3.0	0.7

Table D.13 Summary statistics for SIPP sample by high flyer status, at first month and 18 months (continued)

	Males						Females					
	High flyers			Others			High flyers			Others		
	Period1	Period2	Difference	Period1	Period2	Difference	Period1	Period2	Difference	Period1	Period2	Difference
Job characteristics												
Food service job	100%	75%	−25%	100%	60%	−40%	100%	40%	−60%	100%	47%	−53%
Manager	0%	0%	0%	0%	4%	4%	0%	40%	40%	0%	5%	5%
Private sector	100%	100%	0%	100%	82%	−18%	100%	100%	0%	97%	69%	−28%
SEI score	18	21	3	18	19	1	18	30	12	19	22	3
Income												
Household income (monthly)	$735	$1,193	$458	$1,643	$2,568	$925	$1,129	$3,233	$2,104	$1,414	$1,701	$286
Below poverty	100%	100%	0%	52%	27%	−25%	80%	20%	−60%	63%	52%	−11%
Below 1.5 × poverty	100%	100%	0%	79%	51%	−29%	100%	40%	−60%	84%	77%	−7%
Family poverty ratio	0.5	0.9	0.4	1.0	1.7	0.7	0.8	2.3	1.6	0.9	1.1	0.3
Public assistance												
AFDC/TANF	0%	0%	0%	1%	3%	2%	20%	0%	−20%	27%	17%	−10%
Public housing	50%	50%	0%	8%	10%	2%	75%	75%	0%	30%	29%	−1%
No. observations	4			73			5			75		

Table D.14 Job changes made by high flyers in 18 months

Four-year wage gain	SEI score		Occupation	
	Period 1	Period 2	Period 1	Period 2
Male high flyers				
$19.27	18	19	kitchen workers, food preparation	helpers, construction trades
$15.16	18	21	cooks	supervisors, food preparation and service occupations
$14.33	18	29	cooks	bank tellers
$11.72	18	47	kitchen workers, food preparation	managers, food serving and lodging establishments
$11.64	21	18	food counter, fountain and related occupations	janitors and cleaners
$10.72	18	29	kitchen workers, food preparation	order clerks
$9.26	18	18	cooks	cooks
$6.56	18	18	cooks	cooks
Female high flyers				
$13.46	18	18	cooks	cooks
$11.17	18	21	cooks	cashiers
$11.15	18	19	cooks	miscellaneous and not specified machine operators, n.e.c.[a]
$8.75	18	19	cooks	hairdressers and cosmetologists
$8.10	21	18	food counter, fountain and related occupations	electrical and electronic equipment assemblers
$7.28	21	21	food counter, fountain and related occupations	cashiers
$6.44	18	18	cooks	cooks
$5.88	18	47	cooks	managers, food serving and lodging establishments
$5.81	18	65	cooks	accountants and auditors
$5.11	18	47	cooks	managers, food serving and lodging establishments
$5.02	18	18	cooks	cooks

a. n.e.c. = not elsewhere classified.

Notes

Prologue

1. Scott Winship and Christopher Jencks, "Understanding Welfare Reform," *Harvard Magazine* 107, no. 2 (November–December 2004): 97.

2. As anyone who has dropped by a high school career fair can attest, the U.S. military is an aggressive recruiter of young people. "DOD [the Department of Defense] is the single largest employer and trainer of youth and recruited about 196,000 individuals into active duty in 2001." U.S. General Accounting Office, "Military Personnel: Active Duty Benefits Reflect Changing Demographics, but Opportunities Exist to Improve," Report to the Subcommittee on Personnel, Committee on Armed Services, U.S. Senate, GAO-02-935, September 2002. In the private sector, the restaurant industry boasts the largest number of entry-level workers. According to a Bureau of Labor Statistics report, "Establishments in this industry [food services and drinking places], particularly fast-food establishments, are leading employers of teenagers—aged 16 through 19—providing first jobs for many new entrants to the labor force. In 2002, nearly 22 percent of all workers in food services and drinking places were teenagers, almost 5 times the proportion in all industries. . . . About 45 percent were under age 25, nearly 3 times the proportion in all industries." Bureau of Labor Statistics, U.S. Department of Labor, "Food Services and Drinking Places," *Career Guide to Industries, 2004–2005 Edition*, on the Internet at *http://www.bls.gov/oco/cg/cgs023.htm* (accessed March 21, 2005).

Fast-food restaurants provide many young workers with not just their first job but also their worst-paying job: "The roughly 3.5 million fast food workers are by far the largest group of minimum wage earners in the United States. The only Americans who consistently earn a lower hourly wage are migrant farm workers," writes Eric Schlosser in his book *Fast Food Nation*, a journalistic exposé of the fast-food industry. According to Schlosser, the industry employs "some of the most disadvantaged members of American society," including recent immigrants, the elderly, and people with disabilities. Schlosser also notes that the restaurant industry overall—fast food and non–fast food—is America's largest private employer (the health-care industry has a larger workforce but includes both public and private employers). Eric Schlosser, *Fast Food Nation: The Dark Side of the All-American Meal* (New York: Houghton Mifflin, 2001), 6, 70–71, 295n.

1. Lives, in the Long Run

1. Hamilton is the fictitious name I have given to the community where Jamal (also a pseudonym) lives. Place names and personal names have been changed to honor the agreement for the protection of human subjects that governed the research reported here.

2. This is the fictitious name I have given to the national chain of fast-food restaurants where my original research subjects were recruited.

3. See Richard J. Murnane and Frank Levy, *Teaching the New Basic Skills* (New York: Free Press, 1996). Murnane and Levy describe the shift in expectations through the story of Diamond-Star Motors (DSM), a joint venture of Mitsubishi of Japan and Chrysler Motors. Back in the 1960s, auto companies had very few standards for hiring workers; as one veteran of management at Ford Motor Company put it, "If we had a vacancy, we would look outside in the plant waiting room to see if there were any warm bodies standing there. If someone was there and they looked physically OK and they weren't an obvious alcoholic, they were hired." In the 1980s, firms decided they needed more than "warm bodies." When DSM started hiring for its first wave of production, it received 80,000 applications for 2,900 jobs. The list of skills that DSM required its production and maintenance associates to have included the ability to read at a "high school level," the ability to do math at a "high school level," the ability to solve semi-structured problems and to originate improvements, the ability to work in teams, skills in oral communication, and skills in inspection. Having a high school diploma and a solid work history wasn't enough anymore; now workers had to receive passing scores on a battery of standardized tests, a physical exam, and drug test, and in two role-playing exercises that were supposed to judge their ability to work in teams and inspect

products—and then they had to pass muster in a thirty-minute interview. "The skills reflect the changing nature of production work. The warm bodies of 1967 were expected to perform a small number of routine operations— bolting a door to a frame—and nothing else. If an employee saw a better way of doing things, he kept his mouth shut. Improvements were management's job. If he saw a mistake or a problem, he would try to pass it on to the next work station. 'Once you passed it on, it wasn't your problem anymore.'. . . These routine jobs still exist, but they no longer pay a living wage" (19–23).

4. The names of all firms in this volume have been changed. I have pre-served the essence of the industries, biographies, and locations of persons who appear in this book, while honoring my promise to change their identities.

5. Churning through jobs is relatively common among young workers. During his first ten years in the labor market, the average male worker will hold seven jobs, or two-thirds of his career total. Robert Topel and Michael Ward, "Job Mobility and the Careers of Young Men," *Quarterly Journal of Economics* 107 (1992): 439–479. Job-hopping also appears to be becoming more widespread. Using two data sets from the National Longitudinal Sur-veys, Martina Morris and her collaborators compared the work experiences of young white men who entered the labor market in the late sixties and throughout the seventies (tracked from 1966 to 1981) with a second cohort who entered during the eighties and early nineties (tracked from 1979 to 1994). They found that the likelihood of changing employers during a given two-year period was 46 percent in the first cohort, and 53 percent in the sec-ond cohort. Median job tenure among the second cohort also declined, as did that cohort's total wage growth over the period of observation (measured in terms of the hourly wage increase between ages sixteen and thirty-six). See Martina Morris et al., "Wage Inequality and Labor Market Segmentation: Ev-idence from the National Longitudinal Study Cohorts," Population Research Institute Working Paper 98-07, Pennsylvania State University, 1998, 8, 22. See also Paul Osterman, *Getting Started: The Youth Labor Market* (Cambridge, MA: MIT Press, 1980).

6. In 1980, the average U.S. household charged $885 on its credit cards ev-ery year; in 1990, it charged $3,753. Over that period, the average card-holder's debt increased from $395 to $2,350. (In early 2000, credit card debt accounted for 43 percent of the $1.4 trillion in outstanding consumer debt in America.) Total consumer debt as a percentage of disposable personal in-come also rose, from 65.4 percent in 1980 to 83.5 percent in 1990. Robert D. Manning, *Credit Card Nation: The Consequences of America's Addiction to Credit* (New York: Basic Books, 2000), 11–13, 64–65. In recent years, credit card usage has increased most dramatically among lower-income families, whom credit card companies have aggressively targeted. "The result is not surpris-

ing: 27 percent of the under-$10,000 [income bracket] families have consumer debt that is more than 40 percent of their income, and nearly one in ten has at least one debt that is more than sixty days past due." Teresa A. Sullivan, Elizabeth Warren, and Jay Lawrence Westbrook, *The Fragile Middle Class: Americans in Debt* (New Haven: Yale University Press, 2000), 136–137.

7. In his seven-year study of workers at a New Jersey chemical plant, David Halle points out that many ethnographic accounts of blue-collar life deal with only one stage of the workers' life cycle—usually the point at which workers marry and begin to support young children. "This is the time when economic problems are likely to be most severe; there are children to support, and often the wife stays at home to care for them and so cannot take a paid job. The presence of young children also seriously curtails the couple's leisure time. Thus to consider only workers with young children is to risk mistaking one stage of the marital and life cycle for the essence of 'blue-collar' life." David Halle, *America's Working Man: Work, Home, and Politics among Blue-Collar Property Owners* (Chicago: University of Chicago Press, 1984), xii. Jamal's own life trajectory underscores this point. In 1993 the stretched paycheck and grim job prospects for Jamal likely compounded his family problems. With maturity and greater economic security, the bleak picture of that earlier period has been replaced by a more stable and more agreeable—if perhaps still troubled—portrait of domestic life.

8. Writing in 1978, William Julius Wilson noted that the growth of the government sector was one of the key reasons that African Americans had been joining the white-collar ranks in increasing numbers over the past decade. This expansion, Wilson said, has "meant that a greater percentage of higher-paying jobs (wages and salaries are relatively high because most government services require a trained or skilled labor force) are available to the black middle class. For example, in 1960, 13.3 percent of the total employed black labor force worked in the government sector; by 1970, that figure had increased to 21.4 percent." William Julius Wilson, *The Declining Significance of Race: Blacks and Changing American Institutions*, 2nd ed. (Chicago: University of Chicago Press, 1980), 103.

9. In a 2005 study, researchers at Harvard Law School and Harvard Medical School surveyed 1,771 personal bankruptcy filers in five federal courts in California, Illinois, Pennsylvania, Tennessee, and Texas. They found that more than one quarter of bankruptcy filers cited illness or injury as a specific reason for bankruptcy, while a similar number reported medical bills not covered by insurers that exceeded $1,000. When they included these two categories with those filers who said they lost at least two weeks of work-related income because of illness/injury, or mortgaged a home to pay medical bills, 46.2 percent of debtors could be categorized as experiencing a "major medi-

cal bankruptcy." David U. Himmelstein et al., "Illness and Injury as Contributors to Bankruptcy," *Health Affairs*, February 2, 2005, *http://content.healthaffairs.org/cgi/content/full/hlthaff.w5.63/DC1*. During the 2005 debate over bankruptcy-reform legislation that raised costs for filing and made it mandatory for many families to enter into a repayment plan, Democratic critics of the bill argued that it would harm "honest" people whose finances had been devastated by illness and other unavoidable catastrophes; Republicans criticized the Harvard study for being unrepresentative and using a definition of "major medical bankruptcy" that was too lenient. See Leslie Eaton, "Bankruptcy, the American Morality Tale," *New York Times*, March 13, 2005, Week in Review, 1.

10. In her classic ethnography *All Our Kin*, anthropologist Carol Stack argued that poor families, lacking the resources to survive on their own, relied heavily on kin networks. "Whether one's source of income is a welfare check or wages from labor, people in The Flats [the poor black urban neighborhood Stack studied] borrow and trade with others in order to obtain daily necessities. . . . As people swap, the limited supply of finished material goods in the community is perpetually redistributed among networks of kinsmen and throughout the community." Carol Stack, *All Our Kin* (New York: Basic Books, 1974), 32–33.

11. Kathryn Edin and Laura Lein describe another kind of "fix" used by single mothers who receive public assistance—working off the books. Stopping short of using false identities, some women work in the informal economy—doing things like babysitting, housecleaning, yard work—and choose not to report earnings. Kathryn Edin and Laura Lein, *Making Ends Meet: How Single Mothers Survive Welfare and Low-Wage Work* (New York: Russell Sage Foundation, 1997), 173–175.

12. Prison records sharply depress ex-offenders' prospects of finding good jobs. This is particularly true for minority men. See Devah Pager, "The Mark of a Criminal Record," *American Journal of Sociology* 108, no. 5 (March 2003): 937–975, and David Harding, "Jean Valjean's Dilemma: The Management of Ex-Convict Identity in the Search for Employment," *Deviant Behavior* 25, no. 6 (1993): 571–595.

13. See Steven D. Levitt and Sudhir Alladi Venkatesh, "An Economic Analysis of a Drug-Selling Gang's Finances," *Quarterly Journal of Economics* (August 2000): 755–789. Using financial information recorded over a four-year period by the leader of a now-defunct gang, Levitt and Venkatesh found that street-level sellers earn roughly the minimum wage, while high-level gang members earn far more: about $1,000 a month, and as much as $4,200 to $10,900 a month for the gang leader (770). Only very few can rise to the top, however. In the gang studied, over the period of observation there were between 60 and

200 rank-and-file members, 25 to 75 "foot soldiers" (street-level sellers), 3 officers (including one runner), and a gang leader (763).

14. William Julius Wilson has argued that the decline in marriage rates among African Americans, particularly the black ghetto poor, is linked to falling employment among African American men, which has left black women without suitable marriage partners. In his 1987 book *The Truly Disadvantaged*, Wilson presented a "male marriageable pool index," which tracked the number of employed men per woman of the same age and race, and found a dramatic decline in the index scores for black women, relative to white women, since the 1960s. William Julius Wilson, *The Truly Disadvantaged: The Inner City, the Underclass, and Public Policy* (Chicago: University of Chicago Press, 1987), 83. For a critical review of Wilson's argument, see Robert G. Wood, "Marriage Rates and Marriageable Men: A Test of the Wilson Hypothesis," *Journal of Human Resources* 30, no. 1 (Winter 1995): 163–193.

15. In 2002, 40.8 percent of black women had never married, compared with 21.2 percent of white women and 30.3 percent of Hispanic women; 13.3 percent of black women had divorced, compared with 11.3 percent of white women and 9.3 percent of Hispanic women. American Community Survey Summary Tables (2002), cited in Administration for Children and Families, U.S. Department of Health and Human Services, "Marriage, Divorce, Childbirth, and Living Arrangements among African American or Black Populations," *http://www.acf.hhs.gov/healthymarriage/about/aami_marriage_statistics.htm.*

16. Katherine S. Newman, *A Different Shade of Gray: Mid-Life and Beyond in the Inner City* (New York: New Press, 2003), discusses at length the burdens that grandmothers bear in caring for generations of dependents.

17. Mary Waters and Tomás Jiménez have written about Mexican immigrants to Garden City, Kansas, who arrived in large numbers in response to opportunities in the meatpacking plants. See Mary C. Waters and Tomás R. Jiménez, "Immigrant Assimilation: Current Trends and Future Directions for Research," *Annual Review of Sociology* 31 (August 2005): 105–125. Helen Marrow has discussed a similar migration stream headed to North Carolina and the chicken-processing plants there. See Helen B. Marrow, "New Immigrant Destinations and U.S. Immigrant Incorporation Research," *Perspectives on Politics* 3, no. 4 (December 2005): 781–799. The highest growth rates for the Hispanic population are now in the Midwest and the South: 81.0 percent and 71.2 percent, respectively, compared with 51.8 percent for the West and 39.9 percent for the Northeast.

2. The Best-Case Scenario

1. David Ellwood, "Winners and Losers in America: Taking the Measure of the New Economic Realities," in *A Working Nation? Workers, Work, and Gov-*

ernment in the New Economy, ed. David T. Ellwood and Karen Lynn-Dyson (New York: Russell Sage Foundation, 2000).

2. "Business Cycle Expansions and Contractions," National Bureau of Economic Research, *http://www.nber.org/cycles.html*, September 5, 2005.

3. U.S. Bureau of Labor Statistics *(www.bls.gov)*, "Unadjusted Employment Rate, 16 Years and Over," Series ID: LNU04000000.

4. Ibid.

5. Lawrence Mishel, Jared Bernstein, and Heather Boushey, *The State of Working America, 2002–2003* (Ithaca: Cornell University Press, 2003). "The era of stagnant and falling wages from the early 1970s to 1995 gave way to one of strong wage growth after 1995 as wages changed course, rising strongly in response to persistent low unemployment and the faster productivity growth relative to the 1973–95 period. However, despite the strong wage improvements in recent years, it was not until 1998 that the wage level for middle-wage workers (the median hourly wage) jumped above its 1979 level."

6. Ibid.

7. U.S. Census Bureau, "Historical Poverty Tables," Table Two: Poverty Status of People by Family Relationship, Race, and Hispanic Origin, 1959 to 2002 (numbers in thousands; people as of March of the following year), *http://www.census.gov/hhes/poverty/histpov/hstpov2.html*.

8. The poverty rate of African Americans declined to a historic low of 22.5 percent. Ibid.

9. Community Service Society, "Poverty in New York City, 2000: Hispanics Make Dramatic Gains; For Blacks It's Business as Usual," Data Brief no. 4 (2001), *www.cssny.org/pubs/databrief/databrief09_26_01.html*. New York City statistics are reported as two-year averages in the Current Population Survey because of limited sample size.

10. Ibid. Technically, we refer here to non-Hispanic whites and non-Hispanic blacks, as there are Hispanics in both racial groups. By 2000, poverty rates for non-Hispanic whites and non-Hispanic blacks had returned to their pre-recession levels, 9.1 percent and 26.4 percent, respectively.

11. The fourth Burger Barn is located in Washington Heights, a Dominican neighborhood north and west of Harlem.

12. Statistics in this paragraph are for Manhattan Community District 10 from the 2000 census (compilation by the New York City Department of City Planning). NYC Department of City Planning Community District Profile, Community District 10, December 2004.

13. Ibid. We are using Community District 10, which is central Harlem, to refer to Harlem throughout. In 1990 the household poverty rate for central Harlem was 38 percent, and by 1999 it had dropped to 33 percent.

14. The 1989 statistic is from the U.S. Census Bureau, and the 1999 and 2002 figures are from the New York City Household and Vacancy Survey.

U.S. Census Bureau, New York City Household and Vacancy Survey, *http://www.census.gov/hhes/www/housing/nychvs/nychvs.html.*

15. There was a 14-point drop—48.9 percent to 34.8 percent—in the percent of the central Harlem population receiving some form of government income support. Manhattan Community District 10, from the 2000 census (compilation by the NYC Department of City Planning). NYC Department of City Planning Community District Profile, Community District 10, December 2004.

16. Over this same period, the number of people receiving Supplemental Security Income was constant but the number receiving Medicaid only almost tripled, jumping from 5,716 to 16,874. Ibid.

17. The population increased from 99,519 to 107,109. Median household income was also on the rise during the 1990s, going from $18,608 to $19,924 ($18,608 equals $13,856 in 1989 dollars). This upward trend contrasts with a drop in the city's median household income, which shrank to $38,293 from $38,909 (all figures in 1999 dollars.) Ibid.

18. Census data indicate that 65 percent of central Harlem residents report that they were living in their current residence five years earlier. Authors' calculation from 2000 census.

19. The numerator is the number of people categorized by the U.S. Census Bureau as employed, and the denominator is the population in the age group sixteen to sixty-four.

20. Why was there a drop in the job-holding rate citywide when the unemployment rate was at the same level in 1989 and 1999? (The New York City unemployment rate was 5.1 percent in 1989 and 6.7 percent in 1999.) It may reflect the fact that the improving economic fortunes of some families allowed one partner to stop working.

21. George Borjas, *Heaven's Door: Immigration Policy and the American Experience* (Princeton: Princeton University Press, 2001).

22. The assumption in most of this research is that welfare recipients with these background characteristics do not differ in any important ways from nonrecipients who are in these longitudinal data sets; hence, the experience of the latter is viewed as a fair proxy for the likely future of the former. Since *Chutes and Ladders* is not about welfare recipients per se, the legitimacy of this assumption is not a primary concern. For our purposes, the findings stand as the best account we have thus far of the long-term prospects for low-wage workers who were not embedded in AFDC.

23. Gregory Acs and Pamela Loprest 2001, *http://www.urban.org/url.cfm?ID=410809*; Loprest 2000, *http://www.urban.org/url.cfm?ID=310282*; and Brauner and Loprest 1999, *http://www.urban.org/url.cfm?ID=309065*. For reviews of studies of welfare leavers, and for analysis of welfare reform, see Gregory Acs

and Pamela Loprest, *Leaving Welfare: Employment and Well-Being of Families That Left Welfare in the Post-Entitlement Era* (Washington, DC: Urban Institute Press, 2004).

24. See Ellwood, "Winners and Losers."

25. Richard Kazis, "Opportunity and Advancement for Low-Wage Workers: New Challenges, New Solutions," in *Low-Wage Workers in the New Economy*, ed. Richard Kazis and Marc S. Miller (Washington, DC: Urban Institute Press), 1–15; David Ellwood, *Grow Faster Together, or Grow Slowly Apart: How Will America Work in the 21st Century?* Report of the Aspen Institute Domestic Strategy Group (Washington, DC: Aspen Institute, 2002).

26. Eileen Applebaum, Annette Bernhardt, and Richard J. Murnane, *Low-Wage America: How Employers Are Reshaping Opportunity in the Workplace* (New York: Russell Sage Foundation, 2003).

27. Frank Levy and Richard Murnane, *The New Division of Labor: How Computers Are Creating the Next Job Market* (Princeton: Princeton University Press, 2004).

28. Technology can have virtuous impacts as well. Some employers adopt "high-road" strategies that reduce turnover and increase productivity. Some enlightened hospitals and medium-size manufacturers, for example, have reorganized the labor process to make jobs more interesting and rewarding for workers. What influences an employer's choice between taking the high road or the low? Applebaum, Bernhardt, and Murnane identify a number of factors that go into the decision: local labor market conditions, corporate culture, union pressure, assistance from "intermediary" organizations, and knowledge about available options. See Applebaum, Bernhardt, and Murnane, *Low-Wage America*.

29. Ibid.

30. Susan Lambert, "Lower-Wage Workers and the New Realities of Work and Family," *Annals of the American Academy of Political and Social Science* 562 (1999): 174–190. The report quoted is Paul Kleppner and Nik Theodore, *Work after Welfare: Is the Midwest's Booming Economy Creating Enough Jobs?* Chicago Urban League and Office for Social Policy Research at Northern Illinois University, July 1997.

31. Jared Bernstein and Heidi Hartmann, "Defining and Characterizing the Low-Wage Labor Market," in Kellene Kaye and Demetra Smith Nightingale, *The Low-Wage Labor Market: Challenges and Opportunities for Economic Self-Sufficiency* (Washington, DC: Urban Institute Press, 1999), *http://aspe.hhs.gov/hsp/lwlm99/bernhart.htm*.

32. Bernstein and Hartmann argue that this is far from the whole story. They point out that, quite apart from educational change, an increasing share of the workforce is in the low-wage sector, and wages are down for some

groups of workers regardless of education level. The declining-demand argument implies that employment opportunities for low-wage workers are shrinking. Yet the Bureau of Labor Statistics projects that some of the largest sources of future job growth will be in the low-wage categories (such as cashiers, retail sales workers, and low-wage clerical workers). The evidence for demand shifts seems at best ambiguous. What is clear is that wages have been falling for the least educated. Bernstein and Hartmann, "Defining and Characterizing the Low-Wage Labor Market."

33. Harry J. Holzer, *What Employers Want: Job Prospects for Less-Educated Workers* (New York: Russell Sage Foundation, 1996).

34. Those with the most limited skills have severe employment problems: only 17 percent of extremely low skilled workers (as compared with 40 percent of moderately low skilled workers) make an immediate transition from school to steady employment. See L. Pavetti, *Against the Odds: Steady Improvement among Low-Skill Women* (Washington, DC: Urban Institute Press for the Annie E. Casey Foundation, 1997), and Gary Burtless, "Employment Prospects of Welfare Recipients," in *The Work Alternative: Welfare Reform and the Realities of the Job Market*, ed. Demetra Smith Nightingale and Robert H. Haveman (Washington, DC: Urban Institute Press, 1995).

35. S. Rosenberg, "Male Occupational Standing and the Dual Labor Market," *Industrial Relations* 19, no. 1 (1980): 34–48.

36. Nan Maxwell, "Occupational Differences in the Determination of U.S. Workers' Earnings: Both the Human Capital and the Structured Labor Market Hypotheses Are Useful in Analysis," *American Journal of Economics and Sociology* 46, no. 4 (October 1987): 437–443. According a 1998 survey of employers, most paid $5.50 per hour for a typical entry-level position. Marsha Regenstein, Jack Meyer, and Jennifer D. Hicks, "Job Prospects for Welfare Recipients: Employers Speak Out," August 1998, *http://www.urban.org/url.cfm?ID=308038.* Other studies have found that when women leave welfare for work, they usually take jobs that pay between $5.00 and $6.00 an hour. Michigan employers interviewed for one study noted that the typical hourly wage for the jobs they would be likely to offer welfare recipients was $6.59. See Harry J. Holzer and Michael A. Stoll, *Employers and Welfare Recipients: Evidence from Four Cities* (San Francisco: Public Policy Institute of California, 2000). In any case, these wages are far below the magic $8.00 an hour that experts have deemed characteristic of a "good" job, and that welfare recipients and low-wage workers alike identify as necessary to cover the costs associated with full-time employment. See also James Ricco, Daniel Friedlander, and Stephen Freedman, *GAIN: Benefits, Costs, and Three-Year Impacts of a Welfare-to-Work Program* (San Francisco: Manpower Demonstration Research Corporation, 1994). Also see LaDonna Pavetti, Pamela Holcomb, and Amy-Ellen

Duke, "Increasing Participation in Work and Work-Related Activities: Lessons from Five State Welfare Reform Demonstration Projects," Urban Institute Paper no. 406406, September 1995. See also Harry J. Holzer, *Will Employers Hire Welfare Recipients? Recent Survey Evidence from Michigan* (Madison: Institute for Research on Poverty, 1998), and Kathryn J. Edin, "The Myths of Welfare Dependence and Self-Sufficiency: Women, Welfare, and Low-Wage Work," *Focus* 17 (2): 1–8; Institute for Research on Poverty, University of Wisconsin–Madison, 1995.

37. Young women here are defined as age eighteen to twenty-seven.

38. A good job paid eight dollars an hour for thirty-five hours per week (in 1993 dollars).

39. The picture for women who have received welfare at some point is even bleaker, as only 13 percent were working primarily in a good job by the time they were twenty-seven. Thus Pavetti and Acs conclude that "it is common for young women to make the transition from bad jobs to good jobs and to eventually work steadily in good jobs. However, this is far less the case for women who share the characteristics of women who ever turn to the welfare system for support." LaDonna Pavetti and Gregory Acs, *Moving Up, Moving Out, or Going Nowhere? A Study of the Employment Patterns of Young Women* (Washington, DC: Urban Institute Press, 1997). Even if welfare recipients were to follow the same employment patterns as women who had never been dependent on the welfare system, their lower skill levels would mean that fewer than one-fourth would make the move to a good job by their late twenties. LaDonna Pavetti, "Welfare Reform: An Opportunity to Improve the Lives of Poor Women—But Not a Guarantee," *Policy and Practice of Public Human Services* 56 (1998): 8–12.

40. Jane Waldfogel and Susan Mayer, "Differences between Men and Women in the Low-Wage Labor Market," *Focus* 20 (1999): 11–16.

41. Burtless reviewed twelve years of earnings for women who received welfare in 1979 and concluded that "they experienced very little wage growth during the period." He found an increase from an hourly wage of $6.07 to only $6.72. By contrast, the wages of women not receiving welfare at the start of the period rose substantially, from a baseline of $6.07 to more than $10.00 per hour. G. Burtless, "Welfare Recipients' Job Skills and Employment Prospects," *The Future of the Children* 7 (Spring 1997).

42. Segmented labor market theory describes occupational hierarchy in terms of primary and secondary labor markets. Primary-sector jobs pay higher wages, are more secure, and provide opportunities for advancement. Secondary-sector jobs pay low wages, are insecure, and offer no chances for promotion. David M. Gordon, Richard Edwards, and Michael Reich, *Segmented Work, Divided Workers: The Historical Transformation of Work in the United States*

(Cambridge: Cambridge University Press, 1982). Maxwell, "Occupational Differences in the Determination of U.S. Workers' Earnings: Both the Human Capital and the Structured Labor Market Hypotheses Are Useful in Analysis."

43. M. Cancian and D. Meyer, "Work after Welfare: Work Effort, Occupation and Economic Well-Being," unpublished manuscript, 1998.

44. Connolly and Gottschalk write, "Gains in earnings of the experimentals were primarily the result of increased hours, not increased wages, and the benefits of almost all these programs did not continue after the fifth year. The earnings gains of experimentals over controls during the first three years largely reflected a shorter time to obtain the initial job, not better future outcomes for people who obtained these jobs." Helen Connolly and Peter Gottschalk, "Early Labor Market Experience: Dead-end Jobs or Stepping Stones for Less Skilled Workers?" unpublished manuscript, 1999.

45. Among workers who changed employers, half of those who still had low earnings were working for low-wage employers. F. Andersson et al., *Moving Up or Moving On: Who Advances in the Low-Wage Labor Market?* (New York: Russell Sage Foundation, 2005).

46. Economists disagree, though, about whether low-wage workers do shift jobs any more often than those better placed. Connolly and Gottschalk's analysis of data from the Survey of Income and Program Participation (SIPP) indicates that low-wage workers are as unlikely to leave their "dead-end" jobs as high-wage workers are to leave their well-paid positions. Be that as it may, they do note that moving from one job to another at the appropriate intervals is critical, since long-term loyalty does not pay off for the low skilled while moving from firm to firm does, so long as the new position is not the "same old, same old." Connolly and Gottschalk, "Early Labor Market Experience."

47. Paul Osterman, "Beginning Work: The Youth Labor Market in America," *Wilson Quarterly*, Fall 1994.

48. Eliot Liebow made a related point years ago in his classic study, *Tally's Corner.* He noted that employers expect poor workers to steal and hence keep their wages low to compensate for the pilferage. Ironically, the low wages practically force workers to steal because they cannot make ends meet. Eliot Liebow, *Tally's Corner* (Boston: Little, Brown, 1967).

49. Jo Anne Schneider, "Social Networks, Career, and Training Paths for Participants in Education and Training Programs," technical report prepared for the Philadelphia Private Industry Council, 1997. Harry Holzer and Robert LaLonde present more equivocal results concerning the effectiveness of training programs, citing examples of particular programs that did—and did not— appear to have effects on the mobility and wages of low-wage workers. H. J.

Holzer and Robert LaLonde, "Job Change and Job Stability among Less-Skilled Young Workers," Institute for Research on Poverty, Discussion Paper no. 1191-99, 1999.

50. Acs and Loprest, *Leaving Welfare*, 7.

51. Ibid., 8.

52. About 40 to 50 percent of welfare-leaving families live below the poverty line, a lower percentage than is the case among families on welfare but still far higher than is often acknowledged by those who trumpet the success of welfare reform. Ibid.

53. For *Chutes and Ladders*, a random sample of 186 persons (93 hires and 93 denied applicants for the same jobs) was drawn from the original pool of 300 participants in the *No Shame* study. We were hoping for a yield of 120 people, which was all our budget could sustain. We were successful, in the end, with 103 respondents. Three people refused to participate, and the rest were subjects who had vanished. The response rate, then, was 55 percent.

54. In particular, the follow-up underrepresents individuals in the "other race" category (primarily Africans and West Indians) and slightly over-represents "other Latinos" (mainly Puerto Ricans and South Americans). In all other respects—race, gender, education, and household status in 1993—the follow-up sample was representative of the original study participants.

55. David Lavin et al., *Changing the Odds* (New Haven: Yale University Press, 1996).

56. $N = 59$, managers excluded.

57. $N = 62$, managers excluded. Median wage is $7.49 in 1997 dollars.

58. $N = 46$ for those employed at both the wave 1 and wave 2 interviews.

59. Only two of the fifteen in this group were in jobs paying below the minimum wage.

60. Minimum wage in 1997 was $5.15 ($4.66 in 1993 dollars).

61. In 1997, 62 percent of the sample was female and 62 percent was African American.

62. Twenty-seven percent had jobs paying $5.50 to $9.99 an hour (1997 dollars).

63. David Leonhardt, "Slow Job Growth Raises Concerns in U.S. Economy," *New York Times*, August 7, 2004.

64. The demographics of the wave 3 sample are contained in Appendix A.

65. Of the twenty-eight people who were working in 2002, only one person was working but earning below the poverty line (but other workers in his family raised the family income above the poverty line). In other words, for all but one of the people employed in the sample, simply by having a job they brought their families up above the poverty line. In 2002, New York had the

second highest average wage of all fifty states. Bureau of Labor Statistics, "Employment and Wages, Annual Averages 2002," table 6, *http://www.bls.gov/cew/cewbultn02.htm.*

66. Another way to benchmark the progress of the Burger Barn workers is to look at a higher threshold: 200 percent of the poverty line. In the final follow-up, 22 percent of the sample fell below this threshold, considering their household income and adjusting for family size.

67. The federal government has not updated the poverty line to reflect changes in household income, consumption, and expenditure patterns that have take place since the early 1960s, when the line was created. Nor does the line acknowledge regional differences in the cost of living. See Constance F. Citro and Robert T. Michael, eds., *Measuring Poverty: A New Approach* (Washington, DC: National Academy Press, 1995).

68. See "Building a Ladder to Jobs and Higher Wages," *Community Service Society Report,* 2000, *http://www.cssny.org/pubs/special/2000_10buildingaladder.pdf.*

69. National Low Income Housing Coalition, "Out of Reach, 2001: America's Growing Wage-Rent Disparity," October 2001, *http://www.nlihc.org/oor2001/.*

70. Mark Levitan, *A Crisis of Black Male Employment: Unemployment and Joblessness in New York City, 2003,* Community Service Society Annual Report, February 2004, 12, 13; *www.cssny.org.*

71. Ibid.

72. Ibid., 11.

73. Jane Waldfogel and Susan Mayer, "Gender Differences in the Low-Wage Labor Market," "Male/Female Differences in the Low-Wage Labor Market," in *Finding Jobs: Work and Welfare Reform,* ed. Rebecca Blank and David Card (New York: Russell Sage Foundation), 193–232.

74. Rebecca M. Blank, *It Takes a Nation: A New Agenda for Fighting Poverty* (Princeton: Princeton University Press; New York: Russell Sage Foundation, 1996).

3. High Flyers, Low Riders, and the "Up but Not Out" Club

1. In the 1950s and 1960s, manufacturing hubs in major cities offered well-paying jobs that even men with minimal education could obtain. These jobs began to disappear in the mid- to late 1970s as a process of deindustrialization—the dismantling of America's industrial capacity—set in. See John Foster-Bey, "The Impact of Changing Manufacturing Employment on Living-Wage Employment for Less-Educated Adult Males," Urban Institute Working Paper on Regional Economic Opportunities, 2001; Barry Bluestone and Bennett Harrison, *The Deindustrialization of America: Plant Closings, Com-*

munity Abandonment, and the Dismantling of Basic Industry (New York: Basic Books, 1982); Bennett Harrison and Barry Bluestone, *The Great U-Turn: Corporate Restructuring and the Polarizing of America* (New York: Basic Books, 1988).

It is a matter of debate whether these manufacturing jobs disappeared altogether or stopped paying decent wages; Foster-Bey argues the latter point. Using 1980 census data and 1990 Public-Use Micro Data Sample (PUMS:15) data encompassing ninety-nine of the country's largest metropolitan areas, he finds that manufacturing employment for less-educated adult males actually increased during the 1980s in those metropolitan areas, though their total employment and living-wage employment ratio declined. At the same time, econometric research has shown that employment rates for African American males have dropped in step with declines in manufacturing employment; see, for instance, Harry Holzer and Wayne Vroman, "Mismatches and the Urban Labor Market," in George Peterson and Wayne Vroman, eds., *Urban Labor Markets and Job Opportunity* (Washington, DC: Urban Institute Press, 1992). The deindustrialization of the Reagan years was especially devastating for African American workers, who were represented in America's factory workforce in numbers exceeding their proportion in the population. Not only did the number of America's high-wage, blue-collar jobs (half of them in manufacturing) decline, but so did the quality of the "secondary" jobs that unskilled African American workers increasingly had to rely on—even as the educational requirements for these jobs rose. See Maury B. Gittleman and David R. Howell, "Job Quality and Labor Market Segmentation in the 1980s: A New Perspective on the Effects of Employment Restructuring by Race and Gender," Working Paper no. 82, Jerome Levy Economics Institute, Bard College, March 1993; William Julius Wilson, *When Work Disappears: The World of the New Urban Poor* (New York: Vintage Books, 1997). In contrast, the brief expansion of manufacturing jobs in the first half of the 1990s helped lower unemployment rates among African Americans, Wilson notes (145).

2. "From the early 1960s to 1980, the average company grew from 13.0 employees in 1962 to 16.3 in 1970 and to 16.5 in 1980. At the peak in 1970, roughly 37 percent of Americans worked in firms of 250 or more employees. . . . In the past decade or so, the trend has gone the other way. The average number of employees per firm slipped to 14.8 in 1993 with only 29 percent of workers employed by firms of 250 or more." Michael Cox and Richard Alm, "The Economy's Good News: The Upside of Downsizing," National Center for Policy Analysis, Policy Backgrounder no. 146, February 25, 1998.

3. The service sector is extremely bifurcated, split between high-paying jobs requiring a high degree of skill and low-wage jobs requiring few skills. See Laura Dresser and Joel Rogers, "Rebuilding Job Access and Career Ad-

vancement Systems in the New Economy," Center on Wisconsin Strategy Briefing Paper, University of Wisconsin at Madison, 1997, 2. Dresser and Rogers also note that the decline in firm size has knocked down some career ladders, since by their nature "small firms and firms that are not growing offer fewer opportunities for internal advancement." See also Davis Jenkins, "Beyond Welfare-to-Work: Bridging the Low-Wage Livable-Wage Employment Gap," Great Cities Institute, University of Illinois at Chicago, January 1999.

4. A variety of studies show a strong and growing relationship between educational attainment and earnings. See, for example, Gary S. Becker, "The Age of Human Capital," in Edward P. Lazear, ed., *Education in the Twenty-first Century* (Stanford, CA: Hoover Institution Press, 2002), 3–8. Becker writes, "In the United States during most of the past forty years, college graduates earned on the average about 50 percent more than high school graduates, and the latter earned about 30 percent more than high school dropouts. . . . Wage differences between typical college and high school graduates increased from 40 percent in 1977 to 60 percent in the 1990s. The gap between high school graduates and persons with at least a college education grew even faster, from 50 percent in the late 1960s to about 75 percent in recent years. These are probably the largest increases in U.S. history" (4–5). See also Jennifer Cheeseman Day and Eric C. Newburger, "The Big Payoff: Educational Attainment and Synthetic Estimates of Work-Life Earnings," U.S. Census Bureau Special Study P23-210, July 2002.

5. Firms have always sought some basic characteristics in their workers: dependability, a positive attitude, a strong work ethic. But today's employers are placing growing importance on skills—including mathematics, problem solving, and reading abilities—that many high schools do not teach adequately. The demand for *basic* cognitive skills is growing—skills such as "the ability to follow directions, manipulate fractions and decimals, and interpret line groups"—as opposed to more complex knowledge, such as geometry or advanced algebra. This finding is surprising until one notes that only about half of the nation's high school seniors have mastered computation with decimals, fractions, and percents, and can recognize geometric figures" (263–264). Richard J. Murnane, John B. Willett, and Frank Levy, "The Growing Importance of Cognitive Skills in Wage Determination," *Review of Economics and Statistics* 77, no. 2 (May 1995): 251–266. See also Richard J. Murnane and Frank Levy, *Teaching the New Basic Skills: Principles for Educating Children to Thrive in a Changing Economy* (New York: Free Press, 1996), 8–9. Murnane and Levy argue that today's employers are increasingly turning to college graduates not because college teaches necessary skills, but because college graduates are more likely to have mastered the desired basic skills back in high school.

6. The term *soft skills* came into widespread use in the early 1990s, though it can be traced all the way back to a 1972 U.S. Army training manual. John P. Fry and Paul G. Whitmore, "What Are Soft Skills?" paper presented at the CONARC Soft Skills Conference, sponsored by the U.S. Continental Army Command, Fort Bliss, Texas, December 12–13, 1972, cited in Philip Moss and Chris Tilly, *Stories Employers Tell: Race, Skill, and Hiring in America* (New York: Russell Sage Foundation, 2001). Definitions of the term vary; see Cecilia A. Conrad, *Soft Skills and the Minority Work Force: A Guide for Informed Discussion* (Washington, DC: Joint Center for Political and Economic Studies, 1999). Moss and Tilly define it as "skills, abilities, and traits that pertain to personality, attitude, and behavior rather than to formal or technical knowledge. We group them into two clusters, based on how employers described to us the skills required to perform entry-level jobs. The first cluster, interaction, involves ability to interact with customers, co-workers, and supervisors. . . . A second cluster of soft skills, motivation, takes in characteristics such as enthusiasm, positive work attitude, commitment, dependability, integrity, and willingness to learn" (44). See Wilson, *When Work Disappears*, for a discussion of the difficulty of distinguishing between overt racial discrimination and preferences for certain soft skills in the environment of the inner city (136).

7. Studies of summer youth programs (as well as other forms of short-term, government-subsidized employment aimed at youth) report mixed results. The research suggests these programs have no effect on earnings or crime rates; see, for example, Shawn Bushway and Peter Reuter, "Labor Markets and Crime Risk Factors," in Lawrence W. Sherman et al., *Preventing Crime: What Works, What Doesn't, What's Promising*, a report to the U.S. Congress, prepared for the National Institute of Justice, July 1998. That said, some studies do show modest gains in soft skills and career knowledge. See Thomas J. Smith and Michelle Alberti Gambone, "Effectiveness of Federally Funded Employment Training Strategies for Youth," in U.S. Department of Labor, *Dilemmas in Youth Employment Programming: Findings from the Youth Research and Technical Assistance Project*, vol. 1, Research and Evaluation Report, ser. 92-C (Washington, DC: U.S. Department of Labor, 1992), 15–67.

8. The Family Support Act of 1988 endorsed the human capital approach, required states to establish a job-opportunity and basic skills training program to help needy families with children, and directed states to guarantee child care services to families receiving AFDC if those services were necessary for a family member's employment or participation in a state-approved education or training activity. The Personal Responsibility and Work Opportunity Reconciliation Act (PRWORA), passed in 1996, favors a "work first" approach, under which welfare recipients are placed in jobs as quickly as possible—even jobs paying below-poverty wages—and are limited in the extent to which they

can count education and training toward their work requirements. Proponents of this legislation argued that welfare recipients learn more from an actual job than from any educational program. See Marie Cohen, "Work Experience and Publicly Funded Jobs for TANF Recipients," *Welfare Information Network* 2, no. 12 (September 1998), available at *http://www.financeproject.org/Publications/newwork.htm*.

Interestingly, evidence to date suggests that welfare recipients with less education are less able to meet the new work requirements. Data from Tennessee show that 60 percent of recipients who had their benefits docked because of failure to meet work or child-support compliance requirements did not have a general equivalency diploma or a high school diploma, compared with 40 percent of recipients who left TANF for work. In South Carolina, 36 percent of those who did not complete high school were sanctioned, compared with 22 percent of high school graduates. LaDonna Pavetti and Dan Bloom, "State Sanctions and Time Limits," in Rebecca Blank and Ron Haskins, eds., *The New World of Welfare* (Washington, DC: Brookings Institution Press, 2001), 259.

9. By 1998, 15 percent of unemployed individuals looking for jobs searched the Internet for leads—a rate that exceeded that for most other traditional job-seeking methods, including contacting private employment agencies, contacting friends and relatives, contacting school and university employment centers, checking union and professional registers, and placing or answering ads. About 7 percent of employed workers looked for new jobs using the Internet. Peter Kuhn and Mikael Skuterud, "Job Search Methods: Internet versus Traditional," *Monthly Labor Review* (October 2000): 4.

10. According to a report by the U.S. Department of Education's National Center for Education Statistics, 24 percent of adults who were enrolled in a degree or credential program in 1995 received some cash assistance from their employer. National Center for Education Statistics, *Employer Aid for Postsecondary Education*, NCES 1999-181 (Washington, DC: U.S. Department of Education, June 1999).

11. There are more than 5,500 proprietary schools in the United States that offer job training in fields as diverse as welding, court reporting, and massage therapy, not to mention business and computer training. Susan Folkman Schulz, "Program Completion in Proprietary Schools: A Phenomenological Case Study," Ph.D. diss., Florida Atlantic University, May 2000, 2. Proprietary schools became notorious in the 1990s after several incidents of fraud were revealed involving federal student loans. Instances of alleged abuse continue to make the headlines. See Center for Law and Social Policy, "Written Testimony on H.R. 4283, the College Access and Opportunity Act," May 12, 2004, and Goldie Blumenstyk, "For-Profit Colleges Face New Scrutiny,"

Chronicle of Higher Education, May 14, 2004. See also W. Norton Grubb, "The Long-Run Effects of Proprietary Schools on Wages and Earnings: Implications for Federal Policy," *Educational Evaluation and Policy Analysis* 15, no. 1 (Spring 1993): 28.

12. See Frederik Andersson, Harry J. Holzer, and Julia I. Lane, *Moving Up or Moving On: Who Advances in the Low-Wage Labor Market?* (New York: Russell Sage, 2005). Their research suggests that "access to high-wage firms is a critical part of the success by which initial low earners make progress in the labor market. On-the-job training and wage growth are more rather than less likely to occur at these firms" (144).

13. Richard B. Freeman and James L. Medoff, *What Do Unions Do?* (New York: Basic Books, 1984). See also David Card, "The Effect of Unions on Wage Inequality in the U.S. Labor Market," *Industrial and Labor Relations Review* 54 (January 2001): 296–315.

14. Returning to school at a later age is quite common among students in today's colleges and universities: in 1990, students who were twenty-five years old or older comprised 21 percent of all full-time students over the age of eighteen. Full- and part-time adult students accounted for 43 percent of all students over eighteen. James Monks, "The Impact of College Timing on Earnings," *Economics of Education Review* 16, no. 4 (1997): 419–423. Research shows that experienced adult workers who return to school receive positive returns on community college education—returns that are comparable to (and in some cases higher than) those for continuing high school graduates. Duane E. Leigh and Andrew M. Gill, "Labor Market Returns to Community Colleges: Evidence for Returning Adults," *Journal of Human Resources* 32, no. 2 (Spring 1997): 334–353.

15. See David Halle, *America's Working Man: Work, Home, and Politics among Blue-Collar Property Owners* (Chicago: University of Chicago Press, 1984). In his study of blue-collar workers at an automated, unionized chemical plant in New Jersey, Halle found that workers were generally reluctant to seek promotions into supervision. "About half the workers . . . do not want promotions to the top of even the blue-collar hierarchy. They turn down the chance to become a chief or leader—non-supervisory positions entailing union membership—because they do not want the bother of disciplining other men. Of those workers who have taken the job of chief or leader, another half would turn down, and in some cases have turned down, offers of promotion into supervision. The main reason is that on entering supervision workers lose the protection of the union" (157).

16. See Carol B. Stack, *Call to Home: African Americans Reclaim the Rural South* (New York: Basic Books, 1996), which tells some of the stories of the estimated half million African Americans who left the North to return to their

ancestral homeland in the South—reversing, to some extent, the Great Migration of the earlier part of the twentieth century.

17. See Chris Tilly, *Half a Job: Bad and Good Part-Time Jobs in a Changing Labor Market* (Philadelphia: Temple University Press, 1996). According to Tilly, some 20 million people now work part-time in the United States, more than 6 million of them involuntarily. Worker demand for part-time jobs peaked in the 1970s, but the cheap labor and flexible schedules that part-time work provides have continued to entice employers, who are hiring part-time workers in greater numbers. Tilly attributes this long-term growth to the expanding trade and service industries, which depend heavily on part-time workers.

18. Eighty-two percent of Costco workers are covered by company health insurance, compared with 48 percent of Wal-Mart workers, and Costco pays 92 percent of its employees' health-insurance premium, while Wal-Mart pays 66 percent (the average contribution at large U.S. companies is 80 percent). The annual worker turnover rate is 24 percent at Costco, compared with 50 percent at Wal-Mart. Ann Zimmerman, "Costco's Dilemma: Is Treating Employees Well Unacceptable for a Public Corporation?" *Wall Street Journal*, March 26, 2004.

19. A portion of Costco's workforce—journalistic accounts say between 13 percent and 20 percent—is unionized. Fifty-six of Costco's 430 stores were unionized in 2004. See James Flanigan, "Costco Sees Value in Higher Pay," *Los Angeles Times*, February 15, 2004; Christine Frey, "Costco's Love of Labor: Employees' Well-Being Key to Its Success," *Seattle Post-Intelligencer*, March 29, 2004; and Nina Shapiro, "Company for the People," *Seattle Weekly*, December 15–21, 2004.

20. Back in 1976, only 36 percent of white women and 42 percent of black women, ages eighteen to sixty-four, had worked continuously since school completion. Mary Corcoran, "The Structure of Female Wages," *American Economic Review* 68, no. 2 (May 1978): 165–166. As female labor-force participation has risen over the past few decades, the number of women who choose to leave the workforce because of motherhood has declined. Sigal Alon, Debra Donahoe, and Marta Tienda, "The Effects of Early Work Experience on Young Women's Labor Force Attachment," *Social Forces* 79, no. 3 (March 2001): 1006.

21. See Katherine Newman, *Falling from Grace: Downward Mobility in the Age of Affluence* (Berkeley: University of California Press, 1999).

22. Scholars of the labor market have distinguished three types of skills: firm-specific skills, industry-specific skills, and general skills. "These different skills differ significantly in terms of their asset-specificity (i.e., portability). Firm-specific skills are acquired through on-the-job training, and are least portable. They are valuable to the employer who carried out the training but

not to other employers. Industry-specific skills are acquired through apprenticeship and vocational schools. These skills, especially when authoritatively certified, are recognized by any employer within a specific trade. General skills, recognized by all employers, do not carry a value that is dependent on the type of firm or industry." Margarita Estevez-Abe, Torben Iversen, and David Soskice, "Social Protection and the Formation of Skills: A Reinterpretation of the Welfare State," paper presented at the American Political Science Association annual meeting, September 2–5, 1999. Estevez-Abe and colleagues make the novel case that in countries where businesses have an interest in promoting specific skills, they tend to support welfare-state policies of social protection (employment, unemployment, and wage protection), because without these protections workers would be reluctant to invest in the firm- or industry-specific skills that increase their exposure to labor market risks.

23. See Monks, "The Impact of College Timing on Earnings," and Leigh and Gill, "Labor Market Returns to Community Colleges."

24. The pseudonyms used here are the same as those used in Katherine Newman, *No Shame in My Game: The Working Poor in the Inner City* (New York: Knopf and Russell Sage, 1999).

25. She was actually making more ($31,500) at her previous job as the secretary/personal assistant to the head of a small ad agency, but she left that job because she had a difficult time with her boss.

26. "The largest occupational groups in the American temp labor force are secretarial/office workers and laborers/operators, each of which accounts for around one-third of total employment. The penetration rate of temping is highest in low-wage occupations in general, and especially in data-processing, manual laboring, plant operative work, clerical, and hand assembly/fabrications, where on average around one in ten of all workers in these occupations is a temp." Nik Theodore and Jamie Peck, "Contingent Chicago: Restructuring the Spaces of Temporary Labor," *International Journal of Urban and Regional Research* 25, no. 3 (September 2001).

27. While we found that temp firms played a particularly important role in linking low-wage workers to jobs that paid in the middle range of our outcome groups, for a small number of workers temp firms were their ticket to high-flyer status. See Andersson, Holzer, and Lane, *Moving Up*, who find that "early work experience at a temp agency is associated with higher subsequent earnings for initial low earners" (143). Lanice Taylor, a twenty-six-year-old African American in our study, made $42,200 with full benefits in her job as an administrative assistant for a firm in the entertainment industry. Lanice had hopscotched from one temp job to the next and finally landed the best job she had ever had. Workers like Lanice appeal to temp agencies in a labor market characterized by instability, interrupted wages, and lack of benefits, because

she was a single unmarried worker with no children or other dependents. She could "afford" to take a short-term job.

28. See David Finegold, Alec Levenson, and Mark Van Buren, "A Temporary Route to Advancement? The Career Opportunities for Low-Skilled Workers in Temporary Employment," in *Low-Wage America: How Employers Are Reshaping Opportunity in the Workplace* (New York: Russell Sage, 2003). Under this rubric there are four different categories of temps: short-term temps who want short-term temp jobs; long-term temps who want better, longer-term temp jobs; short-term workers who want to use temp work to find a permanent job as quickly as possible; and selective job seekers who want to use temping to find the right permanent position.

29. According to salary.com, the median salary for a social worker in the United States is $38,331; in New York City, it is $44,847.

30. There is debate within the social science literature about how much of an economic return a worker in America receives from going to community college. See Thomas J. Kane and Cecilia Elena Rouse, "Comment on W. Norton Grubb, 'The Varied Economic Returns to Postsecondary Education': New Evidence from the Class of 1972," *Journal of Human Resources* 30, no. 1 (Winter 1995): 205–221, and W. Norton Grubb, "The Returns to Education in the Sub-Baccalaureate Labor Market, 1984–1990," *Economics of Education Review* 16, no. 3 (1997): 231–245. One point of contention is whether taking community college courses but not completing a degree has any economic benefit. Another is whether a so-called sheepskin or program effect exists, whereby completing a credential has a greater return than acquiring an equivalent number of credits. Kane and Rouse argue that whether or not they complete the degree, individuals who attend a two-year college have wages that are higher than those of comparable high school graduates. Grubb, however, maintains that the effects are varied, and that attending community college for less than one year has an impact that "is usually too small to be statistically significant. Also, contrary to Kane and Rouse's findings, Grubb presents evidence that suggests that program effects do exist: "Completing a certificate is more beneficial than completing one year of college without a credential; an associate degree is more valuable than two years of college, and a baccalaureate degree increases earnings by more than four years of college without the credential" (241). Finally, Grubb asserts that the type of field that an individual enters matters: "Some programs prepare their students for such poorly paid occupations that there is no real economic advantage to attending a community college or technical institute; others—particularly in technical fields and business for men, in business and health for women—have more consistent and substantial returns. Some relatively common fields of study at the sub-baccalaureate level—education (or child care) for women, certain trades and crafts at the

certificate level—provide very little if any increase in earnings over those of high school graduates. Finally, the returns to academic associate degrees, for those who fail to transfer to four-year colleges, are often low or uncertain" (238).

Of course, how much higher education pays has to be weighed against the opportunity cost of leaving or not entering the work world for a period of time—time that could be spent gaining on-the-job experience that also augments wages.

31. The retail industry, in particular, is associated with low wages and high turnover. A congested retail market has brought down profit margins and created pressures for consolidation and cost reduction, driving smaller mom-and-pop stores out of business. Corporate chains like Wal-Mart follow a low-road approach to human resources: "Sales jobs are dead end, starting pay is at or close to the minimum wage, and raises are given yearly but not guaranteed, with a ceiling of 25 to 30 cents an hour. Work schedules are changed constantly, and if demand is slack, workers are required to leave their shift early. Working more than thirty-five hours is considered a major infraction since it incurs federally mandated overtime pay. The low pay is exacerbated by the lack of opportunity to work sufficient hours a week to produce a livable paycheck. At Wal-Mart, full-time is defined as twenty-eight or more hours a week. Thus, while two-thirds of the company's workers are said to be full-time, most are in reality working only part-time. Health benefits are available to full-timers, but they must contribute 40 percent from their own paychecks, so only about three-fourths of the employees are covered." Annette Bernhardt, "The Future of Low-Wage Service Jobs and the Workers That Hold Them," Institute of Education and the Economy Information Brief no. BI-25 (July 1999).

The literature on segmented labor markets provides one way of understanding the gulf between the high-road employment strategies of the hi-tech, knowledge-based economy and the low-road strategies of the service sector. "Jobs in the primary segment are core jobs. These pay higher wages and are more likely to provide fringe benefits (such as health insurance and paid vacations) than jobs in the secondary segment. They also have ladders upward (often within the same firm), whereby workers can steadily improve their earnings and living standards over time. Jobs in the secondary segment, on the other hand, are peripheral jobs. They pay low wages, offer few benefits, tend to be nonunion, and generally have worse working conditions than core jobs in the primary sector. They are also less stable than core jobs, with high job turnover and much churning but little upward mobility. Race- and gender-based discrimination are also more common in the secondary than in the primary segment." Jared Bernstein and Heidi Hartmann, "Defining and Characterizing the Low-Wage Labor Market," in Urban Institute, *The Low-Wage Labor Market: Challenges and Opportunities for Economic Self-Sufficiency*, report prepared for the Assistant Secretary for Planning and Evaluation, U.S. Department of Health and Human Services, December 1999. See also Bennett Harrison and Andrew Sum, "The Theory of 'Dual' or Segmented Labor Markets," *Journal of Economic Issues* 8, no. 3 (1979): 687–706; David M. Gordon, *Theories of Poverty and Unemployment* (Lexington, MA: D.C. Heath, 1972); Michael Piore, "Fragments of a 'Sociological' Theory of Wages," *American Economic Review* 63, no. 2 (May 1973): 377–384; and David R. Howell, "Institutional Failure and the America Worker: The Collapse of Low-Skill Wages," Jerome Levy Economics Institute of Bard College Public Policy Brief no. 29, 1997.

32. Cassandra had had this job for more than a year and a half when we met with her in 2002 (before that she had a number of shorter-term phone customer service jobs, which she got through a combination of friends and job placement agencies).

33. See, for example, Lawrence M. Mead, "Welfare Employment," in Lawrence M. Mead, ed., *The New Paternalism* (Washington, DC: Brookings Institution Press, 1997), 39–88. "Reducing caseloads will not be enough to end welfare because the more the rolls shrink the less employable the remaining recipients become. In Wisconsin, even counties that are the toughest about work have begun to doubt whether the families still on the rolls can work. Perhaps forms of community service short of actual work are needed to structure the lives of people too impaired for regular employment. These adults would be obligated to function in some ways, but not to work for pay or support themselves" (76).

A 2002 analysis of data from the Women's Employment Study, which followed female, single-parent heads of household in TANF cases from one urban county in Michigan, examined the barriers that impede people from leaving welfare, and found that persistent welfare users are less likely to have a high school degree, more likely to have transportation problems, more likely to report domestic violence, and more likely to experience problems with their health or their children's health. Sandra K. Danziger and Kristin S. Seefeldt, "Barriers to Employment and the 'Hard to Serve': Implications for Services, Sanctions, and Time Limits," *Social Policy and Society* 2, no. 2 (2002): 151–160.

34. Employers do often monitor the academic performance of their high school and college workers. Indeed, they may be the adults who are most closely invested in the trajectories of their employees toward higher education. See Katherine Newman, *No Shame in My Game: The Working Poor in the Inner City* (New York: Knopf and Russell Sage, 1999), chap. 5, "School and Skill in the Low-Wage World."

35. In 2003, the last year for which data are available, there were 69,244 drug-and-alcohol treatment admissions (excluding alcohol-only) in New York City. That same year, there were 23,563 admissions to treatment in which heroin was the primary drug of abuse; there were 16,114 such admissions for cocaine, and 13,471 for marijuana. White House Office of National Drug Control Policy, "Profile of Drug Indicators: New York, New York," February 2005, *http://www.whitehousedrugpolicy.gov/statelocal/ny/nyny.pdf.*

36. For a perspective on how low-income single mothers reconcile their need to find work with their need to be a good mother, see Kathryn Edin and Laura Lein, *Making Ends Meet: How Single Mothers Survive Welfare and Low-Wage Work* (New York: Russell Sage Foundation, 1997).

37. Prison records, now quite common among men in poor, minority neighborhoods, constitute a major barrier to employment. Background checks have become easier to perform; it is now a simple matter for employers to check on criminal convictions. See David Harding, "Jean Valjean's Dilemma: The Management of Ex-Convict Identity in the Search for Employment," *Deviant Behavior* 25, no. 6 (1993): 571–595, and Devah Pager, "The Mark of a Criminal Record," *American Journal of Sociology* 108, no. 5 (March 2003): 937–975.

4. All in the Family

1. See Viviana Zelizer, *Pricing the Priceless Child: The Changing Social Value of Children* (New York: Basic Books, 1985). Zelizer notes that as late as the early twentieth century, parents saw their children as "objects of utility" and valued them primarily for their extra labor. While the wages earned by children remained important to working-class families, middle-class reformers gradually put into place laws that banned child labor and made education compulsory, and the "object of utility" was ultimately replaced by the "economically worthless but emotionally priceless child." Carol Stack describes the ways that parents, siblings, and relatives exert forms of social control to keep productive family members from marrying and leaving the household. "When a mother in The Flats has a relationship with a non-economically productive man, the relationship saps the resources of others in her domestic network. Participants in the network try to break up such relationships in order to maximize their potential resources and the services they hope to exchange." The difficulty that a woman encounters in breaking away from the daily obligations of her kin network means that "couples rarely chance marriage unless a man has a job." Carol Stack, *All Our Kin* (New York: Basic Books, 1974), 115, 113.

2. See Thomas D. Cook and Frank F. Furstenberg, Jr., "Explaining Aspects of the Transition to Adulthood in Italy, Sweden, Germany, and the United States: A Cross-Disciplinary, Case Synthesis Approach," *Annals of the Ameri-*

can Academy of Political and Social Science 580 (March 2002): 257–287. Cook and Furstenberg look at the specific contexts of Italy, Sweden, Germany, and the United States, but they also make observations about the "generally similar historical changes" occurring across Western Europe and in North America (259).

3. In Italy, however, this is rapidly becoming normative. Fifty percent of Italian men age thirty live with their parents. Ibid., 261. Cook and Furstenberg note: "Whether employed or not, young adults in Italy live with their parents for longer than in other nations. Veneto has the lowest unemployment in Italy, but even so, more than 60 percent of the unemployed twenty-five- to thirty-five-year-olds living there in 1999 were residing with their parents." See also Marco Manacorda and Enrico Moretti, "Intergenerational Transfers and Household Structure: Why Do Most Italian Youths Live with Their Parents?" Centre for Economic Performance, London School of Economics and Political Science, June 2002, *http://cep.lse.ac.uk/pubs/ download/DP0536.pdf.* According to their data, 85 percent of Italian men age eighteen to thirty-three live with their parents (Table 1).

4. Stack, *All Our Kin*, 46–49. After a teenager gives birth to a child, her mother, her mother's sister, or an older sister may raise that child and take on the title of "mama" (47). The mama in effect acquires the rights and responsibilities of the biological parent. This transfer of parental authority may last even after the child's mother sets up an independent household; efforts to regain custody of the child may be rejected or met with "disapproval, threats, and gossip within the domestic group" (88). When the mother and "mama" are residing in the same household with the child, a power struggle may arise in which the two fight over what is best for the child.

5. A 1999 study by researchers at Mount Sinai School of Medicine analyzed hospital discharge data by zip code, income level, and minority status, and found that hospitalization rates correlated with low median household incomes. The average hospital admission rate for the entire city was 46.26 per 10,000 residents; in the worst ten zip-code areas (which included east Harlem/ south, east Harlem/center, and central Harlem) it ranged from 119.53 to 222.28 per 10,000, and in the least-affected ten zip codes (lower Manhattan and some parts of Queens) it ranged from 0 to 5.64 per 10,000. Areas with high asthma hospitalization rates had higher percentages of minority residents and of children under the age of eighteen, and had average household incomes from $10,256 to $19,383 a year—less than half the city average of $35,673. (Areas with the lowest asthma hospitalization rates had average household incomes of $57,554.) The asthma hospitalization rate for minorities was 7.5 times higher than the rate for whites. L. Claudio et al., "Socioeconomic Factors and Asthma Hospitalization Rates in New York City," *Journal of Asthma* 36, no. 4 (June–July 1999): 343–350; Center for Children's Health and the En-

vironment, Mount Sinai School of Medicine, "Asthma Hospitalization Rates in Poor New York City Neighborhoods Up to Five Times Higher Than the City Average," press release, July 27, 1999.

6. Of 214 welfare-reliant single mothers (then under the AFDC program) interviewed by Kathryn Edin and Laura Lein, 121 said they could not afford to work at least in part because they did not have access to low-cost child care. Of the 165 wage-reliant mothers who were interviewed, the vast majority were able to find more affordable forms of child care. Only 5 percent said they paid market rate for child care; 23 percent received child care subsidies or had found an unlicensed provider willing to accept less than the market rate, 18 percent had a friend or relative who could care for their children for little or no compensation, and the rest had working hours that allowed them to avoid child care or felt their children were independent enough to be left home alone. Kathryn Edin and Laura Lein, *Making Ends Meet: How Single Mothers Survive Welfare and Low-Wage Work* (New York: Russell Sage Foundation, 1997), 80, 94. See also William Julius Wilson, *When Work Disappears: The World of the New Urban Poor* (New York: Vintage Books, 1997), 93–94. More recent research has supported the finding that mothers are influenced by the availability and cost of child care in making labor market decisions; for a review of the literature, see Patricia Anderson and Phillip Levine, "Child Care and Mother's Employment Decisions," in David E. Card and Rebecca M. Blank, eds., *Finding Jobs: Work and Welfare Reform* (New York: Russell Sage Foundation, 2000). At the same time, a 2003 study found that increasing child care subsidies to poor families in which a single mother was working but not on welfare was linked to an increased likelihood of the mother's employment: "A $1,000 increase in the average annual subsidy per single mother with a child under thirteen translates into an estimated 11 percent increase in the probability of employment." Jay Bainbridge, Marcia K. Myers, and Jane Waldfogel, "Child Care Policy Reform and the Employment of Single Mothers," *Social Science Quarterly* 84, no. 4 (December 2003): 789.

7. For varied accounts of how values of work and family clash (or do not) in middle-class families, see Arlie Hochschild, *The Second Shift: Working Parents and the Revolution at Home* (New York: Viking, 1989); Arlie Hochschild, *The Time Bind: When Work Becomes Home and Home Becomes Work* (New York: Metropolitan Books, 1997); Rosalind C. Barnett and Caryl Rivers, *She Works/He Works: How Two-Income Families Are Happy, Healthy, and Thriving* (Cambridge, MA: Harvard University Press, 1998); Kathleen Gerson, *Hard Choices: How Women Decide about Work, Career, and Motherhood* (Berkeley: University of California Press, 1985); and Jerry A. Jacobs and Kathleen Gerson, *The Time Divide: Work, Family, and Gender Inequality* (Cambridge, MA: Harvard University Press, 2004).

8. Of course, the same thing can happen to middle-class families. It is the

essence of middle-class culture to expect to be financially autonomous from one's kin. Siblings do not expect to raise one another's children unless there has been an unexpected death in the family. Parents may try to help their children financially, but they would see themselves as failures if their adult progeny could not support themselves and their own children. Because they do not create and sustain a private safety net of the kind that is routine among the poor—who could not survive without it—middle-class families who fall on hard times are often far more vulnerable. They do not have reciprocal ties to rely on. See Katherine Newman, *Falling from Grace: Downward Mobility in the Age of Affluence* (Berkeley: University of California Press, 1999).

9. A Centers for Disease Control and Prevention report analyzed data from a 1995 survey of women age fifteen to forty-four and found that 38 percent of the entire sample had never married, whereas 10 percent of women age forty to forty-four had never married. The ratio of never-married women in the African American community, however, is considerably higher. Among black non-Hispanic women age fifteen to forty-four, 57 percent had never married, compared with 39 percent of Hispanic women and 34 percent of white non-Hispanic women. Only 52 percent of black non-Hispanic women were married by the age of thirty, compared with 77 percent of Hispanic women and 81 percent of non-Hispanic white women. Matthew D. Bramlett and William D. Mosher, "Cohabitation, Marriage, Divorce, and Remarriage in the United States," National Center for Health Statistics, *Vital Health Statistics* 23, no. 22 (2002): 10, 12. See also Katherine S. Newman, *A Different Shade of Gray: Mid-Life and Beyond in the Inner City* (New York: New Press, 2003).

10. I have preserved the exact spellings in the passages from Latoya's diary because her words convey her emotions clearly, and also so the reader can understand the limits her educational background imposes on her job prospects.

11. Using the National Longitudinal Survey of Youth, Jody Heymann and Alison Earle analyzed a sample of mothers who worked at least twenty hours per week, and found that mothers who had been on AFDC were significantly more likely than mothers who had never been on AFDC to have children with chronic health problems. Of working mothers who had been on AFDC for more than two years, 14 percent had a child with asthma, compared with 11 percent of mothers who had been on AFDC for two years or less and 7 percent of mothers who had never been on AFDC. Forty-one percent of mothers who had been on AFDC for more than two years had at least one child with a chronic condition that required parental attention, compared with 32 percent of mothers who had been on AFDC for two years or less and 21 percent of mothers who had never been on AFDC. Heymann and Earle note that low-wage mothers who take time off to care for their children often suffer in the labor market. S. Jody Heymann and Alison Earle, "The Impact of Welfare Re-

form on Parents' Ability to Care for Their Children's Health," *American Journal of Public Health* 89, no. 4 (April 1999): 502–505. A separate study by Earle and Heymann, also using data from the National Longitudinal Survey of Youth, found that having a child with a health limitation was associated with significantly increased risk of job loss among women who had previously been on welfare. "The effects remained significant after adjustment for age, education, marital status, race, age and number of children, and economic conditions." Alison Earle and S. Jody Heymann, "What Causes Job Loss among Former Welfare Recipients: The Role of Family Health Problems," *Journal of the American Medical Women's Association* 57, no. 1 (Winter 2002): 5–10. See also Jody Heymann, *The Widening Gap: Why America's Working Families Are in Jeopardy and What Can Be Done about It* (New York: Basic Books, 2000), which talks about how parents are fired from their jobs after missing work to care for seriously ill children.

12. The substantial literature on the impact of family structure on children's outcomes presents varied conclusions, with some studies asserting that single parenthood is harmful to children and others arguing that it has no negative effects. One of the most well-respected treatments of this topic, Sara McLanahan and Gary Sandefur's *Growing Up with a Single Parent*, draws on four national data sets and finds that, after controlling for background characteristics, two-parent families are better than one-parent families in terms of graduation rates, early family formation, and labor-force attachment. However, McLanahan and Sandefur also conclude that single-parent families are not a *root cause* of negative outcomes in these areas but are, rather, a contributing factor that increases a child's risk of such outcomes, through the loss of economic resources, parental guidance and attention, and social capital. Sara McLanahan and Gary Sandefur, *Growing Up with a Single Parent: What Hurts, What Helps* (Cambridge, MA: Harvard University Press, 1994). Other notable studies include Kevin Lang and Jay L. Zagorsky, "Does Growing Up with a Parent Absent Really Hurt?" *Journal of Human Resources* 36, no. 2 (Spring 2001): 253–273, and Alison Aughinbaugh, Charles Pierret, and Donna Rothstein, "The Impact of Family Structure Transitions on Youth Achievement: Evidence from the Children of the NLSY," Bureau of Labor Statistics, July 2002.

There is also a growing body of research on "neighborhood effects" on individual outcomes. Research on the Gatreaux Assisted Housing Program, which moved low-income black families out of public housing in Chicago, finds evidence for large neighborhood effects. The children of families who opted to move to the suburbs were about one-fifth as likely to drop out of high school than the children of those Gatreaux families who opted to move to another urban location; rates of welfare recipiency were also lower among suburban movers. Leonard S. Rubinowitz and James E. Rosenbaum, *Crossing the Class and Color Lines: From Public Housing to White Suburbia* (Chicago: University of Chicago Press, 2000). These neighborhood effects appear to operate through a variety of mechanisms. Christopher Jencks and Susan Mayer identify peer influences, collective socialization, and formal institutions as pathways through which neighborhood poverty contributes to negative outcomes for adolescents. Christopher Jencks and Susan E. Mayer, "The Social Consequences of Growing Up in a Poor Neighborhood," in Lawrence E. Lynn Jr. and Michael G. H. McGreary, eds., *Inner-City Poverty in the United States* (Washington, DC: National Academy Press, 1990), 111–186. Other research shows how neighborhood effects operate through their impact on schools; see Nancy Darling and Laurence Steinberg, "Community Influences on Adolescent Achievement and Deviance," in Jeanne Brooks-Gunn, Greg J. Duncan, and J. Lawrence Aber, eds., *Neighborhood Poverty*, vol. 2: *Policy Implications in Studying Neighborhoods* (New York: Russell Sage, 1997). For a recent analysis of the cultural and structural mechanisms that lead to negative adolescent outcomes in poor neighborhoods, see David J. Harding, "Why Neighborhoods Matter: Cultural and Structural Influences on Adolescents in Poor Communities," Ph.D. diss., Harvard University, 2005.

13. In *Falling from Grace*, I described how birth position in a sibling set can shape children's views of, and interaction with, their families. In many of the middle-class, downwardly mobile families I observed, there was a sharp divide between the elder children, who were teenagers when the family slipped into financial crisis, and the younger children, whose formative years fell within the period of collapse. The elder children had known their parents when times were good and the arguments few, and they were also able to escape the household sooner, when they reached adulthood. The younger children did not have the luxury of that larger context—in their minds, their parents had always acted that way. Also, they had to keep living in the home as financial chaos and personality disintegration took hold of the household. Having a different perception of what had come before and after their family's economic meltdown, the younger siblings were more likely than their elder brothers and sisters to blame their parents for what had happened. Katherine S. Newman, *Falling from Grace: Downward Mobility in the Age of Affluence* (Berkeley: University of California Press, 199), 123–124.

14. As Kathryn Edin and Maria Kefalas summarize the literature on the relationship between women's earnings and marriage: "Contrary to [economist Gary] Becker's theory, most studies find that women who earn higher wages—both in general and relative to men—do not marry less. In fact, among disadvantaged populations, women with higher earnings are more, not less, likely to marry." Kathryn Edin and Maria Kefalas, *Promises I Can Keep: Why Poor*

Women Put Motherhood before Marriage (Berkeley: University of California Press, 2005), 199. See, for example, Megan M. Sweeney, "Two Decades of Family Change: The Shifting Economic Foundations of Marriage," *American Sociological Review* 67 (2002): 132–147. Sweeney finds that "improvements in the earnings of both women and men can be expected to *increase* the likelihood of marriage" (144).

Edin and Kefalas also discuss the reasons that low-income women tend to put off marriage for a number of years. Since the cultural upheavals of the 1960s, Americans (of all socioeconomic backgrounds) have come to separate sex, coresidence, and children from marriage, while their standards for marriage and marriage partners have grown higher. Because low-income single mothers hold marriage in the highest regard, they believe they need to get settled financially and find the "right" man before they can consider marriage— conditions that it may take them years to realize. While children can come earlier, "Marriage is the prize at the end of the race" (136).

15. Cohabitation tends to be less stable than marriage. According to a 2002 report by the Centers for Disease Control and Prevention, the probability of a first cohabitation disruption is 39 percent within three years and 49 percent within five years; the probability of a first marriage disruption because of separation or divorce is 12 percent within three years and 20 percent within five years. Bramlett and Mosher, "Cohabitation, Marriage, Divorce, and Remarriage," 49, 55, 14. See also David Popenoe and Barbara Dafoe Whitehead, *Should We Live Together? What Young Adults Need to Know about Cohabitation before Marriage*, 2nd ed. (Piscataway, NJ: National Marriage Project, Rutgers University, 2002); Larry L. Bumpass, James A. Sweet, and Andrew Cherlin, "The Role of Cohabitation in Declining Rates of Marriage," *Journal of Marriage and the Family* 53, no. 4 (November 1991): 913–927.

16. Ana's mother died when she was just a baby, and she never knew her father. Her aunt Matilde, a laundry lady for Dona Eleanor Camancho, used to take Ana along with her when she worked, and she finally hit upon a solution for Ana: she gave her to Dona Eleanor. When she was two years old, Ana went to live with Eleanor, a widow (at thirty-eight) who had already raised three grown sons, and she stayed with her until she left Ecuador for New York. Eleanor was the only mother Ana ever knew, but she was not legally responsible for the little girl. The day Ana started kindergarten, the school wanted to know who her official guardian was. Dona Eleanor would have been only too happy to adopt Ana, but Ana's maternal uncle—Guillermo—refused to allow it, and he listed himself instead.

17. One study of immigrant workers finds that, on arriving in the United States, immigrant husbands and wives both earn and work less than their native counterparts, but with time these wage rates and work hours increase and

eventually overtake those of natives. Francine D. Blau et al., "The Role of the Family in Immigrants' Labor-Market Activity: An Evaluation of Alternative Explanations: Comment," *American Economic Review* 93, no. 1 (March 2003): 429–447. Research on immigrant families highlights how the lengthy workdays of parents can have a detrimental effect on their family life: "Face-to-face interaction between parents and children decreases as both parents are usually out working for long hours." Min Zhou, "Growing Up American: The Challenge Confronting Immigrant Children and Children of Immigrants," *Annual Review of Sociology* 23 (1997): 83. Meanwhile, immigrant children are often expected to contribute to the household from an early age. In her study of Chicago fifth and sixth graders in a low-income, predominantly Mexican immigrant student body, Marjorie Faulstich Orellana notes that children as young as twelve are often expected to help out at home with a range of tasks, including laundry, ironing, cleaning, preparing meals, caring for younger siblings, and translating. Marjorie Faulstich Orellana, "Responsibilities of Children in Latino Immigrant Homes," *New Directions for Youth Development* 100 (Winter 2003): 25–39.

18. The Women, Infants and Children (WIC) Supplemental Nutrition Program provides supplemental food and nutrition products and services for low-income pregnant, breastfeeding, and postpartum women and their children under age five who have a nutritional risk. (Low income is defined as at or below 185 percent of the federal poverty level, which in June 2003 was an income of $33,485 annually for a family of four.) The program's goal is to reduce the risk of poor birth outcomes and improve the health of women and children during critical periods of development. WIC offers nutrition education, breastfeeding promotion, medical care referrals, and supplemental nutritious foods that are high in protein and iron, such as peanut butter, beans, milk, cheese, eggs, cereal, infant formula, and juices. On average, WIC participants receive services for two years. See, for example, *http://www.wicworks.ca.gov/about/detailed.html*.

19. Research on family structure shows that children in families in which only one biological parent is present tend to do worse on assessments of cognitive ability and socioemotional development, though there remains disagreement about how substantial those effects are and whether there is truly a causal relationship linking parental presence and child outcomes. However, even if the children of single mothers do fare worse than their counterparts in married households, there remains the question of whether having the help of a family member as an "extra parent" improves those outcomes. A 1998 study by James B. Kirby and Peter Uhlenberg found that the parenting help of a grandparent or grandparents makes a difference for children of single mothers: "First, presence of a grandparent in single-mother families was asso-

ciated with lower rates of adolescent delinquent behavior. Second, in both single-mother families and non-parent families, adolescent girls had a lower rate of depression when a grandparent was living in the family." Peter Uhlenberg, "Integration of Old and Young," *Gerontologist* 40 (2000): 276–279, and James B. Kirby and Peter Uhlenberg, "The Well-being of Adolescents: Do Coresident Grandparents Make a Difference?" paper presented at the Population Association of America annual meeting, Chicago, April 1998. A 2001 study using data from the Survey of Income and Program Participation found that children who live with a single mother and grandparent(s) generally have the same developmental outcomes—in terms of hospital visits, health, grade repetition, and suspension/expulsion—as children whose mothers remained married, whereas children who live in households where the single mother lives with a male partner but is not married, or where the single mother is neither coresiding nor cohabiting, do worse. Ariel Kalil et al., "Living Arrangements of Single-Mother Families: Variations, Transitions, and Child Development Outcome," Harris School Working Paper Series, University of Chicago, September 2001.

Other studies, however, contest the claim that having more adults in the household leads to better supervision of youth. Children in households composed of single mothers with grandparent(s) have *worse* outcomes as young adults in terms of years of school completed and the risk of having a premarital birth. However, selection bias may be at work. Martha S. Hill, Wei-Jun J. Yeung, and Greg J. Duncan, "Childhood Family Structure and Young Adult Behaviors," *Journal of Population Economics* 14 (2001): 293. A 1994 study found that coresidence with grandmothers had negative consequences for the quality of parenting by mothers and grandmothers. The authors reject selectivity as a "major explanatory factor" and instead contend that psychological processes are at work: "We would argue that there are considerable strains involved in multigenerational families brought about by early mothering and early grandmothering. Grandmothers in African-American multigenerational families (whether coresiding or not) are balancing the demands of adult midlife (work, relationships, parenting, leisure) with new responsibilities to rear the next generation of children, all within the challenges of economic hardship." P. Lindsay Chase-Lansdale, Jeanne Brooks-Gunn, and Elise S. Zamsky, "Young African-American Multigenerational Families in Poverty: Quality of Mothering and Grandmothering," *Child Development* 65, no. 2 (1994): 389.

20. Harlem's share of condominium and co-op sales in Manhattan was 3.6 percent in 2003 and 5.5 percent in 2004, according to the *Prudential Douglas Elliman Manhattan Market Report*. In 2004, 473 condominiums and co-ops were sold in Harlem, compared with just 179 in 1995. The average sale price

in 2004 was $358,657, compared with $261,951 in 2003 and $82,693 in 1995; the median sale price in 2004 was $305,490, compared with $230,000 in 2003 and $68,000 in 1995. Dennis Hevesi, "Real Estate Is Still Surging in Harlem, a Study Finds," *New York Times*, February 23, 2005, B3.

5. The National Picture

1. For details, see Helen Connolly et al., "Wage Trajectories of Workers in Poor Households: The National Experience," May 2004, Boston College Working Paper 555, *http://fmwww.bc.edu/ec-p/wp555.pdf*.

2. The U.S. Census Bureau developed the Survey of Income and Program Participation in the 1970s, mainly to address the deficiencies of the March supplement to the Current Population Survey (CPS). The CPS has long been a key source of information on patterns of employment, income, and poverty, but because it is cross-sectional and administered once a year, it relies on recall over the preceding calendar year. Respondents have a difficult time remembering wages accurately, and those who have irregular sources of income often find it impossible to reconstruct with accuracy what their earnings have been over twelve months.

3. For more information, see U.S. Census Bureau, "Evolution and History of SIPP," at *www.sipp.census.gov/sipp/evol.html*.

4. We do not use the 1984 and 1985 panels because the monthly school enrollment questions were not asked prior to the 1986 panel. The 1989 panel was discontinued after three waves (one year), and the results were incorporated with those of the 1990 panel. We do not use the 1993 panel because we want to have a clear break between the observations of the earlier and later time periods.

5. The Harlem sample consists of the individuals interviewed in Katherine Newman, "In the Long Run: Career Patterns and Cultural Values in the Low-Wage Labor Force," *Harvard Journal of African American Public Policy* 6, no. 1 (1999): 17–62. The terms "Harlem replication" and "base sample" here both refer to our replication of the Harlem sample in the SIPP, which includes all metropolitan areas.

6. Nonmanagerial food service jobs are those in "Eating and Drinking Places" (1980 and 1990 Census of Population Standard Industrial Classification [SIC] code 641) with the following occupational titles (as classified in the 1980 Census of Population Standard Occupational Classification [SOC] system): 436—cooks, except short order; 437—short-order cooks; 438—food counter, fountain, and related occupations; and 439—kitchen workers, food preparation. In the 1990 census, the SOC codes for cooks (436 and 437) were combined into one category (436—cooks).

7. There are not enough SIPP respondents in the New York metropolitan area to narrow the sample further to this one metropolitan statistical area (MSA).

8. See column 1 in Table D.1 (Appendix D).

9. An individual is "first observed" in the first observation of the job that qualifies him or her for the sample.

10. See column 2, Table D.1 (Appendix D).

11. More closely replicating the Harlem sample by limiting ourselves to the New York MSA gives us four males and seven females. Only three males and six females have enough wage information to determine wage growth.

12. See Table D.2 (Appendix D).

13. These are mean starting wages for the subsample used to calculate wage growth (individuals employed at two discrete points in time). The corresponding figures in 1993 dollars (used in Newman, "In the Long Run") are $5.01 for males and $4.68 for females.

14. This procedure, however, requires individuals to be observed in a food service job in the initial period and also to be observed in the panel twelve months later. Since few of these jobs start at the beginning of the panel, even the 1996 panel, which covers forty-eight months, contains few people who can be followed for four years.

15. Table D.3 (Appendix D) shows the distribution of yearly changes in real wage rates for persons employed one year after they are initially observed in a job in the food industry. Columns 1 and 3 show the monetary change in wages and columns 2 and 4 show the percentage change.

16. This includes all wage changes in which wages are observed in two consecutive months, whether or not the person changes jobs.

17. The first four columns of Table D.4 (Appendix D) show the distribution of these growth rates for the 140 men and 145 women in our base sample for whom this measure can be calculated. For women, these data show the same basic patterns found in Table D.3, which is based on the smaller sample. Mean annual wage growth is similar to that found in Table D.3, but the mean percentage change in wages is somewhat higher (4 percent compared with 2.9 percent). There is also substantial diversity around the mean.

18. See Table D.4, columns 5 through 8, which show the same measure.

19. See Table D.5 (Appendix D). Even when we consider the large potential sampling error in calculating a proportion based on thirty-eight observations in the Harlem sample, the SIPP estimate of 11 to 13 percent does not fall within the 95 percent confidence interval around the estimate.

20. For the four high flyers in the Harlem sample with reported wage gains of more than ten dollars, it seems unlikely that measurement error would be large enough to mean their wage gains were actually less than five dol-

lars. Such large misreporting of wage gains would be inconsistent with the ethnographic information. However, four of the fourteen high flyers have wage gains of less than six dollars an hour.

21. To replicate the original sample among SIPP respondents, we chose Industry Group 641, "Eating and Drinking Establishments," and limited ourselves to the three-digit Standard Occupational Classification codes described in Appendix B.

22. It is not possible to determine how the greater diversity of the SIPP sample would affect the relative mobility rates of entry-level workers, since one would need to know the relationship between wage growth and initial wages.

23. Table D.6 (Appendix D).

24. The low wage scale in the food service industry is apparent primarily at the top of the distribution. For example, the ninetieth percentile of initial wages is $9.04 for males in the base sample and $12.53 for the sample that includes all nonmanagerial jobs.

25. Table D.6 (Appendix D).

26. See Table D.7 (Appendix D).

27. This is confirmed in Table D.7. The mean dollar wage change of $0.58 for males in the base sample is somewhat higher than in the expanded samples, but the differences are not substantial. For women, the $0.29 change is actually lower than in any other sample.

28. Table D.8 (Appendix D).

29. Table D.9 (Appendix D). The 1986 through 1992 SIPP panels covered the period from October 1985 to April 1995. Data for the 1996 panel are the same as in the previous tables. They are replicated here for ease of comparison.

30. This is largely consistent with findings in Frederik Andersson, Harry J. Holzer, and Julia I. Lane, *Moving Up or Moving On: Who Advances in the Low-Wage Labor Market?* (New York: Russell Sage Foundation, 2005).

31. Table D.10 (Appendix D).

32. Tables D.8 and D.10.

33. We also ran regressions to estimate the impact of local unemployment rates on the mean wage change and on the probability that a sample member was a high flyer. These regressions allow us to compare outcomes for persons of the same age, race, educational attainment, and marital status. We also controlled for whether the person was living in a metropolitan area, and whether the job they held was a managerial job. These regression coefficients, shown in Tables D.11 and D.12 (Appendix D), indicate that higher unemployment rates have a small but not insignificant effect on wage growth for women and on the probability that a woman is a high flyer. The impact on men, however, is not statistically significant.

34. See Alan Krueger, James R. Hines, and Hilary Hoynes, "Another Look at Whether a Rising Tide Lifts All Boats," in *The Roaring Nineties: Can Full Employment Be Sustained?* ed. Alan Krueger and Robert Solow (New York: Russell Sage and Century Fund, 2001), *http://www.irs.princeton.edu/pubs/pdfs/454revised.pdf.*

35. See Andersson, Holzer, and Lane, *Moving Up,* 25.

36. Ibid., 51–52.

37. Ibid., 56. The authors also examine the kinds of firms that employ the more successful workers in their sample. They find that workers who transitioned out of low-earnings status were much more likely to be employed in construction, manufacturing, transportation and utilities, and wholesale trade than were persistently low earners. Nearly three-quarters of those stuck in the low-wage labor market worked for firms that were located in the bottom quartile in terms of their earnings premiums (61).

38. Ibid., 103. Their results indicate that, generally speaking, low-wage workers who change jobs are more likely to leave the low-wage labor market than those who stay in their original jobs, though there are important caveats: "But the low earners who gain the most in the labor market are those who change jobs early on and then stay in that next job, gaining on-the-job training and accumulating additional job tenure. In general, job-changers are hurt by the loss of some early tenure, though these losses are generally outweighed by the higher returns to tenure in their newer jobs and the higher levels of wages in those jobs more broadly. The higher returns to tenure in higher-wage jobs suggest that both wage growth over time and initial wage levels are enhanced by job changes to higher-wage firms; this implies that workers gain more on-the-job training in such firms and benefit from promotion ladders and other firm policies as well as higher initial wages."

39. Krueger, Hines, and Hoynes, "Another Look at Whether a Rising Tide Lifts All Boats."

40. Table D.13 (Appendix D) shows the characteristics of respondents in the SIPP sample in the first month they are observed in a qualifying job (period 1) and after eighteen months (period 2). We use the eighteen-month time period because it is long enough to observe changes but short enough to maintain sample size. (Since many qualifying jobs start late in the panel, the sample size declines quickly as the window is lengthened.) This time span allows us to track the changes in characteristics of high flyers and the jobs that they hold. For contrast, we show the same set of measures for other sample members. The sample includes all nonmanagerial black or Hispanic food service workers in metropolitan areas who live in families with a combined income at or below 1.5 times the poverty line at some point during the qualifying job. It should be remembered that even large changes or large differences between high flyers

and other sample members are seldom statistically significant, owing to the small sample size.

41. Individuals qualified for the sample if they met all the criteria for the sample definition at some point during a job. The entire job is then included in the sample. Because workers may switch occupations while remaining with the same employer, it is possible for some initial job observations to include managerial positions.

42. See Table D.13 (Appendix D). The increases in monthly household income are the result of higher wages, increased hours, and increases in other sources of family income.

43. When income is adjusted for family size, the results are similar. For male high flyers, the income-to-needs ratio increases from .5 to .9; for female high flyers, the increase is from .8 to 2.3. In contrast, the increase in the income-to-needs ratio for other sample members is .7 for males and only .3 for females.

44. To get a sense of the types of job transitions that led to wage growth, see Table D.14 (Appendix D), which lists the jobs held at periods 1 and 2 by the eight male and eleven female high flyers in the SIPP sample.

45. For a discussion of socioeconomic index scores and for the scores assigned to jobs held by participants in the SIPP sample, see Appendix C.

46. An example of an occupation with an SEI of 18 is janitor, while a food service manager has an SEI score of 47.

6. Streetwise Economics

1. Indeed, the field of behavioral economics has grown up to fill the space between the ordinary realities of human beings as decision makers and the formal rationality of econometrics.

2. See William Julius Wilson's two seminal studies, *The Truly Disadvantaged: The Inner City, the Underclass, and Public Policy* (Chicago: University of Chicago Press, 1987) and *When Work Disappears: The World of the New Urban Poor* (New York: Vintage Books, 1997), and also Elijah Anderson, *Streetwise: Race, Class, and Change in an Urban Community* (Chicago, University of Chicago Press, 1990).

3. See, for example, A. Michael Spence, "Job Market Signaling," *Quarterly Journal of Economics* 87 (August 1973): 355–374.

4. In the third wave of interviews with our *Chutes and Ladders* subjects, we asked the question, "What do you think employers are looking for when they hire people?" Twenty-eight respondents answered the question, and of those individuals three (10.7 percent) identified appearance or dress, and four (14.3 percent) mentioned "people skills" or the ability to communicate well.

5. See Philip Moss and Chris Tilly, *Stories Employers Tell: Race, Skill, and*

Hiring in America (New York: Russell Sage Foundation, 2001). Using data from the Multi-City Study of Urban Inequality, which includes 350 face-to-face interviews with employers in Atlanta, Boston, Detroit, and Los Angeles, Moss and Tilly found that about 20.3 percent of employers had a low opinion of black workers' hard skills (reading, writing, math, and so on), 14.6 percent thought they had poor interaction skills, and 33.4 percent thought they were lazy, unmotivated, or undependable (97).

6. See Erving Goffman, *The Presentation of Self in Everyday Life* (Doubleday: New York, 1959).

7. See Jennifer Hochschild, *Facing Up to the American Dream* (Princeton: Princeton University Press, 1996). Survey data presented by Hochschild indicate that middle-class African Americans—about one-third of the black population—are more likely than poor African Americans to express frustration about racism. See also Ellis Cose, *The Rage of a Privileged Class* (New York: HarperPerennial, 1995). Cose describes a study by researchers at the University of California, Los Angeles, that included surveys of racial attitudes before and after the 1992 Los Angeles riot. "The responses of blacks with a household income of $50,000 and more were especially intriguing. Even before the riot, that group, on average, appeared to be more alienated than poorer blacks. But what stunned the researchers was that after the riot, alienation among the most affluent group of African Americans skyrocketed, rising nearly a full 'standard deviation'—much more than it did for those who were less well off." In a press release, Lawrence Bobo, a UCLA sociologist who directed the survey, added, "These are people of high accomplishment and who have worked hard for what they have achieved. As far as they are concerned, however, what happened to Rodney King can just as easily befall any of them. Given all the dues they have paid, and all the contributions the black middle class has made, these events—especially the jury verdict—came as a jolt of racial injustice." See Lawrence D. Bobo et al., "Public Opinion before and after a Spring of Discontent," in Mark Baldassare, ed., *The Los Angeles Riots: Lessons for the Urban Future* (Boulder, CO: Westview Press, 1994), 103–134. While middle-class African Americans experience racism interactively in their workplaces and middle-class neighborhoods, the residential segregation that cuts the ghetto off from the outside world means that poor African Americans (and Latinos) have little contact with people of other racial or ethnic backgrounds. As a result, they are more willing than their middle-class counterparts to downplay the importance of race. See Katherine S. Newman, *A Different Shade of Gray: Mid-Life and Beyond in the Inner City* (New York: New Press, 2003).

8. See Moss and Tilly, *Stories Employers Tell*.

9. Ibid., 44.

10. Of the twenty-eight respondents in wave 3 who answered the question of what employers looked for when hiring people, twenty (71.4 percent) mentioned hard work/productivity, reliability/dependability, or motivation/determination, while ten (35.7 percent) mentioned competency or efficiency on the job, and three (10.7 percent) mentioned experience. All eight of the high flyers in our sample who answered this question indicated that a strong work ethic, dependability, or motivation were important to employers in making hiring decisions.

11. "While more than one-third of employed people belonged to unions in 1945, union membership fell to 24.1 percent of the U.S. work force in 1979 and to 13.9 percent in 1998." Christopher Conte and Albert R. Karr, "An Outline of the U.S. Economy," U.S. Department of State, February 2001, *http://usinfo.state.gov/products/pubs/oecon*.

12. David Halle, *America's Working Man: Work, Home, and Politics among Blue-Collar Property Owners* (Chicago: University of Chicago Press, 1984), 157.

13. See Frederik Andersson, Harry J. Holzer, and Julia I. Lane, *Moving Up or Moving On: Who Advances in the Low-Wage Labor Market?* (New York: Russell Sage Foundation, 2005).

14. For a discussion of how workers deal with the stigma of "dirty work," see Blake E. Ashforth and Glen E. Kreiner, "'How Can You Do It?' Dirty Work and the Challenge of Constructing a Positive Identity," *Academy of Management Review* 24, no. 3 (1999): 413–434.

15. See Oliver Mendelsohn and Marika Vicziany, *The Untouchables: Subordination, Poverty, and the State in Modern India* (Cambridge, England: Cambridge University Press, 1998); Sukhadeo Thorat and Umakant, *Caste, Race, and Discrimination: Discourses in International Context* (New Delhi: Rawat, 2004); and William Darity, Jr., and Ashwini Deshpande, *Boundaries of Clan and Color: Transnational Comparisons of Inter-Group Disparity* (London: Routledge, 2003).

16. See Yawen Cheng et al., "Association between Psychosocial Work Characteristics and Health Functioning in American Women: Prospective Study," *British Medical Journal* 320 (2000): 1432–1436, in which the authors find that women in jobs with high demands, low control, and low social support tend to have poor health.

17. Michael Marmot, *The Status Syndrome: How Social Standing Affects Our Health and Longevity* (New York: Times Books/Henry Holt, 2004), 112, 120, 122, 121.

18. See, for example, Robert E. Hall, "The Value of Education: Evidence from around the Globe," in Edward P. Lazear, *Education in the Twenty-first Century* (Stanford, CA: Hoover Institution Press, 2002), and Thomas J. Kane and Cecilia Elena Rouse, "Labor-Market Returns to Two- and Four-Year College," *American Economic Review* 85 (3): 600–614.

19. W. Norton Grubb, "The Returns to Education in the Sub-Baccalaureate Labor Market, 1984–1990," *Economics of Education Review* 16, no. 3 (1997): 231–245.

20. Randall Collins, *The Credential Society* (New York: Academic Press, 1979), 191–204.

21. See, for example, David K. Brown, "The Social Sources of Educational Credentialism: Status Cultures, Labor Markets, and Organizations," *Sociology of Education* 74, extra issue (2001): 19–34. "Credential requirements of jobs are less concerned with concrete work skills than with demanding that recruits hold similar, school-taught cultural dispositions to incumbents of positions," Brown argues. "These similarities reduce a variety of organizational recruitment uncertainties. Occupational monopolies are upheld by popular beliefs that mask cultural domination under ideologies of individual merit and technical competence" (20). Other research focuses on what role educational credentials play when employers make hiring and promotion decisions. David B. Bills, "Educational Credentials and Promotions: Does Schooling Do More Than Get You in the Door?" *Sociology of Education* 61 (1988): 58.

22. This belief is supported by research that seems to indicate that the degree itself matters more than the courses taken. See Grubb, "The Returns to Education in the Sub-Baccalaureate Labor Market," 241.

23. See Devah Pager, "The Mark of a Criminal Record," *American Journal of Sociology* 108, no. 5 (2003): 937–975. Using an experimental audit approach in which individuals applied for entry-level jobs and presented themselves as ex-offenders to employers, Pager found that those with criminal records "are only one-half to one-third as likely as nonoffenders to be considered by employers."

24. Anderson, *Streetwise*.

25. In wave 3 we asked the question, "Has there been anyone in particular who's been very influential in your life in these last years?" Thirty-one respondents answered the question, and of those respondents, three (9.7 percent) mentioned a spouse, twelve (38.7 percent) mentioned another family member, eleven (35.5 percent) mentioned a friend or romantic partner, and two (6.5 percent) said "no one."

26. Sandra Smith, "Don't Put My Name on It: Social Capital Activation and Job Finding Assistance among the Black Urban Poor," *American Journal of Sociology* 111, no. 1 (July 2005): 1–57.

7. "This Is the Kind of Life I Want"

1. LynNell Hancock, *Hands to Work: Three Women Navigate the New World of Welfare Deadlines and Work Rules* (New York: HarperCollins, 2002), 86–87.

2. The union number is false to protect her anonymity.

3. This analysis omits respondents who were not asked the question or who did not give a relevant answer. There were seven such respondents in wave 2 and fourteen in wave 3. In the latter case, this was nearly half of the sample.

4. Lawrence M. Mead, *The New Politics of Poverty: The Nonworking Poor in America* (New York: Basic Books, 1992).

5. Interestingly, the only respondents who felt this way were those who were rejected for Burger Barn jobs at the start of the study.

6. See Ellen K. Scott et. al., "My Children Come First: Welfare-Reliant Women's Post-TANF Views of Work-Family Trade-offs and Marriage," Manpower Demonstration Research Corporation, The Next Generation Project Working Paper no. 4, December 2001. This study was based on interviews with eighty welfare-reliant women in Cleveland and Philadelphia. The researchers conclude: "In the face of mandatory work requirements and time limits, women expressed tremendous ambivalence about what they thought working outside the home would entail for their children and families. Although women saw work as potentially beneficial, in our baseline interviews they repeatedly discussed the tensions and dilemmas that working motherhood (mostly working single-parenthood) would pose in their lives. As they talked about various work-family trade-offs, the women consistently focused on what they thought working would mean for their children" (7). See also Katherine Newman, *No Shame in My Game: The Working Poor in the Inner City* (New York: Knopf and Russell Sage, 1999).

7. See Christopher Jencks and Kathryn Edin, "Do Poor Women Have a Right to Bear Children?" *American Prospect* 20 (Winter 1995): 43–52. Jencks and Edin describe the bleak prospects for young, poor women in both the labor and marriage markets and conclude: "As long as America remains committed to competitive labor markets, open borders, and weak labor unions, most marginally employable adults will need some kind of public assistance if they have children."

8. "Nearly half the children on welfare in any given month were born to parents who were married at the time of their birth," Jencks and Edin note, "and most of these parents had enough money to scrape by while they were married." Ibid. See also Kathryn Edin and Maria Kefalas, *Promises I Can Keep: Why Poor Women Put Motherhood before Marriage* (Berkeley: University of California Press, 2005). "Even in poor communities, expectant fathers are still supposed to provide, to 'straighten up,' and to deepen their commitment to the mother, even though they are not legally bound to her. Pregnancy forces these young men to confront their limited ability, and sometimes their lack of willingness, to pay the full price of parenthood" (69). The reactions of young men to a pregnancy run the gamut from denial to anger to an embracing of it.

9. See Celeste M. Watkins, "When a Stumble Is Not a Fall: Recovering

from Employment Setbacks in the Welfare to Work Transition," *Harvard Journal of African American Public Policy* 6, no. 1 (2000): 63–84.

10. Hancock, *Hands to Work*, 86–87. Numerous observers have examined the consequences of welfare reform for recipients and their families. Journalistic accounts include the in-depth profiles written by Hancock and Jason DeParle, who tell the stories of several welfare recipients in New York and Milwaukee, respectively, and how they and their children adjust to the new reality of the welfare-to-work policy. See Jason DeParle, *American Dream: Three Women, Ten Kids, and a Nation's Drive to End Welfare* (New York: Viking, 2004). DeParle sums up the national impact of welfare reform in this way: "To understand the economics of the post-welfare years, you have to juggle two competing ideas. The first is that most poor single mothers fared better than expected. The second is that they continued to lead terribly straitened lives. Earnings surged, welfare fell, and net incomes inched up—but not necessarily enough to keep the lights on" (284).

Social scientists tend to highlight one observation or the other. Scott Winship and Christopher Jencks observe that between 1996 and 2004, the official poverty rate for female-headed families with children plummeted from 42 percent to 34. The prevalence of food-related problems fell among mother-only families between 1995 and 2000; the number of reported problems increased between 2000 and 2002, but the earlier decline was much greater than the subsequent increase. Winship and Jencks conclude: "In economic terms, the social policy changes of the 1990s appear to have helped more single mothers and harmed fewer than most observers . . . expected" (29). Scott Winship and Christopher Jencks, "Did the Social Policy Changes of the 1990s Affect Material Hardship among Single Mothers? Evidence from the CPS Food Security Supplement," John F. Kennedy School of Government Faculty Research Working Paper no. RWP04-027, Harvard University, June 2004. See also Ron Haskins, "Effects of Welfare Reform on Family Income and Poverty," in *The New World of Welfare*, ed. Rebecca Blank and Ron Haskins (Washington, DC: Brookings Institution Press, 2001), 103–136. Examining the impact of welfare reform on children's development, Greg J. Duncan and P. Lindsay Chase-Lansdale find little evidence of harm. In fact, Duncan and Chase-Lansdale argue that welfare reform policies can be an important tool in enhancing child outcomes. Greg J. Duncan and P. Lindsay Chase-Lansdale, "Welfare Reform and Children's Well-Being," in *The New World of Welfare*, ed. Rebecca Blank and Ron Haskins (Washington, DC: Brookings Institution Press, 2001), 391–417.

Other scholars are somewhat less sanguine about the reforms' impact on families. Wendell Primus questions the statement that "most" families are better off after leaving the rolls. He points to two studies, one in Wisconsin and the other using Survey on Income and Program Participation (SIPP) data, that find that only about one-half of the "leaver" population is faring better than they were in the period before reform. Primus also observes that the increase between 1995 and 1999 in the disposable income of the poorest 40 percent of single-mother families was "very modest"—an average of $292—which he attributes to the fact that many families no longer received cash assistance and food stamps even though in general they remained eligible (133). From their study of continuing and former welfare recipients in Michigan, Sandra Danziger and her colleagues find that women who accumulate labor market experience remain vulnerable to economic insecurity: even among those respondents who worked every month, about one-third remained below the poverty line, two-thirds received food stamps, and one-fifth reported two or more experiences of material hardship, such as lacking health insurance or sufficient food for their family. Sandra Danziger et al., "Work, Income, and Material Hardship after Welfare Reform," *Journal of Consumer Affairs* 34, no. 1 (Summer 2000). Some scholars also express concerns that the relatively good fortunes of single mothers in the workforce in the 1990s had more to do with a strong economy than with changes in welfare policies. A 2004 study of the impact of welfare reform on single mothers concludes that the economic expansion of the 1990s and the increase in Earned Income Tax Credit benefits "largely explain the increase in work among relatively well educated single mothers, while work requirements were a much more important factor for high school dropouts." Hanming Fang and Michael P. Keane, "Assessing the Impact of Welfare Reform on Single Mothers," *Brookings Papers on Economic Activity* 1 (2004): 1–95.

11. Scholars have debated to what extent attitudes remain stable over time. Analyzing panel data from the late 1950s, Philip Converse differentiated between two groups of individuals in society, one with a much more stable set of opinions than the other: "There is first a 'hard core' of opinion on a given issue, which is well crystallized and perfectly stable over time. For the remainder of the population, response sequences over time are statistically random" (242). Stated preferences on policy issues were capable of changing dramatically even within the short time frame. Philip Converse, "The Nature of Belief Systems in Mass Publics," in *Ideology and Discontent*, ed. David E. Apter (New York: Free Press, 1964), 206–261.

Subsequent research suggested that attitudes were more stable than previously thought, at least when general orientations toward political, economic, and social affairs were probed (for example, agreement with broad statements like, "Men are equal—maybe not financially or in influence—but equal to one another as to being a person"). Steven R. Brown, "Consistency and the Persistence of Ideology: Some Experimental Results," *Public Opinion Quarterly* 34, no. 1 (Spring 1970): 60–68. Reassessing Converse's panel data, Christopher H. Achen made the case that the weak correlations among respondents' survey responses were due in large part to "measurement error" resulting from vague and/or misunderstood questions. Christopher H. Achen, "Mass Political Attitudes and the Survey Response," *American Political Science Review* 69, no. 4 (December 1975): 1218–1231. John Zaller, in turn, argued that the observed instability did not arise because the respondents (as Converse had suggested) did not possess real attitudes, but because most of them were ambivalent toward issues. John R. Zaller, *The Nature and Origins of Mass Opinion* (New York: Cambridge University Press, 1992). More recent research has taken an intermediate stance between the Converse and Zaller models; see, for instance, Jennifer L. Hill and Hanspeter Kriesi, "An Extension and Test of Converse's 'Black-and-White' Model of Response Stability," *American Political Science Review* 95, no. 2 (June 2001): 397–413.

Related bodies of literature concern the relative stability of different kinds of attitudes, and the stability of attitudes over a person's life span. On this first point, scholars have mapped out a continuum of attitudes from more stable to least stable, with "symbolic" attitudes corresponding to the former description and "nonsymbolic" to the latter. According to the theory, highly symbolic attitudes—such as political party identification—are characterized by their affective content and their development through a conditioning-like process early in life, whereas nonsymbolic attitudes—such as policy preferences—arise from the integration of information acquired in adulthood. See, for example, David O. Sears, "The Persistence of Early Political Predispositions: The Roles of Attitude, Object, and Life Stage," in *Review of Personality and Social Psychology*, vol. 4, ed. Ladd Wheeler (Beverly Hills: Sage, 1983).

12. See Martin Gilens, *Why Americans Hate Welfare*, for a detailed analysis of public attitudes toward welfare, poverty, and work. Gilens notes that African Americans express the same commitment to work as whites: "In 1987 the General Social Survey included a black oversample, which permitted more exact comparisons of blacks' and whites' attitudes. In this survey 74 percent of whites and 79 percent of blacks said that they would continue to work even if they were to get enough money to live comfortably for the rest of their lives. And when asked to rank the importance of given job characteristics, 51 percent of whites and 56 percent of blacks ranked 'working hours are short, lots of free time' last of the five (the other features were high income, no danger of being fired, chances for advancement, and work important and gives a feeling of accomplishment). Based on the attitudes they express on surveys, African Americans are no less committed to the work ethic than are whites" (159). A *Los Angeles Times* survey in 1985 found that 79 percent of nonpoor respondents believed that "welfare benefits make poor people dependent and encour-

age them to remain poor," and a significant number of poor respondents—58 percent—also agreed with this statement (56). Martin Gilens, *Why Americans Hate Welfare: Race, Media, and the Politics of Antipoverty Policy* (Chicago: University of Chicago Press, 1999).

Similarly, interviews with welfare-reliant women in Cleveland and Philadelphia revealed that "they appeared to have accepted the dominant ideology that welfare is bad and work is good." See Scott et al., "My Children Come First." See also Roberta R. Iversen and Naomi B. Farber, "Transmission of Family Values, Work, and Welfare among Poor Urban Black Women," *Work and Occupations* 23, no. 4 (1996): 437–460.

13. These numbers include only those respondents who gave answers that could be coded. Those who were in the sample but who were not asked this question, or who did not give a relevant answer, have been omitted from these calculations. There were twenty-seven respondents who fit these criteria in the first wave of interviews (1993–94), eight in the second wave (1997), and five in the third wave (2001–2002).

14. Two-thirds of the respondents said they would prefer a low-paying job over welfare in both the first and second interviews (1993–94 and 1997). Fifty-eight percent preferred work over welfare in both the second- and third-wave interviews (1997 and 2001–2002). Those who changed their opinion between interview periods tended to move in the direction of supporting *welfare* before 1997, and in the direction of supporting *work* after 1997—that is, when the U.S. economy was moving upward at a brisk clip.

15. Seven out of ten low riders (compared with two-thirds of the overall sample) favored work over welfare in 1997. Nearly three-fourths (compared with two-thirds overall) did so in 2002. (In 1993, 62 percent of the low riders had expressed support for the job option, compared with 68 percent in the overall sample.)

16. See Kathryn Edin and Laura Lein, *Making Ends Meet: How Single Mothers Survive Welfare and Low-Wage Work* (New York: Russell Sage Foundation, 1997).

17. The stigma associated with working in the fast-food industry is pervasive throughout the United States and is a point of special sensitivity in minority communities, where the demand for deference in these service jobs grates against a history of enforced subservience. The stigma is powerful enough to set many young people against the idea of starting their work life under the "golden arches." Yet the industry remains an enormous employer of minority teens, suggesting that thousands find a way to blast past that public image in order to collect a paycheck. See Newman, *No Shame in My Game*.

18. See Katherine Newman, *Falling from Grace: Downward Mobility in the Age of Affluence* (Berkeley: University of California Press, 1999). I argue that work

is the source of honor and identity in American culture, so much so that the loss of a job spells social dislocation even when the economic consequences are minor.

19. See Nelson Aldrich, Jr., *Old Money: The Mythology of Wealth in America* (New York: Knopf, 1988); William Julius Wilson, *When Work Disappears: The World of the New Urban Poor* (New York: Knopf, 1996). See also Jamie Johnson's 2003 HBO documentary, *Born Rich.*

20. There is also a category of work that is not in itself illegal but becomes so if it is performed by a welfare recipient and the pay is not reported as income. For example, some of the women we interviewed braided hair for extra money. This is a rather different sort of illegal work and was viewed much less negatively in the community because the difficulty of surviving solely on public assistance was widely recognized.

21. See Watkins, "When a Stumble Is Not a Fall."

22. Loïc Wacquant, "Scrutinizing the Street: Poverty, Morality, and the Pitfalls of Urban Ethnography," *American Journal of Sociology* 107, no. 6 (May 2002): 1468–1532.

23. See David Halle, *America's Working Man: Work, Home, and Politics among Blue-Collar Property Owners* (Chicago: University of Chicago Press, 1984).

24. See Gilens, *Why Americans Hate Welfare.*

25. See Michael B. Katz, *The Undeserving Poor: From the War on Poverty to the War on Welfare* (New York: Pantheon, 1989), and Herbert J. Gans, *The War against the Poor: The Underclass and Antipoverty Policy* (New York: Basic Books, 1995), for discussions of the distinctions made between "deserving" and "undeserving" poor. In his analysis of public attitudes toward welfare, Martin Gilens presents data that show that most Americans are willing to help people who can't support themselves, but most are also in favor of limiting benefits to only those poor people who need it (that is, deserve it). "In large measure, Americans hate welfare because they view it as a program that rewards the undeserving poor." Gilens, *Why Americans Hate Welfare*, 39, 3.

26. See Joe Soss, "Making Clients and Citizens: Welfare Policy as a Source of Status, Belief, and Action," in *Deserving and Entitled: Social Constructions and Public Policy*, ed. Anne Schneider and Helen Ingram (Albany: State University of New York Press, 2005), in which he describes the contrast between the "professional and accommodating" service that Social Security Disability Insurance clients typically enjoy and the "degrading" treatment that welfare recipients routinely receive. See also Watkins, "When a Stumble Is Not a Fall." Some political commentators have put a positive spin on the fact that poor people today are not applying for assistance that they are eligible for. "If many of the poor are reluctant to sign up for food stamps because they retain the stigma of welfare, it's hard to say they are wrong," writes Mickey Kaus. "A low

'take-up' rate is a good sign, indicating the presence of a work ethic, not a bad sign." Mickey Kaus, "TANF and 'Welfare': Further Steps toward the Work-Ethic State," *Brookings Review* 19, no. 3 (Summer 2001): 43–47.

27. Edin and Lein, *Making Ends Meet*, 5.

28. A New Yorker who worked forty hours per week for the minimum wage, $5.15 an hour, would earn $10,712 a year. In 2003, the federal poverty line for a single-person "family unit" was $8,980; for a family of four it was $18,400. New York is more generous than most other states about extending Medicaid benefits beyond the federal mandates: a family of four living in New York can make up to 150 percent of the poverty line ($27,600) and be covered under New York's Family Health Plus program.

8. Dreams, Deferred

1. For more on this, see Katherine Newman, *Falling from Grace: The Experience of Downward Mobility in the Age of Affluence* (Berkeley: University of California Press, 1999).

2. According to an unscientific, online poll by the job-listing site Jobtrak, 52 percent of college students and recent graduates in 2000 expected to be millionaires by the time they reached forty. Another 19 percent expected to be millionaires later in life; only 29 percent thought it would never happen. Jim McKay, "Young Have Big Plans to Be Rich," *Pittsburgh Post-Gazette*, March 19, 2000, C5.

3. By then, however, Natalie had dropped out of yet another college because she couldn't afford it.

4. These numbers include only those respondents who gave answers that could be coded. Those who were in the sample but who were not asked this question, or who gave no relevant answer, were omitted from these calculations. There were thirty-four such respondents at wave 1, nine at wave 2, and eight at wave 3.

5. Between waves 1 and 2, as well as between waves 2 and 3, interviewees were slightly more likely to come to believe that employers do *not* discriminate than to come to believe that they do.

6. These numbers include only those respondents who gave answers that could be coded. Those who were in the sample but who were not asked this question, or who gave no relevant answer, were omitted from these calculations. There were fifty such respondents at wave 1, twenty-seven at wave 2, and five at wave 3.

7. Recent research appears to support the beliefs of these respondents that they are being evaluated based on their group identity. In a 2003 study by Devah Pager, black and white auditors applied for jobs, at times indicating

that they had a criminal record. Among blacks applicants who did not indicate that they had a criminal record, 14 percent were called back by employers, compared with 34 percent of white applicants who said they had no criminal record—and 17 percent of whites who said they *did* have a record. Devah Pager, "The Mark of a Criminal Record," *American Journal of Sociology* 108, no. 5 (2003): 937–975. As part of their 2003 study, Marianne Bertrand and Sendhil Mullainathan sent out fictitious résumés in response to help-wanted ads in Boston and Chicago newspapers, and found that résumés with white-sounding names (e.g., Carrie, Geoffrey) received 50 percent more calls for interviews than those with African American–sounding names (Keisha, Tremayne). Marianne Bertrand and Sendhil Mullainathan, "Are Emily and Greg More Employable than Lakisha and Jamal? A Field Experiment on Labor Market Discrimination," National Bureau of Economic Research Working Paper no. 9873, July 2003, *http://nber15.nbcr.org.ezp1.harvard.edu/papers/w9873.pdf.*

8. Jennifer L. Hochschild, *Facing Up to the American Dream: Race, Class, and the Soul of the Nation* (Princeton: Princeton University Press, 1996).

9. Of the low riders in the sample, three-fourths said people were judged by their group identity, two-thirds said that employers discriminated, and one-third said they had personally experienced discrimination. In the rest of the sample, more than nine-tenths (95 percent) said people were judged by their group identity, three-fourths said that employers discriminated, and two-fifths said that they had personally experienced discrimination.

10. Jennifer L. Hochschild, *What's Fair? American Beliefs about Distributive Justice* (Cambridge, MA: Harvard University Press, 1981), 21.

11. A wide range of research on the urban ghetto has discussed the social isolation and cultural deprivation experienced by ghetto residents. Conservative scholar Lawrence Mead describes a separate subculture in America's cities: "Much of the urban underclass is made up of street hustlers, welfare families, drug addicts, and former mental patients. There are, of course, needy people who function well—the so-called 'deserving' or 'working poor'—and better-off people who function poorly, but in general low income and serious behavioral difficulties go together. The underclass is not large as a share of population, perhaps nine million people, but it accounts for the lion's share of the most serious disorders in American life, especially in the cities" (22). Lawrence M. Mead, *Beyond Entitlement: The Social Obligations of Citizenship* (New York: Free Press, 1986). For liberal perspectives on the isolation of the poor, see Kenneth B. Clark, *Dark Ghetto: Dilemmas of Social Power* (New York: Harper and Row, 1965), and William Julius Wilson, *The Truly Disadvantaged: The Inner City, the Underclass, and Public Policy* (Chicago: University of Chicago Press, 1987).

12. In wave 1, 92 percent of low riders said they agreed with the statement that anyone can make it; in wave 2, 75 percent did; and in wave 3, 90 percent did. Of the rest of the sample, 85 percent agreed with the statement in wave 1; 75 percent agreed in wave 2; and 86 percent agreed in wave 3.

13. On the hardships of growing old in poor, segregated neighborhoods, see Katherine Newman, *A Different Shade of Gray: Mid-Life and Beyond in the Inner City* (New York: New Press, 2003).

14. Of course the rate at which women have children differs according to their class background. According to David T. Ellwood and Christopher Jencks, 78 percent of high school dropouts born in the years 1960 to 1964 had a child by age twenty-five, and 83 percent by age thirty; in comparison, only 20 percent of college graduates in the group had children by age twenty-five; 50 percent had children by age thirty. David T. Ellwood and Christopher Jencks, "The Spread of Single-Parent Families in the United States since 1960," in *The Future of the Family*, ed. Daniel P. Moynihan, Timothy M. Smeeding, and Lee Rainwater (New York: Russell Sage Foundation, 2004), 25–65.

15. Ibid., 41.

16. Kathryn Edin and Maria Kefalas, *Promises I Can Keep: Why Poor Women Put Motherhood before Marriage* (Berkeley: University of California Press, 2005), 208.

17. Elaine Bell Kaplan discusses the "poverty of relationships" that black teenage mothers endure in their families and with their sexual partners, and their desperation to find supportive, stable connections with others. Elaine Bell Kaplan, *Not Our Kind of Girl: Unraveling the Myths of Black Teenage Motherhood* (Berkeley: University of California Press, 1997). For some teens, the experience of motherhood provides meaning and motivation that can help them stop leading self-destructive lives. Janna Lesser, Deborah Koniak-Griffin, and Nancy L. R. Anderson, "Depressed Adolescent Mothers' Perceptions of Their Own Maternal Role," *Issues in Mental Health Nursing* 20, no. 2 (February 1999): 131–149. In a series of longitudinal studies conducted over twelve years, Lee SmithBattle identifies several types of teenage mothers. One group—those who "invented a future from an impoverished past"—use the occasion of childbirth to reorganize and anchor their lives, SmithBattle writes: "Although at odds with middle-class assumptions, mothering often cultivates a sense of responsibility and purpose in a context which provides few other options." Lee SmithBattle, "Understanding Teenage Mothering: Conventional and Unconventional Wisdom," *Prevention Researcher* 10, no. 3 (2003), *http:// www.tpronline.org/read.cfm?section=articles&id=179*. See also Edin and Kefalas, *Promises I Can Keep*.

18. Edin and Kefalas say concerns like Patty's are very evident among lower-income mothers: whereas middle-class parents have the luxury of fretting about their children's academic and extracurricular development, poor parents

are focused on providing basic necessities and keeping their children out of trouble—mammoth tasks in their own right, given the dangers and temptations present in their neighborhoods.

19. Geronimus argues that early childbearing may be an "adaptive" practice for the African American ghetto poor: "In communities such as high-poverty, urban areas, where income is low and precarious, and healthy life expectancy is uncertain, the vitality of the community may be enhanced by early childbearing norms *coupled with* a normative family structure that is multigenerational and extends the responsibility for children's well-being beyond the biological parents. In the context of collective health uncertainty, African American parents in poverty may experience legitimate worries of leaving their children orphaned or of becoming compromised in their capacity to provide for them. . . . Children may fare best if their birth and preschool years coincide with their mother's peak health and access to social and practical support provided by relatively healthy kin" (159). Arline T. Geronimus, "Teenage Childbearing as Cultural Prism," *British Medical Bulletin* 69 (2004): 155–166.

20. Arline T. Geronimus, "On Teenage Childbearing and Neonatal Mortality in the United States," *Population and Development Review* 13, no. 2 (June 1987): 245, 256.

21. This is even more true in immigrant families from societies in which maturity and adult responsibility come much earlier than in affluent societies like that of the United States.

22. Twenty percent of the women in the sample (four out of twenty) were married, two women were separated, and one woman was widowed.

23. See Roberta L. Coles, "Black Single Fathers: Choosing to Parent Full-Time," *Journal of Contemporary Ethnography* 31, no. 4 (2002): 411–439, and Jennifer Hamer, *What It Means to Be Daddy: Fatherhood for Black Men Living Away from Their Children* (New York: Columbia University Press, 2001).

24. Forty-five percent of black men have never married, compared with 28 percent of non-Hispanic white men and 42 percent of black women. Jesse McKinnon, *The Black Population in the United States: March 2002*, U.S. Bureau of the Census, Current Population Reports, Series P20-541, 2003. See Newman, *A Different Shade of Gray*, for further discussion of the marital status of men and women over their life span.

25. Maria's aspirations are typical among sojourners of any ethno-national stripe—the homeland ever entices—and scholars like Peggy Levitt have described in detail the impact that returning migrants have on their countries of origin: they come back bearing riches, yes, but also the seeds of different ideas and worldviews. See Peggy Levitt, *The Transnational Villagers* (Berkeley: University of California Press, 2001).

26. See Carol B. Stack, *Call to Home: African Americans Reclaim the Rural South* (New York: Basic Books, 1996).

9. Opening the Gates

1. A 1999 study of the labor market in the greater Boston area found that during the economic boom of the 1990s, African American workers with a high school diploma or less education were just as likely as their white or Hispanic counterparts to have been employed at least sometime during the preceding year. Barry Bluestone and Mary Huff Stevenson, "Racial and Ethnic Gaps in Male Earnings in a Booming Urban Economy," *Eastern Economic Journal* 25, no. 2 (Spring 1999): 209–238. That said, the unemployment rate for black men was about twice as high as that for white or Hispanic men; labor force participation is relatively widespread while unemployment remains high because "black men are substantially more likely to cycle in and out of jobs" (213). Bluestone and Stevenson also point out that even in a tight labor market, a huge gap in annual earnings persists among the three groups of men, with black men with a high school diploma or less expected to earn just $12,762, compared with $14,744 for Hispanic men and $23,295 for white men. Barry Bluestone and Mary Huff Stevenson, "Boston in Bloom," *Boston Globe*, July 30, 2000, *http://www.curp.neu.edu/staging/sitearchive/column.asp?id=1282*. See also Barry Bluestone and Mary Huff Stevenson, *The Boston Renaissance: Race, Space, and Economic Change in an American Metropolis* (New York: Russell Sage Foundation, 2000).

2. A report from the Economic Policy Institute describes the changes in the poverty rate over the past few decades: "First, after making impressive progress against poverty in the 1960s, the trend stalled and then generally drifted up from the early 1970s to the mid-1990s. The 1995–2000 period was one of dramatic progress, as poverty fell by 2.5 percentage points, and twice-poverty by 4.3 points (corresponding to 4.8 million fewer poor and 8.6 million fewer twice-poor persons). The 2001 recession and jobless recovery partially reversed these gains." Lawrence R. Mishel, Jared Bernstein, and Sylvia Allegretto, *The State of Working America, 2004–2005* (Ithaca, NY: ILR Press, 2005). Other research finds comparable trends in inequality over this period. As Gottschalk and Danziger note, real earnings and real family incomes rose across the income spectrum for the first time since the 1960s. Whereas the distribution of wages, the distribution of annual earnings, and the distribution of total family income (adjusted for family size) became less equal during the last half of the 1970s and the 1980s, wage inequality stabilized and earnings inequality declined during the 1990s. Family income inequality, on the other hand, continued to rise. Peter Gottschalk and Sheldon Danziger, "Wage Inequality, Earnings Inequality, and Poverty in the U.S. over the Last Quarter of the Twentieth Century," Boston College Working Paper in Economics no. 560, Department of Economics, Boston College, 2003.

3. See, for example, Lawrence Mishel with Matthew Walters, "How Unions Help All Workers," Economic Policy Institute Briefing Paper, Washington, DC, August 2003, *http://www.epinet.org/briefingpapers/143/bp143.pdf*, and Josh Bivens and Christian Weller, "Rights Make Might: Ensuring Workers' Rights as a Strategy for Economic Growth," Economic Policy Institute Issue Brief no. 192, Washington, DC, April 9, 2003, *http://www.epinet.org/Issuebriefs/ib192/ib192.pdf*. These reports by the Economic Policy Institute tout the benefits of unions and labor standards both for workers and for the overall economy. Even former U.S. labor secretary Robert B. Reich, a strong proponent of free trade, has expressed support for international labor standards (albeit according to a sliding scale for economic development). See Robert B. Reich, "Escape from the Global Sweatshop: Capitalism's Stake in Uniting the Workers of the World," *Washington Post*, May 22, 1994, C1.

4. The fortunes of the AFL-CIO, the country's largest federation of unions, have sunk so low that in early 2005 the labor leader John J. Sweeney—once hailed as the salvation of America's labor movement—faced a major uprising within his own organization, with dissidents calling for the headquarters budget to be cut by half so that the money could be returned to individual unions for organizing. Steven Greenhouse, "Labor Chief Emerges from Meeting a Winner, But for How Long?" *New York Times*, March 4, 2005, 16.

5. Ruth Milkman (personal communication, March 2005) contends that in southern California the history of organized labor has left a stronger legacy, which helps to explain some successful organizing campaigns and living-wage strikes among the least likely candidates: home health aides and janitors.

6. Indeed, a number of unions split off from the AFL-CIO in July 2005 over the issue of organizing strategies.

7. In the twenty-five years between 1974 and 1999, the proportion of black children ages six to eighteen who had mothers who did not complete high school fell from 58 percent to 20 percent; the proportion of white children who had mothers without a diploma dropped from 27 percent to 7 percent. Problems remain most acute for Hispanic mothers, who have also been graduating from high school in higher numbers but are still more likely to drop out. In 1999, 49 percent of Hispanic children ages six to eighteen had mothers who lacked a high school degree; in 1974, that percentage was 62. U.S. Department of Education, National Center for Education Statistics, *The Condition of Education 2001*, NCES 2001-072 (Washington, DC: U.S. Government Printing Office, 2001), Table 4-1, quoted in Child Trends DataBank, "Parental Education" (accessed on April 1, 2005), Figure 1, *http://www.childtrendsdatabank.org/indicators/67ParentalEducation.cfm*.

8. Based on their analysis of two national longitudinal data sets, Thomas J.

Kane and Cecilia Elena Rouse conclude that attending a two-year college increases earnings for the average worker by about 10 percent—even without
completing an associate's degree—and the estimated returns to a credit at a
two-year or four-year college are similar, at "roughly 4–6 percent for every
thirty completed credits (two semesters)" (601). See Thomas J. Kane and Cecilia Elena Rouse, "Labor-Market Returns to Two- and Four-Year College,"
American Economic Review 85, no. 3 (June 1995): 600–614. There is some debate in the economic literature, however, over the importance of getting a credential as opposed to just racking up credits. W. Norton Grubb makes the case
for the former: "In particular, while earnings credits [*sic*] without a credential
from community colleges may increase earnings, it matters a great deal what
kinds of credits these are; there is substantial evidence that returns to different
types of community college degrees vary; and there appear to be 'sheepskin' or
'program' effects associated with completing credentials rather than accumulating credits" (222). See W. Norton Grubb, "The Varied Economic Returns
to Postsecondary Education: New Evidence from the Class of 1972: Response
to Comment," *Journal of Human Resources* 30, no. 1 (Winter 1995): 222–228;
Thomas J. Kane and Cecilia Elena Rouse, "Comment on W. Norton Grubb:
'The Varied Economic Returns to Postsecondary Education: New Evidence
from the Class of 1972,'" *Journal of Human Resources* 30, no. 1 (Winter 1995):
205–221; and W. Norton Grubb, "The Returns to Education in the Sub-Baccalaureate Labor Market, 1984–1990," *Economics of Education Review* 16, no. 3
(1997): 231–245.

9. See Christopher Avery and Thomas J. Kane, "Student Perceptions of
College Opportunities: The Boston COACH Program," in *College Choices:
The Economics of Where to Go, When to Go, and How to Pay for It*, ed. Caroline
M. Hoxby (Chicago: University of Chicago Press, 2004), 355–391, for one recent review of the literature on the impact of tuition and financial aid subsidies
on college enrollment. According to Avery and Kane, for every $1,000 change
in college costs (in 1990 dollars), research has found effects on college enrollment rates ranging from 4 to 8 percentage points. An earlier review of
the literature by Larry Leslie and Paul T. Brinkman found that for every
$1,000 change in college costs (in 1990 dollars), there was a corresponding 5
percent difference in college enrollment rates. Larry L. Leslie and Paul T.
Brinkman, "Student Price Response in Higher Education: The Student Demand Studies," *Journal of Higher Education* 58, no. 2 (1987): 181–204; Larry L.
Leslie and Paul T. Brinkman, *The Economic Value of Higher Education* (New
York: Macmillan, 1988). Three studies exploiting between-state differences in
state tuition policy and using three different data sets—the October Current
Population Survey, the National Longitudinal Survey of Youth, and High
School and Beyond—found that a $1,000 change in tuition (1990 dollars) was
associated with, on average, a 6 percent difference in college-going. See Ste-

phen V. Cameron and James J. Heckman, "Life Cycle Schooling and Dynamic Selection Bias: Models and Evidence for Five Cohorts of American Males," *Journal of Political Economy* 106, no. 2 (April 1998): 262–333; Thomas J. Kane, "College Attendance by Blacks since 1970: The Role of College Cost, Family Background, and the Returns to Education," *Journal of Political Economy* 102, no. 5 (1994): 878–911; and Thomas J. Kane, *The Price of Admission: Rethinking How Americans Pay for College* (Washington, DC: Brookings Institution and Russell Sage, 1999). Susan Dynarski has used data on narrower forms of tuition assistance—tuition benefits given to Social Security survivors and the Hope Scholarship program in Georgia—to conduct innovative analyses gauging the effects of benefit programs on college entry. She finds that a $1,000 change in tuition price owing to the Social Security Student Benefit program was associated with an impact of 3.7 to 4.8 percent, while the same change in price owing to the Georgia Hope Scholarship program was associated with a 3.1 to 3.5 percent impact (all dollar amounts were converted by Avery and Kane to 1990 dollars). Susan Dynarski, "Does Aid Matter? Measuring the Effect of Student Aid on College Attendance and Completion," National Bureau of Economic Research Working Paper no. 7422, November 1999; Susan Dynarski, "Hope for Whom? Financial Aid for the Middle Class and Its Impact on College Attendance," National Bureau of Economic Research Working Paper no. 7756, June 2000. See also David T. Ellwood and Thomas J. Kane, "Who Is Getting a College Education? Family Background and the Growing Gaps in Enrollment," in *Securing the Future: Investing in Children from Birth to College*, ed. Sheldon Danziger and Jane Waldfogel (New York: Russell Sage, 2000).

For a contrarian view of the effect that tuition policy can have on college enrollment decisions, see Pedro Carneiro and James J. Heckman, "The Evidence on Credit Constraints in Post-Secondary Schooling," *Economic Journal* 112 (October 2002): 705–734. Carneiro and Heckman make the case that almost all of the college enrollment gap for children of low- and high-income families can be attributed to the fact that high-income families are able to provide more nurturing home environments that develop their children's abilities and make them more college-ready than children who grow up in poorer households. "We find that *at most* 8 percent of American youth are credit constrained in the short run sense"—that is, in critical need of financial aid to help them attend college (707). Carneiro and Heckman uncover the strongest evidence of credit constraint within one subgroup of the student population: those children with low scholastic ability. Among white males whose scholastic performance ranks in the lowest third of the Armed Forces Qualification Test distribution, those students from families with higher incomes were much likelier to enroll in college than their poorer counterparts (724).

Of particular note in Avery and Kane's chapter, cited above, is their discussion of the Harvard COACH program, which sends students from Harvard University into Boston public schools to serve as mentors for high school seniors hoping to be accepted into college. The Harvard students work with the seniors to develop plans for their future and help them complete their college and financial aid applications, thus attempting to overcome information barriers within Boston's poorer communities. High school students in the COACH program tend to overestimate the costs of college, but nonetheless their enthusiasm for attending college is high: at the beginning of their senior year, two-thirds of students said they planned to go to a four-year college right after graduation; by the spring, less than one-third were actually going to go to a four-year college, but more than two-thirds stated that they planned to complete a bachelor's degree eventually.

10. That said, a much higher proportion of Pell Grant funds go to students in their forties and fifties than one might expect. In 2003–2004, 5.9 percent of Pell Grant recipients were forty-one to fifty years of age; 1.2 percent were fifty-one to sixty years of age; and 0.1 percent were older than sixty. Almost 40 percent of Pell Grants awarded that year went to individuals who were twenty-five or older.

11. "Higher Education Act: Reauthorization Status and Issues," *Almanac of Policy Issues*, adapted from an article by James B. Stedman, Congressional Research Service, October 9, 2002, *www.policyalmanac.org/education/archive/crs_higher_education.shtml*, cited in Wendy Fleischer, "Education Policy and the AECF Jobs Initiative," Annie E. Casey Foundation Jobs Initiative Policy Brief no. 3, 2003, 4.

12. For more on this idea, see Fleischer, "Education Policy and the AECF Jobs Initiative," 8.

13. Liz McNichol and John Springer, "State Policies to Assist Working-Poor Families," Center on Budget and Policy Priorities, December 2004, 35, *http://www.cbpp.org/12-10-04sfp.pdf*.

14. Ibid.

15. Ibid., 35–37.

16. Alan Berube and Benjamin Forman, "A Local Ladder for the Working Poor: The Impact of the Earned Income Tax Credit in U.S. Metropolitan Areas," Brookings Institution Center on Urban and Metropolitan Policy EITC Series, September 2001, 1, *http://www.brookings.edu/dybdocroot/es/urban/eitc/eitcnational.pdf*.

17. Ibid., 2.

18. Ibid.

19. McNichol and Springer, "State Policies to Assist Working-Poor Families," 9.

20. Riley's proposal would have raised the amount that a family of four could earn before it was taxed to $17,000, from $4,600 per year; the amount would

have increased to $20,000 after four years. The proposal would have also raised the exemption for each child from $300 to $2,135, increased the tax rate for higher-income individuals ($75,000 or more for singles, $150,000 or more for families) from 5 to 6 percent, and increased or added taxes on property, businesses, automobile repairs, utilities, and cigarettes. The additional revenue would have plugged up the state's $675 million budget deficit and funded efforts to raise reading levels and waive tuition at state universities for Alabama high school graduates with a B average or better. Receiving a mere 32 percent of the vote, the tax proposal was roundly defeated in a September referendum, and a month later Alabama was forced to make drastic cuts in services—18 percent for most state agencies, and 75 percent for other recipients of state funds. Larry Copeland, "Alabama Governor's Tax-Increase Plan Is a Switch with High Stakes," *USA Today*, September 5, 2003, 3A; Tom Baxter, "Alabama Looks at Budget Cuts," *Atlanta Journal-Constitution*, September 11, 2003, 6A; and Adam Cohen, "Editorial Observer: What Alabama's Low-Tax Mania Can Teach the Rest of the Country," *New York Times*, October 20, 2003, 16.

21. McNichol and Springer, "State Policies to Assist Working-Poor Families," 11.

22. Ibid., 12.

23. Ibid., 4.

24. Ibid., 21.

25. Ruth Milkman and Eileen Appelbaum, "Paid Family Leave in California," *The State of California Labor* 4 (2004): 45–67.

26. Ibid., 27.

27. Leslie Kaufman, "City Officials Call Budget 'a Disaster' for Day Care," *New York Times*, March 16, 2005, B5.

28. Ibid.

29. Jennifer Mezey, Mark Greenberg, and Rachel Schumacher, "The Vast Majority of Federally Eligible Children Did Not Receive Child Care Assistance in FY 2000," Center for Law and Social Policy, October 2, 2002, *http:// www.clasp.org/publications/1in7sum.pdf*, cited in McNichol and Springer, "State Policies to Assist Working-Poor Families."

30. "A Michigan study found, after controlling for demographic and other factors shown to affect work, that TANF recipients with subsidized childcare worked 50 percent more months and had more than 100 percent higher earnings than TANF recipients without subsidized childcare." McNichol and Springer, "State Policies to Assist Working-Poor Families," 27. See Sandra K. Danziger, Elizabeth Oltmans Ananat, and Kimberly G. Browning, "Childcare Subsidies and the Transition from Welfare to Work," *Family Relations* 52, no. 2 (March 2004): 219–228, *http://www.npc.umich.edu/publications/working_papers/ paper11/03-11.pdf*.

31. Lynch argues that by improving the skills of those future workers who are born into low-income families, we would raise the GDP, reduce poverty, and improve our competitive position in the world economy. "Within forty-five years," he writes, "the increase in earnings due to [early childhood development] investments would likely boost the GDP by nearly one-half of 1 percent, or $107 billion (in 2004 dollars)." Quoted on the Economic Policy Institute Web site, *http://www.epinet.org/content.cfm/books_exceptional_returns*. See also Robert G. Lynch, *Exceptional Returns: Economic, Fiscal, and Social Benefits of Investment in Early Childhood Development* (Washington, DC: Economic Policy Institute, 2004).

32. Foundation for Child Development, "New American Children: Immigrant Children's Initiative," accessed on April 1, 2005, at *http://www.ffcd.org/ourwork/n-index.html*.

33. Child Trends, a research organization devoted to the study of children, has analyzed the Early Childhood Longitudinal Study of the Kindergarten Class of 1998–99 (ECLS-K) to determine the demographic characteristics of kindergartners who are already trailing behind their peers. They identify several subgroups—boys, non-Hispanic blacks, children living in troubled neighborhoods, and children from educationally disadvantaged, low-income, or single-parent families—that are disproportionately at risk of lagging on various academic and social indicators in kindergarten. In the 1998–99 school year, 2.2 million children—more than half of all kindergartners—lagged in one area; the most vulnerable (who trailed in three areas) constituted 192,000 children, or 5 percent of the total. Richard Wertheimer and Tara Croan, with Kristin Anderson Moore and Elizabeth C. Hair, "Attending Kindergarten and Already Behind: A Statistical Portrait of Vulnerable Young Children," Child Trends Research Brief, Publication no. 2003-20, December 2003, 2, *http://www.childtrends.org/Files/AttendingKindergartenRB.pdf*.

34. David Lawrence Jr., "Pre-K Education: Legislature's Action Is an 'Honorable Start,'" *Miami Herald*, December 17, 2004, *http://www.ffcd.org/news/floridaPrek.html*.

35. Deborah Baker and Barry Massey, "Senate Approves Pre-K as Adjournment Nears," Associated Press, March 19, 2005.

36. Jody Temkin, "If You Think It's Crowded Now . . .; Preschool Enrollment Likely to Rise with Generation Y Babies," *Chicago Tribune*, March 13, 2005, *Education Today*, 1.

37. Ibid.

38. McNichol and Springer, "State Policies to Assist Working-Poor Families," 49.

39. Ibid.

40. Katherine Ross Phillips, "Who Knows about the Earned Income Tax Credit?" Urban Institute Policy Brief no. B-27, January 2001, *http://*

newfederalism.urban.org/html/series_b/b27/b27.html, cited in Alan Berube and Benjamin Forman, "A Local Ladder for the Working Poor: The Impact of the Earned Income Tax Credit in U.S. Metropolitan Areas," Brookings Institution Center on Urban and Metropolitan Policy EITC Series, September 2001, 2, *http://www.brookings.edu/dybdocroot/es/urban/eitc/eitcnational.pdf.*

41. In their classic volume, *Regulating the Poor*, Frances Fox Piven and Richard Cloward argued that a "restrictive cycle" emerges in which public bureaucracies deliberately erect barriers to participation in legal entitlements in order to force people off the rolls and into the labor market. Frances Fox Piven and Richard A. Cloward, *Regulating the Poor: The Functions of Public Welfare*, updated ed. (New York: Vintage Books, 1993).

42. Melvin Claxton and Ronald J. Hansen, "Working Poor Suffer under Bush Tax Cuts," *Detroit News*, September 26, 2004, *http://www.detnews.com/2004/specialreport/0409/26/a01-284666.htm.*

43. Alice Dembner, "Medicaid Recipients Face New Fees," *Boston Globe*, February 27, 2003, B5.

Appendix A: Study Design

1. Rejects who did not report a job at wave 1 but reported employment during that period at wave 2 were dropped; there are only three who fit these criteria, and their average wage was $8.24 (in 1994 dollars) at wave 1. The two rejects from Burger Barn included here are those who did report being currently employed by another employer when interviewed at wave 1.

2. For hires, the average hourly wage growth per year equals the wave 3 wage minus the wave 1 wage in 2002 dollars, divided by nine; for rejects, the average equals the wave 3 wage minus the wave 1 wage in 2002 dollars, divided by eight.

3. The same criteria apply as for the previous calculation of average yearly gains.

4. For hires, this equals the wave 3 wage minus the wave 1 wage in 2002 dollars, divided by nine.

5. For hires, this equals the wave 3 wage minus the wave 1 wage in 2002 dollars, divided by nine.

Appendix C:
Occupational Prestige Scores and the Socioeconomic Index

1. Charles North and Paul K. Hatt, "Jobs and Occupations: A Popular Evaluation," in *Sociological Analysis*, ed. Logan Wilson and William Kolb (New York: Harcourt, Brace, 1949).

2. Otis D. Duncan, "A Socioeconomic Index for All Occupations," in *Occu-*

pations and Social Status, ed. Albert Reiss, Jr., et al. (New York: Free Press of Glencoe, 1961).

3. Paul Siegel, "Prestige in the American Occupational Structure," Ph.D. diss., University of Chicago, June 1971.

4. Gillian Stevens and David Featherman, "Occupational Status Index," *Social Science Research* 10 (May 1981): 364–395.

5. Gillian Stevens and Joo Hyun Cho, "Socioeconomic Indexes and the New 1980 Census Occupational Classification Scheme," *Social Science Research* 14 (October 1985): 142–168.

6. Gillian Stevens and Elizabeth Hoisington, "Occupational Prestige and the 1980 Labor Force," *Social Science Research* 16 (April 1987): 74–105.

7. Kim Nakao and Judith Treas, "The 1989 Socioeconomic Index of Occupations: Construction from the 1989 Occupational Prestige Scores," General Social Survey Methodological Report no. 74, National Opinion Research Center, University of Chicago, 1992.

8. Ibid.

Index